P9-EEC-284

WITHDRAWN

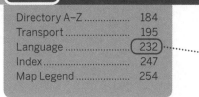

Language

THIS EDITION WRITTEN AND RESEARCHED BY

Regis St Louis

Jean-Bernard Carillet, Dean Starnes

welcome to PNG & Solomon Islands

Exploring the Landscape

Test your mettle on a 10-day trek following the steps of Australian diggers along the Kokoda Track, or summit Highland peaks for a glimpse of both sparkling coasts on a clear day. Prowl through jungle-clad scenery with village guides, en route to thundering waterfalls or in search of magnificently plumed birds of paradise. On the coast, hundreds of islands and atolls cry out for exploration. You can slow-boat your way along pristine stretches of shoreline, overnighting at peaceful villages along the way.

The Life Aquatic

The Solomon Islands and PNG are both world-famous diving destinations, with excellent conditions most months of the year. The biodiversity beneath is astounding, with a colourful array of hard and soft corals and teeming fish life, along with a jaw-dropping collection of WWII plane- and shipwrecks. Live-aboard boats and first-rate dive resorts provide access to sites far from the hordes. The waves are equally uncrowded for surf lovers, with fantastic reef, point and beach breaks scattered around the region's northern shores. There's also fantastic fishing in these pristine waters, with yellowfin tuna, mackerel, sailfish and the legendary Papuan black bass in abundance.

Coral-ringed beaches, smouldering volcanoes and rainforest-covered mountains set the stage for unforgettable adventures, while traditional villages and tropical islands provide magnificent settings for a remote getaway.

(left) An Ulu Island boy enjoying azure waters in East New Britain (p141)
(below) A Malaita Islander (p224) plays a traditional bamboo panpipe

Cultural Wonders

Home to more than 800 distinct languages and lifestyles, Papua New Guinea and the Solomons provide fascinating opportunities to be immersed in traditional cultures. It's well worth planning your trip around over-the-top annual festivals: see colourfully painted and feathered Highland warriors, fearless snake-wielding fire dancers and brilliantly attired island oarsmen chanting to the backdrop of pounding drums. Festivals aside, there are myriad ways to have a paradigm-altering experience: an impromptu *singsing* on the Trobriand Islands, learning about the legends of an eerie skull cave or sharing fruit with new-found friends on a bumpy PMV ride.

Island Idyll

Travel is rarely easy in Melanesia, but the rewards are bountiful. After a few weeks of hard travel you can find your way to a pristine swath of coastline and unwind for a few days in a beautifully sited ecofriendly resort or bush-material village guesthouse overlooking the sea. Spend your days snorkelling coral reefs, walking sandy beaches, paddling up placid rivers or lounging beneath a palm tree. By night, watch the sunset, feast on fresh seafood and watch the sky slowly fill with stars while daydreaming about the great adventures still ahead.

Papua New Guinea & Solomon Islands

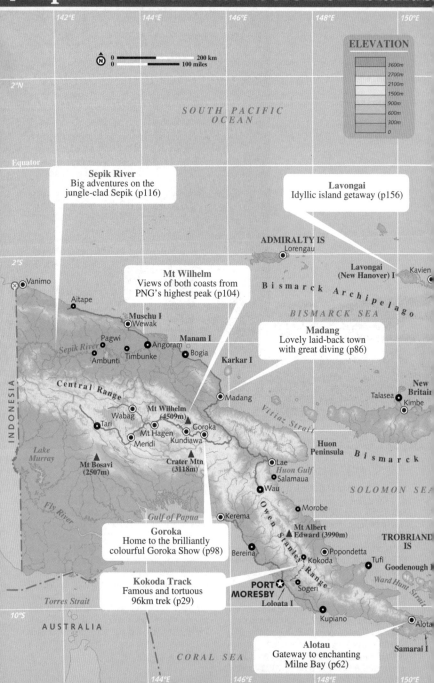

ELEVATION

3600m
2700m
2100m
1500m
900m
600m
300m
0

0   200 km
0   100 miles

Sepik River
Big adventures on the
jungle-clad Sepik (p116)

Lavongai
Idyllic island getaway (p156)

SOUTH PACIFIC
OCEAN

2°N

Equator

ADMIRALTY IS
Lorengau

Mt Wilhelm
Views of both coasts from
PNG's highest peak (p104)

Lavongai
(New Hanover) I

Kavien

2°S

Vanimo

Bismarck Archipelago

BISMARCK SEA

Madang
Lovely laid-back town
with great diving (p86)

Aitape

Muschu I
Wewak

Pagwi
Angoram
Manam I

Sepik River
Bogia

Ambunti
Timbunke

Karkar I

New
Britain

Central Range

Talasea
Kimbe

INDONESIA

Madang

Vitiaz Strait

Tari

Wabag
Mt Wilhelm
(4509m)
Goroka

Mt Hagen
Kundiawa

Huon
Peninsula

Bismarck

Mendi

Lake
Murray

Mt Bosavi
(2507m)

Crater Mtn
(3118m)

Lae
Huon Gulf
Salamaua

Wau

SOLOMON SEA

Fly River

Gulf of Papua

Kerema

Morobe

Mt Albert
Edward (3990m)

TROBRIAND
IS

Goroka
Home to the brilliantly
colourful Goroka Show (p98)

Bereina

Popondetta
Kokoda

Tufi

Goodenough I

Ward Hunt Strait

Kokoda Track
Famous and tortuous
96km trek (p29)

PORT
MORESBY
Loloata I

Sogeri

Torres Strait

AUSTRALIA

Kupiano

Alota

CORAL SEA

Samarai I

Alotau
Gateway to enchanting
Milne Bay (p62)

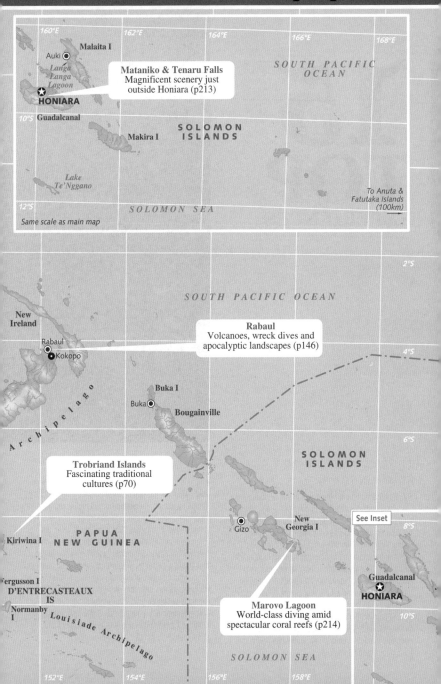

Mataniko & Tenaru Falls
Magnificent scenery just outside Honiara (p213)

To Anuta & Fatutaka Islands (100km)

Same scale as main map

Rabaul
Volcanoes, wreck dives and apocalyptic landscapes (p146)

Trobriand Islands
Fascinating traditional cultures (p70)

See Inset

Marovo Lagoon
World-class diving amid spectacular coral reefs (p214)

15 TOP EXPERIENCES

Diving in PNG & the Solomons

1 PNG and the Solomons rank among the best destinations on Planet Scuba, with an irresistible menu of underwater treasures: luscious reefs festooned with huge sea fans; warm waters teeming with rainbow-coloured and bizarre critters; eerie drop-offs that tumble into the abyss; and a host of atmospheric WWII wrecks – not to mention the thrill of diving uncrowded sites. A handful of beautifully set dive resorts (p25) provide the idyllic gateway to your undersea adventure. To reach even more remote and pristine environments, sign on to a live-aboard vessel.

Kokoda Track

2 It's muddy and gruelling, with maddeningly steep uphill scrambles followed by slippery, bone-jarring descents. Treacherous river crossings ensure feet don't stay dry for long, while the humidity wreaks havoc on even the best-prepared trekkers. Why walk the 96km Kokoda Track (p29)? To follow in the footsteps of giants, recalling the great men who fought and died on this hellish, mountainous stretch. As you pass through remote villages and pause beside evocative war memorials you'll find – like the many who've done it before – the rewards far outweigh the physical challenges.

CASEY MAHANEY/LONELY PLANET IMAGES ©

GREG NEWINGTON/GETTY IMAGES ©

PAUL BEINSSEN/LONELY PLANET IMAGES ©

Seeing a Festival

3 Rio's Carnaval has nothing on the magnificent pageantry of a Highland festival. PNG's biggest fests, such as the Goroka Show (p99), are pure sensory overload, with massive feather headdresses, rustling grass skirts and evocative face- and body paint adorning enormous numbers of participants – over 100 tribal groups at last count – from all across the Highlands. *Singsing* groups perform traditional songs and dances in this pride-filled extravaganza. The thrill of coming face to face with such uplifting traditional cultures is indescribable – and well worth planning a trip around. A Mara man in Goroka

Rabaul

4 One of the prettiest towns in the South Pacific was devastated by Mt Tavurvur, which erupted in 1994 and buried much of Rabaul (p146) under volcanic ash. Today you can wander the abandoned, apocalyptic streets of this once-thriving community, and take in adventures further afield. You can visit Matupit Island (p148), with its village of megapode egg-hunters, go diving in wreck-strewn Simpson Harbour and peer back in time at eerie WWII bunkers hidden in the hillsides. There are great views to be had, particularly from atop the volcanoes looming over town. Simpson Harbour and Mt Tavurvur

Marovo Lagoon (SI)

5 A visual feast awaits you at Marovo Lagoon (p214). A profusion of dive sites at South and North Marovo offer excellent fish action, suitable for all levels of proficiency. The reefs are blanketed with sea fans and act as a magnet for marine species, from tiny critters to marauding pelagics, including manta rays and sharks. South Marovo rewards divers with scenic sites off a cluster of three islands – Kicha, Mbula and Male Male Islands – while North Marovo has a vibrant assemblage of dramatic walls, exhilarating passages and uncomplicated reef dives.

ANDREW MARSHALL & LEANNE WALKER/LONELY PLANET IMAGES ©

Melanesian Markets (SI)

6 Honiara's (p206) expansive Central Market is a wonderful and largely hassle-free place to experience a typical Melanesian city market, with its fruit and vegetable stalls watched over by colourfully clad women and surrounded by the pungent odours of the fish section at the back. Gizo (p219) boasts another intriguing market on the waterfront. Villagers from neighbouring islands arrive each morning by boat to occupy stands under the shade of tall trees. Soak up the atmosphere, feast on sweet bananas, chat with the locals and quench your thirst with coconut water. Honiara

PHILIP GAME/ALAMY ©

Idyllic Islands

7 There are some places where you arrive, put down your pack and think: this is it! This is why I travel. White-sand beaches, swaying palms, the day's freshly caught seafood served by moonlight. Outside Kavieng (p151), a handful of thatch-roof guesthouses scattered on tiny islands near Lavongai provide the type of getaway that would make Robinson Crusoe proud. Days are spent snorkelling coral reefs, surfing virgin waves, visiting welcoming villages and soaking up the pristine island ambience. Overlooking a small bay in PNG

Milne Bay

8 At the eastern edge of the mainland, Milne Bay (p61) is a landscape of remarkable beauty. You'll find scattered islands, coral reefs, lovely palm-fringed beaches, hidden waterfalls, meandering rivers and steep-sided rainforest-covered mountains plunging to the sea. The opportunity for adventure is staggering, with great birdwatching, bushwalking and island- and village-hopping. Alotau is the gateway to it all, and also host of the colourful Canoe Festival, with gyrating *singsing* groups, string bands and people-packed longboats racing across the waterfront.

WILL SALTER/LONELY PLANET IMAGES ©

PAUL HARRIS/GETTY IMAGES ©

PETER HENDRIE/LONELY PLANET IMAGES ©

Big Adventures

9 The craggy ridges of the Bismarck Range culminate with the wind-scoured peak of Mt Wilhelm (p104), the tallest mountain in Oceania. A predawn start has trekkers clambering up its rocky slopes so that they see the mainland's north and south coasts before the clouds roll in. If this isn't challenging enough, rugged types might want to measure their mettle against the infamous Black Cat Trail (p84). First used by 1920s gold rush prospectors, this trail is more bite than bark. Bismarck Range

Mataniko & Tenaru Falls (SI)

10 Magnificent scenery lies within a half-day's travel of Honiara, including Mataniko Falls and Tenaru Waterfalls (p213) – both with lovely natural pools perfect for a refreshing dip. A guide is required for both. If you're fit, opt for the two-hour hike to Mataniko Falls, which are in fact little cascades that tumble into a small canyon. The stunning Tenaru Waterfalls – an easy four-hour walk (return) – rewards visitors with a dreamy tropical ambience and the offer of a refreshing swim in its snug natural pool.

Trobriand Islands

11 Anthropologists have long been fascinated with the Trobriand Islands (p70). Here you'll find a remarkably intact Polynesian culture, with unique traditions – based on a strict matrilineal society – and a distinct cosmology. It's well known for its colourfully painted yam houses, wild harvest festival and celebratory cricket matches (complete with singing and dancing). Visitors here are still a rarity, and they have a fantastic opportunity to stay in local villages and experience the Trobes firsthand, visiting skull caves and coral megaliths, and taking in the pretty island scenery.

Tribal Art

12 Treasure hunters will be spoilt for choice when it comes to the incredible assortment of woodcarvings, bark paintings, masks and other tribal art from across PNG. One of the best destinations for crafts is the Middle Sepik (p132), where master carvers carry on age-old traditions creating shields, masks, figures, canoe prows and story boards. Other artistic traditions flourish in the Trobriands (p70), such as carved ebony walking sticks, bowls and sculptures inlaid with mother of pearl. Oro Province around Tufi (p60) is the go-to spot for tapa cloth – a bark cloth featuring wild designs. A traditional mask from the Sepik

WWII Relics (SI)

13 The Solomon Islands has everything in spades. Above the surface, plenty of WWII relics scattered in the jungle will captivate history buffs. Outside Honiara (p206), the capital, you can visit poignant battlefields and memorials, as well as abandoned amtracks, a Sherman tank, Japanese field guns and the remains of several US aircraft. West New Georgia (p219) also has a fantastic collection of WWII relics, including a sunken Japanese freighter, several large Japanese antiaircraft guns and numerous museums featuring WWII debris and memorabilia. A neglected Japanese war memorial west of Honiara

JERRY GALEA/LONELY PLANET IMAGES ©

PETER SOLNESS/LONELY PLANET IMAGES ©

14

MICHAEL GEBICKI/LONELY PLANET IMAGES ©

15

Madang

14 One of the most attractive towns in PNG, Madang (p86) straddles a small peninsula surrounded by a deep-water harbour littered with WWII wreckage. It might be one of the more tourist-oriented towns in PNG, but the vibe is positively low-key. Huge, bat-filled casuarina trees tower over the streets, the market buzzes with good-natured laughter and a smattering of offshore islands bear sandy stretches on which to throw down a beach towel. Relaxing waterfront guesthouses provide a fine tropical ambience, and there are village stays just outside of town.

Sepik River

15 Besieged on all sides by thick jungle and shrouded in mist, the mighty Sepik (p116) wanders across northwestern PNG like a lazy brown snake full with food. The river is the region's lifeblood, home to a string of villages rich in artistic tradition, and the cultural treasure chest of the Pacific. Here you can hire a crocodile-headed canoe and thread the seasonal waterways from one village to the next, sleeping in stilt homes and exploring the towering *haus tambarans* (spirit houses).

need to know

Solomon Islands
» See p202 for Need to Know information for Solomon Islands

Language
» Tok Pisin (English creole), English, Hiri Motu and 800+ other languages

When to Go

Tropical climate, wet & dry seasons
Tropical climate, rain year round

Rabaul
GO May–Nov

Madang
GO Jun–Sep

Goroka
GO May–Nov

Port Moresby
GO Mar–Nov

Alotau
GO Nov–Jan

High Season
(May–Oct)
» Slightly busier season, with bigger crowds at big-name festivals and higher accommodation prices
» Generally cooler, drier weather, but rainier in Milne Bay
» Best time to hike the Kokoda Track

Shoulder Season
(Apr & Nov)
» Generally hot and humid, but with increasingly unpredictable rain patterns

Low Season
(Dec–Mar)
» The wet season for much of PNG
» Mild weather, less rain in Milne Bay
» Heavy rains, washed-out roads in the Highlands
» Best surfing off the north coast and islands

Your Daily Budget

Budget less than
K300
» Staying in village guesthouses: K50 to K100 per night
» Focusing on one region (rather than flying between areas)
» Eating in local markets; taking PMVs whenever possible

Midrange
K300- 600
» Double room in midrange hotel: K300 to K450
» Flying between regions: K350 to K600
» Hiring local guides for village-hopping, treks, birdwatching

Top End over
K600
» Lodging in a resort: from K500
» Fine dining: K60 to K150 per person
» Adventure: Kokoda Track (from A$3000 for eight days)

Money

» The currency is Papua New Guinea Kina (K). There are ATMs in large towns. Credit cards are accepted at midrange and top-end lodging, restaurants and shops.

Visas

» Most foreign nationals can obtain a 60-day tourist visa on arrival for K100; can also be obtained in advance at PNG diplomatic missions.

Mobile Phones

» Local SIM cards can be used in Australian and European phones. Of the main providers, Digicel has the most extensive network.

Transport

» Travel between regions is mostly by flight (often via Port Moresby). PMVs (Public Motor Vehicles) generally run wherever there are roads.

Websites

» **Lonely Planet** (www. lonelyplanet.com/papua-new-guinea) Destination information, travel forum, photos.

» **PNG Tourism Promotion Authority** (www.pngtourism.org. pg) Official website of PNG's peak tourism body. Has good links.

» **Tubuans & Dukduks** (http://garamut. wordpress.com) Blog covering current events in PNG.

» **National** (www. thenational.com.pg) PNG's main newspaper.

» **PNG Business Directory** (www.pngbd. com) Business and tourism website.

Exchange Rates

For current exchange rates see www. xe.com.

Australia	A$1	K2.21
Canada	C$1	K2.06
Euro	€1	K2.77
Japan	¥100	K2.55
New Zealand	NZ$1	K1.72
Solomon Islands	S$1	K0.30
UK	UK£	K3.27
USA	US$1	K2.06

Important Numbers

Papua New Guinea has different emergency numbers for each city. See individual chapters.

Papua New Guinea country code	☑675
International access code	☑05
Directory Assistance local/international	☑013/0178

Arriving in Papua New Guinea

» **Port Moresby Airport** (p52)
Free transport from most midrange and top-end lodging by advance notice; make a free call from the tourism office at International Arrivals if your hotel van doesn't show up.
Taxis (some have meters, some don't, so negotiate): around K25 to Waigani or Boroko; K35 to Town.

Safety

PNG has a notorious reputation, though the dangers are largely overhyped. For more information on safe travel see p191. Outside Port Moresby, Lae and Mt Hagen, things are much more relaxed. Tribal fighting is still an issue deep in the Highlands but rarely involves outsiders or foreign travellers. Some commonsense tips:

» Don't flaunt your wealth – wear unremarkable clothes and keep your camera hidden. Carry a *bilum* (a traditional string bag) rather than a daypack.

» Always keep at least K50 '*raskol* (bandit) money' in your pocket to appease any would-be thief. Hide the rest of your money in a money belt or your shoe.

» Speak to people rather than be aloof.

» Be especially careful on the fortnightly Friday pay nights when things can get pretty wild.

» If you get held up, try to stay calm. Most robberies are fairly unsophisticated affairs.

if you like...

Festivals & Celebrations

Pounding drums, masked warriors and slow, mesmerising dances are just a few things you'll see at some of the most fantastically colourful festivals, shows and *singsings* on the planet.

Milne Bay Kundu & Canoe Festival Giant, brightly painted ocean-going canoes, costumed dancers and traditional song transform sleepy Alotau into a riotously colourful stage (p63)

Goroka Show One of PNG's biggest fests, the Goroka Show is an alluring mash of feathered headdresses, face paint, *kundu* drums and twirling dancers (p99)

Crocodile Festival An up-and-coming fest in the tiny settlement of Ambunti on the Sepik (p131)

Warwagira Festival New Britain's big bash features string bands, forest spirits and the surreal Baining fire dancers (p143)

Kalam Cultural Festival Get an up-close look at important customs, including bride-price exchanges and initiation rites at this traditional celebration (p94)

Dramatic Scenery

Home to rainforest-covered mountains, misty waterfalls, lush river valleys and sparkling coastlines, PNG and the Solomons have countless places to stop and savour the scenery.

Highlands Hwy Join locals on a bumpy PMV ride from Goroka to Mt Hagen and beyond against a stunning backdrop of towering mountains and verdant valleys (p96)

Lake Kutubu A beautiful highland lake amid countryside of peaceful traditional settlements (p112)

Rabaul The wild volcano-strewn backdrop of Rabaul makes a fantastic setting for a walk; scenic overlooks provide the finest vantage points (p146)

Tufi Steep, fjord-like *rias* showcase nature at its finest – no roads, no towns, just tiny welcoming villages set between topaz waters and the vast untouched interior (p60)

Marovo Lagoon In a word: jaw-dropping. Hundreds of lovely islands covered with palm trees and ringed by coral (p214)

Wildlife Watching

Spotting richly hued birds of paradise in misty mountain forests, snorkelling with graceful manta rays through crystal-clear seas and chasing iridescent butterflies through the bush – it's all part of the great Melanesian wildlife-watching experience.

Tari Basin This world-famous birding site has a staggering array of feathered beauties, including the King of Saxony and other birds of paradise (p114)

Tetepare Island Whether your interest is pygmy parrots, leatherback turtles, dugongs or crocs, this is one of the best places to see wildlife in the Solomons (p221)

Lae Probably the best reason to go to Lae is the fantastic Rainforest Habitat, with raised walkways skirting past some of PNG's greatest flora and fauna hits (p78)

Loloata Island A top place to see well-camouflaged rock wallabies just outside of Port Moresby (p46)

Normanby Island Head to this island in Milne Bay for a chance to see the remarkable Goldie's bird of paradise (p69)

TIM LAMAN / NATURE PICTURE LIBRARY ©

» Goldie's bird of paradise (p69), Milne Bay Province

Walks & Treks

For an unforgettable taste of PNG, grab your kit, lace up your boots and head into the bush. You'll pass through remote villages, spy wildlife and perhaps see hulking WWII relics slowly being reclaimed by the jungle.

Kokoda Trek PNG's most famous overland adventure is 96km of ups and downs, traversing rushing rivers and walking slippery narrow ridges while retracing the diggers' footsteps (p29)

Mt Wilhelm The three- to four-day climb is hard going, but the rewards are great: views of both coasts from the 4509m summit (p104)

Black Cat Track Shorter but tougher than the Kokoda, this little-visited track is for those up for a serious challenge (p84)

North Coast If you want to get well off the beaten path, hire a guide in Alotau and walk your way between villages on Milne Bay's scenic north coast (p67)

Epic Journeys

Travelling around PNG is rarely easy. That said, sometimes the journey is the best part of the experience, whether mingling with villagers at traditional settlements on the Sepik or discovering unimaginable beauty on an island-hopping adventure off the coast.

Sepik River Take a journey along one of the world's mighty waterways, learning about fascinating cultures along the way (p129)

D'Entrecasteaux Islands Load up on petrol and provisions in Alotau, hire a boatman, then head out for a multi-day adventure village-hopping your way around some of Milne Bay's most spectacular scenery (p68)

Boluminski Highway Avid cyclists can hire a bike in Kavieng and set off on the 263km journey down New Ireland's east coast, overnighting in beachfront guesthouses along the way (p157)

Vanimo to Lae For pure adventure, leave the aeroplane behind and hop on a boat and/or rugged 4WD between Vanimo and Wewak then on to Lae (p125)

Village Life

One of the great ways to see PNG is to stay in a village. You'll share meals with villagers and sleep in traditional dwellings made of bush materials. By day, local guides will show you the local highlights – beaches, reefs, waterfalls and rare birds.

Abelam Villages The area around Maprik near the Sepik has striking *haus tambarans*, Apangai has three of these carved wooden beauties, and makes a great base for taking in village life (p126)

Simbai In Madang Province, you can stay in this peasant village, perhaps timing your visit to see the Kalam Culture Festival; those looking for more adventure can head off on a five-day trek from here to the Ramu River (p94)

Trobriands To experience some of the most traditional cultures of PNG, arrange a village stay on Kiriwina Island in the famed Trobriand archipelago (p70)

Kofure One of many beautifully set villages near Tufi, with white-sand beaches, swaying palms and local seafood (p61)

If you like... exploring magnificent, rarely visited places, head to Bougainville, with dense forests, mountainous peaks, waterfalls, caves and lagoons – but little infrastructure (p162)

Surfing

There's great surf in PNG and the Solomons, and you won't have to contend with the crowds found in other parts. On the north coast and the islands, the best waves coincide with monsoon season from November to April.

Nusa Island Retreat Run by a knowledgeable surfing expat, this Kavieng gem is a great spot for a surf getaway. Boats take you daily to the best breaks (p154)

Boluminski Highway You'll find great breaks all along New Ireland's east coast; you can stay in a sweet village guesthouse at Malom or Dalom or the surfer-run Rubio Guesthouse just beyond (p157)

Vanimo Tin outpost across the border from Indonesia with legendary breaks (p124)

Wewak A pretty town with golden sand beaches and reputable breaks on the north coast (p117)

Ghizo Island Great surf, with practically virgin waves (and good diving, too) in the Solomons' western province (p219)

Diving

The diving here is staggering: you'll find a fantastic array of marine life, WWII wrecks and muck-diving, but a fraction of the crowds found in better-known diving destinations. There are live aboard options for those seeking total immersion.

Madang Lovely Madang has loads of great dive spots and a top-notch operator to get you there (p86)

Walindi A top resort, with unforgettable diving in pristine Kimbe Bay, West New Britain (p150)

Tawali First-rate diving and liveaboards in Milne Bay's North Coast (p67)

Rabaul Near Rabaul, you can go wreck-diving in Simpson Harbour, then head to the reefs on the peninsula's western side for coral and coral life (p146)

Marovo Lagoon World-class diving with coral gardens, caves, drop-offs and astounding marine life (p214)

Bonegi Wrecks Diving among two sunken Japanese freighters, one of which is so close to the surface it can be snorkelled (p214)

Island Getaways

With hundreds of islands in these parts, you'll find both resort-style pampering and rustic, Robinson-Crusoe-type getaways. Both offer magical settings complete with a backdrop of beach, reef and rain forest.

Sibonai Guesthouse Hard to get to, but well worth the effort, this peaceful village guesthouse is a great place for birdwatching, snorkelling and seeing the natural beauty of Normanby Island (p69)

Lavongai For a remote getaway, hop a boat from Kavieng out toward the islands near Lavongai: you'll find pretty beaches, peaceful villages, good surf and superb home-cooked seafood (p156)

Muschu Island Swaying palms, coral reefs, a jungle-clad interior and simple village-style lodging (p123)

Tetepare Island A rainforest-covered spot in the Solomons with eco-friendly accommodation that makes a great base for wildlife watching (p221)

Mbabanga Island A Solomons gem with idyllic beaches and a pretty lagoon that's perfect for snorkelling (p222)

month by month

March

The wet season – typically December to March – brings heavy downpours, particularly in the Highlands, mixed with high temperatures. Expect less rain in Milne Bay and on the islands.

 National Surfing Titles

Held in Madang province in mid-March, this surf comp attracts around 100 amateur and pro surfers to ride the big waves brought by the monsoon season.

April

The tail end of the wet season sees fewer showers and brighter skies. Kokoda Track season kicks off, with large numbers of trekkers arriving around Anzac Day.

 National Fishing Titles

From late March to early April, anglers compete in this weeklong game-fishing extravaganza. The competition is rotated between Madang, Lae, Port Moresby and Rabaul (www.gfa.com.pg).

June

The dry season, which runs through September in most parts, is in full swing, with cooler temperatures and fewer showers. Weather can be less predictable in Milne Bay and Lae.

 Spear Fighting Festival

Held on the remote island of Santa Catalina in the Solomons, this three-day event, known locally as Wogasia, takes place in late May or early June and features men from the island's two tribes squaring off and throwing spears at one another. Keep your distance!

 Whit Monday This religious fest happens on the eighth Monday after Easter and is celebrated with fervour all over the Solomons. Expect processions with singing and dancing.

July

July is a generally cool and dry time to visit PNG and the Solomons. The cultural calendar picks up, with some of the best festivals and shows.

 Warwagira Festival

One of the biggest events on the islands, Warwagira takes place during the first two weeks of July in either Kokopo or Rabaul. *Dukduks* and *tumbuans* (masked forest spirits) come out of the sea from canoes at dawn to dance. At night, Baining fire dancers perform.

 National Mask Festival

Held in Rabaul, this fest has been around since 1995 and showcases the unique mask cultures of PNG. Groups from all across the country perform – with ancestor masks, spirit masks and *tumbuan* masks on display.

 Malagan Festival

Held in Kavieng or Namatanai toward the end of July, this festival features unique Malagan art, traditionally made as totems to honour ancestors and the recently deceased. Malagan carvings are rare outside New Ireland and highly prized among collectors.

August

In most of PNG and the Solomons, August is hot and humid, though heavy rain showers are thankfully infrequent. In Lae, however, it's rainy season (May to October).

 Ambunti Crocodile Festival

This small four-day event features cultural groups from the Sepik region performing to promote tourism and crocodile conservation. In addition to colourfully garbed dancing, village crafts and food stalls, there's 'the triathlon' – a 1km run, followed by canoe race, then swimming in crocodile-infested waters!

International Orchid Show

In early August, the grounds of Port Moresby's Parliament Haus come alive with thousands of orchids, including rare and unusual species from both coastal and mountain regions.

Enga Cultural Show

In mid-August, sleepy Wabag comes alive during its colourful Highlands fest. With *singsing* groups, live music and arts and crafts stalls, it's not unlike the larger, better-known Goroka Show.

Tufi Cultural Show

Tufi's big shindig lights up the region in mid-August, when you can see a two-day *singsing*. In addition to brilliantly costumed singing and dancing groups, there are traditional demonstrations of craft-making.

Mt Hagen Show

Held in late August, this Highlands fest is a two-day spectacular. It features elaborate headdresses, colourful make-up and over-the-top costumes, with performing *singsing* groups from all across the country.

September

Still firmly rooted in the dry season, September is the festival season, and usually a cool(er) and pleasant time to visit.

 **National Garamut & Mambu Festival**

In early September, Wewak keeps the dance-loving spirits alive with colourful traditional music and dance. In addition to *singsing* groups, there's the all-important yam-planting ceremonies.

Goroka Show

If you can only make one Highlands fest, the famed Goroka Show in mid-September features big numbers of outrageously feathered and costumed clans staging unforgettable performances. Accommodation should be booked early.

Hiri Moale Festival

On Ela Beach in Port Moresby, this long-running fest is on Independence Day (16 September) and features canoe racing by native Motu groups as well as *singsings* and live music.

Kalam Culture Festival

This traditional festival at Simbai, a tiny Highlands outpost, features male initiation rites, nose piercing and bride-price payments. Held the Wednesday and Thursday after the Goroka Show.

October

The last official month of the dry season, with increasingly erratic weather patterns. The festival calendar is winding down.

Kundiawa Simbu Show

In early October, tiny Kundiawa sees a flurry of activity around its colourful show. Expect a fine assortment of *singsings* with dancers in traditional dress and *bilas* (finery).

Morobe Show

One of the last big *singsings* of the year happens in Lae in late October. Agricultural displays and fiery *singsing* groups are the big draw – perhaps the best reason to come to this rugged coastal city (www.morobeshow.org.pg).

November

Temperatures are climbing in most of PNG. Milne Bay, with its own unique weather patterns, offers cooler weather through January.

Milne Bay Canoe & Kundu Festival

In early November, Alotau, the gateway to the enchanting islands of Milne Bay, hosts a magnificent festival. Brilliantly painted canoes packed with costumed warriors race in the bay, while elaborately garbed *singsing* groups perform on stages.

itineraries

Whether you've got six days or 60, these itineraries provide a starting point for the trip of a lifetime. Want more inspiration? Head online to lonelyplanet. com/thorntree to chat with other travellers.

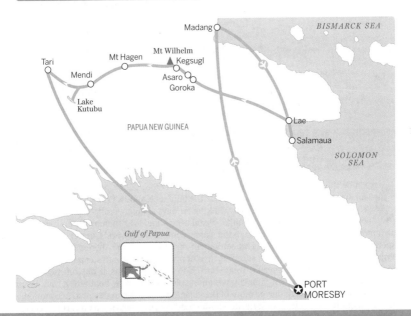

Two Weeks
Mainland Odyssey

Spend a day taking in the highlights of **Port Moresby** before flying up to pretty **Madang**. Spend a couple days diving or snorkelling and exploring nearby islands before going down to **Lae** for a look at the Rainforest Habitat and the picturesque village of **Salamaua**, one hour south. Next, take a bus up the Highlands Hwy to **Goroka** and see the Goroka Show, or visit the mudmen of **Asaro** just northwest of Goroka.

Continue up to **Kegsugl** – Betty's Place is a good base – for the amazing climb up **Mt Wilhelm**. After enjoying the view of both coasts, make the descent for travel onward to **Mt Hagen**, enjoying the spectacular scenery and a game of Highlands darts. If there's no clan warfare, continue along the highway to **Tari** via **Mendi** and stunning **Lake Kutubu**, but if the feisty Southern Highlanders are fighting you'd better do this leg by aeroplane – the beautiful Tari Basin is worth it. Don't miss the Huli Wigmen.

From Tari fly back to **Port Moresby** and, if time allows, spend a final day relaxing on Loloata Island.

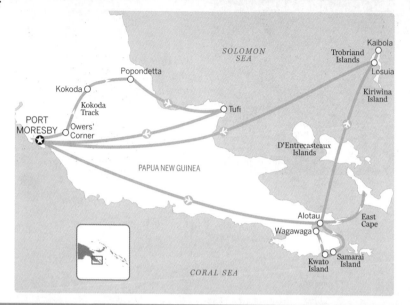

Three to Four Weeks
Eastward Wander

> Enjoy the relative comforts of **Port Moresby** before taking on one of PNG's most memorable – and challenging! – treks: the famous **Kokoda Track**. Get a feel for the challenges faced by the troops by walking for days along this rugged path, traversing chilly streams, visiting old bunker installations and war memorials and stopping at remote villages along the way. Take the classic route from **Owers' Corner**; afterwards, spend a day relaxing in the peaceful settlement of **Kokoda**. From there catch a PMV to **Popondetta** and fly on to **Tufi**, a stunning area of pretty coastline and steep fjord-like *rias*, with a lush, mountainous interior. Treat yourself to a couple nights at the Tufi Resort. Go diving or snorkelling, fish for your dinner, and explore the area by boat and kayak. From here spend a few nights in one or more of the village guesthouses in the area. Accommodation is rustic, but the setting is fantastic – white sand beaches, swaying palms, coral reefs at your doorstep, with guides who can lead you to waterfalls or on birdwatching expeditions.

Afterwards, fly from Tufi back to Port Moresby and on to **Alotau**, gateway to the idyllic beauty of Milne Bay. Spend a day taking in the market, the harbour and fine views from Top Town. Then catch an afternoon boat out to the colonial-era capital of **Samarai Island** and nearby **Kwato Island** – the bungalows of Nuli Sapi make a fine base for exploring the area. Afterwards, head back to Alotau and over to **Wagawaga**. Visit waterfalls, go for a dugout canoe trip on the Dawadawa River and enjoy serene views from Ulumani Treetops Lodge. Afterwards, cross back to Alotau, load up on provisions and fuel and head up to **East Cape** then by boat for an adventure exploring the **D'Entrecasteaux Islands**. Birdwatching, rainforest walks, pretty beaches, coral reefs and peaceful villages are all part of the allure of this little-visited region.

For the final leg of the journey, fly from Alotau up to Losuia on **Kiriwina**, the largest of the Trobriand Islands. Spend three days visiting traditional villages, learning about yam power and magic and perhaps catching a *singsing* or a festive cricket match. Stay at least one night in a village; **Kaibola**, perched near a picturesque beach is a good option. From Kiriwina it's an easy flight back to Moresby.

» (above) Children making their way to school on a once-a-month traditional day on Kiriwina Island (p70)
» (left) The diving in Papua New Guinea is world renowned (p25)

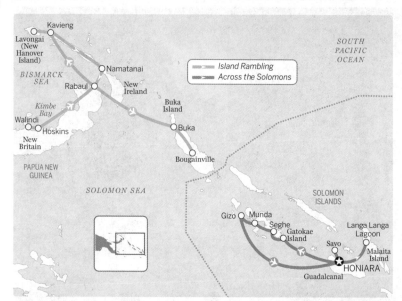

Three Weeks
Across the Solomons

World-class diving, virgin waves and idyllic island retreats: the Solomon Islands is a place for adventurers. Start your journey in **Honiara**. Take in the market, the wharf and national museum, then tack on a tour of the battlefields and pretty beaches outside the capital. Next take a boat to **Savo**, a volcanic island with boiling hot springs, a massive megapode field and pretty, tropical scenery. Spend a few days unwinding here before boating back to Honiara and catching an onward flight to **Gatokae Island**, which provides access to South Marovo Lagoon, a great setting for snorkelling, swimming and simply soaking up the tropical beauty. Catch a boat up to the north end of the lagoon for a stay in one of the pristine ecolodges, then continue by plane from **Seghe** to **Munda**, a fine base for diving, surfing and bushwalking in New Georgia. From here continue west by boat to **Gizo**, a first-rate diving and up-and-coming surfing spot. Fly back to Honiara, then catch a boat to **Langa Langa Lagoon** for a blissfully relaxing night or two on scenic **Malaita Island**.

Three Weeks
Island Rambling

A world away from the Highlands, the steamy island provinces are a fantastic destination for surfers, divers, bush walkers and those wanting an idyllic Robinson Crusoe–type getaway at the ends of the earth. From Moresby fly up to **Hoskins**, and spend a couple of days exploring Kimbe Bay at **Walindi**: diving or snorkelling, birdwatching, bushwalking and soaking in hot springs. Afterwards, fly to **Rabaul**. There, visit Matupit Island to check out belching Tavurvur, the volcano that buried the Pacific's prettiest city, before getting under the water at the WWII-era Submarine Base. Treat yourself to one of Kokopo's pretty resorts – or sleep in the thick of the apocalyptic streetscape at the Rabaul Hotel. Fly on to **Kavieng**, where you can get your fill of surfing or diving, before heading toward **Lavongai** for a remote tropical island getaway. Afterwards, work your way down the Boluminski Highway, stopping at pretty guesthouses (like Dalom) along the way. Continue to **Namatanai** for the boat back to Rabaul and onward flight to **Buka** for a visit to pretty islands in the area. Then continue across to **Bougainville** for a ramble through a beautiful mountainous island with enormous DIY ecotourism potential.

Diving in PNG & Solomon Islands

When to Go

PNG and the Solomons are diveable year-round. Milne Bay: best seasons September to January and April to June.
Average surface sea temperatures: 25°C to 30°C; don't bring more than a 3mm wetsuit. Visibility varies greatly, from 10m to 40m.

Dive Centres

Outfitters are highly professional, with well-trained instructors offering introductory dives, exploratory dives and certification programs. Most dive centres are PADI-, SSI- or NAUI-affiliated, and accept credit cards.
Generally, prices don't include equipment rental; consider bringing your own if you plan on doing many dives.

Live-Aboards

Live-aboard dive boats mostly operate out of PNG. Check the websites for itineraries. Some boats and their base ports:
Barbarian II (www.niuginidiving.com) Lae, Morobe.
Bilikiki (www.bilikiki.com) Honiara, Solomon Islands.
Chertan (www.chertan.com) Alotau, Milne Bay.
FeBrina (www.febrina.com) Walindi, New Britain.
Golden Dawn (www.mvgoldendawn.com) Port Moresby.
Marlin 1 (www.marlin1charters.com.au) Alotau, Milne Bay.

PNG

Papua New Guinea offers truly world-class diving. The marine biodiversity is exceptional, incredibly healthy reefs look like a Garden of Eden and the absence of crowds is a prime draw. Another clincher is the mind-boggling array of WWII wrecks – ships, aircraft and even submarines.

Madang

Of Madang's outer reefs, favourites include **Pig Island** and nearby **Barracuda Point**, **Magic Passage** and **Pig Passage**. You'll likely come across aggregations of barracuda, trevally and sweetlips, as well as photogenic barrel sponges and a variety of soft and hard corals. Some sites are subject to powerful currents, depending on tidal changes.

Much closer to Madang is **Planet Rock**, a submerged seamount around which barracuda, tuna, snapper, jacks and whitetip reef sharks whirl. To the north, just off Wongat Island, the tugboat **Henry Leith** sits upright in 20m and makes for an easy dive, while the coral-encrusted **B25 Mitchell** aircraft lies in less than 15m.

Loloata Island

Port Moresby has probably the best diving of any capital city in the world, with a wide variety of dive sites easily accessible from the dive shop based on Loloata Island (though

Diving in PNG & the Solomons

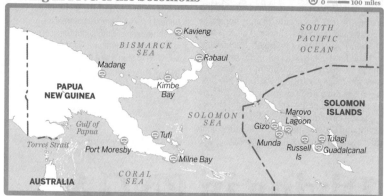

visibility sometimes doesn't exceed 10m). A few minutes' boat ride from your bungalow is a WWII aircraft wreck, the **Boston A20 Havoc**, resting in 18m on a silty bottom. Further south is the 65m-long **Pacific Gas**, formerly a liquid gas carrier, scuttled in 1986 for recreational diving.

More classic dives can be found around Horseshoe Reef, especially the **End Bommie**, famous for its fish life and healthy corals. Another wonderful site (further west) is **Suzie's Bommie**, with a big pinnacle rising from the sandy floor to about 12m below the surface – an oasis of life.

Loloata is also noted for its superb muck diving potential. A few fin strokes from your bungalow, **Loloata Island Jetty** features lots of tiny critters and bizarre fish, from mantis shrimp to dwarf lionfish.

Tufi

Tufi is pure bliss if you're after variety. Fancy muck diving? Try **Tufi Wharf**, just on your doorstep. In the mood for wreck dives? The scattered remains of two PT boats can be seen at 40m directly down the Tufi Wharf. Too gentle for you? Make a beeline for the **S'Jacob**, a Dutch merchant ship that was sunk during a Japanese air raid during WWII – for experienced divers only (she lies in 60m). Fabulous offshore reefs.

Milne Bay

Muck diving, great sheer walls, coral seamounts and lots of pelagic action: it's impossible to get bored in Milne Bay. Visibility is variable and currents might be tricky.

» **Nuakata Island** Pristine reefs and abundant fish life, including marauding pelagics, such as grey sharks, tuna and Spanish mackerel.

» **Boirama Reef** In the passage between Nuakata and Boirama Islands, Boirama attracts large fish.

» **North coast (mainland)** A day trip from Tawali, get a buzz drifting along steep walls and keeping your eyes peeled for sharks and other biggies.

» **Duchess Island** A 45-minute boat ride from Tawali, boasting numerous untouched sites. Expect coral pinnacles ablaze with fish life, elaborate soft corals and regular shark sightings.

Rabaul

One of PNG's finest areas for wreck dives, with a collection of shipwrecks lying in Rabaul Harbour, and reefs along the north coast of the Gazelle Peninsula.

» **Manko Maru** Sunk in 1943, she sits in 35m. The cargo hull can be penetrated.

» **George's Wreck** This coral-encased wreck lies outside Rabaul Harbour. The bow rests on a steep slope in 15m, the stern deck in about 55m.

» **Zero Fighter** She sits at 27m, upright, off a beach to the west of Kokopo.

» **Reimers Reef** Famous for its contoured topography, with overhangs, swimthroughs and canyons; astoundingly dense fish life; and a fabulous mixture of hard and soft corals.

» **Tom, Dick and Harry Reefs** A string of seamounts that plummet to 50m.

Kimbe Bay

Kimbe Bay is famous for towering seamounts crowned by coral formations that project from the continental shelf. The bay is home to more than 350 types of hard coral and 860 species of fish, from cute pygmy horses to massive hammerhead sharks. The tapestry of colours and textures is equally fascinating; soft and hard corals, sea fans, giant sea whips and huge barrel and elephant ear sponges compete for every inch of space on the reef. A sunken **Zero Fighter** adds a bit of variety; it's to the north of the bay, close to the shore.

Strong currents and variable visibility can disappoint. Most sites are a lengthy boat ride away (45 minutes on average).

Kavieng

The large reef system that stretches between Kavieng and New Hanover offers thrilling dives, especially in the passages. There's lots of marine life, including rays, turtles, barracuda, tuna, jacks and grey sharks. Just outside Kavieng, **Echuca Patch** features a large ridge rising from 45m to 12m. A Korean fishing boat, the **Der Yang**, lies on its starboard side close to Echuca Patch, in about 30m. In the same area, **Blowholes** is very atmospheric, with lots of swimthroughs and fish life.

There are a few sunken planes in Kavieng harbour, as well as the **B25 Aircraft Wreck** near Albatross Passage.

Solomon Islands

Diving in the Solomons and PNG is similar, though most dive operations are land-based, whereas PNG is famous for its live-aboards. But what sets the Solomons apart is a unique sense of 'forgotten paradise'.

Guadalcanal

The obvious place to start your diving adventures, with world-class sunken WWII

vessels lying close to the shore. Most sites can be reached by car from Honiara.

» **Bonegi I** About 12km west of Honiara, a giant-sized Japanese merchant transport ship, also known as the *Hirokawa Maru*, lies in 3m descending to 55m, just a few fin strokes offshore.

» **Bonegi II** Also known as *Kinugawa Maru*, the upper works break the surface a towel's throw from the beach, about 500m west of Bonegi I.

» **Searpens** A big ship that lies upside down, east of Honiara.

» **John Penn** Also to the east, this US troopship was sunk about 4km offshore.

Tulagi

Easily accessible from Honiara, Tulagi is a must for wreck enthusiasts, with awesome reef dives as well.

» **USS Kanawha & USS Aaron Ward** A 150m-long oil tanker sitting upright, and a 106m-long US Navy destroyer noted for its extensive arsenal. The catch? They lie deep, very deep (the *Kanawha* in 45m and the *Aaron Ward* in 65m), and are accessible to experienced divers only. Visibility is not the strong point here; expect 15m on average.

» **Twin Tunnels** Two chimneys that start on the top of a reef in about 12m.

» **Sandfly Passage** An exhilarating wall drift dive.

» **Manta Passage** Boasts regular sightings of huge manta rays.

Munda

Offers a good balance of wreck and reef.

» **Corsair** A WWII US fighter that rests undamaged close to the shore on a sandy bottom, in 50m.

» **Casi Maru** A Japanese boat, in less than 20m. Visibility is often reduced due to silt after heavy rains (due to nearby deforestation by logging).

RESPONSIBLE DIVING

» Avoid touching living marine organisms with your body or equipment; practise and maintain proper buoyancy control.

» Take great care in underwater caves; air bubbles can damage fragile organisms.

» Minimise your disturbance of marine animals.

» Take home all your rubbish and any you find as well.

» Never stand on corals, even if they look solid and robust.

» Do not collect seashells or buy any seashell or turtleshell products.

» Use professional dive operators who maintain high safety and ethical standards.

RUSSELL ISLANDS

The Russell Islands are the Solomons' best-kept secret, with absolutely pristine sites, a dramatic topography and stellar visibility due to regular currents. The only way to dive this sensational world is to sign up for a live-aboard cruise with the MV *Bilikiki* (www.bilikiki.com).

» **SBD Douglas Dauntless Bomber** This US plane lies on a sandy bottom in 12m in Rendova Harbour. It's fun to sit in the cockpit.

» **P-39 Airacobra** This well-preserved WWII American fighter was found in April 2011 in 28m.

» **Shark Point** A 25-minute boat ride from Munda, this sloping reef seldom fails to produce sightings of grey reef sharks, silvertips, devil rays, snapper, batfish and turtles. You'll have to go deep (around 50m) to see the marauding sharks.

» **Top Shelf** Features top-notch coral gardens and varied fish life.

» **Susu Hite** A relaxing dive, this lively reef sits in less than 20m – perfect for novices.

» **The Pinnacle** Refers to a massive bommie magnet for rays and grey sharks. Sadly, most corals at this site were damaged during the earthquake in 2007.

» **Mbigo Mbigo** Features beautiful hard and soft corals and, quite often, Galapagos sharks.

» **Cave of the Kastom Shark** Seasoned divers won't want to miss the opportunity to descend vertically through a chimney down to 13m, follow a tunnel and exit at 25m into cobalt open water.

South Marovo Lagoon

South Marovo rewards divers with a host of very scenic sites off a cluster of three lovely islands – Kicha, Mbulo and Male Male Islands – accessible by 15- to 30-minute boat rides from the village of Peava.

» **Vuana House Reef** In front of Vuana Guesthouse. A superb drop-off.

» **Kavolavata Treasure** (Gatokae Island) A unique combination of muck diving and reef diving, with rare species of fish and invertebrates.

» **Toana** (Mbulo Island) Scenic drop-off dripping with luscious corals and sea fans. Another highlight is the dramatic underwater terrain.

» **Coral Gardens** (Mbulo Island) Massive fields of hard corals as well as swimthroughs and caverns.

» **Fantastic Fans** (Kicha Island) The drop-off is embellished with huge sea fans.

» **Picnic** (Kicha Island) A constant parade of reef tropicals, dramatic drop-offs and scenic ridges.

» **Ukala Via** (Male Male Island) Features an underwater point that attracts tons of species.

North Marovo Lagoon

North Marovo Lagoon is Uepi Island Resort territory. This exceptional dive area has dramatic walls, exhilarating passages and simple reef dives within reach of the resort. Daytrips to further dive sites can be arranged.

» **Bapita Sinkhole, Penguin Reef, Taiyo Fishing Boat Wreck, Lockheed P38 Wreck & Dauntless Dive-Bomber Aircraft Wreck** Four dives that are combined during a full-day excursion, near Seghe. The Sinkhole features a vertical shaft that exits at 28m. The P38 is in good condition and, nearby, the Dauntless is in only 10m.

» **Wickham Wrecks** A 90-minute boat ride from the resort, these four wrecks in South Marovo make for a fantastic excursion.

» **BOTCH** Stands for 'Bottom of the Channel'. Drift dive on the sandy bottom of Charapoana Passage.

» **Uepi & Charapoana Points** Iconic dive sites on the ocean side of the passage. Sizzling with electric fish action – sharks, jacks, barracuda, trevally – against a backdrop of corals, sea fans and sponges. Seasoned divers can do the Point to Point, navigating across Charapoana Passage.

» **General Store** 'A bit of everything' on the outer reef. Lots of swimthroughs and small canyons carved into the reef. A photographer's delight, with twistings and turnings, and light plays.

» **Elbow Point** A magnificent drop-off, lavishly draped with sea fans. Likely to spot pelagics.

» **Elbow Caves** A network of gutters carved into the reef wall. Sunbeams play through skylights in the caves – magical.

Gizo

Another not-to-be-missed area is Ghizo Island, further west. Again, the diving is superlative, with a stunning mix of WWII wrecks (bookmark the **Toa Maru**, a virtually intact Japanese freighter that ran aground during WWII) and superb offshore reefs. The 2007 earthquake/tsunami did wreak havoc on a few sites (particularly **Grand Central Station**, north of Gizo, and **Hotspot**, east of Gizo). Just off Fatboys, **Kennedy Island** is a lovely spot to learn to dive, with a parade of reef fish to be observed on the sprawling reef.

Kokoda Track

When to Go

May to September are the coolest, driest and best months to trek, although most companies operate from March to October. Always prepare for rain.

What to Pack

comprehensive trail guide: Clive Baker's *The Kokoda Trek* or Bill James' *Kokoda Field Guide*
comfortable, well-made boots (already broken in)
tent
lightweight sleeping bag
poncho or other wet-weather gear
water bottle, to refill from streams
medical kit
zip-lock bags to keep papers/maps dry

Total pack weight should not exceed 15kg.

Websites

Kokoda Track Authority (www.kokoda trackauthority.org) List of licensed tour operators.
Kokoda Trekkers Forum (www.kokodatrail. com.au/forums) Training tips, advice and testimonials.
Kokoda Commemoration (http://kokoda. commemoration.gov.au) Snapshot history of WWII events.
Kokoda Track Foundation (www.kokoda trackfoundation.org) Opportunities to give back.

Why Do It?

Halfway through you may wonder why you came to walk the Kokoda Track. Your blistered feet will hurt, your clothes will be wet with sweat and by the end of the day you'll undoubtedly be tired and hungry. But what your pictures won't show (assuming you muster the energy to take a few) is your growing sense of awe. For over every steep, slippery step on this 96km natural rollercoaster, Australians, Americans and Japanese fought for their lives; against each other and against the terrain. In 1942 there were no guesthouses, no porters, no relief from dysentery and the constant fear of ambush. To read a synopsis of the Kokoda campaign, see p177.

Crossing the Owen Stanley Range has become a pilgrimage for many Australians, a chance to pay their respects by sharing some of the trials of the men who fought and died here. And what started as a trickle is turning into a tide. In recent years, there has been an average of some 4000 trekkers (95% of them Australian) who gritted their teeth and tackled the mountains. The majority walk as part of an organised group; only the most experienced trekkers could consider walking this track independently.

Apart from the wartime history, relationships built with today's residents of the track, and particularly the guides and carriers who trek with you, are mutually rewarding. They serve as a reminder that the Kokoda Track is about people; not just a distant, heroic military campaign.

Planning Your Trek

Most people walk the track with a company specialising in organised treks (see p31) and all the logistical arrangements will be dealt with by them. The first decision when considering walking the Kokoda Track is whether you prefer a hassle-free, albeit more expensive, guided trek or a cheaper, locally arranged walk. The following advice is a starting point for all walkers.

All trekkers (but not porters or guides) must pay a K300 trekking fee and obtain a permit from the Kokoda Track Authority (KTA; Map p47; ☎323 6165, 685 7685; kokoda trackauthority@global.net.pg, 2nd fl, Brian Bell Bldg, Boroko, Port Moresby) before starting the trip. The KTA is also a great place to 'bump' into guides and porters who sometimes hang around here.

There are basic 'resthouses' in most villages plus various shelters and campsites along the track. Some of the resthouses and camp sites are small, so if you meet another party you might have to camp in the village or move on to the next village.

Most porters are very resourceful and able to find accommodation with *wantoks*. However, ultimately it is your responsibility to bring all the equipment, including tents and utensils, that your party will need. The same is also true for food; your guide will take only the clothes he is wearing.

Organised treks supply the bulk of your food, which accompanies you on the backs of local carriers. It's replenished about halfway along via a chartered flight; there are no trade stores on the track (only at Sogeri and Kokoda). Bring any comfort food yourself and keep it light. And don't forget sachets of rehydration salts – maintaining your fluid and carbohydrate levels is critical.

Whether you are on an organised trek or walking with locals, ensure that you have comprehensive individual medical insurance.

Training

Train for at least three months. Do stair-training, running, and practise hiking with a heavy load. As LP reader galahad_at_large put it, 'Practise by climbing the stairs in an office tower at home. For realism, cover yourself in mud, carry a sack of onions on your back and wear slippery shoes.'

Guides & Carriers

If you're trekking independently, don't do it without a good guide. A personal recommendation is best – the KTA is a good place to start. You could also try asking other trekkers on the www.kokodatrail.com.au.

Kokoda Track – South

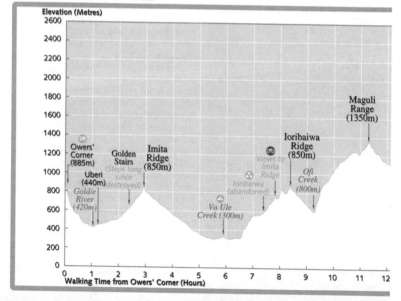

There are dozens of guides and carriers working on the track and most of them are freelancers.

It is also possible to hire carriers at Kokoda, although you can't just expect them to be able to drop everything at a moment's notice and head off. The maximum that a carrier can carry (and is permitted to do so under KTA rules) is 15kg.

Having a carrier might mean the difference between finishing the trek or giving up. One carrier between two or three is a good idea. If the weight becomes too much, you can employ a carrier in most villages along the track, but they are getting busier as the route becomes more popular. Pay guides about K100 per day and carriers about K80 per day, plus K20 per day for food and lodgings; you'll also need to pay their airfares back home.

Organised Treks

You can choose to walk the track with one of dozens of companies, which takes most of the hassle out of the preparation, leaving you to focus on getting fit. Costs depend on the length of the trek, whether it includes airfares from Australia, what equipment is provided and whether you employ a carrier. See the websites for full details and make sure you are comparing like with like.

SAFETY

The Kokoda Track is not PNG's most difficult trek, but it's no walk in the park either. Aim to do it in nine days, not six. Take advantage of the services of local carriers and never walk with fewer than four people. If there is an accident, two can get help and one can stay with the injured. Robberies and conflicts among traditional landowners have led to the track's closure in the past, but in recent years the situation has been fairly calm. Still, it's worth keeping an ear open.

Price is not the only consideration when selecting a trekking company. It's worth asking a few questions before handing over a fistful of kina.

» If you are particularly keen on the military history, a knowledgeable guide is a must. What sites will you be shown? What level of information can you expect from your guide?

» Most trekking companies carry a satellite phone or a two-way radio; if they don't have one and there's a problem, no one can hear your screams.

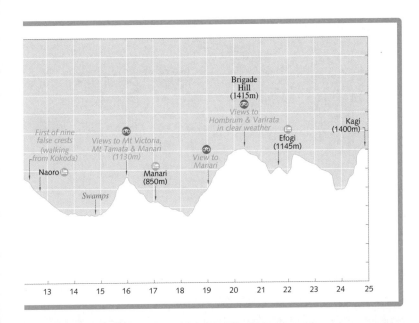

First of nine false crests (walking from Kokoda)

Naoro

Swamps

Views to Mt Victoria, Mt Tamata & Manari (1130m)

Manari (850m)

View to Manari

Brigade Hill (1415m)

Views to Hombrum & Varirata in clear weather

Efogi (1145m)

Kagi (1400m)

13 14 15 16 17 18 19 20 21 22 23 24 25

» How is their safety record? Besides your own insurance – which is essential – what additional insurances do they carry and what does it cover?

» Ask about equipment; if they supply tents it may be possible to inspect them.

» While agony loves company, it's a trail, not a highway. How many people in a group?

» What is their code of ethics? Do they carry out accumulated rubbish? Do they pay guides and porters reasonable wages? Contribute to local communities?

Some of the main players include the following. All prices include transport out of Port Moresby unless otherwise indicated.

Adventure Kokoda (www.kokodatreks.com; from A$3695) This high-profile company is led by Charlie Lynn, son of a WWII Kokoda digger. One of the best operators.

Ecotourism Melanesia (☑323 4518; www.em.com.pg; from A$4000) Perhaps the largest locally owned inbound tour operator in PNG. Not cheap, but has an excellent reputation.

Executive Excellence (www.executiveexcellence.com.au; from A$6350 ex Brisbane) Known by some as the 'men in tights', this Brisbane-based operation employs ex-soldiers and includes a pre-departure training program.

Kokoda Trekking (www.kokodatrekking.com.au; without/with porter A$2700/3280) This PNG-owned company sponsors the Kokoda Challenge. With no expert guides, their trips are cheaper and encourage greater interaction with local guides and carriers, but historical knowledge is limited.

Kokoda Treks & Tours (www.kokoda.com.au; A$3950) When it comes to knowledge of the campaign, Frank Taylor is hard to beat. Treks include a trip to Buna and Gona. Good value.

PNG Trekking Adventures (www.pngtrekkingadventures.com) Highly regarded company operated by long-time Australian expats based in Port Moresby. Tours are limited to 12 to 15 walkers.

Local Operators

Of the many local Kokoda trekking operators, the KTA's recommendations include the following:

Fuzzy Wuzzy Expeditions (☑629 7469, 7127 2458; kokodatrackauthority@global.net.pg) Defol Orere is an experienced tour leader who also works with the Kokoda Track Authority.

Kokoda Holidays (☑340 4294, 7164 3221) This small operation is run by David Soru.

Kokoda Track – North

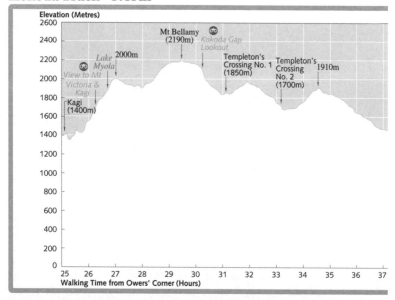

KOKODA CHALLENGE

If you find walking the Kokoda Track challenging, imagine taking it at full speed, running through sweltering humidity, rain showers and darkness, while taking only short breaks in hopes of completing the race not in days but in hours.

The Kokoda Challenge (www.kokodatrekking.com.au/kokodachallenge.html) was first held in 2005, and still remains a small, intimate affair. Some 70 runners – 20 spots reserved for international athletes – compete for top honours. Although some high-ranking ultra-marathoners and trail runners have entered in recent years, the long-running champion is Brendan Buka, a porter from Kokoda, who has set the course record for races in both directions. The fastest run ever was in 2008, when Buka raced from Owers' Corner to Kokoda in a thigh-defying 16 hours and 34 minutes.

The race is held on the last weekend in August each year, with a $2650 admission fee (including accommodation and chartered aircraft out of Moresby). If you can't make it, Australia also hosts its own 96km Kokoda Challenge, held in the Gold Coast hinterlands each year (see http://kokodachallenge.com).

Getting To & From the Trek

The Kokoda Track runs between Owers' Corner in Central Province and Kokoda in Oro Province. At the southern end you'll need a 4WD to reach Owers' Corner, taking the turn-off just before Sogeri – look for a white-painted stone war memorial. At McDonald's Corner there is a strange metal sculpture of a soldier; this is where the road once ended and the track started, but the actual track now starts further on at Owers' Corner. PMVs run from Gordons Market in Port Moresby to Sogeri early in the morning. From there, you'll need to wait and hope for a lift to Owers' Corner or start walking the 16km. The KTA can help arrange transport. Note: the road is often impassable, so be prepared to walk at least part of it if required.

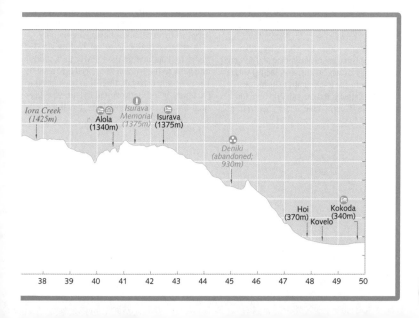

The Trek

Depending on how fit you are, it takes between six and 11 days to traverse the track (walking for about 50 hours from beginning to end). The itinerary shown here is indicative only. It starts at Owers' Corner, but just as many people walk the other way, which involves about 550m more climbing. By making it a longer trip you have more time for side-trips, exploring the battlefields and experiencing village life.

Day 1: Owers' Corner–Va Ule Creek (10km, six hours) The Va Ule Creek campsites are about one to three hours past Imita Ridge. Watch for the extensive weapon pits on the northern face of Imita Ridge, where the Australians made their last stand in 1942.

Day 2: Va Ule Creek–Naoro (17km, seven hours) The track follows the original wartime route over Ioribaiwa Ridge. A memorial is being installed on the ridge and there are many interesting weapon pits, bunkers and relics on the slopes. Naoro has spectacular 270-degree views over the valley and there is a large resthouse.

Day 3: Naoro–Efogi (19km, seven hours) About halfway between these points there are three resthouses in Manari village. After the long climb up Brigade Hill you suddenly come into the open and have a wide panorama down the 1942 battlefield, across to Kagi and Mt Bellamy in the distance and Efogi, just below you. On a clear day you can see all the way back to Hombrum and Varirata, near Sogeri. There are about three resthouses in Efogi, the biggest village on the track.

Day 4: Efogi–Kagi–Mt Bellamy (12km, eight hours) Three hours of climbing and descending past Efogi is Kagi, another spectacular village site. From here, the track climbs to its highest point at Mt Bellamy. You can side-trip from the track to Lake Myola in three to four hours return.

Along the way, and just off the track, is the huge crater where a WWII bomber blew up and scattered aircraft parts in all directions. Your guide/carrier should know the place.

Day 5: Mt Bellamy–Alola (17km, 11 hours) After a long down and up section, the track passes Templeton's Crossings, followed by another up, down and up to Alola – quite a tiring section.

Day 6: Alola–Kokoda (19km, 10 hours) When you reach the Isurava Memorial, allow yourself at least an hour at the old battle site. It's a most impressive and moving place. After the memorial there is an optional two-hour detour to a wrecked Japanese aircraft with its paintwork still clearly visible. It's a steep climb and you'll need a guide.

Shortcuts

If you're looking for the Kokoda experience without taking on the full challenge, you could take a PMV from Port Moresby to the village of Madilogo, which avoids two hard days' walk from Owers' Corner to Naoro. It takes about two hours to reach the track from Madilogo; from there it's one to 1½ hours to Naoro.

For a little taste of the track you can walk down to the Goldie River from Owers' Corner in just an hour or so. If you have the energy, struggle up what was once the Golden Stairs to Imita Ridge.

Another option would be to fly in to Kagi, Efogi or Manari, walk a section and fly out. Flying to Kagi and walking to Manari (one day) would be interesting. These trips are serviced by expensive charter flights only.

A cheaper option is to get to Kokoda (by flight to Popondetta then PMV to Kokoda) and walk to the Isurava Memorial and back. If you're fit, you can walk there and back in a day (10 hours or so). Or overnight in Isurava village or at the Isurava Memorial trekkers hut.

regions at a glance

Central, Oro & Milne Bay Provinces

Villages ✓✓✓
Water Sports ✓✓
Trekking ✓✓✓

Morobe & Madang

Water Sports ✓
Trekking ✓✓✓
Festivals ✓✓

Port Moresby

Culture ✓
Islands ✓
Shopping ✓

Traditional Culture

The *haus tambaran*-style Parliament Haus provides a window into PNG culture, while the nearby National Museum showcases the arts and crafts of this diverse country. Many traditional customs of Moresby's original inhabitants can still be observed in the stilt villages of Hanuabada and Koki.

Tranquil Islands

If you can make friends with a yachty, there are some alluring island destinations a short sail from town. If you find yourself boatless, head to peaceful Loloata Island, where you can overnight beachside, and go snorkelling or diving by day.

Markets & Handicrafts

It's worth planning a trip around the fantastic Ela Beach market, held once a month. At other times, there are smaller markets as well as the excellent PNG Arts, selling weavings and carvings from all across the country.

Sustainable Stays

Move from village to village, staying in thatch-roof guesthouses, spending your days birdwatching, snorkelling, hiking and relaxing on beaches. Tufi and the islands of Milne Bay are the gateways.

Aquatic Adventure

There's superb diving at Tufi and Tawali Resorts, DIY snorkelling adventures in the Trobriands and paddling trips up the Dawadawa River. The Milne Bay Canoe & Kundu Festival is spectacular.

Bushwalks

Home to Kokoda Track, Central Province offers unforgettable adventure. There are great day hikes near Tufi and challenging walks all over Milne Bay – from one-day jaunts to multiday treks.

Surfing & Diving

Madang boasts some excellent diving and snorkelling with a legacy of WWII wrecks and a number of coral-fringed islands. Further up the coast, Ulingan Bay sees seasonal surf and its own slice of sandy nirvana.

Tracks & Trails

Morobe's Black Cat Trail and Bulldog Track are rated as some of the most challenging on the planet. Their 'take-no-prisoners, show-no-mercy' reputations will appeal to those with a wide masochist streak.

Singsing Fests

Singsing groups from around the country converge on Lae in their ceremonial wigs, cowrie shell breastplates and arse gras skirts for the region's premier event, the Morobe Show.

p40

p55

p75

The Highlands

Festivals ✓✓✓
Trekking ✓✓
Culture ✓✓✓

Highland Fests
First held in the early '60, the Highland shows have evolved into one of the world's greatest displays of indigenous culture. Expect hundreds of *singsing* participants dressed in feathers, shells and leaves.

Mountain Treks
With so many mountains on offer, why not tackle the biggest of them all – Mt Wilhelm. The less ambitious might prefer exploring the Crater Mountain Wildlife Management Area and around Lake Kutubu.

Traditional Culture
Beating drums and blood-curdling war songs, the Highlands holds some of the most resilient cultures in PNG, including the Asaro mudmen with their distorted face masks.

p95

The Sepik

Surfing ✓
Culture ✓✓
Arts ✓✓✓

Monsoon Surf
Between mid-October and late April, monsoon-induced swells reach PNG's remote northern coast, creating fine surf breaks. Vanimo is the region's best pick, attracting a growing trickle of experienced riders.

Ancient Rituals
The Sepik River is an 1126km-long cultural smorgasbord, and old customs die hard here. Young men are still cut so that the resulting scars imitate a crocodile's skin; women are still denied entry into the towering spirit houses.

Traditional Arts
Traditional art and spiritual beliefs collide in the Sepik. Skull racks, story boards, cassowary thighbone daggers and unusual masks have made the Sepik villages powerhouses of artistic expression.

p116

Island Provinces

Diving ✓✓✓
Surfing ✓✓✓
Adventure ✓✓✓

Wrecks & Reefs
You can go wreck-diving and explore the coral wonders of East New Britain, book into a first-rate dive resort at Walindi and take in New Ireland's profusion of fish species.

Wonder Waves
With a good range of breaks, Kavieng has fantastic surf and a management plan that ensures the waves never get too crowded. You can also head out near Lavongai where you can surf, fish for dinner and enjoy island life.

Island Adventures
There are plenty of adventures on the islands: treks up volcanoes near Rabaul, multiday bike rides down the scenic Boluminski Hwy and memorable hikes through the mountainous rainforests of Bougainville.

p137

Solomon Islands

Diving ✓✓✓
History ✓✓✓
Getaways ✓✓✓

Undersea Marvels
The Solomons are as beautiful below the waterline as on land. The country is famous for its world-class sunken wrecks, its incredible reefs and abundance of marine life.

WWII Artefacts
A fleet of WWII ship- and plane wrecks rest on the seafloor between Guadalcanal and Tulagi. Tanks, amtracks, memorials and anti-aircraft guns are scattered in the jungle throughout the archipelago.

Enchanting Escapes
We've all dreamt of the ultimate getaway: a vision of dense jungle, a turquoise sea, a few scattered bungalows, healthy local food and the soundtrack of nature. Find yours here.

p202

Papua
New Guinea

❯ Every listing is recommended by our authors, and their favourite places are listed first

❯ Look out for these icons:

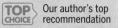 Our author's top recommendation

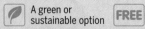 A green or sustainable option

 No payment required

See the Index for a full list of destinations covered in this book.

Papua New Guinea On the Road

> **For the Solomon Islands see p201**

Port Moresby

POP 300,000 / AREA 240 SQ KM

Best Places to Eat

» Rapala (p50)
» Jepello (p50)
» Daikoku (p50)
» Asia Aromas (p50)
» Beachside Brasserie (p50)

Best Places to Stay

» Airways Hotel & Apartments (p49)
» Ela Beach Hotel (p49)
» Jessie Wyatt House (p46)
» Shady Rest (p49)
» Lamana (p49)

Why Go?

First-time visitors to Papua New Guinea's capital Port Moresby can find it confronting and even intimidating, but since all visitors enter PNG through its gritty capital almost everyone ends up spending some time here. Port Moresby is the South Pacific's largest city, and while the sprawling city isn't among the world's great metropolises, it does have redeeming features.

A visit to Parliament Haus, PNG's most impressive building, and the cultural displays at the National Museum are recommended – the mosaic facade of Parliament Haus will excite any photographer in the late afternoon. The National Botanical Gardens are a highlight; when the orchids are blooming, it's perhaps the city's most charming spot.

The city's relative sophistication is a treat before heading bush; or, if you've been wandering through villages for weeks, a meal at one of Port Moresby's good restaurants makes a welcome change from rice, taro and sweet potato.

When to Go
Port Moresby

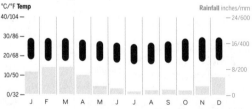

Year-round Hot year-round; average highs between 28°C and 32°C.

Dec–May Wet season with hotter, rainier days.

Jun–Nov Dry season, with slightly lower temperatures.

History

While Port Moresby today has dozens of tribal groups, only two can truly call it home: the Motu and Koitabu. The native people of the Port Moresby area (and much of the eastern tip of the mainland) are descendents of Polynesian people, unlike the predominantly Melanesian population. The Motu are traditionally a seagoing people and didn't arrive until relatively recently, probably less than 2000 years ago. Motu villages were built on stilts over Moresby Harbour. Hanuabada ('Great Village') was the largest of their communities and still exists today. Stilt houses can also be seen at Koki Village near Town and Tubuseraia down the Magi Hwy.

The first European to visit was Captain John Moresby in 1873, after whom the harbour was named. Moresby explored extensively along the south coast and spent several days trading with villagers at Hanuabada. One year later, the London Missionary Society arrived and was soon followed by traders and 'blackbirders', who recruited indentured labourers and were little better than slave-dealers.

In 1888 Port Moresby became the capital of the newly declared British New Guinea, and in 1906 the territory was handed to Australia, itself only five years independent of British rule. Sir Hubert Murray took over administration of Papua, as it was known, until his death in 1940, aged 78, at Samarai Island while still on duty.

Port Moresby was overshadowed by Lae, the supply base for the gold rushes in Wau and Bulolo, and Rabaul until WWII. The Japanese quickly occupied all of northern New Guinea and were rapidly advancing south when Port Moresby became the staging post for Allied troops fighting along the Kokoda Track. Port Moresby remained in Australian hands throughout the war.

After the war, Papua and New Guinea were administered as one territory with Port Moresby becoming the capital largely by default – more attractive alternatives such as Lae and Rabaul had been flattened by Allied bombing.

Dangers & Annoyances

Port Moresby can be a dangerous place, but it's not the hell on earth that many who've never been here make it out to be. The vast majority of visitors to Port Moresby leave unscathed and, if you use your common sense, you should be fine.

Despite this, there are no guarantees and the situation in Port Moresby can change quickly, so always ask the locals when you arrive about what is safe, then make your own choice. Walking around Town and Boroko during daylight hours should be fine, but anywhere else you should walk with a local. Avoid secluded urban areas at any time; *raskols* (bandits) are not strictly nocturnal. The view from Paga Hill in Town is terrific, but don't walk up there on your own. Stay out of the settlements unless you are with one of the residents (that includes Hanuabada). Don't walk around Kila Kila, Sabama or Six Mile at any time. After dark, don't walk anywhere. The most important thing is not to make yourself a target or put yourself in situations where you are vulnerable. It is just common sense.

⊙ Sights

A collection of districts rather than a single city, Port Moresby sprawls around the coast and inland hills. Most of Port Moresby's few sights are in the modest CBD, called Town, and the government district of Waigani.

Hanuabada   NEIGHBOURHOOD

(Map p42) Past the docks to the north lies Hanuabada, the original Motu village. Although it is still built over the sea on stilts, the original wood and thatched houses were destroyed by fire during WWII. They were rebuilt in all-Australian building materials, corrugated iron and fibrocement, but it's an interesting place and the people have retained many traditional Motu customs.

You cannot simply wander around the villages if you are not a guest or if you don't have a local guide – ask your hotel to suggest someone.

Koki   NEIGHBOURHOOD

(off Map p44) The picturesque stilt village of Koki, at the eastern end of Ela Beach, is worth visiting if you can find a local to take you. The best way to do that is by visiting the neighbouring Koki Market, one of the oldest and, after a vast improvement in security, safest markets in the city. Fresh produce and fish straight off the boat are sold here and even if you're not shopping for produce it's a colourful place to watch grassroots-style PNG commerce. It's best not to go alone, and preferable to go with a local. PMVs (public motor vehicles) stop outside the market.

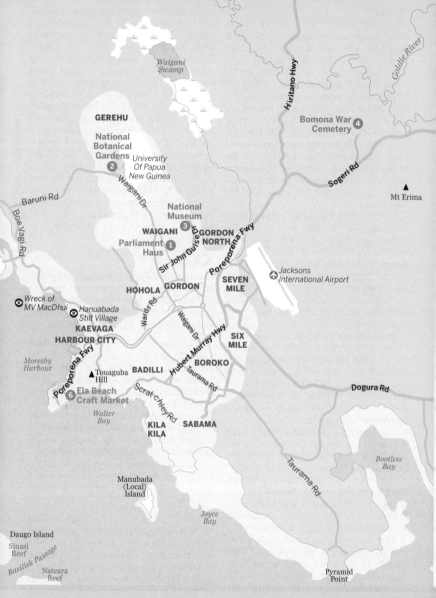

Port Moresby Highlights

1 Gazing up at the towering, mosaic facade of **Parliament Haus** (p44), done in Sepik *haus tambaran* (spirit house) style

2 Seeing the spectacular orchids' explosion of form

and colour at the **National Botanical Gardens** (p44)

3 Discovering cultural treasures tucked away inside the little-visited **National Museum** (p44)

4 Driving out to solemn **Bomana War Cemetery** (p53) and contemplating the tragic losses wrought by WWII

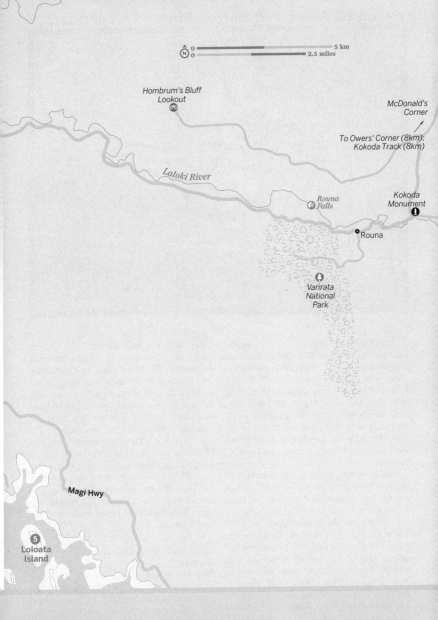

Hombrum's Bluff
Lookout

McDonald's
Corner

To Owers' Corner (8km);
Kokoda Track (8km)

Laloki River

*Rouna
Falls*

Kokoda
Monument

Rouna

Varirata
National
Park

Magi Hwy

5 Loloata
Island

0   5 km
0   2.5 miles

5 Catching a boat out to **Loloata Island** (p46) for some excellent snorkelling, diving and waterfront relaxing

6 Loading up on one-of-a-kind handicrafts brought from all across PNG to the colourful monthly **Ela Beach Craft Market** (p51)

7 Watching whirling dance performances at the lively **Hiri Moale Festival** (p46)

Town & Ela Beach (Port Moresby City)

(Map of Town & Ela Beach area showing streets and numbered locations including Royal Papua Yacht Club, Daikoku & Spa Pua, Weigh Inn Hotel, Container Wharf, Moresby Harbour, Main Wharf, Cuthbertson St, Stanley Esp, Champion Pde, Douglas St, Mary St, Hunter St, Brampton St, Ela Beach Rd, Chesterfield St, Kermadec St, Lawes Rd, Touaguba Hill, Reservoir, Reserve, Ela Beach, Paga Hill Lookout, Bougainville Cres, Armit St, Musgrave St, Chalmers Cres, Bramell St, Ela Beach Recreation Reserve, Walter Bay, To Koki, Koki Market)

FREE **Parliament Haus** BUILDING

(Map p48; Independence Dr, Waigani; ⊗8am-noon & 1-3pm Mon-Fri) The impressive Parliament Haus was officially opened in 1984 with Prince Charles on hand. The main building is in the style of a Maprik, or Sepik-style, *haus tambaran,* while the attached, circular cafeteria building follows Highland design principles. The facade is quite stunning, with a mosaic featuring unmistakably PNG motifs.

The cavernous lobby is entered through doors whose handles are stylised *kundu* drums (an hourglass-shaped drum with lizard skin). Inside, a towering wood carving represents the four regions of PNG, while several glass displays showcase the nation's wondrous insect life, including the native Queen Alexandra's Birdwing (the world's largest with a 30cm wingspan). Photography inside Parliament Haus is forbidden. There's often a guide on hand to explain the building's design and interior elements.

It's possible to visit the chamber and witness parliament when it's sitting. A taxi from Boroko costs about K25 or K30 from Town. Alternatively, take a PMV along Waigani Dr, get out at the white, empty Pineapple Building, and walk about 2km northeast.

TOP CHOICE **National Museum** MUSEUM

(Map p48; Independence Dr, Waigani; admission by donation; ⊗8.30am-3.30pm Mon-Fri, 1-3.30pm Sun) All the exhibits at the museum, just beyond Parliament Haus, sit under a fine film of dust. But you can happily spend an hour or so looking at the displays that cover the geography, fauna, culture, ethnography and history of PNG. There are superb examples of masks, tapa cloths, shields and totems, a magnificent Milne Bay outrigger canoe decorated in cowrie shells, and a display showing how *bilums* are made. Photography is not allowed. The tiny shop just outside the entrance sells carved bowls, walking sticks and *bilums.*

TOP CHOICE **National Botanical Gardens** GARDENS

(Map p42; www.ncbg.org.pg; Waigani Dr, Waigani; adult/child/student K8/2/4; ⊗8am-4pm) At the northern end of Waigani Dr, just beyond the University of Papua New Guinea, the National Botanical Gardens are an island of calm and beauty in an otherwise lacklustre city. There is more than 2km of walkways threading under and through the jungle canopy, well-maintained lawns and gardens displaying both local and exotic plant species, and probably the best collection of

Town & Ela Beach (Port Moresby City)

native and hybrid orchids in PNG. There are also some excellent wildlife displays, such as tree kangaroos, hornbills, cassowaries, a giant python, and a large aviary that houses parrots and birds of paradise (the only chance most visitors get to see them).

St Mary's Catholic Cathedral CHURCH
(Map p44; Musgrave St, Town) This cathedral is not so old but it does have an impressive entrance portal in the style of a Sepik *haus tambaran*.

Paga Point LOOKOUT
(Map p44) The harbour headland, Paga Point, is adjacent to Town. It's worth walking to the top of Paga Hill for the fine views over the town, the harbour and the encircling reefs – but don't go alone.

Ela Beach BEACH
(Map p44) On the southern side of Town is the long, sandy stretch of Ela Beach. The beachfront promenade is a popular walk during the day, though the sands are not full of sunbathers these days. Even locals perceive this area as potentially unsafe.

ISLANDS, BEACHES & REEFS
The wreck of the Burns Philp cargo ship **MV MacDhui** (Map p42) can be seen just breaking the surface in Moresby Harbour, off Hanuabada. It was sunk by Japanese aircraft in the early days of WWII. Its mast now stands in front of the Royal Papua Yacht Club (off Map p44).

Many expats have boats and the yacht club is busy on weekends. If you play your charm cards right, you might be asked out for the day. **Manubada (Local) Island** (Map p42) is popular for weekend beach trips, but carry your own water and sun protection because there is no shade. The **Bootless Bay** (Map p42) area, southeast of Port Moresby, and the other islands around the harbour are also popular; see p46.

There are many interesting places within easy reach if you have access to a boat. **Basilisk Passage** (Map p42) is the deep, narrow entrance to the Port Moresby harbour named by Captain Moresby after his ship, HMS *Basilisk*. The SS *Pruth* was wrecked on nearby **Nateara Reef** (Map p42) in 1924, and there's the beautiful **Sinasi Reef** (Map p42) outside the passage and the adjoining **Daugo Island** (Map p42), also known as Fisherman's Island, which has lovely stretches of white-sand beaches.

🏃 Activities

The diving around Port Moresby is excellent. Bootless Bay has world-class diving over reefs and WWII wreckage. Loloata Island (p46) is a popular holiday spot for divers.

Dive Centre
DIVING

(☎320 1200; www.divecentre.com.pg) The biggest dive operator in Moresby is the Dive Centre, currently based at Gateway (p49). It offers full PADI courses (K1300), equipment, air, and a wide range of diving and snorkelling tours. A two-dive outing including gear costs K275. Very professional.

Spa Pua
SPA

(off Map p44; ☎340 2717; 2nd fl, SVS Foodland Bldg, Harbour City) Recover from hard days of travel at this relaxing spa, which offers a wide range of treatments (massages cost K140 for one hour).

☞ Tours

For organised tours that walk the Kokoda Track see p29. The companies listed here also offer Kokoda trekking, but they do Moresby-based day tours also.

Ecotourism Melanesia
TOUR

(Map p48; ☎323 4518; www.em.com.pg; Lokua Ave, Boroko; half-day tour per person from K300) This is the best of the locally owned tour operators, but by no means the cheapest. They'll customise tours to suit your needs.

Niugini Holidays
TOUR

(☎323 5245; www.nghols.com) Offers professionally run day trips, including three-hour tours of Port Moresby Town (per person A$130), full-day Town and Varirata National Park tours (A$290).

★ Festivals & Events

Hiri Moale
FESTIVAL

Port Moresby's big event is the three-day Hiri Moale Festival, celebrated around September 16 to coincide with Independence Day celebrations. Motu people race giant canoes and celebrate the shift in trade winds that traditionally brought traders home from the Gulf region where they exchanged earth-fired pots for food. There's a Miss Hiri Queen contest. The festival is held at Ela Beach.

🛏 Sleeping

Places to stay are scattered all over Port Moresby and, with few exceptions, are absurdly overpriced. There are places at Seven Mile near the airport, in Six Mile, Boroko, Hohola (sometimes called Waigani) and Town, with a few others scattered in between. Boroko is really the centre of activity in Port Moresby and the most convenient location as almost all PMV routes stop at its big bus stop on the Hubert Murray Hwy, one of only two routes into Town. All but the budget places listed below provide free airport pick-ups and drop-offs.

Jessie Wyatt House
GUESTHOUSE $

(Map p47; ☎325 3646; Taurama Rd, Boroko; r per person K80) Run by the Country Women's Association, this churchy place is popular with Papua New Guineans. It is clean, quiet and homely with a communal kitchen, free tea and coffee, and a fridge in each room. The rooms are few and in high demand.

WORTH A TRIP

LOLOATA ISLAND

About 20km east of Port Moresby, **Loloata Island** (Map p42), in Bootless Bay, is a popular weekend escape – midweek is even better.

After the hurly-burly of Port Moresby, **Loloata Island Resort** (☎325 8590; www. loloata.com; s/d incl all meals from A$235/390; ❄) is the perfect tonic, with first-rate diving as well as snorkelling, fishing and kayaking. There are around 30 dive sites, including wreck dives (notably, a Boston A20 bomber), but many people come simply to do nothing for a few days. Loloata is popular with day-trippers from Port Moresby; weekends can get busy here. A day trip, including return transfers, from Port Moresby, lunch and a diving/snorkelling trip to the reefs around nearby Lion Island costs K165. Accommodation is provided in large, comfortable beachfront bungalows that have panoramic views northeast across Bootless Bay and the Owen Stanley Range on the mainland. The island has many semi-tame wallabies that graze along the walking paths, and there are tree kangaroos and parrots in an enclosure. Diving costs A$75 for one or A$190 for three dives (including equipment); night dives and PADI courses are also available.

Loloata offers a range of tours (such as Varirata National Park, Sogeri, Owers' Corner). To get there, drive out on the Rigo Rd (which meets the airport road in Six Mile) to the Tahira Boating Centre on Bootless Bay. The resort's boats make regular trips to the island. Alternatively, call ahead and the resort bus will collect you from the airport or your hotel.

Boroko

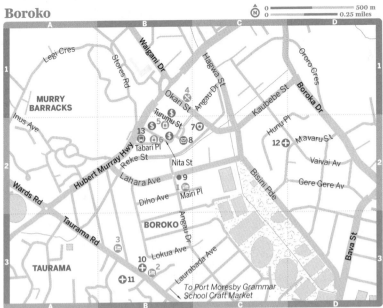

Kangaroo Motel   HOTEL **$**
(Map p48; ☑323 6188; Magila Rd, Six Mile; s/tw without bathroom K100/150, r with bathroom K220-250; ▓) Kangaroo Motel has very basic 'backpacker' rooms, which are narrow, prison-like quarters with fencing above the walls and no windows. The standard and deluxe rooms are cleaner and more inviting, with windows, tile floors and in-room fridges. There's a bar and pokies parlour, and the motel is run by a security firm so safety isn't an issue – though it is in a bad neighbourhood.

Ponderosa Family Hotel   HOTEL **$$**
(Map p48; ☑323 4888; Nuana Rd, Gordons; r K285-435; ▓). In a quiet area, this friendly place has simple, tidy rooms (though the cheapest rooms have very old bathrooms and lack air-conditioning).

Weigh Inn Hotel   HOTEL **$$**
(off Map p44; ☑321 7777; www.weighinnhotel.com; Poreporena Fwy; r K330-390; ▓) This ageing place has a mixed bag of rooms, from poorly lit standards with cinderblock walls to boxy but airier 'premier' rooms. All have TV, fridge and phone. There's a restaurant (mains around K25) and pub that serves daily specials (pot roast, fish and chips) for K18.

Boroko

Sleeping
1 Comfort Inn B2
2 Jessie Wyatt House B3
3 Shady Rest Hotel B3

Eating
Cellar .... (see 3)
4 City Point B1
Mr B Coffee Shop .... (see 5)

Shopping
5 Brian Bell Plaza B2
6 Handicrafts Market B2

Information
7 Boroko Police Station C2
8 Boroko Post Office B2
9 Dove Travel B2
Kokoda Track Authority .... (see 5)
10 Paradise Private Clinic B3
11 Port Moresby General
    Hospital B3
12 Port Moresby Medical Centre C2

Transport
13 Manu Autoport (Boroko PMV
    Stop) B2

Waigani

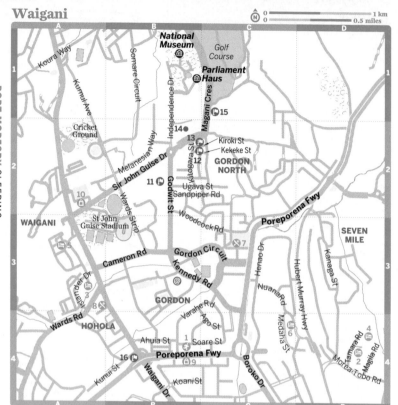

Waigani

⊙ Top Sights
National Museum......................................B1
Parliament Haus B1

✪ Activities, Courses & Tours
1 Ecotourism Melanesia...........................B4

🛏 Sleeping
2 Hideaway Hotel......................................D4
3 Holiday Inn...A3
4 Kangaroo Motel.....................................D4
5 Lamana Hotel...A3
6 Ponderosa Family Hotel........................C4

✘ Eating
Dynasty..(see 10)
7 Gordons Market....................................C3
Hog's Breath..................................(see 10)
8 Jepello...A3

✪ Entertainment
Gold Club...(see 5)

🛍 Shopping
9 PNG Arts...B4
10 Vision City...A2

ℹ Information
11 Australian High Commission.................B2
12 British High Commission B2
13 Indonesian Embassy B2
14 National Library & Archives...................B2
15 New Zealand High Commission............C1
16 Solomon Islands High
   Commission..B4

ℹ Transport
Gordons Market PMV Stop............(see 7)
Thrifty...(see 5)

Comfort Inn
HOTEL **$$**

(Map p47; ☎323 6024; reservations@comfortinn. com.pg; Mairi Pl, Boroko; s/d incl breakfast from K260/360, apt K490; ❄❅) In a quiet location two minutes' walk from central Boroko, the Comfort Inn has friendly service and comfortable if rather unloved rooms.

Hideaway
HOTEL **$$**

(Map p48; ☎323 6888; www.accommodationpng. com.pg; Tamara Rd, Six Mile; r from K350; ❄❅) Rooms here are clean but compact, and have noisy air-con and uninspiring decor. The palm-fringed pool is a nice retreat on sweltering days. The attached restaurant (meals K30 to K40) receives mixed reviews. Hideaway is in an unsafe neighbourhood.

Shady Rest
HOTEL **$$**

(Map p47; ☎323 0000; www.shadyrest.com.pg; Taurama Rd, Boroko; r K298-468; ❄) The rooms here are clean and adequately equipped (large flat-screen TV, phone, fridge), and there are decent dining options (a pizza stand and a restaurant) with indoor and outdoor seating (see p50).

Lamana
HOTEL **$$$**

(Map p48; ☎323 2333; www.lamanahotel.com.pg; off Waigani Dr, Hohola; r K760-800; ❄❅) The nicely designed rooms at Lamana are large and comfortable, and the service is friendly and efficient. There's a good restaurant and a decent nightspot.

Gateway
HOTEL **$$**

(☎325 3855; www.coralseahotels.com.pg; Morea-Tobo Rd, Seven Mile; d K280-455, apt K505; ❄❅) Located one minute's drive from the airport, this member of the Coral Sea chain is a Moresby institution, with comfortable if slightly worn rooms, and there are plenty of facilities. There are a couple of bars and restaurants; the Rattle 'n' Hum pizzeria downstairs serves passable pizzas to a mixed local crowd.

Ela Beach Hotel
LUXURY HOTEL **$$$**

(Map p44; ☎321 2100; www.coralseahotels.com.pg; Ela Beach Rd, Ela Beach; d/apt K704/803; ❄❅) This flash hotel has attractively set rooms in a prime beachfront location. Its redeeming features include the excellent Beachside Brasserie restaurant and Ozzie's Bar (p51), one of Moresby's best live-music venues.

Airways Hotel & Apartments
LUXURY HOTEL **$$$**

(☎324 5200; www.airways.com.pg; Jackson's Pde, Seven Mile; r K825-1125, ste K1350-2200; ❄@❅) Airways is the pick of the top-end hotels, pitching itself as the perfect place for the visitor who wants nothing to do with Port Moresby. It has spectacular views over the airport and the poolside lounge-and-bar area is lovely. Airways offers luxury rooms (ranging from standard rooms through to suites) and classy amenities two minutes from the airport. There are two restaurants, the wonderful KC's Deli (open 7am to 7pm) and bars including Balus Casino Bar, with pool tables and live entertainment, and the Dakota Lounge, inside an old DC-3. Even if you're not staying at the Airways, it's worth dropping by for lunch or a drink.

Holiday Inn
HOTEL **$$$**

(Map p48; ☎303 2000; www.holidayinn.com.au; Islander Dr, Hohola; r K792-858; ❄@❅) Another top-notch option, the Holiday Inn has excellent facilities – a good restaurant, a nightclub, an inviting palm-fringed pool – plus modern rooms.

Crowne Plaza
HOTEL **$$$**

(Map p44; ☎309 3000; www.crowneplaza.com; cnr Douglas & Hunter Sts, Town; r K902-1067; ❄@❅) In the heart of Town, this concrete behemoth has commanding views from its nine floors of neatly fitted-out rooms. The standard rooms are modestly sized, but you could throw a party in the executive suites and apartments, which come with free use of the club lounge. There are restaurants, bars and a cafe.

Grand Papua
LUXURY HOTEL **$$$**

(Map p44; ☎304 0000; www.grandpapuahotel. com.pg; Mary St near Musgrave St, Town; r from K800; ❄@❅) The high-rising Grand Papua brings yet more luxury to the Town scene, with handsomely appointed rooms, a top-notch restaurant (with Moresby's best breakfast buffet) and loads of amenities (including spa services).

✖ Eating

Moresby's restaurant scene has come a long way in recent years. After a few weeks in the provinces eating rice, *kaukau* (sweet potato) and *tinpis* (tinned fish), travellers will find the Moresby dining options a blessing. There are good restaurants in Port Moresby, but little to fill the void between *kai* bars (takeaway food) and pricey restaurants.

A good spot for mealtime browsing is in the newish **Vision City** (Map p48; Sir John Guise Dr, Waigani), a mall with a bakery, food court and several good sit-down restaurants.

HAVE YOUR SAY

Found a fantastic restaurant that you're longing to share with the world? Disagree with our recommendations? Or just want to talk about your most recent trip?

Whatever your reason, head to lonelyplanet.com, where you can post a review, ask or answer a question on the Thorntree forum, comment on a blog, or share your photos and tips on Groups. Or you can simply spend time chatting with like-minded travellers. So go on, have your say.

Rapala   INTERNATIONAL $$$
(Map p44; ☎309 3240; cnr Douglas & Hunter Sts, Town; mains K70-100; ⊙6.30-10pm Mon-Sat) One of Moresby's best restaurants is an elegant, well-dressed affair inside the Crowne Plaza. Top picks include roast duck breast, thyme-scented rack of lamb, mud crab bouillabaisse and other mouth-watering dishes. The design is a pure geometric extravagance, though the views are nice.

Jepello   ITALIAN $$$
(Map p48; ☎323 6800; Inki St, Hohola; meals K27-60; ⊙noon-2pm Mon-Fri & 5-10pm Mon-Sat) Just off Waigani Dr, behind the Interoil Service Station in another dodgy area, is Jepello, Moresby's best Italian restaurant. The fresh pastas and wood-fired pizzas are good, but leave room for the homemade gelato.

Daikoku   JAPANESE $$$
(off Map p44; ☎321 0255; 2nd fl, SVS Foodland Bldg, Harbour City; meals K35-100; ⊙11.30am-2pm & 6-10pm Mon-Sat, 6-10pm Sun) This elegant, long-running spot serves up Moresby's best Japanese fare, with mouth-watering sushi, sashimi and other Japanese favourites. At dinner, chefs will prepare your meal on a hotplate at your table with great skill and showmanship.

Asia Aromas   ASIAN $$
(Map p44; ☎321 4780; Ground fl, Steamships Plaza, Champion Pde, Town; meals K35-60; ⊙11.30am-2pm & 5.30-10pm Mon-Sat) The Chinese and Thai dishes and friendly service here are so good it's worth booking ahead to secure an evening table. Top dishes include Thai curries, braised prawns with butter and garlic, salt and pepper squid and Tom Yum Talay (spicy seafood soup).

Beachside Brasserie   INTERNATIONAL $$
(Map p44; ☎321 2100; Ela Beach Rd, Ela Beach; meals K30-72; ⊙6.30am-10.30pm) The pleasant brasserie in Ela Beach Hotel serves excellent gourmet pizzas as well as chilli prawns, salmon plates, grilled steaks and other international fare.

Cellar   INDIAN $$
(Map p47; Taurama Rd, Boroko; mains K30-45; ⊙6am-10pm) At the Shady Rest Hotel, this place serves an assortment of spicy Indian dishes. Popular picks include tandoori chicken, vegetable samosas, beef vindaloo and chicken masala. Cellar also has changing dinner buffets, with nights dedicated to Indian, pizzas and pastas, regional fare and Aussie barbecue.

Hog's Breath   INTERNATIONAL $$$
(Map p48; Sir John Guise Dr, Vision City, Waigani; mains K33-88; ⊙11.30am-2.45pm & 5.30-10pm) This well-known Aussie chain serves up sizzling steaks, burgers, fish and chips, plus more eclectic fare – Tex-Mex combos, Thai prawn and pawpaw salads, and lamb cutlets. It's one of several good choices inside the Vision City mall.

City Point   ASIAN $$
(Map p47; ☎311 3666; Okari St, Boroko; mains K28-48; ⊙10am-2pm & 5-9pm) New in 2010, this trim modern place serves good Chinese and Malaysian food. Top hits include fried crab with chilli sauce, spicy Sichuan selections and sea cucumber dishes. The lunchtime menu (K17 to K22) provides good value.

Dynasty   CHINESE $$$
(Map p48; ☎302 8538; Vision City, Sir John Guise Dr, Waigani; meals K30-75; ⊙11am-2pm & 6-10pm) This is the top spot for Chinese cuisine. The yum cha is a major draw on Sunday mornings.

Cafe   INTERNATIONAL $$$
(Map p44; ☎309 3000; Crowne Plaza, cnr Douglas & Hunter Sts, Town; mains K35-70; ⊙6.30am-10pm; ❄) Slightly cheaper and more casual than neighbouring Rapala, this Crowne Plaza gem serves grilled barramundi, Thai chicken curry and other multifarious fare. There's also a good lunch or dinner buffet (K67) highlighting different cuisines (Asian, Melanesian, Seafood, Carvery).

Mr B Coffee Shop   CAFE $
(Map p47; 1st fl, Brian Bell Plaza, Boroko; mains K5-10; ⊙9am-5pm Mon-Fri, 9am-1pm Sat) Colourful artwork and masks adorn the walls of this tiny local favourite, which is a fine refuge

from Boroko's chaotic streets. It serves sandwiches, savoury pies, pastries and good Goroka coffee.

Espresso Bar CAFE $
(Map p44; Ground fl, Deloitte Tower, Douglas St, Town; ☺7.30am-5pm Mon-Fri, 8.30am-2pm Sat) This tiny place provides good coffee and light meals.

Gordons Market MARKET
(Woodcock Rd, Gordon) One of Port Moresby's largest produce markets. It's a ragged place, best visited with a local.

☆ Entertainment

Port Moresby has a few live-music venues and some discos and nightclubs. The *Post Courier* publishes the 'What's On' entertainment guide on Wednesday.

Royal Papua Yacht Club PRIVATE CLUB
(off Map p44; ☑321 1700; Poreporena Fwy) This large, airy place is the last bastion of postcolonial white elitism, with expats and a few visiting yachties mixing over cold beer and good bistro fare (mains K28 to K57) on the deck overlooking the harbour. It's tough to get in here unless a member signs you in, so try to make a contact before venturing over.

Gold Club CLUB
(Map p48; ☑323 2333; Lamana Hotel; off Waigani Dr, Hohola; ☺11am-5am) This club has live music a couple of nights a week, but otherwise it's given over to DJs and dancing. The open-air dance floor surrounded by layers of bars creates a festive ambience. The music is good and there's no riff-raff. A top spot.

Ozzie's Bar CLUB
(Map p44; ☑321 2100; Ela Beach Hotel, Ela Beach; ☺9am-2am) With live music Wednesday, Friday and Saturday nights, Ozzie's is a laid-back and unprepossessing place where you can mix it with locals who love to dance.

Pondo Tavern BAR
(Map p44; ☑309 3000; cnr Douglas & Hunter Sts, Town; ☺11am-4.30am) Low-key spot underneath the Crowne Plaza with live music on Thursday nights, and decent pub grub (mains K17 to K23) served on the enclosed patio.

🛍 Shopping

Handicrafts Market MARKET
(Map p47; Tabari Pl, Boroko; ☺8am-5pm) Boroko's dusty central square is the best place to buy *bilums*, Highland hats, carvings, kina-shell breast plates, shell jewellery and the like. Moresby's sellers are used to the ways of tourists and will happily engage in some friendly negotiation, but protracted haggling is considered rude. See p192 for more on bargaining.

Ela Beach Craft Market MARKET
(Map p44; ☑325 2838; Ela Beach International School, Ela Beach Rd, Ela Beach; ☺7am-noon last Saturday of every month) This is the best market in PNG, with all the paintings, carvings, baskets, shells and weavings you can poke a *koteka* (penis gourd) at. Barbecued food and traditional dancers (at about 10am) contribute to the carnival atmosphere.

Port Moresby Grammar School Craft Market MARKET
(off Map p47; ☑323 6577; Leander St; ☺8am-noon 2nd Sat of every month) Another monthly event with good crowds and a party atmosphere.

PNG Arts HANDICRAFTS
(Map p48; ☑325 3976; Poreporena Fwy, Gordons; ☺9am-4.30pm Mon-Fri, 9am-3.30pm Sat, 10.30am-2pm Sun) The long-running PNG Arts warehouse has a huge collection of wares from all over the country. The prices are reasonable, credit cards are accepted and freight and documentation can be organised.

ℹ Information

Emergency
Ambulance (☑111)
Fire (☑110, 321 3658)
Police (☑000)

Internet Access
Only the priciest hotels ($$$) offer internet access. Apart from these, Port Moresby has few internet cafes, their connections are only moderately quick and they keep short hours.
IT Station (Map p48; RH Hypermarket, Kennedy Rd, Gordons; per hr K12; ☺8am-4.45pm Mon-Fri, to 2.45pm Sat)
Micom (Map p44; Douglas St, Town; per hr K12; ☺9am-5pm Mon-Fri, 10am-1pm Sun)

Libraries
National Library & Archives (Map p48; ☑325 6200; Independence Dr, Waigani; ☺9am-4pm Mon-Fri, to 1pm Sat, 1-4pm Sun) An independence gift from Australia, this library houses a huge PNG collection.

Medical Services
Whatever the situation, it's probably worth calling one of the two clinics first.

Paradise Private Clinic (Map p47; ☑325 6022; Taurama Rd, Boroko; ⊙24hr)

Port Moresby General Hospital (Map p47; ☑324 8200; Taurama Rd, Korobosea)

Port Moresby Medical Centre (Map p47; ☑325 6633; portmoresbymedicalservice@gmail.com; cnr Vaivai Ave & Mavaru St, Boroko; ⊙24hr) Best place in an emergency. Can arrange medivac and has a decompression chamber on site.

DENTISTS

Dr Richard Pickworth (Map p44; ☑321 1137, after hours 321 6328; Ground fl, Moguru Motu Bldg, Champion Pde, Town) Good reputation.

Mills Dental Care (Map p44; ☑320 0600, after hr 7697 5933; 1st fl, Deloitte Tower, Douglas St, Town) Emergency service (24hr) available.

Money

ANZ and Westpac are more efficient than Bank South Pacific, where you'll likely grow old waiting to change your money. If you're changing cash or travellers cheques, ask for the international desk. See p190 for more on money.

TOWN

ANZ (Map p44; cnr Champion Pde & Musgrave St, Town) ATMs are more reliable than Westpac's. Can use Visa and MasterCard.

Bank South Pacific (Map p44; cnr Musgrave & Douglas Sts) Agents for Western Union.

Westpac (Map p44; cnr Musgrave & Douglas Sts) Agent for Amex. In theory, ATMs work for Visa, MasterCard, Cirrus, Visa/PLUS, Maestro. There's a charge of K20 to change cash.

BOROKO

ANZ (Map p47; Hubert Murray Hwy) Has ATMs.

Bank South Pacific (Map p47; cnr Nita St & Angau Dr)

Westpac (Map p47; Nita St)

Post

Boroko Post Office (Map p47; Tabari Pl, Boroko; ⊙8am-4pm Mon-Fri, 8-11.30am Sat)

Post Office (Map p44; cnr Cuthbertson St & Champion Pde, Town; ⊙8am-4pm Mon-Fri, to 11.30am Sat)

Tourist Information

Kokoda Track Authority (Map p47; ☑323 6165; www.kokodatrackauthority.org, 2nd fl, Brian Bell Plaza, Boroko; ⊙9am-4pm Mon-Fri) Statutory body that administers activities related to the Kokoda Track – it collects and distributes trekking fees, liaises with landowners etc. Good place to contact if you're looking for a guide or want to join a trek.

NCD Tourism Office (Jackson's International Airport; ⊙8.30am-4.30pm Mon-Fri) Small, underfunded National Capital District tourism office.

PNG Tourism Promotion Authority (TPA; Map p44; ☑320 0211; 5th fl, MMI Haus, Champion Pde, Town; ⊙8.30am-4.30pm Mon-Fri) Provides limited information on accommodation; it's mainly about marketing and promotion.

Travel Agencies

Dove Travel (Map p47; ☑325 9800; Angau Dr, Boroko; ⊙8.30am-4pm Mon-Fri) This Catholic-run agency is pretty well connected with all forms of transport in PNG, plus international flights. Can also suggest cheap sleeping options if you're desperate.

ⓘ Getting There & Away

Air

Flights link Port Moresby to virtually everywhere in PNG and anywhere Air Niugini flies internationally (see p195).

Some airline offices in Port Moresby:

Air Niugini (Map p44; ☑321 2888; www.airniugini.com.pg; Ground fl, MMI House, Champion Pde, Town)

Airlines PNG (Map p44; ☑321 3400; www.apng.com; 1st fl, Pacific Place, Musgrave St, Town)

Qantas (Map p44; ☑308 3200; www.qantas.com.au; Cuthbertson St, Town)

Travel Air (Map p44; ☑323 8530; www.travelairpng.com; Steamship Compound, Waigani Dr)

Boat

There are no regular passenger boats sailing out of Port Moresby. Many freighters do have passenger facilities but none of the shipping companies officially allow passengers. If you want to go to the Gulf, ask around the smaller boats at the jetties north of the main wharf. Heading east towards Milne Bay, you could go to Kupiano and look for a small boat or canoe. A series of hops along the south coast could, after nights in villages and days waiting under palm trees, get you to Alotau (p62).

Car

You can't really drive anywhere else from Port Moresby (except Kerema). There are several companies renting cars and 4WDs in Port Moresby. See p53 for details.

PMV

Rural PMVs leave from Gordons Market (Map p48) and head west as far as Kerema (K40, five hours) and east along the Magi Hwy. PMVs also leave here for Bomana War Cemetery (p53; bus 16) and destinations along the Sogeri Rd.

ⓘ Getting Around

To & From the Airport

The hotel minibus is the easiest way to get between the airport and where you're staying. All but the smallest establishments have one and if you contact them ahead, or call from the airport, you'll soon have a free ride. In the international terminal arrivals hall, go into the NCD Tourist Office where you can use the phone for free. In the domestic terminal, buy a phonecard from the shop beside the cafe.

Taxis wait outside both terminals and, unless you find a taxi with a meter, you'll need to negotiate the fare before you leave. A taxi to Waigani or Boroko should cost K25, and to Town it's about K35.

Car & 4WD

The airport is full of companies renting cars and 4WDs, and the major names also have offices in several top-end hotels. Prices start at around K175 per day and K0.80 per km for a manual Mitsubishi Lancer (plus insurance at K50 per day for a collision damage waiver excess of K2000). Port Moresby can be a confusing place to navigate at first, so be sure to have a map and take out full insurance. Police checkpoints are common after dark but shouldn't be a problem if you have your licence. For more information, see p199.

Avis (☑324 9400; www.avis.com.pg) Offices at the airport (domestic and international terminals).

Friendly Car Hire (☑683 6238) Utikas Pok runs this small operation – much cheaper than the big boys – and he'll deliver a car to you.

Hertz (☑302 6822; sales@leasemaster.com. pg) Desks at the airport and Gateway Hotel.

Thrifty (Map p48; ☑325 5550) Offices at the airport, Airways Hotel & Apartments and Lamana Hotel.

PMV

Port Moresby has an efficient PMV (public motor vehicle) service, though you'll see very few white faces in the windows. Most expats will advise against using PMVs, but they're quite safe provided you stick to certain routes and be careful about where you disembark. PMVs run frequently from about 6am to 6pm but stop suddenly at nightfall; be careful not to be caught out. The flat fare is K1 to K2 for trips around Moresby. The main interchange point is **Manu Autoport** (Map p47) in Boroko; look for the pedestrian overpass and crowds of people. In Town, the main stop is on Douglas St, and at Gordons it's near Gordons Market. PMVs get crowded at peak hours and especially on Friday evening.

PMVs run set routes and have route numbers (and sometimes the destination itself) painted on the front. They go both ways. Some useful routes include the following:

Route 4 From Hanuabada, through Town, Koki and Boroko to Gordons Market.

Route 7 From Gerehu, past Waigani, Gordons and Erima to Seven Mile.

Route 9 From Gerehu and Waigani to Four Mile/Boroko, East Boroko and then to Three Mile (this is the bus to get from Boroko to the Botanical Gardens).

Route 10 From Hanuabada to Town, Badilly, Sabama, Manu, Three Mile, Four Mile/Boroko (Jessie Wyatt House; past the hospital and the CWA Hostel), and on to the airport at Seven Mile. Avoid getting on or off in the Kila Kila and Sabama areas, which are relatively unsafe.

Route 11 From Town to Two Mile Hill, Boroko, Waigani (not all stop at the government offices) and Morata.

Route 12 From Gerehu to Waigani, Hohola, Three Mile and Manu.

Route 15 From Tokarara to the government buildings in Waigani, Gordons, Erema, Seven Mile, Six Mile, Five Mile and Four Mile/Boroko to Hohola.

Route16 From Gordons Market out to Bomana Prison, past the War Cemetery.

Route 17 From Gordons to Four Mile/Boroko, Three Mile, Sabama and Bari.

Taxi

Port Moresby has no shortage of taxis, and you'll usually be able to find one outside a hotel or the airport, and in Boroko. Sample fares: Town to Boroko or Waigani, K20; Town to the airport, K30.

If you need to book or call a taxi, reputable companies include **Ark** (☑323 0998, 7122 5522), **Comfort** (☑325 3046) and **Scarlet** (☑323 4266).

AROUND PORT MORESBY

Sogeri Road

There are some interesting areas near Port Moresby along or just off the Sogeri Rd, which veers to the right (east) off the Hubert Murray Hwy a couple of kilometres past the airport. It's quiet during the week, so it's best to travel on the Sogeri Rd with a local – there have been occasional robberies.

It's 46km to Sogeri but there is enough to see to make it a full-day trip. The first stop is the large and carefully tended **Bomana War Cemetery** (Map p42; ☑328 1536; ☺8am-4pm), where 4000 PNG and Australian WWII soldiers are buried; American soldiers who died in PNG were usually shipped home for burial. It's a serene yet sobering place. PMV 16 from Gordons Market (Map p48) runs past the gate.

Around Fourteen Mile, you reach the small new **Adventure Park PNG** (☑311 2471; half-/full day K20/30; ☉9am-4pm Sat & Sun), which has two waterslides, a petting zoo, a cafe and a lake where you can fish for your dinner (fishing rod hire available). Next door is the **National Orchid Gardens** (☑325 5049; adult/child K10/5; ☉8am-4pm Sat & Sun), where you can see a broad variety of flowering orchids, as well as a few resident cassowaries.

A few kilometres beyond the cemetery, the road winds up the impressive **Laloki River gorge** and you're soon more than 600m above sea level. There are several viewing points looking into the gorge and up to the **Rouna Falls** and power station. Just beyond is a track leading to the run-down Kokoda Trail Hotel (p54).

Continue a bit further to the turn-off to the run-down **Varirata National Park**, which spreads across 1000 hectares at over 800m elevation. It's 8km from the turn-off, along a battered but 2WD-accessible road. There are some poorly maintained trails and an excellent lookout back to Port Moresby and the coast. The birdwatching here can be rewarding, with an array of kingfishers and Raggiana birds of paradise as highlights.

A few kilometres down the dreadful Kokoda Track road (navigable by 4WD only) is a turn-off left (west) back towards Port Moresby. This is the Hombrum Bluff road that runs along the top of the Laloki River canyon wall. It leads to **Hombrum Bluff Lookout**, which rises 1300m and was used as a retreat for the military brass during WWII. Below is Seventeen Mile, which was an important base camp for more than 400 soldiers.

Back on the Kokoda Track road you can drive past **McDonald's Corner** where there's a small memorial that marks the start of the Kokoda Track. It was here that Australian WWII soldiers disembarked from their trucks and began the long muddy march. Later the rough road was pushed further through to **Owers' Corner**, and you can drive here too... if your poor car hasn't suffered enough! Be

careful out here. There are no road signs so ask villagers for directions, and if it rains you'll be stuck good and proper.

There's nothing worth stopping for in Sogeri for, but a couple of kilometres along another diabolical dirt road the **Crystal Rapids** (admission per vehicle K20) make a pleasant swimming and picnic spot.

🛏 Sleeping & Eating

Bluff Inn   MOTEL **$$**
(☑328 1223; www.bluffinnmotel.com; Sogeri Rd; s/d/tr K165/220/250; ❉) Run by an English expat, this sprawling motel by the river at Seventeen Mile has basic cabin-style rooms that are fair value. The restaurant (meals K10 to K42) serves tasty pub fare (including fat burgers, steaks and fish and chips), and is a popular expat gathering spot on weekends (with occasional live bands).

Sogeri Lodge   GUESTHOUSE **$$**
(☑325 5440; sogent@global.net.pg; s/d with shared bathroom K175/250) Popular with Kokoda trekkers, Sogeri has clean, simple, fan-cooled rooms and a pleasant restaurant (mains K20 to K45) with a terrace offering fine views.

Kokoda Trail Hotel   LODGE **$$$**
(☑323 6724; www.kokodatrailhotel.com; r K350, bungalow K450-650) The plushest option on the Sogeri Rd is this Aussie-owned lodge that's often booked out by trekkers. Amid lush landscaping, the rooms here are bright and nicely equipped (fan, TV, fridge), and the restaurant (mains K25 to K60) has tasty dishes, including pan-fried barramundi, and superb views over the river.

❶ Getting There & Away

PMVs leave from Gordons Market (Map p48) semi-regularly. The road is surfaced to Sogeri and all the way down to the Varirata National Park, however the section from Sogeri to Owers' Corner – the start of the Kokoda Track – is suitable for 4WDs only.

Central, Oro & Milne Bay Provinces

POP 550,000 / AREA 67,940 SQ KM

Includes »

Best Places to Stay

- » Napatana Lodge (p63)
- » Ulumani Treetops Lodge (p66)
- » Nuli Sapi (p68)
- » Tufi Resort (p61)
- » Tawali Resort (p67)

Best Village Stays

- » Sibonai Guesthouse (p69)
- » Kofure (p61)
- » Okaibama (p73)

Why Go?

These eastern provinces have it all – dazzling reefs, an arsenal of historic WWII sites, jungle-clad mountains, and good-spirited and genuinely hospitable people. Outdoor adventure comes in many forms with superb bushwalking, birdwatching, island-hopping, diving and much more.

Papua New Guinea's foremost attraction, the legendary Kokoda Track, seesaws for 96 unrelenting kilometres between the Central and Oro Provinces. Further east, at Tufi and north of Alotau, some of the world's most biologically diverse reefs will have you gasping on your snorkel's mouthpiece.

Turning north, across the Solomon Sea, you'll find the famed Trobriand Islands, home to the exotic Milamala Festival of 'free' love, cricket and – above all – yams. Alotau, the capital of Milne Bay Province, is one of the safest and most attractive towns in the country and home to the Milne Bay Canoe & Kundu Festival, during which island warriors paddle ocean-going canoes in races guaranteed to have your heart racing.

When to Go

Kokoda

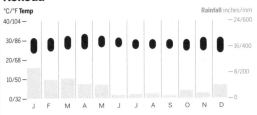

Jan–Mar High winds in Milne Bay; cyclone season in Coral Sea area.

May–Sep Dry, cooler weather in Central Province, ideal Kokoda trekking weather. Rain in Milne Bay.

Oct–Dec Calm, dry weather in Milne Bay.

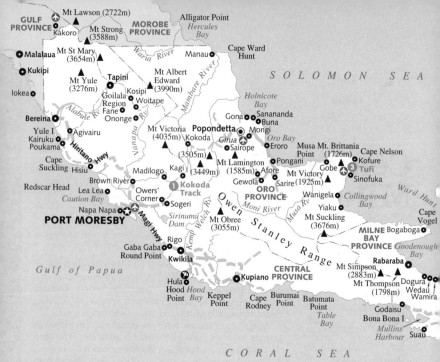

GULF PROVINCE
Mt Lawson (2722m)
Kakoro
Mt Strong (3588m)
MOROBE PROVINCE
Alligator Point
Hercules Bay
Malalaua
Kukipi
Mt St Mary (3654m)
Waria River
Manau
Cape Ward Hunt
Mt Yule (3276m)
Tapini
Goilala Region
Kosipi
Mt Albert Edward (3990m)
Fane
Woitape
Ononge
Mambare River
Mt Victoria (4035m)
SOLOMON SEA
Iokea
Bereina
Yule I
Kairuku
Poukama
Agivairu
Hiritano Hwy
Alabule Rv
Cape Suckling
Hisiu
Madilogo
Kagi
Kokoda
(3505m)
Popondetta
Girua
Sairope
Mt Lamington (1585m)
Afore
Gewola
Sarire
Mt Victory (1925m)
Gona
Sanananda
Buna
Mongi
Eroro
Pongani
Gobe
Kofure
Tufi
Sinofuka
Musa Mt. Brittania (1726m)
Cape Nelson
Oro Bay
Holnicote Bay
ORO PROVINCE
Brown River
Lea Lea
Owers' Corner
Kokoda Track
(3449m)
Owen Stanley Range
Moni River
Wanigela
Yiaku
Musa Rv
Wanigela
Collingwood Bay
Ward Hunt
Redscar Head
Napa Napa
Sogeri
PORT MORESBY
Magi Hwy
Sirinumu Dam
Kemp Welch Rv
Mt Obree (3055m)
Mt Suckling (3676m)
Cape Vogel
MILNE BAY PROVINCE
Bogaboga
Goodenough Bay
Rigo
Gaba Gaba
Round Point
Kwikila
Gulf of Papua
Kupiano
CENTRAL PROVINCE
Mt Simpson (2883m)
Rababara
Mt Thompson (1798m)
Dogura
Wedau
Wamira
Hula
Hood Point
Hood Bay
Keppel Point
Cape Rodney
Burumai Point
Batumata Point
Table Bay
Godaisu
Bona Bona I
Mullins Harbour
Suau
CORAL SEA

Kuiaro
Dagadaga (Pearl)
China Strait
China Strait
West Channel
Galahi I
Bonaloahilihili I
Kwato I
Kwato Mission
Magesina (Magehau)
Sariba I
See Samarai I Enlargement
Kwaiam I
Logea I (Rogeia)
Bonalia Bay
East Channel
Deka Deka I
Yama Reef
Luluni Point
Manta Ray Cleaning Station
Gona Bara Bara I
Doini I
Tobu I
Arch Is
0   5 km
0   3 miles

Customs Wharf
Samarai Island
Old International Wharfs
Christopher Robinson Memorial
Samarai I Wharf Dive Site
Bwanasa Women's Association Guesthouse
SITCO Wharf (Boats to Kwato I & Alotau)
Market
Sports Ground
Power House
Lookout
Old Hospital
Memorial Hall
Customs & Immigration Office
Police Station
0   200 m
0   0.1 miles

Central, Oro & Milne Bay Provinces Highlights

① Retracing WWII battles over the rugged Owen Stanley Range on the infamous **Kokoda Track** (p29)

② Watching spirited dance groups followed by a magnificent race on the waterfront at the **Milne Bay Canoe & Kundu Festival** (p63) in Alotau

③ Staying in a seaside village among the amazing volcanic *rias* (fjords) of **Tufi** (p60)

④ Hiking to waterfalls, snorkelling coral reefs and spying birds of paradise outside of island communities on the **D'Entrecasteaux Islands** (p68)

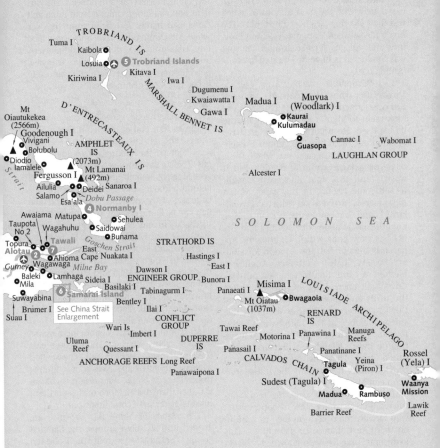

See China Strait Enlargement

⑤ Catching a wildly colourful cricket match on the **Trobriand Islands** (p72) and immersing yourself in the islands' unique culture

⑥ Wandering the forlorn waterfront of **Samarai Island** (p67) then exploring picturesque nearby islands

⑦ Taking in the abundance of marine life on a dive at **Tawali** (p67)

History

The coastal people and islanders of this region have traded for centuries in extensive barter networks, the most famous of which was the *kula* ring (see boxed text, p71). The *hiri* trade between Motuans in Central Province and villages further around the gulf was conducted in huge two-masted *lakatois* (sailing boats).

In 1606 Spanish mariner Luis Vaéz de Torres, after whom the Louisiade Archipelago was named, abducted 14 children and took them to Manila in the Philippines to be baptised. He was followed by an array of explorers, including the famous Frenchman Antoine d'Entrecasteaux, who left his name on a large group of islands. But it wasn't until 1847 that Europeans sought to settle the region. In that year, Marist missionaries arrived on Muyua (Woodlark) Island, but the locals, it seems, were unenthusiastic about Christianity and the Marists were gone within eight years. Apparently undeterred, the London Missionary Society (LMS), Catholics, Anglicans, Methodists and finally the Seventh-Day Adventists opened for business between the 1870s and 1908. Most notable among them was Reverend Charles W Abel, a dissident member of the LMS, who in 1891 founded the Kwato Extension Association on Kwato Island, near Samarai in the China Strait. This was the first church to provide skills training to the indigenous people of Milne Bay.

Apart from men of God, the region attracted a less savoury crew of opportunists who forcibly removed local men to work in northern Australian sugar plantations. This loathsome practice was known as 'blackbirding' and continued well into the 20th century. Errol Flynn, who spent his formative years ducking and diving around New Guinea from 1927 to 1933, later wrote of the 'confidence' required to persuade local elders to allow their men to be carted off.

On the north coast early European contacts with the Orokaiva people were relatively peaceful, but when gold was discovered at Yodda and Kokoda in 1895, violence soon followed. A government station was established after an altercation between locals and miners, but the first government officer was killed shortly after he arrived. Eventually things quietened down and the mines were worked out. Then came the war (see boxed text, p62).

Milne Bay became a huge Allied naval base and a few American landing craft and several memorials can still be seen. The gardens and plantations inland from Buna and Gona had barely recovered from the war when Mt Lamington's 1951 eruption wiped out Higaturu, the district headquarters, and killed almost 3000 people. The new headquarters town of Popondetta was established at a safer distance from the volcano.

Geography

The region stretches down the 'dragon's tail' at the eastern end of mainland Papua New Guinea and out into the Coral and Solomon Seas, taking in the hundreds of islands and atolls of Milne Bay Province. On the south coast Port Moresby is built around one of several natural harbours and sits in the centre of a large area of dry grasslands; swamps and tidal flats can be found elsewhere on the coast.

The mainland is divided by the Owen Stanley Range, which rises rapidly from the northern and southern coasts to peaks of 3500m to 4000m. Not surprisingly, major roads are few: the Magi and Hiritano Hwys extend from Port Moresby, while in Oro Province the only road of any length runs from the capital, Popondetta, to Kokoda, from where it's all about leg power.

Mt Lamington, near Popondetta, remains a mildly active volcano and further east there are volcanoes near Tufi. The section of coast around Cape Nelson has unique tropical 'fjords' *(rias);* their origin is volcanic rather than glacial. Much of this northern coast is made up of coral limestone.

The islands of Milne Bay Province are divided into six main groups: the Samarai group; D'Entrecasteaux group; the Trobriand Islands; Muyua (Woodlark) Island; the Conflict and Engineer groups; and the 300km-long Louisiade Archipelago. They range from tiny dots to mountainous islands such as Fergusson, Normanby and Goodenough, which, while only 26km wide, soars to 2566m at the summit of Mt Oiautukekea, making it one of the most steeply sided islands on earth.

CENTRAL PROVINCE

Stretching for more than 500km either side of Port Moresby, Central Province lives in the shadow of the national capital. Overlooked by tourists and long ignored by politicians, infrastructure is, even by local standards, *bagarap* (buggered up).

Hiritano Highway

The now impressively pot-holed Hiritano Hwy once connected Port Moresby with Kerema, far to the west in Gulf Province. Locals now abandon the road at Malalaua for dinghies that ferry them the last 70km. If you do consider driving the whole highway, only do so in the dry season and bring an extra 4WD with a winch to pull free your first vehicle from the waist-high mud. There is talk of road repairs but in these parts talk is cheap, and road repairs are expensive.

This area is home to the Mekeo people, who are noted for their colourful, dancing costumes and face-painting. On ceremonial occasions the men paint their faces in striking geometric designs.

If you fancy munching on a marsupial, watch for the Vanuamai people selling roasted wallaby (K10 for a set of ribs) along the roadside. They taste pretty good – the wallabies that is, not the Vanuamai people; no one has been eaten around here for decades.

Kokoda

The Owen Stanley Range rises almost sheer as a cliff face behind the Oro Province village of Kokoda, where the northern end of the track terminates. It's a sleepy place and the grassed area in the centre of town houses a small museum that has photos and descriptions of the campaign. Ask around to have it opened. Grace Eroro (✆7113 6598), who runs a small guesthouse, is a great source of information. Opposite the post office is a branch of the Kokoda Track Authority where trekking permits can be bought if you haven't already done so in Port Moresby. Trekkers finishing the trail should also report here to be officially stamped off the trail.

🛏 Sleeping & Eating

There are a couple of resthouses in Kokoda and all of them allow you to pitch your tent on their camping grounds.

Limited food and, mercifully, beer is usually available from Kokoda's trade stores; send a runner ahead to organise ice.

Kokoda Memorial Hospital   GUESTHOUSE $
(dm/camping per person K50) The first guesthouse after exiting the trail (to your right) is part of the Kokoda Memorial Hospital, which has some dormitories with toilets, showers, gas stoves and kitchen utensils.

Money goes towards much-needed medical supplies. You can reserve ahead by contacting Camp 39.

Camp 39   GUESTHOUSE $
(✆7382 3309, 629 7130; dm/camping per person K30) Named after the legendary 39th Battalion, Camp 39 is a friendly, pleasantly sited spot with a grassy lawn (for camping) and a large open thatch-roof building where you can sleep on a mat. Meals available (around K60 per day). Facilities are basic, though the Kennia family plan to add flush toilets and a shower.

Priscilla's Place   GUESTHOUSE $
(✆329 7653; priskokoda@daltron.com.pg; r per person incl breakfast K100) Priscilla's has private rooms in traditional thatch-roof buildings with basic shared facilities. Lunch (K15) and dinner (K25) also available.

Grace Eroro's Guesthouse   GUESTHOUSE $
(✆7113 6598; r per person K50) About 2.5km along the road to Popondetta is Grace's place, run by the big-hearted Grace Eroro. Grace welcomes travellers and was in the process of constructing an eight-room bunkhouse when we passed through. At the moment, accommodation is simple (but flush toilets and showers are planned), or you can camp on the lawn and bathe in the river. Meals cost extra.

❶ Getting There & Away

Most people fly into or out of Kokoda on a flight chartered by their tour company. PMVs (public motor vehicles; K20, 3½ hours) leave Kokoda for Popondetta around the ungodly hour of 3am.

ORO PROVINCE

Oro Province is sandwiched between the Solomon Sea and the Owen Stanley Range. It's physically beautiful but an uninspiring capital and poor transport connections mean few travellers make it here.

The world's largest butterfly is found in Oro Province, the Queen Alexandra's birdwing. You might think that you've seen some big butterflies in PNG, but these are monsters, with wingspans of nearly 30cm. The first specimen collected by a European was brought down by a shotgun! That butterfly, a little damaged, is still in the British Museum. The Queen Alexandra's birdwing is now a threatened species. It lays its eggs on a particular species of vine that is poisonous to most birds and animals; the butterfly is poisonous as well.

Popondetta

Popondetta is a ragged town, without much appeal for tourists, although some come to see the area's WWII history – Buna and Gona are within an easy day trip. The Oro Guesthouse and Birdwing Butterfly Lodge can provide information and help arrange guides for trips to Buna or Gona. The looming 1585m Mt Lamington is currently off-limits to bushwalkers following heavy rains that have washed out the walking trails.

Popondetta is not a place to be wandering around alone at night.

🛏 Sleeping & Eating

Oro Guesthouse   GUESTHOUSE $$
(☑629 7127; r incl breakfast, dinner & laundry K226-280; ❄) The best option in Popondetta has tidy guestrooms, excellent local information (including nearby village stays) and decent meals. It's a 10-minute walk from town but PMVs will sometimes drop you here if you ask. There are discounts for Kokoda Track walkers (K119).

**Birdwing Butterfly
Lodge**   GUESTHOUSE $$
(☑629 7477; birdwing@online.net.pg; r K286; ❄) Friendly place, 1.5km northeast of town on the road to Gona, with clean rooms with fridge and TV. Meals are extra, though there's a kitchen for guests.

Comfort Inn   HOTEL $$
(☑629 7222; r K292-422; ❄) Simple rooms with tile floors, fridge and TV that open on to a garden-like exterior. It has the only restaurant in town (mains K25 to K65).

❶ Getting There & Away

Air

Girua airport is 15km from town. **Air Niugini** (☑329 7022), next to the post office, has flights to and from Port Moresby (K295, 40 minutes, daily). **Airlines PNG** (☑629 7638) flies to Port Moresby and Tufi.

Boat

All boats leave from Oro Bay.

PMV

PMVs for Kokoda (K20, 3½ hours, about 11am) leave from beneath the large trees outside Oro Motors in the centre of town. PMVs for Oro Bay (K9, 45 minutes) and the airport (K4, 20 minutes) leave from the main road.

Oro Bay

Oro Bay is the province's main port. It became a major American base after the Japanese had been prised out of Buna and Gona, though the bustle of those days is long gone. Today it's a quiet place with occasional banana-boat traffic up and down the coast, and a larger boat travelling weekly to Lae (p77).

If your ship doesn't come in, the **Oro Bay Guesthouse** (r per person K100) is on the water's edge near the wharf, but it's a 30-minute walk around the bay to the PMV boats.

The **Edna Resort Centre** (r per person K120) has a few simple two-room bungalows. Contact the Birdwing Butterfly Lodge for bookings.

Rabaul Shipping (Star Ships) has a weekly boat to Lae (18 hours) and another to Alotau (K160, economy class only) calling at all ports in between, including Tufi (K130). Banana boats to Tufi (K100) run if the winds aren't too high and usually leave mid-morning.

Tufi

Carefree and far away from the world, Tufi is one of PNG's best-kept secrets. On the stunningly beautiful Cape Nelson, where steepsided *rias* penetrate the land like the fingers of a grasping hand, this picturesque spot has a more relaxed atmosphere than any city in the country. Once home to fishing and rubber industries, the settlement now heavily relies on tourists drawn to the Tufi Resort.

The area, however, is much more than the resort. Several villages within two hours of Tufi welcome guests to their bush-material guesthouses, some of them set under swaying palm trees beside sandy beaches, which is a truly idyllic way to spend a few days. If you're around in mid-August you might catch the Tufi Cultural Show, a relatively intimate *singsing* (celebratory dance/festival) with groups mainly from Oro Province. Contact Tufi Resort for dates.

The cape was formed by ancient eruptions of its three volcanoes and the lava that flowed down into the sea creating the *rias*, for which the cape is now famous.

⊙ Sights & Activities

Diving is one of Tufi's great attractions, with consistent 30m-plus visibility. Maloway,

EXPLORING THE COAST AROUND TUFI

One of the highlights of visiting Tufi is staying in villages that dot the coastline on either side. You could spend weeks wending your way along the coast in this way, staying at **village guesthouses** (r per person K150) en route. The accommodation is basic, with mosquito nets and local food (the seafood is tasty), but most visitors rate it as far more memorable than staying at the pricey resort. Boat transfers cost extra. The guesthouses can also arrange fishing and snorkelling; bring your own gear. It's best, though not essential, to contact them ahead, and this is most easily done through Tufi Resort.

Most of the villages offer treks, birdwatching, snorkelling, fishing and participation in *singsings* (celebratory dances/festivals). Some of the better village stays include the following:

» **Kofure** (30min outrigger canoe ride north of Tufi) Long-running guesthouse with white sands, palm trees, snorkelling and canoeing the *rias* (fjords).

» **Garewa** (1hr outrigger canoe ride south of Tufi) Gorgeous beach, waterfall, lobster feasts.

» **Jebo Guesthouse** (1hr dinghy ride south of Tufi) White-sand beach, waterfall, canoeing, spotting birds of paradise.

» **Kamoa Beach Guesthouse** (15min outrigger canoe ride to the mouth of Tufi ria) Pretty beach.

» **Tumari Guesthouse** (45min dinghy ride south of Tufi) Brown-sand beach, but sweet and welcoming village; good birdwatching opportunities.

Cyclone Reef and Marion Reef are memorable, and the muck diving under Tufi wharf is exceptional. Nearby are some WWII ships easily accessible in shallow water, while the famous B17 'Black Jack' bomber is down the coast. Tufi Resort has dive boats and a fully equipped dive shop. The dive season is from September to May. From June to August, high winds make diving difficult.

Local villages can provide outrigger canoes (the standard form of transport) if you want to go fishing, and Tufi Resort's dive boat also does fishing trips.

There is a network of tracks in the area ideal for trekking. Many follow the *ria* around the coast. Other tracks can be quite difficult; you must be fit. Tufi Resort can arrange a guide and village stays, or you could take your chances and ask around yourself. The villages and the resort can arrange boats to pick you up at various locations at the end of your walk.

Orchids, birds and butterflies can also been seen in the surrounding jungles and, again, Tufi Resort can arrange guides to view these.

🛏 Sleeping & Eating

Tufi Resort RESORT $$$
(☏276 3631; www.tufidive.com; s/d incl meals K495; ❄☙❄) Located a short distance from the airstrip, this upmarket resort has a relaxed atmosphere, with pleasantly designed rooms, an airy bar and restaurant, and a cliffside barbecue area with spectacular views across the *ria*. Diving, fishing and cultural outings are the main attractions, and the resort encourages people to get into the local villages for an even more memorable stay. Wi-fi available (for the absurd price of K110 per day). Reserve well in advance.

❶ Getting There & Around

Airlines PNG flies to and from Port Moresby (K392 to K525) on Monday, Wednesday and Friday.

For information on small boats to and from Oro Bay. Between Tufi and Wanigela you can hire a banana boat (K150, 30 minutes). Getting to the villages around Tufi is usually done on foot or by outrigger canoe; you'll be expected to help with the paddling.

Rabaul Shipping (Star Ships) boats from Alotau stop here on their weekly run between Alotau and Oro Bay.

MILNE BAY PROVINCE

At the eastern end of mainland PNG, the Owen Stanley Range plunges into the sea, and islands are scattered across the ocean for hundreds of kilometres further out. This is the start of the Pacific proper – tiny atolls, coral reefs, volcanic islands, swaying palms and white beaches. It's safe, secluded and unfailingly friendly.

More than 435 islands give the province 2120km of coastline, but poor transport infrastructure and limited arable land have hindered the region's development.

To many Australians, Milne Bay is synonymous with the 1942 WWII battles fought here between Japanese and Australian forces (see boxed text). Today the only bombs falling from above are likely to be coconuts.

The far-flung Trobriand Islands are proving to be culturally resilient and as exotic a destination as the father of modern anthropology, Bronsilaw Malinowski, first described them to be.

Culture

Milne Bay is home to large numbers of Polynesians and Motuans who have successfully grafted traditional beliefs on to contemporary church teachings, which can be confusing for the uninitiated. Witchcraft is widely respected and still practised, especially on the islands. Contract killings can still be arranged with local witch doctors, who sometimes employ the spiritual powers of cyanide from disused mining operations.

In most island societies land ownership falls under matrilineal lore; family rights are passed down through the mother. Clan leaders and the paramount chief are still men, but behind the scenes women wield considerable power.

In many of the region's tribes, people were traditionally buried standing up with their heads poking out of the ground. Their heads were then covered over by clay pots. When the heads eventually separated from the bodies, the pots were removed and the skulls were then placed in a skull cave. These caves are common in the area and clay pots are a traditional (and popular) regional artefact.

Alotau

Alotau is a sleepy little town built on the hillsides of the northern shore of Milne Bay. It became the provincial capital in 1968 when administrators were moved from overcrowded Samarai Island.

Alotau and the coastal strip either side played a pivotal role in the WWII Battle of Milne Bay and there are several memorials and relics here. The town's sights might soak up some time, but the real attractions lie beyond Alotau, amid the beautifully set capes, coves and islands of Milne Bay.

◉ Sights & Activities

Harbour   LANDMARK
The harbour is the most colourful part of town and it's worth exploring. There are one-man canoes, brightly painted island boats, work tugs and passenger vessels.

Viewpoint   LOOKOUT
For a bird's-eye view, walk up the steps in town to the hospital, take the right fork and keep going for a couple of hundred metres.

BETWEEN THE SEA AND A HARD PLACE: THE BATTLE OF MILNE BAY

In 1942, at 11.30pm on 25 August, the Japanese Imperial Army started invading Milne Bay. In just two landings a few days apart, the Japanese established a 2400-strong army near Ahioma. Unlike Kokoda, the battle of Milne Bay was not to be a protracted affair; it would be over in just 12 days.

The Japanese fought skirmishes with the Allies and their base suffered early casualties under a fierce RAAF aircraft–led barrage. On the moonlit nights of 26 and 27 August the Japanese attacked, forcing the Australian battalions to withdraw to the Gama River. Pressing their advantage the Japanese attacked again the next night, this time pushing the Allies backwards to the converted No 3 airstrip, amid furious fighting.

Three times the Japanese charged wildly across the open before a hail of fire, and they were repulsed each time. The tide of the battle had turned, the Australians had been reinforced and the attackers became the defenders. The Australians launched counterattacks and the Japanese sent warships to help their embattled troops. A week later the Japanese Navy called its invasion off and started evacuating troops. It is estimated that 750 Japanese and 161 Australians were killed at Milne Bay; many more were wounded.

In the broad canvas of the Pacific war, it was not a major victory. Its significance as the first Allied land victory in the Pacific boosted morale far beyond Milne Bay's bloodied shores.

Cameron Secondary School   BUILDING
At the other end of town, Cameron Secondary School welcomes visitors to its cultural village in the afternoon between 2.30pm and 3.30pm, when students have finished their studies and are free to show guests around. Donations should be made to the school library and not to the students themselves.

Swimming Beaches   BEACHES
There are several good black-sand swimming beaches to the east of town towards Ahioma, although they're not obvious from the road. PMVs run past.

🖝 Tours

Patty's Tours   TOUR
(☎7209 0576; pattystours@kulamail.net) Operating out of Napatana Lodge, Patty can take you on a great variety of customisable adventures – birdwatching, waterfall hikes, WWII tours, East Cape excursions, village visits and island-hopping trips out on Milne Bay.

Milne Bay Magic Tours   TOUR
(☎641 0711; milnebaymagictours@global.com.pg; Charles Abel Hwy) Offers a range of tours including a WWII tour of the Battle of Milne Bay and a creek bed filled with abandoned Japanese landing craft. There are also tours of local bat caves and trips to Samarai and Kwato Islands.

Florah Todurawai   GUIDED TOUR
(☎698 0738 or through Napatana Lodge; per day around K50) Florah is an excellent and very affordable local guide. She accompanies tourists on day-long or multiday trips, and takes the hassle out of catching PMVs.

Driftwood   FISHING TOUR
(☎641 0098; http://driftwoodpng.com; full-day fishing safari per person A$250-400). Milne Bay has a number of game fish worth casting for – giant marlin, sailfish, mackerel, barramundi and the Papuan black bass. This charter operating from a boutique hotel of the same name (p65) offers both saltwater and freshwater fishing safaris.

✹ Festivals & Events

**Milne Bay Canoe &
Kundu Festival**   FESTIVAL
The Milne Bay Canoe & Kundu Festival (first full weekend in November) is definitely worth seeing. Ocean-going barges bring canoes from as far away as Daru to compete for pride and prize money. Dozens of canoes, some with

40-plus warriors, adorned in traditional dress and paddling to the beat of island drums, leave a powerful impression. The dance performances are even more spectacular with brilliantly attired groups from all around Milne Bay. The races are held amid much rivalry and celebrated with just as much revelry.

🛏 Sleeping & Eating

Apart from the *kai* bars (cheap takeaway food bars) in the centre of town, with their usual fare of fried chicken, stews and greasy chips, the hotels and guesthouses are the only food and drink options around. *Mabewa,* a fruit indigenous to Milne Bay, is sometimes sold at the town market.

TOP CHOICE Napatana Lodge   LODGE $$
(☎641 0738; www.napatanalodge.com; Charles Abel Hwy; flashpackers s & d K220, bungalows from K308; ❄🐾🛜) Napatana is the pick of Alotau's accommodation, and has 'flashpacker' rooms with private bathroom, cable TV, porch and tea-/coffee-making facilities. The bungalows are even more comfortable, with private balconies and crisp, clean bedding. A huge drawcard is the amount of information on hand and the staff can help arrange any number of day or overnight trips. Upstairs, the Napatana bar (meals K28 to K44, open 7am to late) is the place to rub shoulders with expats and nationals alike. There is always something going on – a pub quiz, some kind of raffle, a joker night or sport on the open-air TV. Friday night's fish'n'chips and Saturday night's seafood buffet are excellent.

Bibiko Farm   GUESTHOUSE $$
(☎7293 5983; www.bibikofarm.com; Charles Abel Hwy; r per person from K60) Located 8km from town on the road to the airport, this family-run spot has four traditional bungalows with shared bathrooms that are excellent value for Alotau. The friendly Mataio family is a great resource, and can help you arrange guides (per day from K50) for hikes, island excursions and village visits.

Saugere   GUESTHOUSE $
(☎641 0165; s/d K77/110) Located on the waterfront west of Napatana, Saugere has a casual and hospitable atmosphere. There are two beds per room with shared bathrooms; meals available on request.

Beto Transit House   GUESTHOUSE $
(☎348 1699; fbenoma@hotmail.com; r K80-100) This well-worn place has extremely basic

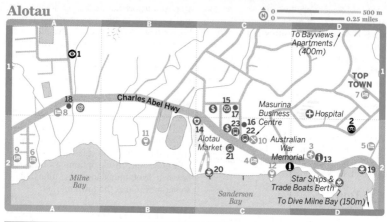

Alotau

rooms (think thin mattresses and small, inadequate fans) with shared bathrooms, but it's a familial and popular place with locals. Guest kitchen.

Bayviews Apartments   GUESTHOUSE **$$**
(📞641 0401; bayviews@kulamail.com; s/d from K140/250; ❄) Expect a warm welcome, but cold water. The budget rooms are in a self-contained house while the other rooms are larger, lighter and airier, but still fairly basic. A toast-and-tea breakfast and airport

transfers are included in the tariff. Meals are available and self-caterers appreciate the large kitchen.

Education Milne Bay   GUESTHOUSE **$$**
(📞641 0146; lulu.ebenis@emb.com.pg; r/bungalow/apt from K160/275/350; @🔊) Although primarily geared towards groups on community development courses, solo travellers are also welcome here. The simplest rooms are small, all-timber affairs with twin beds and shared bathrooms. Two bungalows (one

with a kitchen) and several self-contained apartments are nicely maintained. There's a simple eatery (sandwiches, drinks) and internet cafe in the lovely Wanigili centre.

Masurina   LODGE $$
(☎641 1212; www.masurina.com; s/d incl breakfast from K305/370; ❄@☎) The large, ageing rooms and apartments are comfortable enough and have a distinct feel of Australia c 1973. Some of the apartments sleep five and are ideal for families. Rates include continental breakfast, laundry and airport transfers, and there's a decent restaurant on hand (meals K35 to K48).

Alotau International Hotel   HOTEL $$$
(☎641 0300; www.alotauinternationalhotel.com. pg; Charles Abel Hwy; r K418-550; ❄@☎☎) For size and facilities these rooms, each with a balcony and bay view, are pretty good. They are, however, more comfortable than characterful. Babysitters can be arranged, and there's internet access (per hour K20). **By the Bay Restaurant** (mains K30 to K40; ☺6-10pm) has a tasty menu of Western fare (burgers, fish'n'chips, sandwiches, pizzas).

Driftwood   BUNGALOWS $$$
(☎641 0098; http://driftwoodpng.com; bungalow K605) Five minutes' drive from town, Driftwood is an upscale spot with eight attractively designed, freestanding bungalows with pleasant hardwood decks (four of which are perched right over the water). There's an elegant restaurant with seafood highlights also jutting over the water (meals K28 to K50). It has its own wharf and game-fishing boats.

Malabu Cafe   BAR $
(☎641 0900; malabu@online.net.pg; Masurina Business Centre; ☺8am-4.30pm Mon-Fri, to 1.30pm Sat) This *kai* bar has affiliations with Butia Lodge on the Trobriand Islands.

🍷 Drinking

Cameron Club   BAR
(☎641 1088; ☺4-10pm Mon-Thu, to midnight Fri & Sat) Located near the waterfront west of the town centre, this large, cavernous space is a local favourite and vaguely reminiscent of a rugby clubhouse. There are large snooker tables in the corner, and you can hire racquets for the squash or tennis courts from the bar.

The Jetty   BAR
(Alotau International Hotel; ☺5pm-midnight Mon-Sat) The Jetty is built on a wharf next to the Alotau International Hotel.

🛍 Shopping

Trobriand Islanders come to Alotau to sell their carvings and they'll find you around town. There are small handicraft shops at the top hotels.

Dive Milne Bay   HANDICRAFTS
(☎641 1421; Charles Abel Hwy) Has the town's best collection of Trobriand lime pots, walking sticks and bowls. It's located about 700m past the tourist office on the road to East Cape.

ℹ Information

Emergency
Ambulance (☎641 1200)
Fire (☎641 1055, 641 1014)
Police (☎641 1391; Charles Abel Hwy)

Internet Access
Education Milne Bay (per hr K10; ☺8am-5pm Mon-Fri, to noon Sat) In the upstairs of the lovely Wanigili Centre.
Internet Cafe (Charles Abel Hwy; per hr K20; ☺8am-4.30pm) Next to the Tanolele Holdings petrol station.

Money
Bank South Pacific has two ATMs and charges K50 for cashing travellers cheques.
   Westpac has an ATM and charges K20 for cashing travellers cheques. It also offers currency exchange for euros, and Australian, New Zealand and US dollars.

Tourist Information
Gretta Kwasnicka-Todurawai (Napatana Lodge, Charles Abel Hwy) Gretta is a veteran traveller and knows what independent travellers need. She has produced a binder detailing all kinds of excursions around Milne Bay.
Milne Bay Tourist Bureau (☎641 1503; Charles Abel Hwy; ☺8am-4pm Mon-Fri) Hopelessly under-resourced centre, but the friendly women here do a fine job in pointing travellers in the right direction. They can advise on accommodation, help arrange village stays and provide transport tips.

ℹ Getting There & Away
Air
Air Niugini (☎641 1100; Masurina Business Centre, Charles Abel Hwy) has one or two daily flights between Port Moresby and Gurney (K458, 50 minutes).
   Airlines PNG (☎641 1591 in Alotau, 641 0013 in Gurney) has daily flights to/from Port Moresby (K290 to K440), and several weekly flights to/from Losuia on the Trobriands (K290 to K560).

Boat

Given the poor maintenance, over-crowded conditions and recent ferry disasters by still-operating firms, we don't recommend travelling by boat. If you're determined, you can ask around at the wharf or try your luck on a vessel operated by **Rabaul Shipping** (Star Ships; ☎ 641 0012; Masurina Business Centre, Charles Abel Hwy), which operates throughout Milne Bay Province.

PMV

PMVs run along the coast to East Cape (K7, from 9am) and on to the north coast.

Getting Around

Alotau's airport is at Gurney, 15km from town.

Taxis travelling from the airport to town cost K35, but most hotels provide transfers for around K30 or for free. PMVs run to town from the nearby main road (K3), but they're infrequent. PMVs to the airport leave from near the Bank South Pacific.

Alotau is well served by taxis. **Bay Cabs** (☎ 641 1093) is the main taxi company and sometimes provides car hire.

Avis (☎ 641 1273; Charles Abel Hwy) has an office next door to Napatana Lodge.

East Cape

East Cape is at the very eastern end of mainland New Guinea. It's a quiet but picturesque village, where banana boats (exposed speed boats) or dinghies come and go for Normanby Island (K25) and others, including nearby Yamba Island with its famous 13-trunk coconut palm (photo fee K20). There's terrific snorkelling and diving in this area and a skull cave (K5), which is an hour's walk away. Guesthouses usually send a boy to show the way.

Many people come here as a day trip from Alotau. The first East Cape–bound PMV (K9) departs Alotau around 10am and the last one returns around 3pm, Monday to Saturday. It's about two hours each way along a metal road that passes many pretty villages and black-sand beaches.

If you're planning on snorkelling some of the reefs, hire your gear and buy your own zoom (petrol; buy 12 litres) in Alotau (where it's cheaper). Banana boats can be hired (K30) at the water's edge to motor you to secluded beaches and reefs.

Opposite the Dulia Stoa, **Bernhard's Guesthouse** (s K50) is a simple beachside hut that has a pleasant veranda. Both places can supply sheets and simple meals (K15), but generally it's bring-your-own all the way.

From East Cape, you can hire a boat to Nuakata Island, which has a reef that's a biodiversity hot spot (independent marine reef surveys recorded 429 species of reef coral; more than the variety found in the entire Great Barrier Reef). Nuakata has several guesthouses, including the lovely **Bomatu Guesthouse** (contact Napatana Lodge ☎ 641 0588 or Milne Bay Tourist Bureau) located on a sandy beach on the island's eastern side.

Wagawaga

On the southern shore of Milne Bay, this tiny settlement in a cove often called Discovery Bay sits below the steeply rising mountains of the southern peninsula. It's a popular day trip for snorkellers, who swim around the mostly submerged *Muscoota,* a WWII coal transport ship that sprang a leak and sank here in 1946.

There are a number of **waterfalls** but some of these, depending on the landowner's disposition, may be off-limits. Warren Dipole from Ulumani Treetops Lodge can arrange guides as well as canoe trips up **Dawadawa River,** which come highly recommended.

Enjoy the stunning panoramic views from **Ulumani Treetops Lodge** (☎/fax 641 0916; www.pngbackpacker.com; s K80-180) that span over the jungle and beyond to Milne Bay. If Warren knows you are coming, he'll collect you from the beach in his 4WD. Otherwise it's a very steep 30-minute (if you take the shortcuts) walk to the lodge. Accommodation is in two buildings: the upper is in the treetops, sleeps eight (four comfortably) and has a great balcony for birdwatchers. Down the hill is a traditional-style building with its own balcony but simpler rooms (single K80) and piping-hot, communal showers. The meals are good and they are served on the verandas. Warren has masks and snorkels and can organise tours.

PMV boats motor across the bay from the market wharf (K7, 45 minutes, daily except Sunday). They depart when everyone has finished their day's shopping between 3pm and 4.30pm. Returning, they leave Wagawaga around 7am.

You can drive from Alotau in about an hour, and Warren collects his guests from the airport for K100 each way.

North Coast

The north coast is a string of villages, beaches and reefs that reward those willing to explore. There are several good walks, and with enough time you could travel by foot, PMV and dinghy all the way from East Cape to Tufi. Increasing numbers of villages have basic accommodation, including: Boianai, Wagahuhu, Awaiama, Wedau and Bogaboga at Cape Vogel.

Speak with Gretta at Napatana Lodge (p63) or the Milne Bay Tourist Bureau (p65) to contact the villages and any guides required.

PMVs operate from Alotau as far as Topura, from where you need to walk or take dinghies if you want to go further west.

Tawali Resort   RESORT $$$
(☑641 0922; www.tawali.com; s/d incl meals from US$202/246; ✳🛜) On a coral-fringed headland overlooking Hoia Bay, this beautifully set resort lives and breathes diving. The resort is completely hidden from the sea, but the views from the main building and rooms are exceptional. A series of covered boardwalks connects the 15 bungalows.

You can also visit Tawali as a day trip from Alotau (per person K110 return transport by minibus and boat; lunch buffet K61). Other activities include rainforest bushwalks and visits to skull caves.

Samarai Island

Samarai is a speck of an island at the southern tip of the Milne Bay mainland. Just 24 hectares in the China Strait, Samarai has seen better times. In its colonial heyday it was said to be one of the most beautiful places in the Pacific, and although no one is saying that now, it's still an intriguing place. It's much like an overgrown and untended garden that still retains a legacy of its former, ordered beauty. The island predates Port Moresby and was the provincial headquarters until 1968, when local government realised it had outgrown the tiny island and left for greener pastures. Two years later the international wharf closed and the town's been going to seed ever since.

◉ Sights & Activities

The main thing to do on Samarai is just wander around soaking up the faded glory. From the wharf, head towards the hill and, at the northeast corner of the sports ground, you'll pass the memorial to Christopher Robinson, the one-time administrator who committed suicide in 1904. The inscription notes he was 'as well meaning as he was unfortunate and as kindly as he was courageous' and that 'his aim was to make New Guinea a good place for white men'. Near the southeast corner of the grounds, a road leads up to the abandoned hospital and, just north of here, a small hill with great views of the island and China Strait. Near the sports ground, and south of the wharf, is Samarai's oldest-surviving building, the Anglican church.

Samarai Island Wharf   DIVE SITE
The rotting piers of the Samarai Island Wharf offer spectacular muck-diving. The marine life is incredible and as you drift carefully between the piers you'll be surrounded by schools of brightly coloured

---

DIVING TAWALI

There are impressive wall drop-offs, overhangs and caverns along the limestone coastline within a short boat ride from Tawali. Most sites have abundant soft and hard corals, sponges and masses of fish. There are also a couple of muck-dive sites nearby but arguably the best dive spots are on the open-water pinnacles with their impressive pelagic action.

Occasionally (around August) there are stingers in the water whose long, near-invisible, threads are impossible to avoid and leave all exposed flesh red and welted.

For more on diving, see p26. For more immersive action, book a trip on one of Tawali's dive boats:

MV Chertan (www.chertan.com; per person per day US$296) Sleeps 10 passengers and runs scheduled trips lasting from four to 24 days. Reserve well ahead.

M/Y Spirit of Niugini (www.spiritofniugini.com; per person per day US$398-425) A well-appointed dive catamaran with large rooms and private bathrooms. Because the catamaran can handle rough seas, it is possible to go as far as the outer-reef chains of the Conflict and Engineer Groups.

fish. Below them, pipefish and various odd nudibranchs can be seen. Be sure to bring a snorkel and mask.

🛏 Sleeping & Eating

If you don't fancy your chances of making friends with the locals, there is only one place to stay on Samarai Island.

Bwanasu Women's Association Guesthouse   GUESTHOUSE $
(☑642 1042; r per person K90) At the top of the stairs leading up from the north side of the sports ground, Bwanasu Women's Association Guesthouse is rapidly approaching 'run-down' but the staff here are fantastically friendly. The rooms are simple and the shared bathrooms have only cold water; all of this is in keeping with the derelict and abandoned atmosphere of the island itself. Meals cost K12 to K15. Staff can also help arrange boat transport to visit other islands.

❶ Getting There & Away

The easiest way to get to the island is to jump aboard one of the public dinghies at Sanderson Bay (K30, 1½ hours, daily except Saturday). The boats depart from Alotau around 3pm and return between 7am and 8am the next morning.

Near Samarai Island

China Strait and the surrounding islands have a reputation for witchcraft and, despite the influence of missionaries, superstitions linger. Strange lights, ghost ships and sirens (the singing kind) all crop up.

Just west of Samarai, Kwato Island was once an educational centre and home to a thriving boat-building industry. The remnants of the old machinery lie where they were discarded in the tall grass and today the island can be eerily quiet.

The Reverend Charles Abel and his wife, Beatrice, founded a nonhierarchical church in 1891. Even though they 'belted' the Bible pretty hard, it wasn't until the 1930s that the last of the nearby cannibal tribes was 'saved'.

If you follow the old tree-lined road until it clears the forest, you'll come to a stone-walled church that was built in 1937 from materials brought from Scotland.

Ask around Samarai Island Wharf for a boatman to take you across.

Not far west of Doini Island is Gona Bara Bara Island, and just off the northwest shore is a dive site known as the Manta Ray

Cleaning Station. Just a few metres below the surface, there is an isolated bommie (a natural spire, covered in coral, rising from the sea floor). Around the bommie, giant, graceful mantas (some with wing spans of up to 5m) are cleaned by tiny wrasses; it is one of the best places on earth to see this happening. Snorkelling is also possible, though high winds make it (and diving) difficult between June and September. Unfortunately only dive charters are visiting here, although it may be possible to arrange a snorkelling trip with local boat operators in Samarai Island.

On Logia Island, right across from Samarai Island, Nuli Sapi (☑7324 1726; nulisapi@gmail.com; bungalow K250; ☺Oct-May) is a peaceful new site run by a couple of well-travelled expats. Lodging is in one of several attractively designed bungalows (several perched right over the water) with modern cold-water bathrooms (there's also a shared hot-water shower available). Days are spent fishing, snorkelling, canoeing, visiting villages and island-hopping. Meals are also available and feature fresh-caught seafood. To get there, take the public afternoon boat from Sanderson Bay in Alotau to Samarai, and someone from Nuli Sapi can whisk across to pick you up. Private boat transport also available.

Another good option in the region is Gumoisu (r per person incl meals K80), a simple homestay option on a beautiful point, a 15-minute dinghy ride from Samarai. The friendly hosts can take you birdwatching or bushwalking, or you can hire their small dinghy for fishing, swimming and nearby island-hopping. Contact the owners through Nuli Sapi.

D'Entrecasteaux Islands

Scattered across a narrow strait from the PNG mainland, the D'Entrecasteaux group was named by French explorer Antoine d'Entrecasteaux, who sailed through in 1793 while searching for his missing compatriot, La Pérouse. The three principal islands, from northwest to southeast, are Goodenough (Nidula), Fergusson (Moratau) and Normanby (Duau). The islands are extremely mountainous, covered by dense jungle and contain a number of active geothermal fields. Sanaroa and Dobu are the most significant of the smaller islands and there are numerous reefs, shoals and atolls.

D'Entrecasteaux islanders are still largely subsistence horticulturalists, living in small, traditional villages and fishing the coastal waters. People of this area participated in the *kula* ring of exchange (see boxed text, p71) and travelled widely to other islands in their seagoing sailing canoes.

The whole archipelago is off-the-beaten-track travel at its best. It can be difficult to contact anyone on the islands because the phones rarely work. Try the Milne Bay Tourist Bureau (p65) instead. If you are happy with basic island accommodation, you could spend weeks exploring coastal villages, sleeping with families on sleeping mats and sharing their food. To mount such an expedition, hire one of the dinghies at East Cape (K200 to K300 per day, including crew), stock it with a couple of drums of petrol (brought in Alotau where it's cheaper), some 1kg bags of rice and tinned fish, and follow the whales, dolphins or dugongs that live here.

Village guesthouses on the islands typically charge around K100 per person per day, including meals and activities.

ⓘ Getting There & Away

Rabaul Shipping (Star Ships) has irregular service to all three principal islands, which includes port of calls at Salamo on Fergusson and Esa'ala on Normanby. Easier to organise are the dinghies that run early afternoons from East Cape across to Sewa Bay, Normanby Island. Let the captain know about your intended destination as these public boats travel to many destinations other than Saidowai. It is also possible to travel between Diodio on Goodenough Island and Cape Vogel on the mainland's north coast. If the seas are rough, consider your options carefully as boats have been swamped and their passengers drowned.

NORMANBY ISLAND

Esa'ala, the district headquarters, is at the entrance to the spectacular Dobu Passage. It's a tiny place, with a couple of shops, a market and a trade store. A reef just offshore offers excellent snorkelling. The friendly **Esa'ala Guesthouse** is on the beach near the main wharf.

One of the most accessible and picturesque bays in the region is **Sewa Bay**, a 45-minute boat ride (K30) from East Cape. During WWII the Allies based warships here among seven tiny islands in the harbour. The beautiful Goldie's bird of paradise is endemic to the island and can be seen at the Buyeti display site (a three-hour walk from

Sibonai), but you'll need a guide to show you where it's located. Snorkelling around the tiny islands of Emanalo, Autoyou and Tou-we is particularly rewarding because of the extremely high biodiversity found in these waters. There is a guesthouse at Bunama village that provides dinghies and canoe trips to the reefs that surround the village. Out of Alotau, the guide **Fred Francisco** (☎7334 9526) arranges excursions to Sewa Bay, with hikes to rock-carving sites, birdwatching and snorkelling. He can also be contacted through Gillian at Bayviews Apartments in Alotau.

In **Saidowai village**, in the northern corner of the bay, local activist Mombi Onesimo is encouraging tourism as an alternative to Malaysian rosewood logging. His **Saidowai Guesthouse** (contact Napatana Lodge ☎641 0588) is an excellent place to base yourself as Mombi arranges guides to local attractions, snorkelling trips, canoe-fishing expeditions, and treks to see Goldie's bird of paradise and the Bwasiaiai hot springs.

Another recommended village guesthouse on the island is further south in **Sibonai village**. The recommended guide Waiyaki Nemani runs the **Sibonai Guesthouse** (☎7395 9892; waiyaki.nemani@gmail. com), beautifully set amid primary rainforest. Waiyaki can take you wildlife-watching, snorkelling and bushwalking. The bird life here is spectacular.

There are other village guesthouses at Welala, Bwakera, Poponawai and Ulowai Beach. All of these guesthouses are within a day's walk from one another and provide meals; however, you will need to bring bedding, a mosquito net and torch.

FERGUSSON ISLAND

Fergusson is the largest island in the group and the highest peak is 2073m, with two other lower ranges from which the island's many rivers and streams flow. It is notable for its hot springs, bubbling mud pools, spouting geysers and extinct volcanoes.

The hike from Warluma to the caldera of **Mt Lamanai** takes about 1½ hours and affords fantastic views over an immense crater. Take a local guide (ask around to arrange for one). Particularly active thermal springs can be found at Deidei, opposite the main town of **Salamo**.

The **Salamo United Church Women's Guesthouse** offers basic accommodation.

Boats cross the beautiful Dobu Passage between Esa'ala and Salamo daily (around K10).

GOODENOUGH ISLAND

The most northwesterly of the group, Goodenough is one of the most steeply sided islands on earth, with Mt Oiautukekea reaching 2566m at the summit. There are fertile coastal plains flanking the mountain range and a road runs around the northeast coast through **Vivigani**, site of the major airstrip in the group. About 10km south of Vivigani, **Bolubolu** is the main settlement, with a simple guesthouse. In the centre of the island there is a large stone, covered in mysterious black-and-white paintings, which is said to have power over the yam crops.

Trobriand Islands

In 1914 a young anthropologist called Bronsilaw Malinowski set sail for the impossibly remote Trobriand archipelago. When WWI broke out, he suddenly found himself cut off from the outside world and, being an Austrian Pole in a British controlled area, unable to leave. The story goes that not being sure which side he was on (or even wanted to be on), he spent the next three years immersed in his fieldwork. On his eventual return, that fieldwork bore fruit as one of the most famous and influential books in anthropology, *The Argonauts of the Western Pacific*.

Despite the dozens of anthropologists, missionaries, TV crews and tourists who have since followed Malinowski, the Trobriands remain one of the most culturally intact places you could possibly find. Although an understanding of reproduction and modern medicines is common, islanders still maintain a world view that includes the belief that in order for a woman to become pregnant, she must first be infused with the spirit of a departed ancestor. A strict matrilineal social system, enormous and highly decorated yam houses, exquisite carvings and the colourful festivals of clan prestige will keep your head turning.

Known locally as the Trobes, the people take their name from Denis de Trobriand, an officer on D'Entrecasteaux's expedition. The Trobriands are low-lying coral islands, in contrast to their mountainous southern neighbours. Trobriand Islanders have a distinct Polynesian appearance and there are scattered remains of stone temples that resemble those of Polynesia. Trade between the islands had strong cultural and economic importance, and the pre-European traders crossed vast distances of open sea in canoes, exchanging fish, vegetables, pigs, stone axes, a rare jade-like stone from Muyua (Woodlark) Island and volcanic glass from Fergusson Island. The *kula* ring (see boxed text) is the most famous of these trade routes.

It's good manners to let the paramount chief know you have arrived. If you are there for reasons other than tourism, you should request an audience with him to explain why you've come. It's enough to ask almost anyone to pass on the message to the chief; it will reach him.

✷ Festivals

Milamala Festival   FESTIVAL

Mention to any mainlander that you are off to see the Milamala Festival and you'll be greeted with raised eyebrows, queasy smirks and any number of puns along the lines of exactly whose yams are ripe for harvesting. Ever since Malinowski published his provocatively titled *The Sexual Life of Savages in northwestern Melanesia* (1929), the West has been fascinated with (some say, fantasising about) the thought of free love with sex-starved, bare-breasted maidens in a tropical paradise.

However, on the island it's more about the yams and the celebration of a bountiful crop. Yams are harvested and stored between June and August. The crop yield (along with the chief's whim and, increasingly, monetary incentives from the government) dictate whether or not there will even be a Milamala, and dates are notoriously difficult to pin down.

When it is held, the Milamala may culminate in a week or two of canoe racing, cricket matches, ribald dancing and, yes, free love. Before you get too excited, it's worth noting that visitors with boiling loins usually have to make their own entertainment because, while yams are considered objects of great beauty, *dim dims* (white people) are not.

KIRIWINA ISLAND

The largest of the Trobriand Islands is Kiriwina, which is home to the district capital of **Losuia** and the airstrip. Kiriwina is relatively flat, although there is a rim of low hills (uplifted coral reefs) along the eastern shore. The central plain is intensely cultivated and, with the island's population growing fast, there are concerns that cutting trees to plant gardens will devastate the island.

The airport is in the north, where the US Air Force had two bases during WWII. South of here, on the west coast, Losuia is the only

KULA RING

Extending around the islands of Milne Bay Province is an invisible circle, or *kula* ring, that binds the islands together in a system of ritual exchange. The ring encompasses the Trobriand, Muyua (Woodlark), Louisiade, Samarai and D'Entrecasteaux islands. Things have changed now, but in the past, the *kula* ring involved the trade of red-shell necklaces, called *bagi* or *soulava*, in a clockwise direction; and white shell armlets, *mwali*, in an anticlockwise direction. Each trader had a *kula* partner on their nearest neighbouring island in each direction. Once a year, the trader and a delegation from his clan journeyed to the island of his *kula* partner to receive gifts in elaborate public ceremonies. On a separate significant date he would be visited by another *kula* partner who would be presented with the prized gifts. Accompanying these voyages were other ceremonial objects and surplus fish and yams to be exchanged with neighbouring islands. Since the *bagis* and *mwalis* rarely left the circle, this system ensured a distribution of wealth among the islanders.

The exchange mostly occurred between traditional families of high status and thus helped to reinforce clan-based hierarchies. Today some people are required to journey to the island home of a traditional *kula* partner bearing ritual gifts in a banana boat rather than the traditional sailing canoe.

real town and is generally known as 'the station'. It has a wharf, police station, health centre and several trade stores. It's more like a sprawling village than a town.

◎ Sights & Activities

Going north from Losuia is 'inland' to the locals. This area has most of the island's roads and villages. Omarakana, about halfway between Losuia and Kaibola, is where the island's paramount chief resides. You'll know you're there by the large, intricate, painted yam house and the couple of cars outside his Western-style bungalow built on stilts. He can often be found sitting on a chair under his house, surrounded by his clansmen. The paramount chief presides over the island's oral traditions and magic, and strictly maintains his political and economic power. He also oversees the important yam festival and *kula* rituals. As a sign of respect, keep your head lower than his and consider bearing a gift of *buai* (betel nut) or cigarettes (cash is also accepted).

Megaliths made of a coral composite have linked the Trobriands to possible early Polynesian migrations. You can see them, but not without a guide – speak with one of the guesthouses to make arrangements.

At Kaibola village, at the northern tip of Kiriwina, you can swim and snorkel at the picture-postcard beach, which has some coral. About 1½ hours' walk from Kaibola is Kalopa Cave, near Matawa village. There are several deep limestone caves housing burial antiquities and skeletal remains. Stories are

told of Dokanikani, a giant whose bones are said to be buried with those of his victims in one of the caves. PMVs run from Losuia to Kaibola (K3, one hour, several times daily). Near Bweka, a former guesthouse run by John Kasaipwalova, sits above a sacred cave of crystal-clear water. You can get permission from the owner (and pay a small fee of K5 or so) to swim in the cave.

The road south of Losuia is dotted with villages but seldom sees motorised transport. Wawela is on a beautiful, curving sand beach edging a cool, deep, protected lagoon. On a falling tide, beware of the channel out to sea from the bay: the current can be very strong. To get here you'll need to rent a bike from Butia lodge or charter a PMV for a few hours.

War relics, including the scattered remains of a couple of planes, can be seen near Butia lodge; ask one of the staff to show you around.

Of the islands off Kiriwina, Kaileuna Island is the easiest and cheapest to access as boats carrying betel nuts travel from Losuia most days. The villages of Kaisiga, in the south, and Tawema to the north, have beautiful white-sand beaches and predictably relaxed locals. Ask around the wharf from about 10am to see if a boat is going.

The offshore islands are worth visiting if you are lucky enough to find a boat full of people going that way. Labi Island is particularly nice for swimming, as is the larger Kitava Island. If you wish to hire a boat ask around the wharf, although as fuel prices are sky high it won't be cheap.

YAMS, SEX & CRICKET

Bronislaw Malinowski's celebrated books, *The Argonauts of the Western Pacific, Coral Gardens and Their Magic* and *The Sexual Life of Savages in northwestern Melanesia,* were published after WWI, and revealed much about the intricate trading rituals (see boxed text, p71), yam cults and sexual practices of the Trobriand Islands. Malinowski found a matrilineal society, in which the chief's sons belong to his wife's clan and he is succeeded by one of his oldest sister's sons. The society is strictly hierarchical, with distinctions between hereditary classes and demarcations in the kind of work each person can perform.

Yams

Yams are far more than a staple food in the Trobriands – they're a sign of prestige and expertise, and a tie between villages and clans. The quality and size of your yams is important. Many hours are spent discussing yam cultivation, and to be known as a *tokwaibagula* (good gardener) is a mark of great prestige.

The yam cult climaxes at the harvest time, which is usually July or August. The yams are first dug up in the gardens, then displayed, studied and admired. At the appropriate time, the men carry the yams back to the village, with the women guarding the procession.

In the villages, the yams are again displayed before being packed into the highly decorated yam houses. Each man has a yam house for each of his wives and it is his brother-in-law's responsibility (in other words, his wife's clan's obligation) to fill his yam house. The chief's yam house is always the biggest, most elaborate and first to be filled.

Sex

Malinowski's tomes on the Trobriand Islanders' customs led to Kiriwina Island being given the misleading title of the 'Island of Love'. It is not surprising that such a label was applied by inhibited Europeans when they first met Trobriand women, with their free-and-easy manners, good looks and short grass skirts, but it led to the inaccurate idea that the Trobriands were some sort of sexual paradise. The sexual customs are different to many other places, but are not without their own complicated social strictures.

Teenagers are encouraged to have as many sexual partners as they choose until marriage, when they settle down with the partner who is chosen as suitable and compatible. Males leave home when they reach puberty and move into the village *bukumatula* (bachelor house). Here, they are free to bring their partners back at any time, although they usually opt for somewhere more private. Even married couples, subject to mutual agreement, are allowed to have a fling when the celebrations for the yam harvest are in full swing.

Aside from all this activity, it's said that few children are born to women without permanent partners. The people do not believe there is a connection between intercourse and pregnancy – a child's spirit, which floats through the air or on top of the sea, chooses to enter a woman, often through her head.

All this apparent freedom has negligible impact on visitors. Freedom of choice is the bedrock of Trobriand Islands life, so why would any islander choose some unattractive, pale *dim dims* who can't speak like a civilised human, doesn't understand the most fundamental laws and will probably be gone tomorrow?

Cricket

Trobriand Islands cricket developed after missionaries introduced the sport as a way of taking the islanders' minds off less-healthy activities. It's since developed its own style, which is quite unlike anything the Melbourne Cricket Club ever had in mind. There is no limit to the number of players, meaning you can wait days for a bat. Trobriand cricket is played with much dancing, singing and whistle blowing, making it rather difficult to concentrate on line and length. When asked what the song meant it was translated to us as 'I don't know why we are dancing, the fool is already out!' If there's a game scheduled while you're there, don't miss it!

🛏 Sleeping & Eating

The following accommodation options have electricity by generator usually from about 6pm to 10pm. Restaurants are nonexistent, with most visitors eating at their guesthouse. Do seek out Lydia, who bakes tasty coconut bread and sells it around the village in the morning.

Butia　　　　　　　　　　　LODGE **$$**
(☑641 0900, in Alotau; malabu@online.net.pg; s/d incl 2 meals K195/350) Located near the airport, on either side of an abandoned WWII-era airstrip, Butia lodge offers the cleanest and most comfortable accommodation on the island. The lodge has its own van, which can be hired for excursions (all-day hire including guide and driver K350). The restaurant and bar are in an attractive, open-sided building supported by 18 posts, each carved with a Trobriand legend. The food is superb, mixing traditional vegetables (yes, yams), fish and masses of mouthwatering mud crabs. Village stays can also be arranged for around K100.

Kiriwina　　　　　　　　　　LODGE **$$**
(☑7360 8603; bungalow K60, r K175-350; ❄) Overlooking a stony beach, not far from Losuia, Kiriwina has 18 simple but pleasant rooms opening on to a shared veranda. A few bungalows made of bush material sit in the grassy yard; these are a good-value option if you don't mind sharing the (cold-water) facilities. The restaurant (meals K25 to K35) has a pleasant deck down by the water. The lodge also has an old bus for hire (per day K300), as well as bicycles (per day K25). The staff can help with dingy hire to visit other islands (per day K250 plus fuel), as well as village stays (per day from K20).

Cindarella's　　　　　　　　GUESTHOUSE **$**
(☑7313 6538 or 7135 5414; r per person incl meals K140) Opposite the cricket field (to the west), big-smiling widow Cindy and her daughter Janet have opened their home to visitors. The small house has two bedrooms, sleeps three or four, and is the heart of her extended family's compound. There is always a 'boy' on hand to show you around and the home-cooked meals are a treat!

VILLAGE STAYS

Most visitors opt to stay at least one night in a village and find it a fantastic experience. Be sure to establish what you're paying for in advance with the village chief.

Butia lodge arranges village stays at Kaibola for about K100 per person per night, including basic food and activities (guided walks and the like). Butia can also transport you to and from the village, but this costs extra.

You could arrange a village stay yourself by speaking with the chief of the village that you'd like to stay in. Burex offers **traditional-style rooms** (per person incl meals K100) on stilts at Kaibola Beach. Contact Tobulowa at Okaiboma to spend the night in one of the basic **beach huts** (per person incl meals from K20) located there. Almost any other village will take you – just ask.

For more on staying in villages, see p185.

🛍 Shopping

Trobriand Islands carvings are famous throughout the whole of PNG. Certain villages specialise in particular styles, ranging from bowls and stools to elaborately carved walking sticks. The best carvings are made from ebony, and much of what you see will be decorated with pearl-shell inlays. Ebony is an extremely hard and brittle timber, and difficult to work, so carving with it requires exceptional skill from the artisan.

A master carver is a position of high prestige in the Trobriands and, like dancers, singers and many other roles, is a role bestowed upon people at birth. A carver cannot fell his own timber, as this role belongs to another, and must purchase it from the landowner where it is grown.

Obweria village specialises in intricately carved walking sticks and bowls. A good walking stick might cost K300 or more. **Bwetalu village** produces particularly fine stools, although these can be quite bulky and difficult to transport.

Yalaka village sells striking lime pots that are small and easy to carry. These gourds are decorated with a distinctive black pattern that runs around the girth of the gourd and are fitted with a boar's tusk stopper. Most pots are around K15, depending on size and quality, and a must for the discerning betel-nut-chewer.

Other than carvings and lime pots, you can get shell money and *doba* (banana leaf money incised with patterns); still used by some women as negotiable currency.

Artisans meet arriving planes hoping to sell their wares and sometimes beautiful bowls can be found then. They'll also come and find you wherever you're staying!

ⓘ Information

Butia and Kiriwina lodges are your best sources of information. Ask at these places about any cricket matches, weddings, mortuary feasts or any other festivities that may be possible to visit. Rebecca Young is particularly helpful (and also the Airlines PNG representative) and can arrange *singsing* groups and a 'mini-Milamala' with her village contacts.

ⓘ Getting There & Away

Airlines PNG connects Losuia with Alotau (K212 to K575) and Port Moresby (K212 to K575). Flights currently run on Tuesday, Thursday and Sunday.

Weather permitting, Rabaul Shipping (Star Ships) sails the *Samarai Queen* from Alotau to Losuia (K125, 19 hours) and back once a week, though schedules are erratic and the crossing can be treacherous.

ⓘ Getting Around

Although the island's few PMVs meet all arriving flights, they are otherwise infrequent. Getting out to the various villages can be a considerable problem if your accommodation is unable to arrange transport. Groups may be advantaged by hiring a vehicle on a daily basis (K250 to K350) – talk to one of the guesthouses about this possibility. Almost all private vehicles (there aren't many) operate as de facto PMVs.

Most of Kiriwina's main roads are in fairly good condition. Cycling is a great way to see the island – Kiriwina lodge has six bicycles for hire for K25 a day.

Morobe & Madang Provinces

POP 905,000 / AREA 62,470 SQ KM

Best Places to Stay

» Madang Lodge (p89)

» Summer Institute of Linguistics Guesthouse (p78)

» Tupira Surf Club (p93)

Best of Culture

» Morobe Show (p78)

» Smoked Bodies of Men-yamya & Aseki (p84)

» Kalam Culture Festival (p95)

Why Go?

If you have just rolled down from the Highlands on an arse-spanking PMV (public motor vehicle), Morobe and Madang, with their beaches and bays, will be a welcome change. Both offer plenty of scope to grab a snorkel, slap on some sunscreen and banana boat–hop your way between bays.

Geographically speaking, Morobe and Madang are quite similar – both rise from pristine beaches off Papua New Guinea's northern coast into a series of thickly forested hills, imposing mountain ranges and, ultimately, the Highlands.

But that is where their similarities end. Lae, the abandoned child of the gold-rush era, grew up hard. In the 1940s she was invaded by the Japanese and bombed by the Allies and is only now finding her feet as an economic and industrial hub.

Madang, situated on a small peninsula jutting into a tranquil harbour, is Lae's younger, prettier sister and despite being heavily bombed in WWII, has retained much of her sunny, carefree ways.

When to Go

Madang

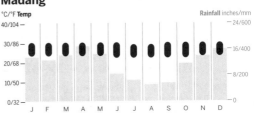

Jun–Sep The dry season offers the best visibility for divers in Madang.

May–Oct During the Lae–Finschhafen area's wet season there is lots of rain.

Late Oct The Morobe show draws *singsing* groups from around the country.

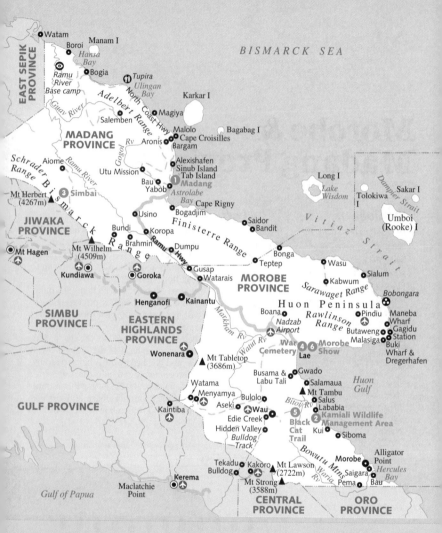

Morobe & Madang Provinces Highlights

① Suiting up to dive the wrecks and carnage of WWII or snorkelling over the psychedelic reefs around **Madang** (p88)

② Watching leatherback turtles scramble ashore at **Kamiali Wildlife Management Area** (p84) under a full moon

③ Being one of the first to witness the beetle-bejewelled *singsings* of the isolated **Simbai** (p94) villages high in Bismarck Range

④ Calling into Lae to pay your respects at the **War Cemetery** (p76) and checking out the critters at the **Rainforest Habitat** (p76)

⑤ Falling into the ocean, exhausted and euphoric after conquering the infamous **Black Cat Trail** (p85)

⑥ Swaying to the rhythm of the drums as you watch Anga warriors dance during the **Morobe Show** (p78)

History

Ancient axe heads that have been found suggest people have been living in this part of PNG for about 40,000 years.

The first European to spend any length of time on the PNG mainland was Russian biologist Nicolai Miklouho-Maclay. He arrived at Astrolabe Bay, south of the present site of Madang, in 1871 and stayed for 15 months before leaving to recover from malaria. More rapid change occurred when the German New Guinea Company established a settlement at Finschhafen in 1885. It was a disaster, with malaria, boredom and alcohol taking a heavy toll. The company moved north, first to Bogadjim on Astrolabe Bay, and then Madang, before finally conceding defeat to the mosquitoes and decamping for the relative comforts of New Britain.

The legendary prospector 'Sharkeye' Park is credited with discovering gold near Wau in 1921. By the mid-1920s the gold hunters were flooding in, arriving at Salamaua and struggling for eight days up the steep and slippery Black Cat Trail to Wau, a mere 50km away. Malaria, the track itself and unhappy tribesmen claimed many lives.

In 1926 a richer field was discovered at Edie Creek, high in the hills above Wau. To squeeze the most out of these gold-rich streams the miners turned to aircraft and within a few years more air freight was being lifted in PNG than the rest of the world combined.

Lae was a tiny mission station before the gold rush but soon became a thriving community and during WWII Lae, Salamaua and Madang became major Japanese bases. In early 1943 the Japanese, reeling from defeats at Milne Bay and the Kokoda Track, attempted to take Port Moresby by attacking towards Wau, marching over the mountains from Salamaua. The Battle of Wau was fought hand-to-hand after the ammunition ran out.

MOROBE PROVINCE

Morobe Province is the industrial heart of PNG and gateway to both the Highlands and Islands. A string of village guesthouses along the beautiful Huon Coast is a great opportunity to get off the beaten track and for those up to the challenge, the historic Black Cat Trail will challenge the most avid outdoor enthusiast.

Intense WWII fighting has bequeathed a legacy of battlefield relics from submerged shipwrecks to downed aircraft. Culturally, the region boasts 171 distinctive languages and is home to the Anga people, renowned throughout PNG as fierce warriors.

Lae

Lae is PNG's second-largest city and, despite having a sizeable industrial base, is vastly more attractive than Port Moresby. Like other PNG cities, the streets are filled with people and it can be hard to imagine what the crowds are doing. No one seems to be in a rush; happy to chat with friends and amble around town.

Most shops can be found in either of the two commercial mini-centres – Top Town and Eriku. There are also a few shops down the hill in China Town; named after the Chinese community who once lived here.

AMELIA EARHART

Amelia Earhart became many things to many people during her short life – bestselling author, women's rights advocate, an international celebrity and even a fashion icon – but the world best remembers her as a spirited aviation pioneer and the first woman to fly nonstop across the Atlantic.

Her first flight was off a ramp on the roof of her family's toolshed in what was meant to be a home-made rollercoaster. Her last was from Lae on her second attempt to be the first person to circumnavigate the globe at its widest point in a plane.

Having successfully completely 35,000km of a journey that had taken her from America to New Guinea via South America, Africa, India and Southeast Asia, Earhart and her navigator, Fred Noonan, had only to cross the Pacific to successfully complete their goal. Her subsequent disappearance has spawned many theories but all that is known for certain is that on 2 July 1937 Earhart and Noonan left Lae bound for Howland Island and were never seen again.

Lae

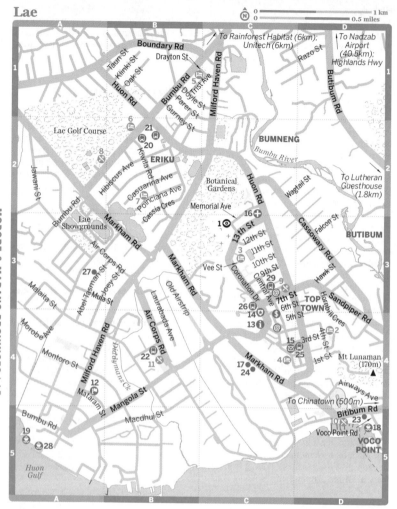

⊙ Sights

Rainforest Habitat   ZOO
(☑475 7839; www.habitat.org.pg; adult/child K10/5; ⊙8am-4pm) Visiting the Rainforest Habitat is like stepping into a microcosm of PNG's most exotic flora and fauna. It comprises about 3000 sq metres of reconstructed rainforest inside a covered shade house. It incorporates a pond, raised walkways, and an abundance of plants and birds. Most people come to see the **bird of paradise**, although the real star is 'Argo', the huge and largely inactive saltwater **crocodile**. Outside is a mini zoo with cuscus, tree kangaroos and cassowaries. To get

there, take a Unitec PMV from Eriku and ask to be let off at the main gate. From here it's a 15-minute walk to Gate 2, where the habitat is located. The Unitec security guards will soon point the way.

Lae War Cemetery   MEMORIAL
(Memorial Ave; ⊙7am-4pm) The Lae War Cemetery, just south of the Botanical Gardens, is meticulously maintained by the Australian government. There are 2808 graves here, 2363 of which are Australian, the rest being Indian, New Zealand or British. An Anzac (Australian New Zealand Army Corp) Day

Lae

dawn service is held here yearly commemorating those who lost their lives during WWII. If the war seems rather distant and unreal, pay a visit and read some of the headstones; the tributes can be quite moving.

Botanical Gardens   GARDENS
(Milford Haven Rd; admission K10; ⊙8am-5pm) The Botanical Gardens offer a pleasant stroll through a small patch of rainforest and grassland in the centre of Lae. The huge, vine-covered trees host colourful birds and butterflies, and the gardens have an exotic orchid collection. Officially, it's closed on weekdays but the guards at either the main northern gate (near the RAAF DC-3) or the southern gate (near Lae War Cemetery) usually let you in. Avoid coming here alone.

Unitech   CULTURAL BUILDING
(www.unitech.ac.pg; Independence Dr, Taraka) About 8km from the centre of town and located in some nicely landscaped parks and gardens, Unitec has a number of notable buildings, including **Duncanson Hall** with its 36 Sepik-style carved pillars, and **Matheson Library**, one of the largest libraries in the South Pacific and home to a small collection of artefacts.

The university also hosts a biannual (even years) traditional *singsing* (celebratory festival/dance) whose participants are mainly students from around the country.

⌂ Tours

Melanesian Arts Gallery   TOUR
(☑472 1604; melansian.arts@global.net.pg; Markham Rd) Karen Quinn, at Melanesian Arts Gallery, is a woman with her finger on Morobe's pulse. If you want to walk the Black Cat or just around town, with advance notice Karen can arrange the necessary guide and transport.

Pagini Tours   TOUR
(☑472 1071; www.paginitours.com.pg; Lae International Hotel, 4th St) Expat Fred Cook runs a one-man operation, Pagini Tours, out of the Lae International Hotel. He specialises in small-group day trips around Lae and can, with advance notice, arrange game-fishing charters.

★ Festivals & Events

Morobe Show   FESTIVAL
(www.morobeshow.org.pg; admission Sat/Sun K8/10) The Morobe Show has become arguably the

best-organised cultural show in PNG. It's usually on the full-moon weekend in late October (check the website for exact dates). There are no tourist prices here, though photographers can gain access to the performance field (and the shaded members' stands) by purchasing a 'gold' pass for K160. Saturday is devoted to agricultural displays and the *singsing* is held on the Sunday.

🛏 Sleeping

Most sleeping options are in Top Town or Eriku.

TOP CHOICE Summer Institute of Linguistics Guesthouse   GUESTHOUSE $

(SIL; ☎472 2939; lae-guesthouse_png@sil.org; Poinciana Ave, Eriku; s/d/tr/q K165/195/225/255, s/d without bathroom K100/130; ✳️🖥️) This a great option for groups and families, with self-contained rooms that have several beds and a clean bathroom and kitchen. Budget rooms are similarly clean and share a communal lounge, kitchen and bathroom. Book well in advance as it is often full.

Lutheran Guesthouse   GUESTHOUSE $

(☎472 2556; Busu Rd, Ampo; dm K95) Set in lush, tropical grounds on the outskirts of town, this homey, sky-blue guesthouse is 200m off the main road. It's a great budget option, and while rooms are shared you can often end up with a room to yourself. The gates close from 11pm to 5am, and a hearty home-cooked dinner (K20) is served at 6pm. It's too far to walk, so take the 13A PMV to Butibum in Ampo (pronounced 'umpo') from the PMV stop beside the post office.

Lae Travellers Inn   HOTEL $$

(☎479 0411; laetravellersinn@global.net.pg; Vee St; d/tw K268/278, r without bathroom K150; ✳️) Clean, quiet, professional and centrally located, this is the pick of Lae's midrange options. Standard rooms have satellite TV and a kettle, while the 'budget' rooms have a fan and shared bathroom. The connected Peaches Coffee Shop (meals K22 to K40) serves tasty, no-fuss mains and simple breakfasts.

Salvation Army Guesthouse   MOTEL $

(☎472 2487; Huon Rd, Eriku; r K190-280; ✳️) Set in sprawling grounds near the shops and PMVs at Eriku, each of the self-contained, motel-style units sleeps two and comes with kitchenettes that were at their best 20 years ago. The staff are very friendly.

Lae International Hotel   HOTEL $$$

(☎472 2000; www.laeinterhotel.com; 4th St; r K550-715, ste K1075-1430; ✳️@🖥️) Self-described as 'an oasis of luxury', the International is easily the smartest digs in town – not that the competition is particularly steep. But with spacious rooms, tennis courts, a pool, travel agency, business centre, tropical gardens, three restaurants, a sports bar and a couple of tree kangaroos thrown in for good measure – what more could you want?

Pilgrim Village Guesthouse   HOTEL $

(☎/fax 472 8076; Drayton St; s/d incl breakfast K120/150) Set around a courtyard, this place has a few rooms that specialise in well-worn decor and a strict adherence to 1960s style. The rooms are small but there is a communal lounge.

Melanesian Hotel   HOTEL $$$

(☎472 3744; www.coralseahotels.com.pg; 2nd St; r/ste K616/880; @🖥️) The 'Mello' has four-star aspirations, three-star amenities and a five-star price tag. On weekends rooms are slightly discounted from the rack rates listed here.

🍴 Eating

The cheapest meals can be found at any of the numerous *kai* bars (cheap takeaway food bars) dotted around town and most have a few plastic tables and chairs inside. A greasy plate of *kaukau* (sweet potato), *aibika* (greens) creamed with coconut and chicken comes heaped with a lot of local conversation and costs around K12.

As there are no taxis and it is unsafe to walk at night, the reality of dining out in Lae makes it likely you'll eat where you sleep.

TOP CHOICE Bunga Raya Restaurant   CHINESE, MALAY $$

(Lae Golf Course, Bumba Rd, Eriku; mains K20-40; ☺lunch & dinner) One of the most popular restaurants in Lae, the Bunga Raya draws a faithful crowd who come for the large selection of Chinese and Malay stir-fried classics. The lunchtime specials are particularly good value (K20 to K22) and see you right with a tasty heaping of veggies and meat served with either rice or noodles.

Lae Yacht Club   INTERNATIONAL $$

(Butibum Rd; meals K25-50; ☺lunch & dinner) The airy, informal 'Yachty' is in a prime position on the harbour and is good for both drinking and eating. Its Tuesday- and Friday-night

FINSCHHAFEN AREA

The town of Finschhafen was the German New Guinea Company's first attempt at colonising New Guinea. Unfortunately, things didn't go well and nothing remains of the original settlement aside from a lone Lutheran Mission building. Today Finschhafen refers to the district and the collective series of peaceful coastal towns within it. The principal settlement is Gagidu Station, 3km from Buki Wharf and about 30km from Maneba.

Towards the end of WWII the area was used as a staging post for US troops and vast numbers of GIs passed through. The war's abrupt end left millions of dollars worth of aircraft and equipment redundant, so the whole lot was bulldozed into a huge hole; ask at Dregerhafen High School, about 4km south of Gagidu Station, for directions.

Although there isn't a lot to do in Finschhafen, its proximity to Lae and abundance of white sandy beaches make it a great weekend escape. Butaweng waterfalls and Langemack Bay are the pick of the mainland swimming spots.

There is little in the way of formal accommodation other than a couple of family-run guesthouses in Gagidu Station – ask the locals to point them out. The only way to get to Finschhafen (either Maneba or Buki Wharf) is by boat; for details, see p82.

Tough-as-nails PMV trucks run between Gagidu and Maneba over a diabolical road (K7, 1½ hours) and from Buki Wharf to Gagidu Station (K2.50).

MOROBE & MADANG PROVINCES LAE

barbecues are excellent value (your choice of steak plus chips and salads for K42 to K50). The clientele is largely (but not solely) drawn from the dwindling expat community and even though it's a members-only club, you're likely to be buzzed in if you ask politely.

Main Market MARKET $
(Air Corps Rd; 7am-4pm Mon-Fri, to noon Sat) The main market is a riot of colourful fruits and fresh vegetables – just keep your wits about you while you shop (see warnings below).

Food Mart SUPERMARKET $
(7th St; 7am-7.30pm) You will think you have died and gone to supermarket heaven at Food Mart, especially if you have just come in from the bush.

 Shopping

**Melanesian Arts Gallery &
Tour Agency** ARTS & CRAFTS
(www.melanesianarts.com.pg; Markham Rd) Located beside the old airstrip, the Melanesian Arts Gallery & Tour Agency is crammed from floor to rafter with an excellent array of artefacts. Besides the obligatory penis gourds you can pick up items from all over PNG, including Sepik masks, Highland shields and Tami Island bowls. Prices are reasonable and shipping can be arranged.

Information

Lae has a reputation for danger and it pays to be more cautious than normal while you're here. Bag snatchers and pickpockets are common

in the market and travellers are often targeted because of their perceived wealth. Having said that, there's no reason why men can't walk around most parts of town during the day, though keep valuables on your person to a minimum. Women should be doubly cautious and, if possible, walk with a friend (preferably someone big and burly) for extra safety.

The area east of Voco Point should be avoided, including the beach.

Emergency
Ambulance (111)
Fire (472 4333/4818)
Police (479 1068; Coronation Dr)

Internet Access
Destiny Internet Cafe (7th St; per hr K20; 8am-5pm Mon-Fri, to 2pm Sat) Tucked inside a white and red building on the ground floor with reasonable connections. It also burns CDs.

Medical Services
Tusa Private Hospital (472 4688; 13th St; 24hr) For emergencies.

Money
Bank South Pacific (cnr Central Ave & 6th St) Credit card advances over the counter. Charges 1% commission on travellers cheques and is the agent for Western Union.

Westpac (cnr Central Ave & 6th St) Charges a 1% commission to cash travellers cheques and has an ATM.

Post
Post office (cnr 2nd & 3rd Sts; 8am-4pm Mon-Fri, to 11.30am Sat)

Tourist Information

Morobe Provincial Administration Division of Sports, Culture and Liquor Licensing (☎473 1713; Governmental Bldg, Coronation Dr; ⊗9am-4.30pm Mon-Fri) Now that the Morobe Tourism Bureau has closed, tourist information falls to these guys. It can be hard to get hold of a staff member to answer your questions – try asking for Mr Joe Kavera or Mrs Nanu Tomalau.

Travel Agencies

Travel Mate (☎479 3000; Lae International Hotel, 4th St) Avoid the queues at Air Niugini and purchase your tickets in comfort here for the same price.

❶ Getting There & Away

Lae is the best-connected city in PNG.

Air

An old airstrip lies at the foot of the steep hill to the west of Top Town and was, for many years, Lae's main airport. Today the city is served by Nadzab airport, the war-time airstrip 42km northwest of Lae's town centre.

It is probable that the Air Niugini and North Coast Aviation town offices will be forced to relocate within the lifetime of this book and Travel Air will begin operations from Lae.

Air Niugini (www.airniugini.com.pg) Town (☎430 1820; Markham Rd); Nadzab airport (☎475 3055) Has direct flights to Port Moresby (K480, 45 minutes, several times daily) and Madang (K433, 35 minutes, Wednesday and Saturday) that connect to the Madang/Wewak flight. To the islands, it flies to Manus (K595) and Hoskins (for Kimbe; K543) on Thursday; Rabaul (K699) every Thursday and Sunday; and Kavieng (K745) on Sunday only. For all other destinations you'll have to go to Port Moresby first.

Airlines PNG (☎475 3147; www.apng.com; Nadzab airport) Offers daily services to Port Moresby (K482), Goroka (K234), Mt Hagen (K391) and Tabubil (K1003).

North Coast Aviation Town (☎472 0516; www.nca.com.pg; Markham Rd); Nadzab (☎475 3006) Mainly services the Morobe, Gulf and West New Britain Provinces.

See the relevant towns later in this chapter for details on MAF and North Coast Aviation routes.

Boat

As the busiest port in the country, Lae is the best place in PNG from which to sail off into the sunset. Banana boats (exposed speed boats) run northeast as far as Finschhafen (K70, three hours) from Aigris Market (not wharf) at Voco Point. Banana boats heading southeast to Salamaua (K30, one hour), Morobe Station and then occasionally on to Oro Bay leave from the main wharf off Bumbu Rd beside Lae's main container terminal. They leave when full from 7am and do not carry life jackets or any kind of safety equipment. Assess the weather carefully.

Lutheran Shipping (Luship; ☎472 2066; fax 472 5806; luship@global.net.pg; Voco Point Rd) Luship has three boats servicing the Morobe coast and publishes a largely unreliable schedule at the beginning of each month. The MV *Gejamsao* leaves for Finschhafen on Monday, Thursday and Saturday (deck/cabin class K70/110, three hours) at 10am. It returns to Lae on Tuesday, Friday and Sunday. The MV *Mamose Express* also calls into Finschhafen on occasional Mondays and Thursdays on its way to Lablab (Umboi Island; deck/cabin class K96/120, overnight) and Wasum (West New Britain; deck/cabin class K110/120, overnight). Twice a month it also sails to Kimbe and Rabaul. Luship also run the MV *Rita* out of Madang, travelling to Vanimo.

Rabaul Shipping (Star Ships; ☎472 5699; Abel Tasman St) Prior to the 2012 ferry disaster when the *Rabaul Queen* sank off the coast of Finschhafen, Star Ships sailed to Rabaul (deck/cabin class K340/440, 40 hours) via Kimbe (deck/cabin class K210/335) on Monday and Friday. There was also an additional Wednesday service to Kimbe and an on-again, off-again Sunday boat to Alotau (per person K340) via Oro Bay (per person K190). If a replacement boat is found, a weekly timetable will be pinned outside its office. Strangely, and somewhat inexplicably, in 2011 non-Papua New Guineans needed permission from management to travel. It remains to be seen if this rule will be rescinded.

PMV

Most PMVs for Goroka (K30, four hours) and Madang (K50, five hours) leave between 8am and 9am daily from the **Eriku long-distance bus stop** opposite the Salvation Army. There are fewer services on weekends.

There are now PMVs travelling in convoy at night. They are intended for those wishing to reach Mt Hagen (K50, 12 hours) or further without overnighting in Goroka. Buses depart from Lae at 6pm, hooking up with the Madang buses at Watarais and arriving in Mt Hagen at 6am. Travelling at night, however, is not advised – convoy or not.

The road to Wau is not sealed but is generally good, with spectacular scenery as the road skirts the Bulolo River. Trucks to Bulolo (K15, three hours) and Wau (K22, four to five hours) collect passengers between 8am and 9am and again at around 1pm from the empty lot near the police station in Top Town.

❶ Getting Around

There are no taxis in Lae, but **Pilgrim Village Guesthouse Bus** (☎472 8076) will run you around if you call (trip within town K20).

To/From the Airport

Most visitors use one of the airport bus services, which collect you from your hotel and complete the journey at alarming speed – usually only 30 minutes. **Butibam Shuttles** (☎724 97236) is popular at K25 a trip, while the guards on **Guard Dog Security** (☎475 1069) would make Rambo look under-equipped (K93).

Local PMVs (K4, 45 minutes) leave from the main market, but with no taxis, getting to or from the market with your luggage can be a hassle.

PMV

PMVs around Lae cost K0.50 to K1 to Unitec. There are three main local PMV stops. One is in Eriku (for Unitec) on Huon Rd. Another is on 7th St in Top Town and the third is next to the main market on Air Corps Rd (good for Voco Point).

Salamaua

The lovely peninsula an hour south of Lae is Salamaua. There's little to suggest this tranquil village once played such a significant part in the development of Wau and Bulolo in the gold-rush days, or a pivotal role in the course of the Pacific War. You can walk to, or dive on, a few interesting war relics. Follow the steep trail to four **Japanese gun emplacements** and what remains of the original town cemetery in the peninsula's hills. The trail begins in the northwest corner of the school oval. Near the start of the path is the now-blocked entrance to a Japanese tunnel.

If you want a full day's walk, **Mt Tambu** has spectacular views and a huge battlefield where the Australians met the Japanese as they advanced towards Wau.

Salamaua bay has a scattering of reefs and coral formations, although you will need to bring your **snorkelling** equipment to appreciate them.

Most days there are boats from Lae to Salamaua (K30, 1½ hours) and the **Black Cat Trail** ends (or starts) at Salamaua; for details, see p85.

🛏 Sleeping & Eating

The village store sells rice, noodles and SP Lager (the generator even works the fridge from 6pm to 10pm!).

Salamaua Guesthouse GUESTHOUSE **$**
(Haus Kibung; dm K66) Has bungalows with shared bathrooms plus a couple of larger family rooms. Bring your own food and use the well-equipped kitchen or ask someone to cook you a local meal.

Wau & Around

In the 1920s and '30s New Guinea's gold rush made the mining towns of Wau (pronounced 'wow') and Bulolo thriving centres of industry (see p76). Not any more. A gold mine discovered a few years ago at nearby Hidden Valley had promised to boost the local economy but much of the wealth has ended up in Lae and unemployment in the area remains sky-high.

Wau's climate is a welcome change from the stifling heat and humidity of the coast and it is far safer and friendlier than Lae down the road. At an altitude of about 1300m, the abundant pines give a refreshing slant on equatorial vegetation. Most who come here do so to tackle either the Black Cat (p85) or Bulldog Trails (see boxed text, p86); two of PNG's most rewarding and challenging treks.

⊙ Sights & Activities

B17 Bomber HISTORIC SITE
(Trekking fee per person K50, compulsory Black Cat Trail Association guide K25) On 8 January 1943 an American B-17E Flying Fortress, crippled by flak sustained while attacking a Japanese convoy near Lae, crashed while searching for the Wau airstrip. The remains are in fairly good condition on a hillside, a four-hour return trek from Biawen Junction, 13km from Wau. Transport to the trailhead can be arranged through Wau Adventures (K275 including waiting time).

☞ Tours

Wau Adventures ADVENTURE TOUR
(☎710 07536; www.wauadventures.com.pg) Wau's only tour company specialises in helping trekkers tackle the Black Cat and, with a stout 4WD at its disposal, also run tours to war relics, including the WWII fox holes dug by Australians at Slippery Ridge. It's best to contact the company in advance, but if you do show up unannounced, staff can be contacted via Donna's Stoa, close to where the PMVs stop in the centre of town.

🛏 Sleeping & Eating

Wau Adventures Guesthouse GUESTHOUSE **$$**
(☎710 07536; www.wauadventures.com.pg; per person without bathroom incl meals K250) Run by the tour company of the same name, this small bunkhouse can accommodate 10 people in three bedrooms that share a cosy communal lounge. The home-cooked meals

WORTH A TRIP

HOPPING ALONG THE HUON GULF COAST

The clear blue waters of the Huon Gulf coast are blessed with a number of white sandy beaches and villagers so laid-back they barely get vertical. Indeed, to even describe life here as merely relaxed is an understatement, akin to describing Errol Flynn (who once made his way to these parts) as merely having 'a way with the ladies'.

Being ultra-relaxed can have its drawbacks. Transport is a touch on the inconsistent side and little things such as electricity don't always work. But, hey, this really is off-the-beaten-track PNG at its best.

But before sailing into that sunset, be sure to speak with Maine Winny from Culture Link PNG Adventures (☏727 94907; mainewinny@gmail.com; culturelinkpng@global.net. pg). He is based in Lae and promotes the village guesthouses along the Huon Gulf coast. Maine can book accommodation by radio and give you the low-down on whose boat is running where. With a bit of planning, it's possible to hop between villages all the way to Oro Bay in Oro Province.

Trips down the coast start at Lae's main wharf off Bumbu Rd, and your conveyance is almost always a PMV banana boat. There's no schedule, but a general rule is that the further the destination, the less frequently it runs. There are about seven guesthouses along the coast and most charge around K65 per person per night and can provide basic meals for an additional K20. Our favourite is Kamiali Guesthouse (per person incl meals K85), 30km south of Salamaua in Lababia village. The attraction here is the 69,000-hectare Kamiali Wildlife Management Area. The area comprises forests, mangroves, sandy beaches, coral reefs, waterfalls, rivers and lakes, and includes the steep David Suzuki Trail through some pristine forest. From November until March, leatherback turtles (permit per person K20) scramble ashore to dig deep nests and lay as many as 100 eggs. These incredible reptiles that can live to a great age weigh up to 500kg and measure up to 2m in length. It is a truly extraordinary sight.

are delicious and hearty. The guesthouse is a few minutes out of town and you need to phone (or email) ahead so staff can prepare for your arrival.

Valley View Guesthouse　　　GUESTHOUSE $$
(☏474 6312, 725 83616; per person without bathroom incl meals K275) A 10-minute walk from town on the road to Bulolo, this informal, breezy guesthouse has large rooms, comfy beds and enough of the owner's personal effects scattered about to give it a very homey feel.

❶ Getting There & Away
Air

North Coast Aviation once flew to Wau from Lae and Port Moresby but *raskols* (bandits) burnt down its Wau building and at the time of writing it was uncertain if flights would resume. Thanks to the Hidden Valley Mine, both Air Niugini and Airlines PNG now fly from Port Moresby to Bululo (K374) frequently.

PMV

PMVs to Lae (K22, four to five hours) leave Wau between 6am and 7am most days from near Donna's Stoa. They run via Bulolo (K7, one hour).

Black Cat Trail

The Black Cat Trail was used by miners in the 1920s (p76) and its difficulty lies in the 'no-matter-what' route straight from Salamaua to its objective – the Black Cat mine, northeast of Wau. The miners took eight days to cover the 50km, and parts of the track were later used by Australian soldiers during WWII.

These days the middle sections of the Black Cat are seldom used by anyone, and the trail itself is often overgrown or obstructed by landslips and fallen trees. Most people actually access the Black Cat using the Skin Diwai Trail that starts 13km from Wau at Biawen Junction and joins the Black Cat proper near Godogasui.

Using this trail gives trekkers the option of walking via a crashed B17 bomber (p83) or opting for an easier route via the Banished Donkey rest stop to Charlies Rest, the campsite for the first night. The second day's six-hour walk will bring you down to Skin Diwai, an old military camp with a few interesting war relics. Expect a long third and fourth day over some very rough terrain as you make a steep descent to the village of Go-dogasul and then Mubo in the Bitoi Valley. Alternatively walk through Mubo and camp at a four-hut settlement known as Nui Kamp. Look out for the unexploded ordinance from WWII and expect multiple river crossings on this day. The final day involves a 1½-hour trek to Komiatum, where villagers build bamboo rafts (K100) for trekkers, allowing them to travel to Salamaua (p83) in relative style.

Note that this track shouldn't be attempted by inexperienced walkers. There is a series of traverses with loose footing and long drops below, plus several crossings of the Bitoi River, but as long as you are fit, enjoy a challenge and are not afraid of heights, the Black Cat is definitely doable.

Tours

The following companies have Black Cat experience.

Executive Excellence (www.executiveexcellence.com.au) A well-respected Australian operator.

Papua New Guinea Trekking Adventures (325 1284; www.pngtrekkingadventures.com)

Wau Adventures (710 07536; www.wauadventures.com.pg) Based in Wau and a reliable source of local knowledge. For more details, see p84.

ⓘ Information

Costs

The Black Cat Trail Association represents the landowners and charges K200 per person for both the Black Cat and Bulldog Trails. This trekking fee is payable to the association's chair-

man, **Ninga Yawa** (710 13612; ninga.yawa@gmail.com), or Wau Adventures in Wau or Dick Ruben in Salamaua. In addition you will also have to pay a K10-per-person camping fee wherever you pitch your tent.

Guides & Porters

Guides (K100 per day) are compulsory but porters (K90 per day) are optional. Trekkers are responsible for feeding everyone they hire.

Neither guides nor porters will bring much beyond a bush knife and a few clothes, so you will also need to supply packs to carry your equipment and arrange a tarpaulin for your guides to sleep beneath.

Practicalities

While the average annual rainfall in Wau is around 1600mm, it is between 2500mm and 3000mm for most areas of the trek. Even during the dry seasons (mid-May to September) waterproof gear (including boots with good grip) should be carried. The trail also passes through exposed grassy areas and a wide-brimmed hat and sunscreen are essential on sunny days. As all of the village guesthouses are in disrepair you will need to carry tents, sleeping bags and foam mattresses. There is little in the way of food that can be brought en route so carry all that you need.

Obviously, it makes sense to walk from Wau *down* to Salamaua but no matter which direction you come from, you will need to pay the public transport fare of your guides and porters back to their villages.

ⓘ Getting There & Away

It is 13km from Wau to the trailhead at Biawen Junction. As there are no PMVs, your only real option is arrange transport through Wau Adventures (per car K275).

WORTH A TRIP

THE SMOKED BODIES OF MENYAMYA & ASEKI

Menyamya, in the heart of Anga country, is *truly* remote. Those who make the significant effort to get here usually come to see the smoked bodies (per person K50, photography K350) at Aseki or Watama, nearer to Menyamya. The Anga used to smoke their dead and leave the mummified bodies in burial caves and cliff ledges to watch over their descendants. While this practice has died out with the advent of Christianity, the skeletal remains and what is left of their leather-like skin still keep guard from where they were placed years ago.

PMVs travel from Bulolo up to Aseki and then on to Menyamya (K40, nine hours) through some extremely rough and absolutely spectacular country. The road actually bypasses Aseki so, if you're going there, make sure the driver knows to take you into the village. Alternatively a day trip can be made with Wau Adventures (p84) but it's a long 10-hour return trip and costs K3000 for the car.

If demand warrants it, North Coast Aviation flies into both Menyamya and Aseki.

MADANG PROVINCE

Madang Province is PNG in miniature. It has coastal people, islanders, mountain people and river dwellers. The fertile coastal strip is backed by some of the most rugged mountains in PNG – the Adelbert and Schrader Ranges to the north, and the Finisterre Range to the south.

Madang

Madang is a little shyer and more reserved than her older sister Lae. Like a Melanesian maiden from a cliché in a South Pacific musical, Madang was once dubbed the 'Prettiest town in the Pacific' and while she retains her charms – perched on a peninsula as she is, surrounded by picturesque islands and sprinkled with parks, ponds and water-lily-filled waterways – her youthful beauty has faded.

Madang's warm, wet climate and fertile soil produce luxuriant growth. Many of the huge casuarina trees that tower over the Madang streets escaped WWII relatively unscathed but Madang itself wasn't so lucky and the town had to be rebuilt after it was virtually destroyed during the Japanese occupation and subsequent fighting.

Sights

Madang Museum   MUSEUM
(☑422 3302; Modilon Rd; admission K5; ⊗8am-noon & 1-4.30pm Mon-Fri) In the same building and operated by the Madang Visitors & Cultural Bureau, this small but fascinating place is worth visiting. Look for the ceremonial headdress from Bosmum village on the Lower Ramu River. These are worn during the 'cleansing of the blood', the time in which blood is drawn from a boy's tongue and penis as part of an initiation rite to manhood.

Flying Fox Roosts   WILDLIFE
(Kasagten Rd) You can't miss Madang's bats, they're everywhere; wheeling overhead all day, constantly disturbed by the town noises below and local boys who like to take pot shots at them with their slingshots (apparently the bats taste delicious). Locals told us that these *Kwandi* (spectacled flying foxes) moved into town in the mid-1970s, although no one could say why.

**Coastwatchers' Memorial
Beacon**   MEMORIAL
(Kalibobo Point lighthouse) The 30m-high Coastwatchers Memorial Beacon, visible 25km

out to sea, is a reminder of those who stayed behind enemy lines during WWII to report on Japanese troop and ship movements. It's a rather ugly concrete memorial, but the 3km beachfront road south of the memorial is the most pleasant walk in Madang.

Activities

Excellent visibility, stunning tropical coral and fish life and countless WWII wrecks make the **diving** and **snorkelling** around Madang world-famous. Local favourites include Barracuda Point, Magic Passage, Planet Rock and Eel Gardens. There's also good snorkelling just off Family Beach and off the rocks at Madang Lodge and Smugglers Inn Resort, but watch the swell and the tides because the rocks, coral and sea urchins can be hazardous.

For more information on diving in Madang, see p25.

The best **swimming beaches** are along Coronation Dr, particularly **Family Beach** and **Machine Gun Beach**, but even these are more rock than sand. If you want to throw down a towel on actual sand, head to nearby Krangket Island (p91).

Niugini Diving Adventures   DIVING
(☑422 2655; mtsoperations@mtspng.com; Madang Resort Hotel, Coastwatchers Ave) Niugini Diving Adventures is now the only operation in town and has plenty of local experience. Prices listed here are based on a minimum of two divers; solo travellers can pay a surcharge (K80) if need be. Rates include: PADI open-water certification (K1050), one-/two-dive packages (K150/270) and snorkelling excursions (K90 including gear). Night diving and speciality courses are also available. Dive gear costs K60 per day to hire.

Tours

Madang Visitors & Cultural Bureau (p90) offers plenty of suggestions and practical advice for day tours and excursions.

Melanesian Tourist Services   TOUR
(MTS; ☑424 1300; www.mtspng.com; Coastwatchers Ave) Madang Resort Hotel's Melanesian Tourist Services runs **village tours** (half-/full day K90/180; minimum 2 people required) to the south coast stopping at lookout points, war memorials and Bilbil village to buy pottery. Its **harbour cruise** (half-/full day K90/180; minimum 2 people required) uses banana boats to visit the rusting wreckage of Japanese landing craft before calling at Krangket Island for snorkelling. MTS also has a dedicated

BULLDOG TRACK: IN THE FOOTSTEPS OF HISTORY

The WWII Bulldog Track, intended to link Wau with the south coast, winds its way from Edie Creek to Bulldog, from where you had to travel by river. When completed in 1943 the track was actually a road capable of bearing large trucks. It has deteriorated since and has been cut by landslides and jungle. Depending on how much of it you want to walk, the Bulldog Track takes from three to nine days and passes through a stunning array of landscapes and villages. It is a bona fide adventure requiring considerable fitness and should not be undertaken lightly.

Recently the Hidden Valley mine has denied track access, making it logistically difficult to undertake without the assistance of one of the tour companies listed in the Black Cat Trail section (see p85).

gamefishing charter (half-/full day for 4 people incl lunch & drinks K2250/4500), as well as the **Kalibobo Spirit**, a 98-foot, luxurious live-aboard boat that is available for diving, fishing and Sepik exploratory cruises.

★★ Festivals & Events

Divine Word University Cultural Show FESTIVAL
(admission K15, ⊙official start 9am, usual start 11am) Usually held on the third or fourth Saturday in August (check with the Madang Visitors & Cultural Bureau), the Divine Word University Cultural Show is smaller than its highland cousins but still a lively riot of colour, feathers and traditional attire. Be sure to stay until the end when the highland *waipa* dance is celebrated with gusto and performers won't rest until everyone – fellow students, tourists and family supporters alike – are up and dancing with them.

🛌 Sleeping

If you're looking for further budget options, the guesthouses on Krangket Island (p91) are worth considering and easily reached.

TOP CHOICE Madang Lodge HOTEL $$
(☑422 3395; www.madanglodge.com.pg; Modilon Rd; s K320-450, d K370-520, s/d without bathroom K99/150; ❄✉🛜) With something for everyone and with great snorkelling nearby, this is one of the best places to stay in PNG. The backpacker rooms are simple, fan-cooled affairs, while the top-end, semidetached bungalows have a kitchenette, cable TV and air-con. Scattered about the grounds you'll find a stunning array of orchids, a seaside pool, carver's workshop, coffee shop and a newly built waterfront restaurant that serves delicious meals. A hotel shuttle can run you into town (K4), or jump on a PMV that stops outside.

CWA Guesthouse GUESTHOUSE $
(☑422 2216; madang.cwa@global.net.pg; Coastwatchers Ave; dm/s/tw K55/85/110) Occupying a prime slice of real estate on the waterfront near the town centre, this church-run guesthouse may be rather basic but is spotlessly clean and the staff genuinely friendly. You can borrow a book (K1) and there is a Saturday morning coffee shop on-site. Meals aren't served but there's a communal kitchen.

Fabies Guesthouse GUESTHOUSE $
(☑718 11616; Coronation Dr; d K250, s/d without bathroom K110/150; ❄) Fabies is the newest guesthouse in town and has spic and span rooms in a renovated family home that share a communal TV lounge. It's virtually opposite Machine Gun Beach and the only place in this price range with air-con. Meals are available (K20).

Madang Resort Hotel and Kalibobo Village Resort RESORT $$$
(☑422 2655; www.mtspng.com; Coastwatchers Ave; s incl breakfast K320-694, d incl breakfast K385-759; ❄🛜✉) Madang Resort and Kalibobo Village are owned by the same people, sit side by side, share facilities and are run jointly. Both share the enormous waterfront grounds, three pools, some brilliant orchid gardens and various wildlife menageries. This is the most tourist-orientated accommodation in the province.

Madang Star International Hotel HOTEL $$$
(☑422 2656; www.madangstar.com.pg; Regina Ave; r/apt K450/600; ❄✉) The landowners of Star Mountain (where the Ok Tedi mine is located) have taken some of their profits and hope to turn their copper windfall into gold. Aimed squarely at the business end of the market and being brand new, the rooms are spacious, immaculate and still smell of fresh paint.

Madang

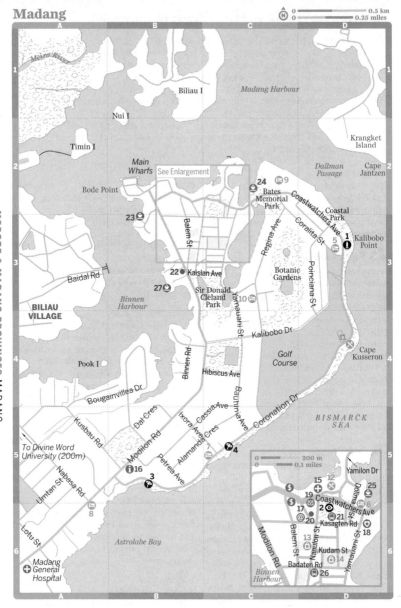

MOROBE & MADANG PROVINCES MADANG

Coastwatchers Hotel HOTEL $$$
(☎422 2684; www.coralseahotels.com.pg; Coast-watchers Ave; r K420-523; ❄☎☀) As the name implies, this Coral Sea Hotel enjoys ocean views – but not from every room. It's a modern, tasteful complex adjacent to the Coastwatchers' Memorial Beacon and the golf course. The rooms are large and some are split over two storeys, ideal for families or groups. There's good dining in Coasties Restaurant and Bar upstairs on the open-air veranda. On a muggy night it catches a

Madang

MOROBE & MADANG PROVINCES MADANG

pleasant breeze, and the lazy fans and cane furniture add to the tropical ambience.

✕ Eating

The overall standard for restaurant dining in Madang is probably PNG's best outside of Port Moresby. All of the major hotels have attached restaurants and bars.

Eden Restaurant   CHINESE $$
(Coronation Dr; meals K25-35; ⊙lunch & dinner Mon-Fri, dinner Sun) Admittedly, this restaurant doesn't make much of a first impression; it's right on the foreshore but cleverly designed to have no views at all. People don't come for the view, however, but for the fantastic lunchtime specials and a bowl of fiery seafood *laksa* (curry noodles). For views, pop next door to the Madang Country Club and buy yourself a beer.

Ocean Restaurant   CHINESE, MALAY $$
(Coastwatchers Ave; mains K25; ⊙lunch & dinner Mon-Fri, dinner Sun) Get here early to secure a table on the small harbour-side veranda at lunch (lunch specials K14 to K18) – for our money, the most atmospheric dining in town. Next door is the Madang Club; officially you need to be member, or at least be signed in by

one, but a bit of bravado will usually see you pass security to the Friday quiz night.

🛍 Shopping

Bilbil clay pots are a local speciality. Highlanders come down with some *bilums* (string bags) and hats, and you'll see Buka-ware and items from the Sepik. Have a look through the market and in the carvers' huts attached to Madang Lodge and Madang Resort Hotel for souvenirs.

The **market** (⊙closed Sun) has fruit and vegetables as well as some clothing, *bilums* and local shell jewellery. It's possible to buy snorkelling gear from the sports shop in **Beckzle Plaza** (Madang Department Store, Nanulon St).

ⓘ Information

Emergency
Ambulance (☑111)
Fire (☑422 2777/2245)
Police (☑422 3233/3243, 149 Yamauani St)

Internet Access
Page Mate (Kasagten Rd; per hr K15; ⊙8am-4pm Mon-Fri, to noon Sat) Fast satellite connections, CD writing capabilities but no Skype.

Medical Services

Pharmacies are well represented.

Family Clinic (☑422 1234; Coastwatchers Ave) Has an Australian doctor on staff.

Money

All major hotels cash travellers cheques, often at a rate that's competitive with the banks, and major credit cards are widely accepted. Both banks listed following have ATMs that accept international credit cards.

ANZ (Coastwatchers Ave)

Bank South Pacific (Coastwatchers Ave)

Post

Post office (Nuna St)

Telephone

Telikom (Nuna St) Next to the post office. It has public phones outside.

Tourist Information

Madang Visitors & Cultural Bureau (☑422 3302; www.tourismmadang.com; Modilon Rd; ☺8am-noon & 1-4.30pm Mon-Fri, on request Sat & Sun) This is one of the best resourced information centres in the country. The friendly staff have up-to-date information on accommodation and attractions throughout the province, including hard-to-reach destinations such as Simbai and Karkar Island.

Melanesian Tourist Services (MTS; ☑424 1300; www.mtspng.com; Madang Resort Hotel, Coastwatchers Ave) Runs local tours (p88) and books airline tickets.

❶ Getting There & Around

To/From the Airport

The airport is 7km from Madang. Most of the hotels and guesthouses have complimentary airport transfers and will meet your flight when you arrive. 8B PMVs run along Independence Dr and into town (K1).

Air

Planes don't fly between 5pm and 8pm (when the flying foxes leave their roosts) for fear of bat strike.

Air Niugini (☑422 2699; www.airniugini.com. pg; Nuna St) has twice-daily flights into Madang from Port Moresby (K588, one hour), daily flights to/from Wewak (K462, 40 minutes), and Thursday and Sunday flights to Lae (K433, 30 minutes) that continue to Rabaul (K781). The Sunday flight continues to Kavieng (K618) and the Thursday flight travels to Kimbe (K657).

Travel Air (☑422 0488; www.travelairpng. com; Beckzle Plaza, Nanulon St) is the phoenix that arose from the defunct Airlink. At time of research it had just commenced operations and

from Madang it was possible to only fly to Port Moresby (K340, daily).

MAF (☑422 2229) and **Island Airways** (☑422 2601) are both based at the airport and service many small communities in remote areas. Their schedules vary with passenger requirements but if you are heading to the Finisterre or Bismarck Ranges or the Ramu Valley (Aiome, Simbai or Teptep), these are the guys to see. Island Airways also flies to Mt Hagen. It is possible to arrange charter flights with either company.

Boat

Small boats run to the islands in Madang harbour from an inlet behind the CWA Guesthouse and next to the Madang Resort, hourly or so from 7am to 5.30pm (K1 to K5).

Lutheran Shipping (Luship; ☑422 2577; luship@global.net.pg; Modilon Rd) operates a weekly service on the MV *Rita* to Wewak (1st/2nd class K180/144, usually Monday night departure), which, twice a month, continues on to Vanimo (1st/2nd class K300/250) via Aitape (K255/216). A schedule is pinned to its notice board at the start of the month.

Rabaul Shipping (Star Ships; Modilon Rd) had a Tuesday boat to Wewak (K155) that, once or twice a month depending on demand, continued to Vanimo (K300). The sinking of its ferry in 2012 is likely to disrupt this service until a new boat is found.

PMV

On the north coast the road is sealed to Bogia. PMVs travel to Siar village (K3, 35 minutes), Riwo/Jais Aben (K3, 45 minutes), Malolo (K5, one hour) and Bogia (PMV 17L or 17M; K20, five hours) from the PMV stop opposite the Ho Kid store on Kasagten Rd. Bogia-bound PMVs usually leave between 1pm and 2pm.

Heading south along Madang's main thoroughfare, the road becomes the Ramu Hwy and rises over the tortuous Finisterre Range into the vast Ramu Valley on its way to Lae; and via the Highlands Hwy, deep into the central mountains. This is very spectacular driving and the only 'interstate' in the country.

Buses gather around the market at 8am and the door guys yell out their destinations 'LaeLaeLaeLae' and 'HagenHagenHagen' with a great sense of theatre. The fare to Lae is K40 (five hours) and to Goroka K40 (five hours). The overnight buses to Mt Hagen (K60) rendezvous with Lae buses at Watarais, where they form a convoy – presumably for safety.

Local buses include the 6A, which runs to Barasiko market at the Lae junction; 6B, which continues 3km up the North Coast Hwy; and 6C, which goes to Yabob village. All cost K0.50 to K1.

Taxi

It's possible to count the taxis in Madang on one hand and you could go for weeks without actually seeing one. If you do need a taxi, call **Ark Taxis** (☑721 42315, 422 1636), which will send one of its five cars.

Krangket Island

Krangket Island, across Dallman Passage from Madang, is a large island with several villages and a beautiful lagoon ideal for swimming and snorkelling. There's a popular picnic spot, which was a former rest area for wounded Australian soldiers in the days following the Japanese surrender in WWII. The snorkelling (bring your own snorkelling gear) near Krangket Island Lodge is well worth the K5 locals charge day-trippers.

Boats from Madang (K1, 15 minutes) drop their passengers about 45 minutes' walk from the Krangket Island Lodge, though you should be able to negotiate passage to the lodge end of the island.

The island's best accommodation is **Laid-ex Guesthouse** (☑7277 3624; r K25), a simple village guesthouse operated by Makos Los. There's a total of six rooms – all fairly basic – and a kitchen for preparing your own food. At the other end of the island, the **Krangket Island Lodge** (☑729 40264; bungalow K80) is operated by the Dum clan (pronounced 'doom'). It consists of a few bush cottages tucked away from the village. They're rustic and with every passing year, increasingly run-down.

Balek Wildlife Sanctuary

This **wildlife management area** (☑715 34883; admission K10; ⊗7am-5pm) is 10km south of Madang. It's featured in scenes from the 1996 film production of *Robinson Crusoe* with Pierce Brosnan. There's a sulphur creek that flows from a huge limestone formation. Spirits are said to inhabit the site and the water has curative properties. The water is incredibly clear and you can feed eels and turtles with bananas and fresh meat. Catch a 15B PMV from town (K2).

Ohu

The **Ohu Butterfly Habitat** (☑726 85248; admission K10; ⊗7am-3pm), 15km southwest of Madang, is a community conservation and research project where butterflies, including

NORTH COAST HIGHWAY

The whole north coast offers a smattering of beaches, excellent diving and snorkelling, and some great hills and rivers to explore. The road runs north of Madang as far as Bogia, from where you catch speedboats to Angoram and ultimately make your way to Wewak.

PNG's famous birdwing varieties, feed on the nectar of the flowering *aristolochia*. The butterflies are best seen in the morning from 7am to 10am. Catch a 13B PMV (K2) from Madang to the 'Medo' drop-off, from where it's a 70-minute (5km) walk.

Jais Aben Area

Divers rave about the north-coast sites, such as the US freighter *Henry Leith* in 20m of water near Jais Aben Resort, and the nearby minesweeper *Boston*. The 'waterhole' is an enclosed lagoon connected to the open sea by a large underwater tunnel and offers dramatic snorkelling. Sinub and Tab Islands are also recommended snorkelling spots but landowners ask a K5 levy. Unfortunately, Aquaventures, the local dive shop, closed but Madang's Niugini Diving Adventures (p88) can arrange trips to these sites.

The **Jais Aben Resort** (☑423 3111; www.jaisabenresort.com; r K295-550; ❀@☎) is 20km from Madang, off the main road. It's a pretty place on its own little peninsula, with small beaches and lawns. The beachside bungalows are large and comfortable, with enclosed verandas and seafront outlooks. The newer 'deluxe' bungalows are flashier and have air-con. There's a beachfront bar where burgers and steaks are served, and a fine restaurant whose changing menu incorporates local and international dishes.

Town and airport transfers are free for guests. PMV 17A runs along the main road from Madang (K1) but stops 1km shy of the resort. This road is occasionally prone to *raskol* hold-ups.

Alexishafen

Alexishafen Catholic Mission is off the North Coast Hwy to the right, 23km north of Madang. The name 'Alexishafen' is derived from the combination of the German word

Around Madang

N 0 ___ 2 km
0 ___ 1 miles

To Baragam (26km);
Bogia (153km)

Sek
Harbour

Sek
I

WWII Japanese
Aircraft Wrecks

Alexishafen

Amron

Mililat
Harbour

Kau Rainforest
Museum &
Conservation Area

Sinub I
Wonad I
Tobad I

Jais Aben
Resort

Nobonob
Mission

Lutheran
Mission

Nagada
Harbour

North Coast Hwy

Siar

Siar I

Samun I
Krangket
I

Madang
Airport

Bilian I

Madang
Harbour

Dallmen Passage

Baidai Rd

Biliau
Village

Binnen
Harbour

Madang

See Madang Map (p88)

Japanese War
Memorial

Lookout

Yabob

Yabob
I

Ramu Hwy

To Balek Wildlife Sanctuary (7km);
Ohu Butterfly Habitat (12km);
Lae; The Highlands

Bilbil

BISMARCK
SEA

for harbour, *hafen,* and the first name of a Russian princess, Alexis. The graveyard here stands as a reminder of the early missionary period. Beyond the mission you can see the old overgrown missionary-built airstrip.

Like so much of the area, Alexishafen was badly damaged during the war. The WWII Japanese airstrip (a little off the road to the left, between the mission airstrip and Alexishafen) is now threatened by the encroaching jungle. Only bomb craters and the odd aircraft wreck hint at the saturation bombing that destroyed the base. The most impressive of these aircraft wrecks is the Japanese *Donryu,* next to the bomb crater that destroyed it. Nearer to the road is the fuselage of an early Junkers mission aircraft.

Malolo

The North Coast Hwy continues north to the old Malolo (*mah*-lollo) plantation, 42km up the coast, site of the upmarket **Malolo Plantation Lodge** (☎542 1438; www.pngtours.com; all-inclusive s/d/tw US$812/1048/1048; @). The **black-sand beaches** along the coast are indicative of volcanic activity on Karkar and Manam Islands. There's good swimming, but watch the currents.

Keki Eco-Mountain Lodge (☎724 31879; Salemben; r per person K40), perched high on a ridge, has two traditional bungalows each with double rooms and cooking facilities. At around 900m above sea level it's a great place for birding, and birds of paradise often sit atop the lodge roof. It's difficult to get to, though – catch a 17E PMV from Madang to Bunabum Junction, which is 26km from the lodge, and phone ahead for a lift.

Ulingan Bay

The area around Ulingan Bay is particularly good for **surfing**, with a number of right- and left-hand breaks. It's best suited to intermediate or advanced riders as most of the waves break over coral reefs (reef booties are recommended).

PNG's second National Surf Titles were held at the **Tupira Surf Club** (☎714 07101; www.tupirasurfclub.com; per person incl meals & surfing fees K250) in 2011. During the peak surfing months (November to April), the Tupira Surf Club operates a guesthouse that overlooks a perfect right-hander and can accommodate 10 people in five simple, fan-cooled rooms. The newly installed generator

THE BETEL NUT RUN: BOGIA TO ANGORAM

The best way to get from Bogia to the Sepik region is to catch a *buai* (betel nut) boat from Mandi Bay, Boroi or Awar (K100 per person, five hours depending on the size of the boat, its load and the size of the motor pushing it). Mandi Bay is perhaps the most convenient as it's only 15 minutes by vehicle from Bogia. Most boats leave between 6am and 7am. Don't travel during rough weather as boats do sink with disastrous consequences.

If you have spent the night at Anua Negu Lodge, it can be very difficult to find a PMV at 5.30am to get you to Mandi Bay in time for the 6am boats. Thankfully Anua Negu Lodge provides transfers for K20, but you should check that its jeep is operational before deciding to stay here. If it is not, a better bet is to travel all the way to Mandi Bay from Madang and ask locals for a place to stay. There is a small hut with a lockable door and concrete floor where you can spend the night but it's *very* basic, without a bed or even a mattress. The village has no toilet, so do as the locals do and go in the sea.

Coming the other way, you'll have to ask around at Angoram for a 'Bogia-bound *buai* boat' (trying say that quickly). Since many of the betel nuts are grown in the Yuat River region, not all boats call at Angoram but you shouldn't have to wait more than a day or two to find passage. The guesthouse owners in Angoram can help you ask around. Once you arrive in Bogia (at either Mandi Bay, Boroi or Awar) it's sometimes possible to jump on a waiting PMV that's heading towards Madang (K20, five hours), although it's more likely you'll have to overnight in Bogia.

and bar make it a social place, and most who come here do so as part of an all-inclusive, week-long package booked directly with the surf club or through World Surfaris (www.worldsurfaris.com).

Karkar Island

Karkar Island is one of the most fertile places in the country and home to some of the most productive copra plantations in the world. The volcano erupted violently in 1974 and again in 1979, killing two vulcanologists, but it is possible to climb to the crater (1831m, 12 hours return). Bring plenty of sunscreen to combat the heat that bounces off the bare basalt and seek permission from the villagers as the crater has religious significance. The climb is easier from Mum village, but there are better views if you start from Kevasob village. Local guides are available.

A road encircles the island and takes four hours to drive around. You can also walk around, but treat the river crossings with caution. When it rains on the mountain, water comes down these rivers like a wall. Karkar is encircled by a reef and has good beaches and snorkelling, although you'll need to bring your own equipment.

The high school and the airstrip are at the government station at Kinim.

Tugutugu Guesthouse (725 81507; s/d K80/130) is about 3km from Kulili wharf (45 minutes by foot) and 10km from Kinim

wharf. It is set in beautiful grounds and is a 15-minute walk to a white sandy beach. On the other side of the Island, Sona Guesthouse (719 94538, 433 1197; s/tw K110/150) has accommodation in a former family home and, although food is available, guests are welcome to bring their own and use the kitchen.

Getting There & Away

In Madang **Kulili Estates** (423 7461; Modilon Rd) has a Monday, Wednesday and Friday 11am boat to Karkar Island (five hours, K20) from a small pier just north of Lutheran Shipping. Daily PMV boats also operate from here to Karkar Island.

Bogia, Hansa Bay & Manam Island

Bogia is 185km northwest of Madang and the departure point for Manam Island. The road is sealed all the way to Bogia but peters out a short distance thereafter before the mighty Ramu River.

In 2004 the Manam Island volcano erupted, displacing 6000 people who fled to the safety of the mainland. Only 2000 or so have returned. It's possible to visit the still-smoking island and explore the carnage. Anua Negu Lodge can arrange a speed boat (K400, one hour) to run you there and back or you can take a PMV boat from Mandi Bay (K15 to K35, depending on where you are dropped) but you will need to find a friend to overnight with, as there are no official guesthouses on the island.

Hansa Bay is a popular diving spot past Bogia, where the wreckage of 35 Japanese freighters and US aircraft lie in a shallow harbour. The upper deck of the 6000-tonne *Shishi Maru* lies in just 6m of water, two anti-aircraft guns on the bow point upwards and brass shell castings litter the deck. Two fire engines are sitting in the hold, just before the bridge, where they were waiting to be unloaded. Niugini Diving Adventures (p88) in Madang doesn't usually come here but it is the closest operator and may be open to convincing.

🛏 Sleeping & Eating

Anua Negu Lodge   GUESTHOUSE $
(Nigugini Electrical Gas; ☎711 45577, 422 2005; jtibong@gmail.com; s/d/tw K150/180/180, s/tw without bathroom K80/100) Mere metres from the waves, this lodge is the obvious place to stop for travellers overlanding between Angoram (on the Sepik River) and Madang. There is generator-supplied electricity, a kitchen that guests can use for an additional K20 fee and, for those who can't face yet another pack of instant noodles, meals can be arranged with advance notice. The lodge offers jeep tours to Hansa Bay (K250), where it is possible to snorkel US and Japanese war wrecks (gear hire K5), and day trips to the smoking volcanic island of Manam (K400). Canoes can also be hired to paddle to nearby islands (K20).

ⓘ Getting There & Away

From Bogia to Madang the 17L and 17M PMVs (K20, five hours) run at around 6am and return from Madang between 1pm and 2pm. The minibuses cost slightly more, but they are quicker and more comfortable than the trucks.

For information on travelling between Bogia and Angoram on the Sepik River, see the boxed text (p94).

Simbai

An isolated and interesting place in central Madang Province, the big attraction here is an opportunity to witness the everyday workings of a rural village cut off from the rest of the world. Don't, however, expect 'natives in loincloths' – instead you'll find a people, despite their isolation, both well informed and politically savvy. That and really cool *singsings*.

◉ Sights & Activities

Simbai to the Ramu River   TREK
The Ramu is one of PNG's great rivers and its broad valley is sugar cane and cattle country. The Ramu Sugar Refinery is a major industrial development, designed to make PNG self-sufficient in sugar.

It's possible to walk and raft from Simbai to the Ramu River base camp in five to six days. This route, developed by the Simbai villagers, only opened in 2007 and represents a fantastic opportunity to experience something truly unique. Guides are essential (K50 per day) and porters are optional (K30 per day).

Dickson Kangi (see below) is the man to contact about arranging this trip or Ecotourism Melanesia (p46) in Port Moresby.

🎎 Festivals & Events

Kalam Culture Festival   FESTIVAL
Simbai's cheif attraction is this festival, first held in 2005. In 2006 there were nine tourists, in 2011 only 15. Held on the Wednesday and Thursday following the Goroka Show (mid-September), the idea is tourists can travel from one to the other and experience two, quite different cultural festivals. Simbai's allows visitors to witness traditional ceremonies that are normally closed to tourists – adult initiation rites, bride-price exchanges and pig-killing festivities. The headdresses used in the festivities are made from the emerald green carapaces of beetles and are as spectacular as they are cumbersome.

🛏 Sleeping

Kalam Guest House   GUESTHOUSE $
(per person K75) This community-built guesthouse is the only place to stay. It's 15 minutes from Simbai Station, and constructed from bush materials. Local meals, which are mostly vegetarian (K15 to K25), are provided but you may want to fortify these with your own snacks.

ⓘ Information

There is no mobile phone coverage in Simbai but contact the Madang Visitors & Cultural Bureau (p90) or **Esron Dotch** (☎713 57801) well in advance so the village can prepare for your arrival. In Simbai contact **Dickson Kangi** (☎768 65205), who speaks on behalf of the chief, Ernest Simgi.

ⓘ Getting There & Away

Simbai is 45 minutes from Madang airport by Island Airways Cessna (K390) or about 30 minutes from Mt Hagen with MAF (K410).

The Highlands

POP 1.9 MILLION / AREA 62,500 SQ KM

Includes »

Best Places to Stay

» Ambua Lodge (p115)

» Tubo Lodge (p112)

» Mt Hagen Missionary Home (p107)

Best of Culture

» Goroka Show (p99)

» Mt Hagen Show (p106)

» Huli Wigmen (p114)

» Asaro Mudmen (p98)

» Enga Cultural Show (p110)

Why Go?

When European explorers made it into Papua New Guinea's rugged interior in the 1930s, they didn't find the unbroken tangle of mountains they had expected. Instead they stumbled into broad, heavily cultivated valleys lined with sawtooth mountains and home to a million-plus people.

Today many aspects of traditional highland culture remain, and clan and tribal loyalties still run deep. During the region's celebrated Highland shows, Western *sekonhan klos* (second-hand clothes) are exchanged for flamboyant feathers, shells, wigs and skins. Massive investment in the natural gas fields near Tari will undoubtedly bring change but, until then, only in the wild dreams of an anthropologist will you see such a gathering of tribes.

The rugged mountains first climbed by early explorers are now accessible and those with determination can conquer even Mt Wilhelm, the tallest of them all. From its craggy summit, it's easy to understand why Highlanders love their land as fiercely as they do.

When to Go

Goroka

°C/°F **Temp**

Rainfall inches/mm

Year-round The area's high altitude ensures a 'perpetual springtime', with fresh veggies and low humidity.

May–Nov The dry season sees an easing of rain, although heavy showers are still possible.

Aug–Sep Tourism ramps up as travellers arrive for the Highland shows.

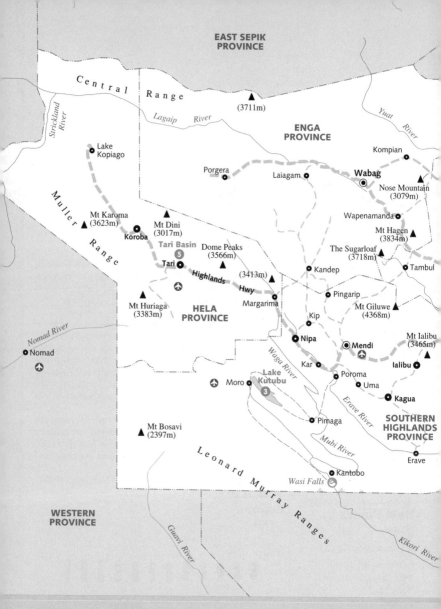

EAST SEPIK
PROVINCE

Central Range

Strickland River

Lagaip River

(3711m)

Lake Kopiago

ENGA PROVINCE

Yuat River

Porgera

Laiagam

Kompian

Wabag

Nose Mountain
(3079m)

Muller Range

Mt Karoma
(3623m)

Mt Dini
(3017m)

Koroba

Tari Basin

Dome Peaks
(3566m)

Tari

Highlands Hwy

(3413m)

Wapenamanda

Mt Hagen
(3834m)

The Sugarloaf
(3718m)

Tambul

Kandep

Mt Huriaga
(3383m)

HELA
PROVINCE

Margarima

Kip

Pingarip

Mt Giluwe
(4368m)

Nipa

Mendi

Mt Ialibu
(3465m)

Nomad River

Nomad

Kar

Poroma

Uma

Ialibu

Kagua

Waga River

Lake Kutubu

Moro

Pimaga

Erave River

Mubi River

SOUTHERN
HIGHLANDS
PROVINCE

Mt Bosavi
(2397m)

Erave

Leonard Murray Ranges

Kantobo

Wasi Falls

WESTERN
PROVINCE

Guavi River

Kikori River

The Highlands Highlights

① Scrambling up **Mt Wilhelm** (p104) in the predawn gloom to catch the sunrise light up both the north and south coasts.

② Photographing the beautifully adorned performers at one of the Highland shows in **Goroka** (p99) or **Mt Hagen** (p106).

③ Chilling out at the seldom-visited **Lake Kutubu** (p112) and visiting the local villages.

BISMARCK
SEA

Schrader Range

Aiome

MADANG
PROVINCE

Utu Mission

Madang

Simbai

Mt Herbert
(4267m)

Jimi River

Bom

Cape
Rigny

Bogadjim

Baiyer River

JIWAKA
PROVINCE

Tabibuga

Bismarck

Ramu River

Usino

WESTERN
HIGHLANDS
PROVINCE

Wamol

Mt Wilhelm
(4509m)

Bundi

Brahmin

Koropa

Range

Ramu Hwy

Dumpu

Mt Hagen

Banz

Highlands
Highway

Minj

Kerowagi

Kegsugl

Gembogl

Waghi

Gusap

Kup

Waghi

Kundiawa

Daulo
Pass

Asaro

Mt Otto
(3546m)

Goroka

Asaro River

Gumine

River

Chuave

Bena Bena

Yonki

Valley

Pararabuk

Kilau

Lufa

Henganofi

Kainantu

Kuminga

Kaugel River

Ukarumpa

SIMBU
PROVINCE

EASTERN
HIGHLANDS
PROVINCE

Pangia

Mt Michael
(3647m)

Tua River

Crater Mountain
(3280m)

Okapa

Obura

Mt Piora
(3557m)

Purari River

Mt Murray
(2254m)

Wonenara

Aure River

GULF
PROVINCE

Mt Akana
(3380m)

Marawaka

Mt Yelia
(3384m)

0   50 km
0   25 miles

N

④ Bouncing along the
stunning **Highlands Highway**
with a truck full of betel nut–
chewing locals.

⑤ Exploring the **Tari Basin**
(p114) in search of legendary
birds of paradise only to find
them upstaged by the local
Huli wigmen.

History

In 1930 Mick Leahy and Mick Dwyer came to the Highlands searching for gold and walked into the previously 'undiscovered' Eastern Highlands. Three years later, Leahy returned with his brother Dan and they stumbled upon the huge, fertile and heavily populated Wahgi Valley.

The film *First Contact* (1983) includes original footage of this patrol by Mick Leahy and is a priceless record of the first interaction between Highlanders and Europeans.

Missionaries followed the Leahy brothers, and government stations were built near present-day Mt Hagen and in the Simbu Valley, near present-day Kundiawa, although gold was never discovered in any great quantities.

Not until the 1950s were these changes really felt, and even then many areas remained largely unaffected until the 1960s and even into the '70s. The construction of the Highlands Hwy had a huge impact on the lives of Highlanders, as did the introduction of cash crops, particularly coffee. The Highlanders had long been traders and skillful gardeners and adapted to the cash economy with remarkable speed, but ritual warfare has always been an integral part of Highlands life and to this day payback feuds and land disputes can erupt into major conflicts.

Dangers & Annoyances

Parts of the PNG Highlands are genuinely high in altitude. You should give yourself a few days' acclimatisation at lower altitudes before taking on any serious mountain climbing or excessive physical activities if you are to avoid acute mountain sickness.

Bus travel through the Highlands is not nearly as dangerous as the expat community will lead you to believe, but there is an element of risk. Very occasionally there are hold-ups, buses are ambushed and the passengers are robbed. During times of political tension and tribal war seek advice from the locals in each town before heading to the next town in a PMV (public motor vehicle). West of Mendi can be particularly volatile, so be careful.

The Highlands is a 'dry region' and alcohol cannot be purchased outside licensed premises, such as hotels, clubs and resorts. However, there's a booming black market in beer and all of PNG has a problem with wickedly strong, home-brewed alcohol and violence.

EASTERN HIGHLANDS PROVINCE

Undulating grass-covered hills and neat villages of low-walled round huts are the defining characteristics of the Eastern Highlands. Listen carefully for the secrets whispered by the tufts of grass fixed to the peaks of the roofs of these houses.

The most heavily populated of all the provinces, the region has had longer contact with the West than the other Highland provinces, and was the first to feel the impact of the missionaries, prospectors, mercenaries and misfits who have visited these parts.

Goroka

Goroka has grown from a small outpost in the mid-1950s to a major commercial centre, and is now the main town in the Eastern Highlands Province.

Mountains encircle the town, which in turn almost encircle the airport. Leafy streets, a pleasant climate and all the essential services combine to make it one of PNG's most attractive towns. More relaxed than Mt Hagen, safer than Lae, and caught between both means there are decent roads in and out of town.

Goroka's main cash crop is coffee and you'll see it growing under the canopies of larger trees in the hills throughout the district.

◉ Sights & Activities

JK McCarthy Museum MUSEUM
(admission K10; ☺8am-noon & 1-4pm Mon-Fri, 8am-noon Sat, 1-3pm Sun) JK McCarthy was one of PNG's legendary patrol officers and wrote one of the classic books on New Guinea patrolling – *Patrol into Yesterday*. Among the exhibits are pottery, weapons, clothes and musical instruments, and even some grisly jewellery – Anga mourning necklaces of human fingers. 'Peer through the mists of time' courtesy of a fascinating collection of photos, many taken by Mick Leahy when he first reached the area in 1933. There are also WWII relics, including a P-39 Aircobra.

Asaro Mudmen CULTURAL VILLAGE
Asaro village, northwest of Goroka, is famous for its mudmen – warriors who traditionally covered themselves in grey mud and wore huge mud masks before heading off on raids. It's a very striking image, and the Asaro men re-create the scene for tourists. The

number of mudmen is in direct proportion to the number of kina-paying tourists. The following tour operators can arrange mudmen tours.

Raun Raun Theatre   HISTORIC BUILDING
(☎532 1116; Wisdom St) The theatre is a superb building, which blends traditional materials and modern architecture. It's located on parkland about 500m due north of the post office. Performances are irregular, but you might get lucky.

Mt Kis Lookout   VIEWPOINT
A track just off Wisdom St climbs to an excellent lookout, Mt Kis, so-called because it's the lovers' leap of Goroka. There are two large water tanks halfway there, and a ladder you can climb to catch spectacular views of the distant valleys through the pine trees and the Highlands' mist. Unfortunately, the area is a favourite hideout of *raskols* (bandits) and even locals now avoid it. It's worth checking to see if the situation has improved.

👉 Tours

Many of the local tour operators are a one-man band, without an office and notoriously difficult to contact. Look for their notices on hotel message boards. Some of them are trustworthy and some have achieved local notoriety for failing to pass on tourist fees to the villages they visit. The two operators listed following are ethical and reliable.

Goroka Trek & Tours   CULTURAL TOUR
(☎532 1281; www.pngexplorers.com; goroka@png explorers.com; Shop 12B, Bird of Paradise Hotel, Elizabeth St) The most prominent and best organised of the local tour operators, with Japanese- and English-speaking guides. Day trips include visits to the Asaro Mudmen (minimum two people, K350 per person), Simbu village, local caves and waterfalls. They can also arrange four-day package deals to Mt Wilhelm.

PNG High Country Tours   ADVENTURE TOUR
(☎719 86042) Samuel Lulu runs tours and treks around the jungles and caves of the Eastern Highlands and out towards Simbu. He offers village accommodation in the Namasaro Unggai district west of Goroka and can organise Asaro Mudmen day trips.

🎭 Festivals & Events

Goroka Show   CULTURAL SHOW
(www.gorokashow.com; per day/2 days adult K100/150, child aged 3-11 K25/50) The Goroka Show is held over the Independence Day weekend (mid-September) at the National Sports Institute's Sports Oval. It attracts more *singsing* (celebratory dance/festival) groups than the Mt Hagen show and there are also bands and other cultural activities, as well as some elements of an agricultural show. The show is the glamour event on the social calendar for many performers and it is extraordinary how many feathers one person can squeeze on a headdress. Performers receive a payment from the proceeds and you are neither expected nor encouraged to tip individuals. Make accommodation arrangements early as many places (especially top-end hotels) are booked out months in advance. Prices, like a Highland headdress, go sky-high.

🛏 Sleeping

Lutheran Guesthouse   GUESTHOUSE $
(☎532 1171; fax 532 1124; luthguesthausgka@ global.net.pg; McNicholl St; dm incl breakfast K95)

KURU

Kuru was a disease unique to the Fore area southwest of Kainantu. Attacking the central nervous system, the disease persisted in the body for a year before causing death. Dubbed 'the laughing disease', its victims died with a peculiar smile on their faces. It only affected one language group and was limited to women and children. It is known to have existed since the early 1900s but reached epidemic proportions in the 1950s when more than 200 cases were reported. Years of epidemiological research by Goroka's PNG Institute of Medical Research finally solved the riddle of the disease's cause.

Kuru was linked to diet and feasting behaviour; specifically it was caused by the ritualised cannibalism of the brain tissue of dead clan members by women and children. Kuru is said to be linked to mad cow disease.

Due to changed dietary and ritual behaviour, there's only been a handful of cases in recent years, the last reported in 1997.

Goroka

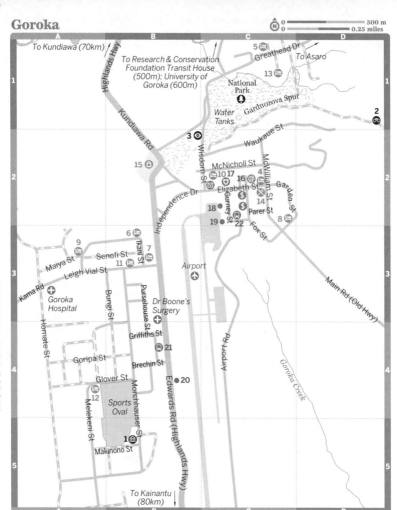

Right in the centre of town behind the post office. Clean and straight, the two-storey house has tidy shared rooms and facilities.

Pacific Gardens Hotel   HOTEL **$$$**
(📞 532 1139; pacifichotel_res@datec.net.pg; Mokara St; r K295-495, ste K595; @) In the grounds of a vast, hilly expats' residential estate with lovely lawns, jungle backdrop and adjacent river, this hotel's premier rooms (K495) are the nicest in town and cheaper than what is on offer at The Bird. Its only drawback is the 10-minute walk (or K20 hotel shuttle) to town, although airport transfers are included. The

restaurant (meals K35 to K45) is also highly rated with a lovely garden terrace.

Research & Conservation
Foundation Transit House   GUESTHOUSE **$**
(RCF; 📞 532 3211; fax 532 1123; Kyle St; dm K60) This good-value, dorm-style accommodation has two bunks per room, free laundry, a shared kitchen and a TV in the common room. Profits go to support the community development within the Crater Mountain Wildlife Management Area (see boxed text, p103) and staff can help you plan a trip there. Catch town bus 3 and get off near the university.

Goroka

THE HIGHLANDS GOROKA

Bird of Paradise Hotel
HOTEL $$$

(📞532 1144; thebird_reservations@coralseahotels. com.pg; Elizabeth St; r K446-567, ste K704; 🛜❄) 'The Bird' is getting a bit tatty round the edges but otherwise ageing gracefully. The rooms are large, comfortable and decorated with an odd assortment of mismatched furniture. Besides the inclusion of an iron and ironing board, there is precious little difference between the standard and premier rooms. Either way, the rooms facing the garden are better than those facing the street.

National Sports Institute
HOSTEL $

(📞532 2391; fax 532 1941; natspoin@daltron.com. pg; Glover St; s/d K66/110) If you don't mind being this far from the town centre, this is a good budget option. Bathroom and kitchen facilities are shared and it's a lot like a university dorm with segregated buildings for men and women. The spacious grounds are fairly quiet except when the Goroka Show is on next door. Meals are available from the student cafeteria (K22 to K33).

GK Lodge
HOTEL $$

(📞532 3819; gkklos@global.net.pg; Garden St; s/d/ tw K198/220/275; ⊘closed Sun) This place hasn't been redecorated since independence, but the rooms are large and homey. The rate for solo travellers is a bit steep, but it's fair value for couples. Oddly, you can't check-in on Sundays.

Diwai Hut Lodge
HOTEL $$

(📞532 3840; fax 532 3850; Greathead Dr; s/d/tw incl breakfast K198/245/285) The Diwai has a pleasant outlook within earshot of the Zokozoi River (you can't actually see it) but it's a good 10 minutes' walk from the town centre. Rooms are comfortable, if plain, have tea- and coffee-making facilities and a small fridge. Meals are available (dinner K47).

Kanda Resthouse
HOTEL $$

(📞532 2944; kanda@global.net.pg; Numune Pl; r/ste K350/450) The whole place is bright and breezy; from the lemon and lime colour scheme on the outside to the large, airy rooms (each with a double and single bed). The suites all have kitchens complete with fridge, gas cooker and microwave, although there's also a small restaurant on-site (mains K47).

Emmanuel Lodge & Guesthouse
HOTEL $$

(📞532 3466; fax 532 1654; Ikani St & Numune Pl; s/d without bathroom K100/140, ste K330) This place has two locations and two faces. The Ikani pad has a series of self-contained units, each with two rooms – a double bed in one, two singles in the other – and a kitchen. Around the corner, the Numune Pl annexe has some basic bed-in-a-box rooms with shared bathrooms and no atmosphere.

Mendikwae Lodge   GUESTHOUSE **$$**
(☎720 60812; Leigh Vial St; r with/without bathroom K240/180) Each room can sleep three in a double and single bed and shares a large communal lounge. Thanks to the well-equipped kitchen, self-caterers might enjoy it, but overall the place is a bit run-down.

✕ Eating

Besides *kai* bars (cheap, takeaway food bars), eating options outside the hotels are few. The market sells an array of fresh fruit and vegetables, peanuts and probably a cuscus or two.

 Mandarin Restaurant   CHINESE **$$**
(☎Elizabeth St; meals K16-30; ⊘lunch & dinner) Opposite the Bird, the Mandarin serves tasty, veggie-packed dishes that would do the home country proud. Meals are served in a variety of sizes and prepared to be shared. A small plate with a side of rice or noodles is enough for one.

The Terrace Bar and
Restaurant   INTERNATIONAL, BUFFET **$$$**
(Bird of Paradise Hotel, Elizabeth St; mains K25-50; ⊘breakfast, lunch & dinner; 🛜) The Bird's terrace bar is *the* place to rendezvous and central to the social life of Goroka's well heeled. There's a nightly themed buffet (K35), of which the Sunday carvery is the pick, and a popular lunch salad buffet (K25 to K35). The 'Grill' has a la carte steaks in varying sizes and cuts – ours came from an animal we suspect died of old age.

🔒 Shopping

There are several supermarkets and shops clustered between the post office and the Bird of Paradise Hotel. Souvenir sellers camp outside the Bird, stringing up their *bilums* (string bags), hats, spears, bows, masks, Buka-ware and jewellery on the wrought-iron fences of the provisional government building. Some mild haggling is acceptable here.

Market   MARKET
(⊘closed Sun) The open-air market is interesting to walk through and you'll see piles of potatoes and exotic leafy greens as well as more familiar tomatoes, capsicums (bell peppers) and avocados. *Bilums* and Highland hats are sold, as are spools of intensely colourful twines and strings used in *bilum* manufacture. Watch out for pickpockets.

ℹ Information

Emergency
Ambulance (☎111)
Fire (☎532 1111/3) Near the airport terminal.
Police (☎532 1443; Elizabeth St)

Internet Access
Computer Shop (Elizabeth St; per 15min K5.50) Has the best connections in town with CD-burning facilities.

Medical Services
There are several pharmacies in town.
Dr Boone's Surgery (☎532 3544, 724 39318; Edwards Rd; ⊘8am-5.30pm Mon-Fri, to 3pm Sun) A safer bet than the Goroka Hospital.

Money
Travellers cheques can be cashed at the bigger hotels as well as banks – compare rates. The bigger hotels accept major credit cards, as do ATMs.
ANZ (Elizabeth St)
Westpac (Fox St) Also maintains a more private ATM in the lobby of the Bird of Paradise Hotel.

Post
DHL (Elizabeth St)
Post office (Elizabeth St)

Travel Agency
Travel Connections (☎532 3422; travelconnect01@gmail.com; Shop 17, Bird of Paradise Hotel, Elizabeth St) Ticketing agent for international and domestic flights.

Tourist Informatiom
The **East Highlands Province Tourism Bureau** (Shop 19, Bird of Paradise Hotel, Elizabeth St) opened in 2011 but every time we called the door was locked with no sign of life inside. Presumably it will spring into action during the Goroka Show, but it looked doubtful it would have much in the way of information. The men who sometimes hang around the steps, despite what they claim, don't work for the office.

ℹ Getting There & Around

Air
Airlines PNG (☎532 2532; www.apng.com) Flies to Lae (K234) and Mt Hagen (K372) daily.
Air Niugini (☎532 1444; www.airniugini.com.pg) All of Air Niugini's flights are routed via the daily Port Moresby flight (K609).
MAF (Mission Aviation Fellowship; ☎532 1080; Edwards Rd) Flies to Lae (K450), Mt Hagen (K370), Madang (K330) and a host of highland airstrips, including Haia at Crater Mountain.

Car & PMV
Goroka is well served by PMVs and the Highland Hwy. It's an easy trip to Mt Hagen (K30, four

hours) in the west or down to the coastal cities of Lae (K30, five hours) and Madang (K40, five hours) in the east.

PMVs gather at the market area early in the morning, but more leave as the day wears on. The road out to Mt Hagen is fairly flat through Asaro, but it then hairpins its way up to Daulo Pass (2450m). The pass is cold and damp, but the views are spectacular.

Although the town is small enough to walk around, PMVs run up and down the stretch of main road, Edwards Rd (Highlands Hwy) and to the university (K0.5).

SIMBU PROVINCE

Simbu (pronounced *chim*-bu, and sometimes spelt that way) derived its name when the first patrol officers gave steel axes and knives to the tribespeople, who replied *simbu* – very pleased. Despite its rugged terrain, it's the second most heavily populated region in PNG. The people have turned their steep country into a patchwork of gardens spreading up every available hillside. Population pressures are pushing them to even higher ground, threatening remaining forests and bird of paradise habitats. Most people in the province speak a similar language – Simbu dialects make up PNG's second-largest language group.

Kundiawa

Kundiawa was the site of the Highlands' first government station, but has been left behind by Goroka and Mt Hagen. Although it's the provincial capital, Kundiawa is pretty small. There's a bank, post office, small supermarket, bakery (with decent coffee) and that's about it.

Caves around Kundiawa invite exploration, but as some were once used as burial places you shouldn't visit them without consulting local advice as they may be *tambu* (forbidden). Assuming you get permission, some of the more promising spelunking spots include the **Keu Caves**, close to the main road near Chuave, and the **Nambaiyufa Amphitheatre** for its rock paintings, also near Chuave.

Mt Wilhelm Hotel (☎535 1062; ctambagle@ live.com; s/d K180/200) doesn't have much competition and is a bit run-down, but it's the best place to stop if you don't make it all the way to Kegsugl, the trailhead to climb Mt Wilhelm. Despite its 'Mt Wilhelm' name, the staff at the hotel are spectacularly uninformed about climbing the mountain itself. The hotel restaurant has a small selection of generously proportioned meals (K25 to K40) and some colourful murals to give it a splash of artistic flair.

ⓘ Getting There & Away

Air

The airport is quite spectacular, on a sloping ridge surrounded by mountains. **Air Niugini** (www.airniugini.com.pg) theoretically flies to/ from Port Moresby (K605) on Tuesday, Thursday and Saturday, although no flights had actually landed here for more than a month at time of research. Would-be passengers were instead heading to Goroka or Mt Hagen.

PMV

There are PMVs to Goroka (K15, three hours) and Mt Hagen (K15, two hours). The trip to Kegsugl (for Mt Wilhelm) takes 4½ hours and costs K25 to K50, depending on the driver. PMVs for Kegsugl leave from the Shell petrol station, others stop on the highway near the police station.

WORTH A TRIP

CRATER MOUNTAIN WILDLIFE MANAGEMENT AREA

In the tri-border area, where the Eastern Highlands, Simbu and Gulf provincial borders meet, is the Crater Mountain Wildlife Management Area. This is one of the best places in PNG to experience the spectacular countryside, wildlife and village culture.

The area encompasses 2700 sq km, ranging from lowland tropical rainforests on the Purari River to alpine grasses on the slopes of Crater Mountain. You can hike between the various villages, but it's serious trekking. There are three villages (Haia, Herowana and Maimafu) with basic **guesthouses** (per person K30) that provide beds (bring your own sleeping bags) and kerosene stoves (bring your own food). **The Research & Conservation Foundation Transit House** in Goroka (p100) can radio each village and help organise guides (K25 per day plus K2 per kilo you ask them to carry) and make your flight arrangements with MAF (one way K275). Scheduled flights are, however, infrequent and you may have to charter a plane, which is considerably more expensive.

Mt Wilhelm

For many, climbing to the 4509m summit of Mt Wilhelm is the highlight of a Highlands trip. On a clear day, you can see both the north and south coasts of PNG. It is the tallest peak in PNG and often billed as the tallest in Oceania (even though several mountains in Indonesian Papua surpass it as, technically, all of Indonesia belongs to Asia).

Even if you don't intend to tackle the summit, the region around the base offers fantastic walking and dramatic landscapes.

Climbing the Mountain

Planning

While not technically difficult, this popular climb is hard work. Preparation is important and the dangers should not be underestimated. Climbers in this region have died and the skeletal remains of a previous trekker and a memorial plaque to another are passed about an hour from the summit. Don't try to climb the mountain on your own no matter how fit you are – a guide is essential.

Would-be guides are plentiful and you'll be approached by men offering their services the moment you reach Kundiawa. It is better (and cheaper) to wait until you arrive in Kegsugl before hiring someone. This way you're guaranteed to get a local who knows the landowners and has climbed the mountain many times before. All of the guesthouses listed in this section can arrange guides (K100 per day) and porters (K60 per day). Porters (or carriers, as they are locally called) will only haul your bag as far as the base camp huts. Whomever you hire will expect to share your food, so bring enough to feed everyone.

If the weather is fine, the climb takes two days, but frequently the weather causes delays. The dry season (April to October) is the best time to climb. If you've just come up from the coast, allow yourself time to acclimatise to avoid altitude sickness – the main reason why many don't make it to the summit.

The final ascent starts in the black of early morning so that climbers get to see the dawn and both coasts before the clouds roll in. It can get very cold on the mountain (and may even snow), and can easily become fogbound. Sunburn and hypothermia are hazards.

You need to take sufficient food, equipment, warm clothing, water containers (there's no water past the lakes), a torch, gloves, candles, toilet paper and a warm sleeping bag. The base camp huts are stocked with kerosene stoves, cooking utensils and musty mattresses.

Besides the DIY approach we've just described, it is also possible to book an organised, all-inclusive trek with any of the following tour companies.

Goroka Trek & Tours (☑532 1281; www.pngexplorers.com) Based in Goroka (see p99).

Investa Treks (www.kokodatrack.org.au)

PNG Holidays (www.pngholidays.com.au)

SPEAKING IN TONGUES: SIL INTERNATIONAL

SIL International (formerly the Summer Institute of Linguistics) is a missionary organisation that aims to translate the Bible into every language in the world. Given the extraordinary number of languages in PNG – 820 distinct languages at last count – SIL has a lot of work to do here.

Before translation begins, the language's distribution, number of speakers and other vital statistics are catalogued to help understand the language's health. This is particularly important, as some languages are critically endangered and may be spoken by as few as 12 individuals. The results of these linguistic surveys are published on www.ethnologue.com.

SIL's translator-missionaries, who are usually husband-and-wife teams, typically spend 15 to 20 years in a remote village, learning the language, developing a written alphabet and translating the Bible. The institute is working on 190 languages today and has completed translations for 94.

Although active throughout the country, SIL's PNG headquarters are based in Ukarumpa in the Aiyura Valley, about 30 minutes by PMV from Kainantu (Eastern Highlands). It's worth visiting to see 'little America' in the midst of PNG.

PNG Trekking Adventures (www.pngtre kkingadventures.com.au)

The Climb
Beginning at the end of the road just past the Camp Jehovah Jireh guesthouse at Kegsugl, a **track** (trekking fee per person K10) leads up through a mountain rainforest and then along an alpine grassland glacial valley to the twin lakes of **Pindaunde** and two huts collectively known as **Base Camp**. It is customary to spend at least one night here before tackling the summit the next morning. Some say it's better to spend another day acclimatising and exploring the area before the final push.

If you catch an early morning PMV from Kundiawa, it is possible to reach Kegsugl by noon and walk (four to five hours) to Base Camp in the afternoon.

From the Pindaunde Lakes Base Camp, it's a long, hard walk to the summit – anything from five to nine hours. Parts of the trail are treacherously steep so take care with your footing at all times. It can get cold, wet, windy and foggy at the top, so bring warm clothes, a hat and some gloves. Clouds roll in after dawn so summit-climbers start out as early as 1am.

The summit itself isn't particularly impressive and isn't visible until you are only 30 minutes from it and, if you are to make it (many don't), go slow! Even if you don't make it all the way to the top, the views of the craggy **Bismarck Range** and the silvery Pindaunde lakes below – from even halfway up – are worth the sweat, and possibly a few tears.

The descent back to the huts takes about four hours, but some people go all the way back to Kegsugl, a further 3½ hours downhill.

🛏 Sleeping
Kegsugl
East Kegsugl Guesthouse   GUESTHOUSE $
(☏734 85915; per person without bathroom K60) Across the road from the airstrip and next to the high school, this guesthouse is a great option. The hosts, Josephine and Arnold (Rambo to his friends), make guests feel welcome with small touches such as strawberries from their garden. There are three rooms with two beds in each and enough blankets to keep an Eskimo warm in a blizzard. Meals with home-grown veggies are an extra K10.

Betty's Place   GUESTHOUSE $
(☏/fax 545 1481, 710 05432; bhiggins@digicelpa cific.blackberry.com; per person with/without meals K240/90) This lovely place, about 1km from Kegsugl and near the start of the trail, is situated on a ridge with superb views over the valley. A generator provides electricity and it's surprisingly comfortable with hot showers and amazing surrounds. There's a trout farm and commercial vegetable gardens, and the meals at Betty's are splendid.

Camp Jehovah Jireh   GUESTHOUSE $$
(☏714 55394; per person incl meals with/without bathroom K280/200) Just up the road from Betty's Place, this newly established camp has a series of interconnected bunkrooms made from split bamboo and local materials. The jungle setting is very pretty and is the closest of the guesthouses to the trailhead but the furthest from the PMV stop in Kegsugl village, just under 2km downhill.

Pindaunde Lakes Base Camp
National Parks Board Huts   HUT $
(per person K80) Halfway up Mt Wilhelm from Kegsugl are two fairly basic huts that are used for overnighting. Bring your own sleeping bag and food. There is no electricity, but you can cook over the bottled-gas stove provided. Guides and porters stay free, although some in Kegsugl will tell you otherwise. Your guide will be given the key for one of the huts when you pay your hut fee down in Kegsugl.

ℹ Getting There & Away
Kegsugl is 57km northeast from Kundiawa along a razorback road that has to be seen to be believed. PMVs to Kegsugl (K25 to K50, 4½ hours) leave Kundiawa from the Shell petrol station. They return to Kundiawa about 6am the following day.

The guesthouses listed above can send a private car to collect you from Kundiawa (K400), Mt Hagen (K800) or Goroka (K800).

Walking to Madang
You can walk to Madang from the Highlands, but it's unwise to go without a guide (K100 per day). The turn-off for the Bundi road and the trek to Brahmin (and Madang) is between Gembogl and Kegsugl. You can walk right down to Madang – but most people catch a PMV at Brahmin. A relatively easy route goes through Pandambai and Bundikara to Bundi. From Bundi the route goes to the Brahmin Mission, from where you can catch a PMV to Madang. The whole route takes three or four days, overnighting in local guesthouses along the way. You will

THE HIGHLANDS WALKING TO MADANG

need to bring your own food and pay for your guide's transport back to Kegsugl.

Any guide worth his boots in Kegsugl will also know this route.

WESTERN HIGHLANDS & JIWAKA PROVINCES

The people in this area are fiercely proud, with strong tribal loyalties and complicated clan affiliations. In part, it was because of such divisions that three districts split from the Western Highlands and formed Jiwaka Province in 2012.

Mt Hagen is by far the region's largest town (and the capital of the Western Province) and it wasn't that many years ago when farmers could be seen proudly strutting through Hagen's market in traditional clothing. The men favoured wide belts of beaten bark with a drape of strings in front and a rear covered by a bunch of leaves attached to a belt (known collectively as a *tanket* or *arse gras*). Women wore string skirts and hung cuscus fur 'scarfs' around their necks. Such attire is now reserved for *singsings* and political rallies but the proud swagger lives on. *Singsings* are still an integral part of life and a great opportunity to witness the Highlanders' singular sense of style – make every effort to see one.

Mt Hagen

Despite its environs, Mt Hagen is not nearly as attractive as Goroka. It's PNG's third biggest city. 'Hagen', as it's often called, was a patrol station before WWII, and has boomed in the last 40 years as Enga and the Southern Highlands have opened up. Now it's an unruly city with major squatter settlements and many itinerant people. As in Lae and Port Moresby, Hagen's streets are packed with people.

The city's ambience can vary from the usual PNG relaxed vibe to periods of heavy tension during elections or interclan disputes.

◉ Sights & Activities

Hagen Market MARKET
(⊘8am-4pm Mon-Sat) This is one of PNG's biggest and most varied markets and a great place to buy *bilums* and Highland hats. There's also a vast range of fresh produce on sale and if you're lucky you may also see cuscus, pigs and birds trussed up on poles

or in enclosures. It's busy each day and thieves work the crowd. They're mostly kids working in tandem – one might distract you while another snatches a bag or wallet. The atmosphere in the market can be edgy, and the best way to make friends is to buy stuff.

Tours

Paiya Tours TOUR
(☑542 3529, 768 58183; www.paiyatours.com) Locally run from the Magic Mountain Lodge (p108).

PNG Eco-Adventure Tours CULTURAL TOUR
(☑736 06260; skyfdn@hotmail.com) A Hagen-based operation that offers tours to remote villages including those around Lake Kutubu.

Trans Niugini Tours TOUR
(☑542 1438; www.pngtours.com; Kongin St) One of the main inbound tour companies in PNG, organising tours and activities across the country. It's well organised, professional and rather expensive. Its packages include meals and activities, and guests are ferried to its six ecolodges by private aircraft and stay in absolute luxury. The lodges are Tari's Ambua Lodge (p115); the Sepik's Karawari Lodge (p136) and its boat the *Sepik Spirit* (p130); Malolo Plantation Lodge (p92) north of Madang; Bensbach Wildlife Lodge in the Western Province; and Mt Hagen's very own Rondon Ridge (p108).

✷ Festivals & Events

Mt Hagen Show CULTURAL SHOW
(general admission K4, adult 2-day pass K300) It's not as big as the Goroka Show, but the Mt Hagen Show is definitely a must-see. It's held annually, on the third weekend of August. The cheap 'general admission' won't allow you access to the *singsing* groups until 11am, and then only from the surrounding banks.

The two-day pass allows you to arrive early (around 8am) and see the groups dressing and donning their feathered headdresses. Vigorous impromptu performances at this time can often be more powerful, even ribald, compared with the formal stuff dished up in the arena. Contrary to what you might be fearful of, there's no general bird of paradise slaughter just before show time – the feather headdresses and costumes are extremely valuable and rarefied heirlooms.

The performers are happy to pose for photographs (they don't charge) but at times it feels like a photographic free-for-all. There

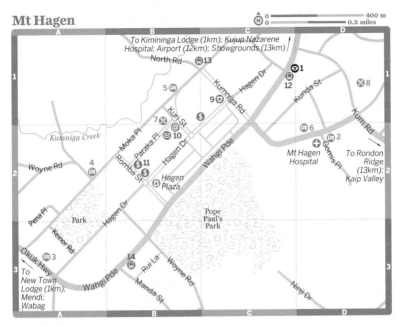

Mt Hagen

are some quality artefacts on sale outside the showgrounds and *mild* bartering here won't offend local sensibilities. Locals prefer the live bands and contemporary music on stage in a natural bowl just outside the showgrounds – follow your ears and watch your camera in the crowds.

Tickets can be brought from Trans Niugini Tours and major hotels prior to the show.

Sleeping

During the weekend of the Mt Hagen Show, rooms are scarcer than tree kangaroos in Port Moresby. Be sure to book at least three months ahead.

Mt Hagen Missionary Home
TOP CHOICE
GUESTHOUSE **$**

(☎542 1041; mhmh@daltron.com.pg; Kumniga Rd; dm/r K100/300) The pick of the budget bunch. Each room sleeps four in two bunk beds and has its own bathroom. It's friendly, secure, very clean and central. For an additional K22 you'll get a hearty dinner, and transport can be arranged to the Mt Hagen Show for K30 per person.

Hotel Poroman
HOTEL **$$**

(☎542 3558; www.hausporoman.com.pg; Moka Pl; r K250-350; @) A great midrange option,

Mt Hagen

◎ Sights
1 Hagen Market...C1

🛏 Sleeping
2 Anglican Guesthouse D2
3 Highlander Hotel.................................A3
4 Hotel Poroman.....................................A2
5 Lutheran Guesthouse B1
6 Mt Hagen Missionary Home...............D2

✕ Eating
7 Best Buy...B1
8 Hagen Club D1
Palmuri Restaurant ....(see 3)

ⓘ Information
9 Police Station C1
10 Post Office B2
11 Westpac B2

ⓘ Transport
Air Niugini ....(see 11)
Budget...(see 3)
12 PMVs to Airport, Kundiawa &
Goroka...C1
13 PMVs to Baiyer River..........................B1
14 PMVs to Wabag, Mendi & Tari B3

the Poroman may have fairly basic rooms but the staff are super friendly and the gardens are an excellent place to unwind after the crowds on Mt Hagen's streets. There's a bar and an excellent restaurant (meals K27 to K40), and tariffs include airport transfers.

Highlander Hotel   HOTEL $$$

(542 1355; www.coralseahotels.com.pg; Okuk Hwy; r K495-765; @) The Highlander, part of the Coral Sea chain, has all the amenities you'd expect from a 1st-class hotel, including pool-side restaurants, bars, tennis and volleyball courts, and a 24-hour foreign-exchange desk. The 60 rooms are self-contained and a little soulless but the foyer and restaurants got a major upgrade in 2010 and are easily the smartest in town.

Magic Mountain Lodge   GUESTHOUSE $$

(542 3529, 768 58183; www.paiyatours.com; cottage K200) Surrounded by lush jungles and a patchwork of vegetable plots, the traditionally built cottages manage to provide all the essential comforts while retaining a genuine ecofriendly vibe. Pym Memindi, the owner, has years of experience under his belt and can arrange everything from village visits to jungle treks. The lodge is a 30-minute drive (transfers K150) out of Mt Hagen on the road to Wabag.

Kimininga Lodge   HOTEL $$

(542 2399; www.wampnga.com.pg/kimininga; Highlands Hwy; s K250-350, d K280-380) Run by a local landowner group, Kimininga Lodge is comfortable, if a little plain. In addition to the 37 self-contained rooms there is an apartment capable of sleeping four. Airport and town transfers are included in the price, and there's a licensed restaurant that serves pizza and Indian but the service is terribly slow.

Hagen Airport Motel   HOTEL $$

(545 1647; irmakap@online.net.pg; Highlands Hwy; r K240;) This motel, near the airport, has 20 rooms that sleep three in a double and single bed. It's clean and friendly, although nothing out of the ordinary. The restaurant (meals K30 to K70) and hotel are 'alcohol-free zones'. You can grab a lift on its truck, which travels into town daily.

Anglican Guesthouse   GUESTHOUSE $

(542 1131; skacpng@online.net.pg; cnr Kumniga Rd & Gomis Pl; dm K40) This church-run guesthouse is safe and well located, but the bunkrooms are dark, the mattresses old and the rooms smell funny.

Lutheran Guesthouse   GUESTHOUSE $

(542 2137; Moka Pl; s/d K150/180) Right in the middle of town, this is a rather noisy option and the rooms are no longer kept as clean as they once were. Nonetheless, of the town cheapies, this is a safe bet with good security. A laundry service and meals (breakfast K15, dinner K30) are also available.

Rondon Ridge   LUXURY HOTEL $$$

(542 1438; www.pngtours.com; all-inclusive s/d US$812/1206; @) Rondon Ridge is the newest of Trans Niugini Tours' luxury lodges, located at 2164m on Kum Mountain, 13km southeast from Hagen. There are magnificent views of the Hagen Range and the Wahgi Valley from each of the 12 units. Up here it's comfort all the way – modern bathrooms, electric blankets, continental quilts and a cosy fireplace in the common lounge. All activities, transfers and meals are included in the rates.

✖ Eating & Drinking

The town centre has lots of *kai* bars (cheap takeaway food bars) selling lamb flaps so greasy that not only are they capable of clogging your arteries, they could damn the Sepik.

TOP CHOICE Banz Kofi   CAFE $$

(near Airport; mains K20-45; ☺breakfast & lunch Mon-Sat) If you're wondering where the expat community hangs out, you'll find them sipping coffee and nibbling cheesecake in this uber trendy cafe. It isn't signposted but it's opposite Avis near the airport – just knock on the metal gates by the stone wall and someone will let you in.

Hagen Club   PUB $$

(Kum Rd; mains K28-50; ☺lunch & dinner) Serves cold beer and good pub-style light meals during lunch, and cold beer and European dishes during dinner. The Mt Hagen Ball is held here to coincide with the Mt Hagen Show. Bring your tux, dancing shoes and see the manager for a ticket (single/double K194/240, including dinner).

Palmuri Restaurant   INTERNATIONAL $$$

(Highlander Hotel, Okuk Hwy; mains K35-60; ☺breakfast, lunch & dinner; @) The Palmuri is Hagen's most upmarket restaurant. It offers delectable delicacies such as Mt Wilhelm trout, triple-stacked pancakes, a seafood-style buffet (K65) every Thursday and a separate pizza menu.

Best Buy SUPERMARKET, BAKERY $
(Paraka Pl; pies K4; ⊙7am-6pm Mon-Fri, to 4pm
Sat & Sun) The biggest and best-stocked store
in town, although it can't compete with the
market when it comes to veggies and fruit.
The on-site bakery is good value with a good
selection of pies, sausage rolls and cakes.

❶ Information

Aside from *raskols*, tribal warfare can break out
over coffee production, land disputes, pigs or
gardens. Clan warfare never embroils outsiders,
confining itself to the protagonists, but it can
make things unstable and unpredictable. During
the day, Mt Hagen is reasonably safe. Nobody
hassles or asks for money, but the town is
thronged with security guards and dogs around
banks and shops. Don't approach the dogs –
they are not accustomed to unfamiliar people.

It's not, however, safe at night and the market
area is rife with cons and pickpockets at any time.

Emergency
Ambulance (☑111)
Fire (☑542 1311/15)
Police (☑542 1233, 542 1343; Kumniga St)

Internet Access
Computer Shop (Ground fl, Komkui Bldg, Kuri
St; per 15min K5.50) Snappy connections.

Medical Services
There are several pharmacies in town.
Kujup Nazarene Hospital (☑546 2341, 546
2228; Kujup) Located 45 minutes east on the
Highlands Hwy, Dr Jim Radcliff comes recom-
mended by the local missionaries.

Money
Besides the following banks listed, which all have
ATMs, there is also an ATM inside the Highlander
Hotel that allows you to withdraw money in com-
parative safety.
ANZ (Hagen Dr)
Bank South Pacific (Romba St)
Westpac (Romba St)

Post
Post office (Paraka Pl)

❶ Getting There & Around
Air
The airport is at Kagamuga, about 10km from
Hagen's centre. Minibuses run often from the small
market next to the airport to the Hagen Market (K1).
For an additional K1 the driver will often drop you at
your hotel. Major hotels provide transfers.
Air Niugini (☑542 1444, 542 1039; www.
airniugini.com.pg; Romba St) Has flights four or
five times daily to Port Moresby (K407).

WORTH A TRIP

KUMUL LODGE

Located 40 minutes from Mt Hagen,
and closer to Hagen or Wapenamenda
airstrip than to Wabag, **Kumul Lodge**
(☑542 1615; www.kumul-lodge.com; s
K151-179, d K156-200) is geared towards
birdwatchers, and you can see birds of
paradise in the grounds of the lodge.
The bungalows, built from bush materials, are comfortable, self-contained
and have large windows and balconies
overlooking the surrounding forest. The
restaurant is a little pricey for what you
get and you'll be charged for every cup
you drink from the self-service tea and
coffee bar. Transfers and birding guides
can be arranged with the lodge.

Airlines PNG (☑545 1407, 542 1547; www.
apng.com; Airport) Has daily flights that connect Mt Hagen to Port Moresby (K472), Lae
(K428), Tabubil (K747), Kiunga (K730) and
Goroko (K326). Also offers flights on Thursday
and Saturday to Moro (K404) and Wewak
(K471).
MAF (Mission Aviation Fellowship; ☑545 1477;
png@maf.org.au; Airport) Offers interesting connections from Mt Hagen to all sorts of remote
destinations, including Tari (K440, Thursday),
Vanimo (K1230, Monday) via Wewak (K700),
Simbai (K240, Friday) and Goroka (K370, Tuesday). Mt Hagen is MAF's principal base.

Car
There are no taxis in Mt Hagen but a number of
car-rental agencies are located near the airport.
Car insurance is not available in Mt Hagen.
Expect to pay around K600 per day for a 4WD,
double cab or Toyota Hilux.
Avis (☑545 1350; fax 545 1525; www.avis.
com.pg; Airport)
Budget (☑542 1818; reservations@budget.
com.pg; Highlander Hotel, Okuk Hwy)
Hertz (☑542 1320; Airport)
Wangdui Hire Car (☑545 1112; Airport)

PMV
Roads heading west from Mt Hagen towards
Mendi and Wabag have been prone to ambushes
in the past and it is worth seeking advice from
your place of accommodation before jumping on a west-bound PMV to Mendi (K20, 3½
hours) or Wabag (K20, four hours). The asphalt
disintegrates into metal and then dirt before
it is resurrected 45 minutes before Mendi. It is
possible to reach Tari (K50, 11 hours) in one day
if you start early.

In the other direction there are buses to Kundiawa (K15, two hours) and Goroka (K30, four hours).

PMVs going east, to Kundiawa and Goroka, leave from the market. PMVs going west, to Wabag, Mendi and Tari, leave from the highway near the Dunlop building.

Wahgi Valley

Thirty thousand years ago the Wahgi Valley had some of the most advanced farming practices, and social and political organisations on earth. Today descendants of those early farmers still rely on technologies developed by their forefathers. If you are interested in why, despite their apparent head start, the farmers of the Wahgi Valley don't rule the world, read Jared Diamond's critically acclaimed *Guns, Germs and Steel,* which untangles the thorny issues (none of them race-related) that enabled only some cultures to produce mighty civilisations. There are numerous references to Highland farmers throughout the book.

Wamol village is a great place to experience an age-old way of life. Here you can see the pig and cassowary huts, the sugar-cane gardens and witness *karim leg* – a traditional courtship song of the Wamol people.

From Hagen catch a PMV to Wahgi Bridge Junction (K10, one hour) and change to a Nondugul Station–bound PMV but get off at Wamol (K5, 30 minutes), from where it is a 20-minute walk.

ENGA PROVINCE

Enga is the highest and most rugged of all PNG's provinces, and even other Highlanders refer to Engans as 'mountain people'. The provincial capital of Wabag is more of

DARTS

Darts is serious business in the Highlands and great fortunes are won and lost on a single throw. Men play darts at roadside 'clubs' where a dozen dartboards are fixed to posts sticking out of the ground. The rules are more or less the same as for regular darts, but you stand a lot further away – Highlands darts is something between regular darts and javelin throwing. Sometimes you can see men in traditional costume playing at village darts clubs.

an outlying town to Mt Hagen than a major centre. The two other main centres are Wapenamanda and Laiagam.

Enga is unique in that it has only one major linguistic and ethnic group, and the shared ethnicity of the Enga speakers overshadows the province's minority tribes such as the Ipili speakers (around Porgera) and Nete speakers.

Porgera, the giant gold and copper mine in the far west, has brought about rapid change for some, but most people still grow cash crops – coffee, pyrethrum and cool-weather European vegetables – in their steep mountain gardens. Porgera is all but spent, but other nearby mineral finds mean the mining town will be there a long while yet.

Wabag

People tend to sit around a lot in Wabag – outside houses, by the road, wherever. Life in general is slow in PNG but it is even slower in Wabag. The shops have all the main necessities, but the cost of transport makes things a little expensive.

The town itself has little to attract tourists, except a cultural centre and the mighty Lai River barrelling through town, but from the hills around Wabag are stunning – jagged mountains, gushing rivers and picturesque villages nestled in the mountains.

At the large **cultural centre** (◷8am-4pm theoretically), art gallery, museum and workshop, you'll see young artists making sand paintings – the principal work on display.

The main (and cynics might say, only) reason to visit Wabag is the annual **Enga Cultural Show**, a smaller version of the Mt Hagen and Goroka Shows. Like the Mt Hagen Show, it is held in mid-August, presumably with the hope of drawing some of the Hagen crowds to Wabag. It's a tactic that seems to be working, and a slowly increasing number of tourists spend a day at each of the two shows. While this show doesn't draw as many *singsing* groups, those who do attend are no less spectacular, and the setting, largely free of tourists (especially on the first day), is more intimate.

🛏 Sleeping

Wabag Guesthouse GUESTHOUSE **$**
(⌂547 1210; r K150, s/tw without bathroom K60/90) The guesthouse has several single and double rooms with shared facilities and a self-contained room that sleeps two. The kitchen is clean and well equipped.

Dae Won Wabag Hotel   HOTEL **$$**

(☑547 1140; fax 547 1033; Highlands Hwy; s K130-180, d K130-240) Wabag's only formal hotel. It's on the Mt Hagen side of town and there's a communal lounge area and kitchen, as well as a restaurant.

🛈 Getting There & Away

Air

Although the Wabag airstrip is closed, **Air Niugini** (☑547 1274) flies to Wapenamenda (an hour's drive away on the highway towards Mt Hagen via PMV) from Port Moresby on Monday, Tuesday and Thursday for K599.

PMV

PMVs travel between Mt Hagen and Wabag (K30, four hours). The road to Porgera and the mine is in good service, but PMVs rarely go there. A few PMVs go to Mendi via Laiagam and Kandep over a very rough road with frequently washed-out bridges.

SOUTHERN HIGHLANDS PROVINCE

Southern Highlands Province is made up of lush, high valleys between towering limestone peaks. Mt Giluwe (4368m), the second-highest mountain in PNG, sits on the province's northeastern border. The limestone hills and high rainfall are ideal for the formation of caves. Some caves of enormous depth and length have already been explored and it is a distinct possibility that some of the deepest caves in the world are still awaiting discovery in this region.

The Mendi area is the most developed region of the Southern Highlands but Europeans did not explore it until 1935. It was 1950 when the first airstrip was constructed and 1952 before tribal warfare was prohibited. The Mendi tribes then focused their attention on attacking government patrols and were still fighting them in the mid-1950s.

Dangers & Annoyances

Historically the Southern Highlands (and the newly formed Hela Province) were beset with lawlessness and tribal fighting. Mendi's hospital closed, the banks pulled out, making it an easy target for the sensationalist stories the international media loves so much.

These days many of the clans have sorted out their differences and the region enjoys relative security. Nonetheless, because the area is unpredictable and potentially dangerous, it would be foolhardy to rely solely on any advice given here; instead we recommend that you ask the locals about the current situation and be prepared to curtail your travel plans if the circumstances warrant it.

Mendi

Despite being the provincial capital, Mendi is a relatively small town, built around an airport. It shelters in a long green valley, surrounded by beautiful limestone peaks. There is not much to keep you hanging around here – it's really just the starting point for a trip into the Tari Basin or Lake Kutubu.

Mendi isn't as volatile as it was a few years back and recently it has been relatively well behaved. Nonetheless, the general vibe is that it's only a few stiff drinks away from sliding back to its warring ways. If a war is on, it will be confined to the aggrieved parties, but you'd do well to quickly move on.

🛏 Sleeping & Eating

The most visible place to stay is the large, sky-blue hotel, and in previous reincarnations this was *the* place to stay in Mendi. Unfortunately, it now attracts an unsavoury crowd who like to drink, fight and urinate in the hallways (although not necessarily in that order) and we recommend you try the guesthouses near the airport, which are quieter and safer.

Mendi Valley Guesthouse   HOTEL **$**

(☑/fax 549 1345; s/d without bathroom K125/135) This small hotel is right next to the Air Niugini office. The rooms are small, containing nothing more than a bed and a light bulb, but cleaner than most others in town, and it's a short walk to the market and PMV stand. If you order ahead, the girls on reception will rustle up a plate of something fried with rice (K20).

Christian Guesthouse   GUESTHOUSE **$$**

(☑549 2253; gandy@digicelpacific.blackberry.com; s/tw K150/250) If you follow the road that runs beside the airport runway out of town for about 10 minutes, you'll come across this little gem. The twin rooms are large enough to host a whole tribe and boast two double beds, tea- and coffee-making facilities, fridge and TV. Staff will prepare meals for around K25 a pop and you are far enough away from town to get a quiet night's sleep.

Kiburu Lodge COTTAGES $$

(549 1077; kiburulodge@gmail.com; r with/without bathroom K330/198) Kiburu, the province's only tourist-quality hotel, is a few kilometres south of town on the Highlands Hwy, just beyond the turn-off into Mendi. It has six chalets with 12 self-contained rooms in a quasi-traditional style set in pleasant grounds surrounding a large, hand-dug, waterlily-filled pond. The bunkrooms with shared bathrooms aren't in the same league, but share the same pleasant gardens and octagonal restaurant (mains K35 to K45) with its pot-bellied stove. The staff can contact Eric Pape, who guides trips to see local avian fauna and nearby caves.

ℹ Information

Mendi's **police station** (549 1333), post office and Bank South Pacific are in the middle of town. There are a number of good *kai* bars and shops in town, although no large supermarkets.

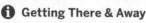

ℹ Getting There & Away

Air

The Mendi airstrip is often unserviceable, mostly in the mornings, because of fog. **Air Niugini** (549 1060; www.airniugini.com.pg) has Monday and Friday flights to/from Port Moresby (K692).

PMV

PMV trucks and more comfortable buses run back and forth between Mt Hagen and Mendi (K20, 3½ hours) with reasonable regularity. The road to Tari goes via Nipa and is a spectacular six- to eight-hour drive (K30). Unfortunately there is no love lost between the good folk of Nipa and Tari and roadblocks are regularly erected by the villagers of Nipa to extract compensation from the villagers of Tari for some misdeed. During such times, westward travel from Mendi is impossible.

SOUTHERN HIGHLANDS CULTURE

The Huli are one of the biggest clans and their homelands are among PNG's most remote and undeveloped regions. Most Huli have had little more than a single generation of contact with the outside world. Though not typical of all Highlanders, the Huli make an interesting case study (for more information, see p114).

Black Brides

Mendi brides wear black for their wedding – they're rubbed down in black tigaso tree oil and soot, and they wear this body colouring for a month after the wedding. The tigaso tree oil is very valuable. It comes from Lake Kutubu and is traded all over the area. During this time neither bride nor groom work, nor is the marriage consummated. This gives the bride time to become acquainted with her husband's family and for the groom to learn 'anti-woman' spells to protect himself from his wife.

Throughout the Highlands, women are traditionally distrusted by men, who go to extraordinary lengths to protect themselves and maintain their status. Sexual relations are not undertaken lightly – contact with women is believed to cause sickness and men usually live in separate houses and prefer to cook their own food. Boys can be removed from their mothers' houses at a very young age. Women travellers should bear these customs in mind because in many places they are still strictly upheld.

Blue Widows

A dead man's wife, daughters, mother, sisters and sisters-in-law coat themselves with bluish-grey clay while in mourning. The wife carries vast numbers of strings of the seeds known as 'Job's tears'. One string a day is removed until eventually, with the removal of the last string, the widow can wash herself of her clay coating and remarry – about nine months after her husband's death.

Long Houses

Long houses, known as *haus lains*, are built along the sides of Mendi ceremonial grounds and used as guesthouses at *singsings* (celebratory dance/festivals) and pig kills. They can be up to 150m long, although 70m is the usual length, and are built beside the stone-filled pits in which the pigs are cooked.

THE HIGHLAND'S NEW GOLD RUSH: THE LNG PROJECT

At times it seems that should you pick up any newspaper in PNG, somewhere within its pages you'll find a story about the liquefied natural gas (LNG) project that is being built to capitalise on the huge natural gas reserves near Tari.

By the time the taps are turned on in 2014, Exxon Mobil will have built not only a gas processing plant, but an airport, eight gas wells, training facilities, 700km of pipelines, massive storage tanks and a new port. It will have created 850 jobs, injected US$15 billion into the country during its construction and is expected to double the country's GDP.

It will also have cleared 2800 hectares of tropical rainforest and will begin to pump out an estimated 3,100,000 tonnes of CO_2 emissions annually.

As well as environmental concerns, locals are apprehensive about royalty-sharing agreements and the even distribution of funds between the landowners. With so much money at stake, and given the Highlander's warlike disposition and the government's widespread corruption (in 2011 PNG was ranked 154 out of 182 countries by Transparency International), negotiations were never going to be easy. Tensions between tribes, the government and the mining company are a constant source of news.

There have been calls for more transparent accountancy and larger royalty payouts; sites have been stormed and operations shut down by angry landowners trying to have their grievances heard. The government has promised regional stability; Exxon Mobil is looking for a return on its investment and the Highlanders are demanding a larger slice of the pie. Many of these ingredients were the precursors to the war that erupted in Bougainville in the late 1980s (see boxed text, p161) and it will take skilful negotiations to stop this gas field turning into a minefield.

Lake Kutubu & Around

According to legend, the lake was formed when a fig tree was cut down by a woman looking for water. The story goes that whatever the tree touched turned to water – hence the lake. Today it's oil that's causing a ripple in this previously remote area. The establishment of oilfields near Lake Kutubu has caused a sudden influx of big money, which in turn has attracted itinerants in search of work.

The influx of money is sure to affect the locals who have, until recently, maintained a largely traditional way of life, and in some villages people still live in sex-segregated buildings. It is also possible to visit the skull caves of Bebere and Kosame, where traditional burial rites are still observed. Custom dictates that the bodies of dead relatives are placed into the hull of a canoe and interred in a cave until the flesh has rotted from the bones. The skeletons are then removed, cleaned and displayed on the walls of the caves.

It is also possible to trek to Wasi Falls from Lake Kutubu via an overnight stop in the Foimeana village of Kantobo. Treks can be arranged through Tubo Lodge. Wasi Falls is the local name for a series of waterfalls that includes the Bisi Falls, the largest

in PNG, which plummet over 100m into a limestone basin.

Perched on a peninsula that forms a fork in the lake, Tubo Lodge (☎275 5778, 763 63351; www.tubo.com.pg; s without bathroom K100, d & tr K300) has commanding views of the surrounding forest-clad hills and the lake itself. After years of neglect it has recently been overhauled and is now rather comfortable. Village visits, birdwatching trips, treks and cultural excursions can be arranged here. It is also possible to swim in the lake, although women should wear a *laplap* (sarong) to respect local customs.

The closest airstrip is at Moro and Airlines PNG (www.apng.com) flies from Port Moresby (K335) and Mount Hagen (K199) three times a week. Staff from Tubo Lodge meet arriving planes with advance notice and will even meet travellers in Mendi and accompany them back to the lodge by PMV (ask to be dropped at Tubaka; four hours, K20). Access to the peninsula is by canoe from Tugiri and a 300-step climb.

HELA PROVINCE

This region is particularly beautiful and traditional cultures thrive, especially in the Tari Basin where many people retain their traditional

THE HIGHLANDS LAKE KUTUBU & AROUND

ways and men are famous for their intricately decorated wigs (see boxed text, p114).

The most remote province of the Highlands, Hela was created in 2012 when three districts broke away from the Southern Highlands to form their own province. Although the split was a culmination of a number of factors, money and underlying tribal tensions associated with the construction of the liquefied natural gas (LNG) project (see boxed text) was a key driver.

Tari

Tari is one of the few towns in PNG where some people still wear traditional dress, and the Huli wigmen and their distinctive clothing are a must-see.

Before photographing anyone, traditionally dressed or not, ask permission. Locals are usually happy to be snapped and do not ask for payment (although this doesn't apply to the wigmen). Still, make your thanks known and if you offer to send copies of the pictures, do. The main market day is Saturday and this is a particularly good time to meet locals in their finery.

The town itself is little more than a handful of buildings. There is a post office, **police station** (☑540 8022), a few large but basic shops and a hospital.

◉ Sights & Activities

There's a tiny **museum** in a stockaded compound and most of the items in the small display are for sale. The place is a sort of old men's home and a couple of older fellows show you around and accept your donation. The covered structure in the compound is the grave of a former provincial premier, and you'll see similar (but usually smaller) structures all around the Tari area.

Birdwatching   WILDLIFE
The **Tari Basin** and the **Tari Gap** are world-renowned birding spots, and because the altitude ranges from 1700m to 2800m through a variety of habitats there is a high diversity of species. Tari is particularly blessed with birds of paradise, including the King of Saxony and the blue bird of paradise. Sir David Attenborough visited the area when making his documentary *Attenborough in Paradise* and really put the place on the maps of twitchers.

The best of the birds can be seen between July and October when their plumage is at its zenith.

Huli Wigmen   CULTURAL
The Huli men are famed throughout PNG for their elaborate dress and spectacular wigs (see boxed text). Most of the wig schools are some distance from the town itself and dif-

---

A GREAT HAIR DAY

The Huli are the largest ethnic group in the Southern Highlands, with a population of around 55,000 and territory exceeding 2500 sq km. Huli don't live in villages but in scattered homesteads dispersed through immaculately and intensively cultivated valleys. The gardens are delineated by trenches and mud walls up to 3m high, broken by brightly painted gateways made of stakes. These trenches mark boundaries, control the movement of pigs and also hide troops of warriors in times of war. As usual, the women do most of the work, while men concentrate on displaying their finery, plotting war and growing their hair.

Traditional Huli culture is highly developed and strikingly executed in dress and personal decoration. Huli men wear decorative woven wigs of human hair. The hair is the wigman's own, grown over many months while living with other unmarried men in isolation from the rest of their community. Under the tutelage and guidance of a master wigman, spells are cast, diets are prescribed and rituals adhered to – all to ensure a healthy head of hair. Many Huli wigmen have more than one wig, but all wigs must be grown before the man marries. Designs are indicative of a wigman's tribe. The Huli cultivate yellow, everlasting daisies that are used to decorate their wigs; they also use feathers and cuscus fur for added panache.

The Huli men wear a band of snakeskin across the forehead, and usually a cassowary quill through the nasal septum. Their faces are decorated with yellow and red ochre. Kina shells are worn around the neck, a decorative belt and *bilum* (string bag) cloth cover the privates, and their rear is covered by a bunch of leaves attached to a belt (known collectively as a *tanket* or *arse gras*).

ficult to find, so you will need to organise transport with your guesthouse or join a tour. Often some of the bachelor boys supplement their income by travelling to town to demonstrate how they grow and care for their hair.

Tours

Ambua and Warili Lodges run tours into the surrounding countryside, although Ambua Lodge does not really cater to casual drop-ins.

Birding tours take in the Tari Gap from the road and a few trails in the rainforest.

Cultural tours are far more varied and depend largely on your budget and what you want to see. Besides visiting the wigmen, tours may include visits to the widow village, *singsings*, spirit and sun dances, and initiation and courtship ceremony re-enactments. Warili Lodge charges K630 per person, per day for one- to three-person tours that include 4WD transport. Ad hoc tours can usually be organised through the smaller guesthouses for less money but they are less organised and will depend largely on whom you meet.

Sleeping & Eating

Ambua Lodge   LUXURY HOTEL **$$$**
(542 1438; www.pngtours.com; all-inclusive s/d/tw US$812/1206/1206; @) The showpiece of the Trans Niugini Tours operation, Ambua offers commanding views across the Tari Basin and Huli homelands. In 2001 it was listed as one of the 10 best ecotourism facilities worldwide by *National Geographic Adventure* magazine. At 2100m, the lodge enjoys a refreshing mountain climate and attracts many birdwatchers and orchid enthusiasts. Guests are accommodated in individual, luxury, bush-material huts. The huts have a great 180-degree view and are surrounded by flower gardens with a backdrop of mossy

forest. Grand opulence in such rugged circumstances is certainly impressive. Ambua is beyond the means of many travellers and most guests come as part of a Trans Niugini package on its private plane.

Warili Lodge   GUESTHOUSE **$$**
(715 98104; www.papua-warili-lodge.com; per person incl meals K180) This lodge is an excellent place to stay, with comfortable rooms made from bush materials. The three-course dinners are delicious, served in a large, thatched room with an atmospheric open fire. The lodge is a 45-minute drive from town and owner Steven usually collects his guests if he knows they are coming. If arriving by PMV, jump out when you see his sign. Tours are also offered.

Kalute Guest House   HOTEL **$$**
(732 52330, 768 8012; Anopi Rd; tw K200) This is one of the many new places that have sprung up to cater to visiting LNG workers. Rooms are quiet and clean with tight security. Guests can cook their own food, although meals are also available (dinner K30). Birding and cultural tours can be arranged here.

Getting There & Away
Air
Air Niugini (540 8023; www.airniugini.com.pg) flies daily to/from Port Moresby (K990). **MAF** (730 08972, 736 45312) has Thursday flights to Tabubil (K560), Kiunga (K520) and Mt Hagen (K440). If telephone lines are down in Tari, book through its Mt Hagen office.

PMV
PMVs leave Tari from the market early each morning (excluding Sunday) and pass Warili Lodge on their way to Mt Hagen (K50, 11 hours) via Mendi (K30, seven hours). PMVs also run from Tari to Koroba for around K10.

The Sepik

POP 530,000 / AREA 79,100 SQ KM

Includes »

Best Places to Stay

» In Wewak Boutique Hotel (p120)

» Auong Guesthouse (p123)

» Vanimo Surf Lodge (p125)

Best of Culture

» Garamut & Mamba Festival (p120)

» Crocodile Festival (p131)

» Middle Sepik *Haus Tambarans* (p132)

» Maprik *Haus Tambarans* (p126)

Why Go?

The mighty Sepik is one of the great rivers of the world. In serpentine fashion it flows for 1126km through a largely undisturbed environment of swamplands, tropical rainforests and mountains. However, the Sepik is more than just a river – it's also a densely populated repository of complex cultures, dying languages and the most potent art in the Pacific.

As you motor around one of the endless river bends, the scale of the river, the towering facades of the *haus tambarans* (spirit houses), the bird life, the eerie lagoons and the beautiful stilt villages make it all too easy to believe that you've travelled clean out of the 21st century and straight into an adventure.

The Sepik region also takes in the sleepy provincial capitals of Wewak and Vanimo, two beachside towns that attract a small trickle of surfers who come to tame the seasonal swells.

When to Go
Wewak

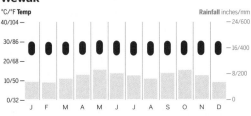

Jun–Oct The dry season has fewer mosquitoes but temperatures vary greatly between regions.	**Mid-Oct–late Apr** Monsoon swells bring waves between 1m and 2.5m to PNG's northern coast.
Dec–Apr Expect drenching rain at any time, but during the wet season it's virtually guaranteed.	

History

The Sepik's first contact with the outside world was probably with Malay bird-of-paradise hunters – the feathers from these beautiful birds were popular in Asia long before fashionable European millinery incorporated them into late-19th-century women's headwear.

The first European contact came in 1885, with the arrival of the German New Guinea Company. Dr Otto Finsch named the river Kaiserin Augusta, after the wife of the German emperor.

The Germans established a station at Aitape on the coast in 1906, and in 1912 and 1913 sent a huge scientific expedition to explore the river and its vast, low-lying basin. They collected insects, studied local tribes and produced maps of such accuracy that they're still referred to today. Angoram, the major station in the lower Sepik, was established at this time.

The early 1930s saw gold rushes in the hills behind Wewak and around Maprik, but development and exploration ceased when WWII started.

The Japanese held the Sepik region for most of the war. Australian forces pushed along the coast from Lae and Madang, and the Japanese withdrew to the west. In early 1944 the Americans seized Aitape and the Australians moved west from there. When a huge American force captured Hollandia (now Jayapura in West Papua) in April, the Japanese in Wewak were completely isolated. A year later, in May 1945, Wewak fell and the remaining Japanese withdrew into the hills. Finally, with the war in its last days, General Adachi surrendered near Yangoru. The formal surrender took place a few days later on 13 September 1945 at Wom Point near Wewak. Of 100,000 Japanese troops, only 13,000 had survived.

EAST SEPIK PROVINCE

East Sepik Province is much more developed than Sandaun Province and includes the most-visited and heavily populated sections of the Sepik, as well as several large tributaries. It was here, in 1945, that the Japanese finally surrendered to the Allies and various vehicles of war can still be seen, rotting where they were left.

Vanilla, once a lucrative crop for Sepik villagers, has seen its price spiral downwards in the last few years. A scarcity of buyers and a glut on the international market have seen the 2004 record highs of US$500 per kilogram nose dive to a mere US$20 per kilogram in 2010, placing additional hardships on impoverished communities.

Wewak

As Wewak was once the site of the largest Japanese airbase in mainland New Guinea, it was subject to a barrage of bombs during WWII.

A short distance inland the coastal mountains of the Prince Alexander Mountains separate the Sepik Basin from the narrow band of flat land and headland peninsula on which Wewak is built.

Wewak itself is an attractive town, and while most people pause only long enough to arrange their Sepik expedition and stock up on provisions, it does have its charms. A series of beaches with golden sand and backed by swaying palm trees start here and stretch along the coast.

⊙ Sights

Mission Point to Cape Boram WATERFRONT
(Map p122) Near the main wharf lie the rusting remains of **MV Busama**. Further down at Kreer, on the road to the airport, there's the wooden hulk of a Taiwanese fishing junk. On the beach between Kreer Market and the hospital are some rapidly disappearing rusting Japanese landing barges. The **Japanese War Memorial** marks the mass grave of many troops. The soldiers' bodies were later exhumed and returned to Japan.

Japanese Memorial Peace Park PARK
(Map p122) This peace park contains a memorial and a fish pond. Tok Pisin doesn't have a word for peace; 'peace' sounds like *pis,* which means fish. Thus, most locals refer to the park as *pis park,* which is perhaps appropriate given the fish pond and the general ambivalence that many modern Papua New Guineans have towards WWII.

🏃 Activities

Swimming & Snorkelling BEACH
Wewak's beaches are excellent – long stretches of sand that fall away gently under the water. The water is clean and clear, warm and very inviting.

There's excellent snorkelling around the Wewak headland, over the outer reef and off the nearby islands. Like many coastal

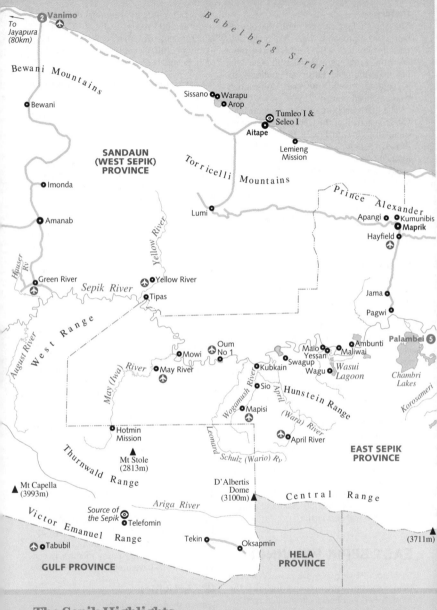

The Sepik Highlights

1 Trailing your fingers in the legendary **Sepik River** (p129) as your canoe threads through narrow channels to remote villages

2 Finally making it to **Vanimo** (p124) and some of the best surf in the country

3 Laughing with the kids as you immerse yourself in the lifestyle of a **Chambri Lakes** (p136) village

4 Buying a totem from a master carver in **Tambanum** (p134), one of the many

BISMARCK SEA

Tarawai I
Walis I
Vokeo I
Kairiru I
Muschu Passage
Dagua
7 Muschu Island
Cape Wom
Cape Moem
Mountains
6 Wewak
Yangoru
Passam
Darapap Entrance
Mendam
▲ Bam I
Hawain R
Nagam River
Marienberg
Murik Lakes
Watam
Angoram
Sepik
River
Chimondo
Anwar
Timbunke
Chambri Lakes
1 Sepik River
Bogia
4 3
Tambanum
Kambot
Yuat River
Yip
River
Korogopa
Amboin
Keram River
Ramu River
Yimas
Schrader Range
MADANG PROVINCE
ENGA PROVINCE

0 — 100 km
0 — 60 miles
N

Middle Sepik villages steeped in artistic tradition

5 Being invited inside a sacred *haus tambaran* (spirit house) at **Palambei** (p133)

6 Snoozing in the shade of a coconut palm on a **Wewak** (p117) beach after roughing it for a week on the river

7 Barbecuing your freshly caught fish on the deserted and idyllic **Muschu Island** (p123)

Wewak Town

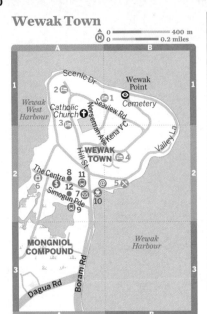

places in PNG, the diving conditions around Wewak are sensational – reefs, wrecks, tropical fish – but there's no organised diving industry in Wewak.

Surfing
SURFING

Between mid-October and late April monsoon swells bring waves between 1m and 2.5m to PNG's northern coast, and there are several good breaks around Wewak. Some of the hotels have surfboards, but they're pretty battered – surfers usually bring their own.

Tours

For tours to the Sepik, including those offered by Wewak-based operators, see p130.

Festivals & Events

Garamut & Mamba Festival
CULTURAL SHOW

Wewak's Garamut (drum) and Mamba (bamboo flute) Festival is usually held on the first weekend of September, and features song and dance as well as yam-planting ceremonies.

Sleeping & Eating

There are good accommodation options among Wewak's hotels and guesthouses. You can stay in town at a couple of decent hotels, but there's no reason not to stay on the beach a few kilometres from town towards the airport. Daytime buses from here to town are frequent and cheap, and the beach is brilliant.

Eating options, beyond daytime *kai bars* (cheap takeaway food bars), are confined to the hotels and yacht club.

TOP CHOICE In Wewak
Boutique Hotel
BOUTIQUE HOTEL $$$

(Map p120; ☎456 2100; inwewak@global.net.pg; Seaview Rd; s K319, d/tw K429-605, f K605; ✳@☎) If you're looking to splurge, this would be the place to do it. This gleaming white, spotlessly clean, plantation-style hotel is easily the best accommodation in town and the only place with a pool. Private decks, furnished with trendy outdoor lounges, front all rooms except the small singles. Beautifully framed Sepik Art can be found throughout the hotel including The Cocoa Café (mains K20) and the Vanilla Room Restaurant (mains K40 to K50; dinner only). The latter serves the most creative dishes in Wewak, including Australian scotch fillet and crocodile tail in green coconut curry. Discounts on accommodation are sometimes available to those who ask.

SIL Guesthouse
GUESTHOUSE $

(off Map p122; ☎456 2176/2416; per person without bathroom K55, apt K150) Located in Kreer Heights, the SIL Guesthouse is clean, secure and comfortable but is often full. Besides the standard rooms, there are several furnished two-bedroom flats with kitchens, bathrooms and TV. To get there, take a town bus to Kreer Heights and then ask for directions.

Sepik Surfsite Lodge   HOTEL $
(Map p122; ☑456 1516; adventurepng@datec.net. pg; r K100-200; ✱) The prime, beachside location and the *haus win* (open-air structure like a gazebo) restaurant (mains K40) are the chief draws here. The room situation, however, is a bit odd and the place feels like a cross between a cheap Aussie motel and a construction site. A new hotel was planned and partially built on stilts above the existing rooms, but when funds dried up progress stalled and now an ageing, partially built complex hovers over the old hotel below. The cheapest rooms come with shared, cold-water-only facilities come in two flavours; fan-cooled and those with air-con. The more expensive rooms are essentially the same but are self-contained with hot water and air-con. The manager, Alois Mateos, is a great Sepik expert and owner of Sepik Adventure Tours (p130) and Ambunti Lodge (p132).

Warihe Guesthouse   GUESTHOUSE $
(Map p120; ☑/fax 456 1153, 693 7201; s/tw without bathroom K80/120) The rooms are airless boxes but they are clean airless boxes with fans, which is more than can be said about some rooms in town. There was once a rowdy bar here but that's been closed and the new management keeps this place free from troublemakers.

Airport Lodge   HOTEL $$
(Map p122; ☑456 2373; airportlodge@datec.net. pg; s/d K205/218, s/d without bathroom K170/182; ✱) The cheaper rooms with shared facilities were a bit musty on the nose but those with small private bathrooms passed the sniff test and came with TVs. There's a large aviary in the tropical gardens and when the cockatoo gets to screeching, you'll be tempted to turn it into a headdress. The beach bar is under a large shade sail and it's a great place for lunch and a beer. The restaurant offers a choice of three mains (K40 to K60) in the evenings.

Paradise New Wewak Hotel   HOTEL $$
(Map p120; ☑456 2155; fax 456 3411; Hill St; s/d/ tr K196/240/280; ✱) There hasn't been anything 'new' about the New Wewak Hotel for some time. Situated atop the headlands, overlooking the ocean, this old hotel has some large and, despite their age, comfortable rooms with fans, fridges, phone, air-con and private bathrooms. The open-air, *haus*

win restaurant (mains K30 to K35) and bar has great views to Robin Island and serves fare of the 'steak 'n' chip' variety.

Talio Lodge   HOTEL $$$
(Map p122; ☑456 3155; info@taliolodge.com; Boram Rd; r K480-500; ✱) The newest hotel in town, Talio Lodge consists of a series of overpriced prefabricated rooms that look like shipping containers with decks and a ranch slider door. They're smart, modern and impersonal inside. They come with/without small kitchenettes (K500/480).

Windjammer Hotel   HOTEL $$$
(Map p122; ☑456 2548; windjammer@datec.net. pg; Boram Rd; r K181-495; ✱@) Once one of Wewak's finest hotels, the Windjammer had a large collection of Sepik art adorning its walls before it was sold some years ago. These days the rooms are badly in need of modernisation to justify their prices. A fire in 2011 destroyed much of the hotel, but at the time of writing the main lobby and restaurant were being rebuilt and should be up and running by this book's publication.

Wewak Guesthouse   GUESTHOUSE $
(Map p122; ☑456 1497; Cathedral Rd; s/d K100/150) Mrs Barry (you won't be on a first-name basis) runs her guesthouse with a titanium fist. It's one of the cheapest places in town and was last cleaned about the same time the country got independence. She usually charges backpackers K50 per person (not the 'official rates' we've listed) and quite frankly that's all these rooms are worth.

Seaview Hotel   HOTEL $$
(Map p120; ☑456 1131; fax 456 1281; Hill St; s/tw K250/280, tw with air-con K350; ✱) The Seaview has had incarnations as a hotel and police barracks, but it's a hotel again now, though the police barrack vibe still lingers. The à la carte restaurant (meals K40) has views to the town and the sweeping arc of the harbour but the service is very slow. Tariffs include airport transfers.

Wewak Yacht Club   PUB $
(Map p120; meals K20; ☉lunch & dinner Mon-Sat, dinner Sun) The yacht club overlooks a nice part of the harbour, though there aren't too many yachts tied up here these days. Most of the patrons are Wewak locals and an odd expat or two who come for drinks and simple pub-style meals. Dances are held here every couple of months, and while the club is for members, tourists are welcomed.

THE SEPIK WEWAK

Wewak Harbour & Around

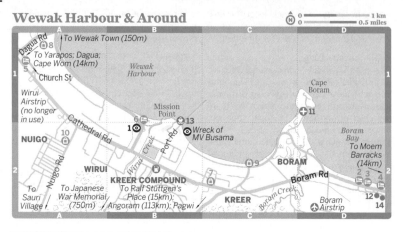

Wewak Harbour & Around

🛍 Shopping

Nobody comes to the Sepik without buying at least one carving and buying just one is often a good strategy. Sepik pieces are often heavy and large, and are a drag to lug around the country. The Airport Lodge and Sepik Surfsite Lodge have small craft shops, and Wewak is adequately supplied with supermarkets, chemists and clothing stores.

Markets   MARKET
The **main market** (Map p120), at the west end of the town's main shopping strip, is pretty colourful thanks to the multitude of umbrellas used to shade the merchants. There are a few *bilums* (string bags) and occasionally some small trinkets for sale; otherwise it's largely all local produce on offer. The dried fish can get fairly 'ripe' in the hot sun but it's worth poking around here to see if anyone

has brought in a live baby crocodile to sell – usually with its snout tied shut.

There are several other markets around Wewak, of which **Kreer market** (Map p122), on the airport road just before it turns inland, is the most interesting. **Chambri market** (Map p122; Boram Rd) sells *buai* (betel nut) and a few artefacts. There is also **Dagua market** (Map p122) and **Nuigo market** (Map p122), which both sell *buai, pitpit* (edible wild cane) and sometimes woven pandanus satchels.

Ralf Stüttgen's Place   ARTEFACTS
(off Map p122; ☎456 2395, 682 0051; Tower) Ralf, a naturalised citizen, has been knocking around PNG for some time; first as a missionary and more recently as an artefacts dealer. His house is overflowing with dogs, storage boxes, carvings, books, WWII

memorabilia and ethnic art. His vast array of Sepik carvings has been collected over a lifetime from 50 different villages and even if you don't buy something from him, he could probably point you to the right village if you're after a particular style. Ralf's place is on a 400m ridge overlooking the coast at Tower (there's a radio mast), 15km inland from Wewak. Take PMV 2-3 (K2) to Tower from the main market.

Information

ANZ (Map p120; ☑856 1100) One of several banks with ATMs in Wewak town.

Hospital (Map p122; ☑856 2166) On the point at Cape Boram.

Police (☑456 2633)

Post office (Map p120; ☑856 2290; cnr The Centre & Boram Rd)

Sorup Telecenter (Map p120; 2nd fl, Fisheries Bldg; per 5 min K10; ☺8am-4pm Mon-Fri) It's not easy to spot but it's upstairs above the old Gala ice-cream shop. On some days a piece of string and a couple of cans would work better.

Getting There & Around

Air

PMVs heading to and from town (K0.50) stop just outside the airport's gates on Boram Rd.

Air Niugini (Map p120; ☑456 2233; fax 456 2203; www.airniugini.com.pg; The Centre) Has daily connections to Madang (K462, 40 minutes) and on to Port Moresby (K751),and a Wednesday flight to Vanimo (K352, 35 minutes). There is also an office at the Airport.

Airlines PNG (Map p122; ☑/fax 456 1153; www.apng.com; Airport) Operates a Thursday and Saturday flight to Port Moresby (K1051) via Mt Hagen (K470) and Moro (K759). At Mt Hagen it's possible to transfer to Goroka- and Lae-bound planes.

MAF (Mission Aviation Fellowship; Map p122; ☑456 2500, 7359 4209; png-wewak@maf.org; Airport) Flies to many remote airstrips in the East Sepik Province including Ambunti (K360) and Amboin (K360) every Tuesday and Thursday. It also flies to Mt Hagen (K700) on Monday and Vanimo (K750) on Wednesday.

Boat

Lutheran Shipping (Luship; Map p122; ☑456 2464; luship@global.net.pg) Connects Wewak to Vanimo (1st/2nd class K180/144) via Aitape (1st/2nd class K150/102) fortnightly and Madang (1st/2nd class K180/144) weekly.

Rabaul Shipping (Star Ships; Map p120; ☑456 1160; Simogun Pde) Operates the MV *Kokopo Queen* between Madang and Wewak. Schedules are erratic but generally there is a weekly boat

to Madang (K155) and, once or twice a month, it continues to Vanimo (K155).

Car & PMV

The **main PMV stop** (Map p120) is next to the main market, but the 3-10PMVs bound for Maprik (K20, four hours) leave between noon and 1am Monday to Saturday from near the post office.

For travel to the Sepik access towns of Pagwi, Timbunke and Angoram from Wewak, see p131. If you want to travel west to Vanimo overland, see the boxed text (p125).

Around Wewak

CAPE WOM

Fourteen kilometres west of Wewak, **Cape Wom International Memorial Park** (admission K5; ☺7am-6.30pm) is the site of a wartime airstrip and where the Japanese surrender took place. There's a war memorial flanked by flagpoles on the spot where Japanese Lieutenant General Adachi signed the surrender documents and handed his sword to Australian Major General Robertson on 13 September 1945. On the west side of the cape there's a good reef for **snorkelling** and a nice stretch of sand for **swimming**.

There's no transport that reaches here – you could catch a PMV bound for Dagua (a village further west) at the Wewak main market and get off at the turn-off to the cape at Suara. From the turn-off it's a 3km walk. There's a ranger at the gates but you shouldn't come here alone.

MUSCHU ISLAND

Just off Wewak's coast are the beautiful and often overlooked islands of Muschu and Kairiru. Palm trees, turquoise waters, nearby reefs and a left-hand point break (November to March) make this one of Papua New Guinea's best-kept secrets.

Hidden in the jungle is a couple of Japanese anti-aircraft guns and a **plane wreck**. There isn't much left of the plane; some scattered debris, two hulking engines and a propeller. Further inland, two jeeps lie abandoned alongside the **Japanese Road**, now overgrown with regenerating jungle.

From the main village of **Sup** it's a five-hour walk to the area's school and a deep and wonderfully clear **swimming hole**.

To stay at **Auong Guesthouse** (George Maiet's Guesthouse; ☑7297 8746; auong.guest house@gmail.com; Sup village; per person K40) ask for George around the small beach opposite Wewak's post office. He'll run you across to the island (K25 each way) to his beachside guesthouse. Accommodation is in a simple, but spotlessly clean bungalow, a stone's throw from an unspoilt, coral-fringed beach. George's wife, Josephine, makes delicious meals (K18 to K20) and his sons guide guests (K20) to local sights. George also has a set of scuba equipment (K80), a surfboard and a snorkel set (K25) for hire.

In Wewak, speed boats leave from the beach opposite the post office at around 3pm for Muschu (K15 to K25 each way).

SANDAUN PROVINCE

Sandaun (pronounced 'sundown') Province is so named because it's in the northwest of PNG – where the sun goes down. Formerly called West Sepik Province, it's largely undeveloped, but agricultural activity around Telefomin and timber development near Vanimo have brought rapid change. Gold is mined inland. There are opportunities to surf and enjoy the beaches here but it's a very remote part of PNG.

Vanimo

Vanimo is a tiny outpost on the western edge of a remote country; most travellers who get this far go on to Jayapura in Indonesia. The town's Indonesian influence is quite marked in the goods for sale in the shops as much as the fabrics hanging in the market.

The Malaysian logging company, Vanimo Forest Products, is logging the province and on most days you'll see two or three barges in the port, stacked high with kwila, a native hardwood that has been felled in the surrounding jungles.

◉ Sights & Activities

Surfing   SURFING
(Surf Area Management Plan or SAMP; fee per person per day K30) Vanimo has some of the best surf in PNG, and it's one of the main reasons why people visit this town. The surf is seasonal, from October through to April, when monsoon swells bring waves between 1m and 2m.

Most surfers head straight to Lido, a small village on the headland 6km from Vanimo and the home of the local board-riding clubs – Sunset Surf Club and Vanimo Surf Club – as well as the Vanimo Surf Lodge, the organisation that collects the SAMP fees.

Lido has two excellent reef breaks (a right and a left) and gets consistently good surf. Five minutes up the coast at Warimo Village there are two lefties and two righties – both reef breaks, and further along at Yako Village there's a fast hollow left.

There's no surf rage in PNG and the scene is just in its infancy. Generally it's BYO boards but Vanimo Surf Lodge may be able to sort you out. For more on surfing in PNG, see p187.

Local Walks   BEACH
There's a pleasant two-hour walk around the headland, but carry water and sun protection. People in the villages here don't get a lot of tourists or even a lot of local passersby, so be respectful as you enter an area and ask before taking the plunge on any of the local beaches.

Another good walk is west along Vanimo's main beach from the airport. After 40 minutes you come to a limestone headland draped with vines – wade around it to the beautiful beach on the other side. There's a rusting Japanese landing barge just offshore.

Narimo Island   BEACH
Narimo Island can be seen offshore from the Vanimo Beach Hotel. This is an excellent place for picnics and swimming. The hotel may be able to arrange a boat to take you there or ask about boat hire at West Deco village near the main wharf on the other side of the peninsula.

🛏 Sleeping & Eating

In addition to the following formal accommodation, locals, particularly those in Lido village, offer homestays for around K60 per person including local meals (although you may want to supplement these with snacks).

TOP CHOICE CBC Guesthouse   GUESTHOUSE $
(Christian Brethren Church Guesthouse; ☎7125 1526; per person without bathroom K66) Easily the best (as it is the only) budget option in town. It isn't signed but take the road between the provincial government buildings and the church that heads up the hill, turn right at the first fork and left at the next fork. The driveway is the first on your right and of the three houses that share this driveway, the guesthouse is the one highest up the hill. Chances are the caretaker, Cecilla Kamaso, won't be around but if you call her mobile, she'll pop over and give you the keys. The simple rooms are fan-cooled and share a communal kitchen.

MISSED THE BOAT? WEWAK TO VANIMO OVERLAND

Most people either fly between Wewak and Vanimo or take one of the passenger boats. Unfortunately, flying is expensive and the boats only run once or twice a fortnight, leaving many travellers stranded and scratching their heads wondering if it's possible to travel overland between the two towns. The short answer is 'Yes'.

From Wewak a rough dirt road runs west as far **Aitape**, a tiny coastal town established by the Germans in 1905 and of significant strategic importance in WWII. In 1944 an Australian division pushed inland against considerable Japanese opposition to establish a base in the Torricelli Mountains. From there they pushed the Japanese eastward until Wewak fell on 22 May 1945.

As fierce as that fighting was, it was the 1998 tsunami that really laid waste to the Aitape coastline. The huge wave swallowed everything within 500m of the shoreline, killed more than 2200 people and left 10,000 homeless in an instant.

PMVs don't travel this route but 4WDs looking for passengers usually park near the small Wewak beach where the boats to Muschu Island pull up. If you ask around for the next 4WD heading to Aitape (K50, six hours), you should find something on most weekdays and even the occasional car heading the whole way to Vanimo (K150, 14 hours). We counted 39 small rivers and streams that needed to be forded between Wewak and Aitape, three of which were sizeable enough to stop traffic after heavy rain.

From Aitape you have a choice of continuing westward along an even rougher forestry road (K100, eight hours) or catching a banana boat (K100, 5½ hours). As the road is often rendered impassable, boats are sometimes your only option. They leave when full most weekdays from the inlet near the centre of Aitape town. Coming from Vanimo they leave from the beach near the Vanimo Beach Hotel and skippers sometimes pin notices on trade stores' notice boards advertising departure dates. The boats are often dangerously overloaded and it's only safe to travel on them during calm weather. On sunny days be sure to wear sunscreen or bring an umbrella for shade; five hours of tropical sun can do ugly things to unacclimatised skin.

There's a couple of places to stay in Aitape, the best of which is **Jamson's Guesthouse** (☑457 2245; emichael@daltron.com.pg; s/d without bathroom K90/140), with its plain but comfortable fan-cooled rooms.

TOP CHOICE **Vanimo Surf Lodge** LODGE **$$**

(☑7393 9762, in Australia 0411 823 500; www.vanimosurflodge.com; per person incl meals without bathroom K330) Opened in 2011 and within a frisbee throw of some of Lido's best breaks, this lodge is aimed squarely at the surfing market and many of its clientele come here on package deals with **World Surfaris** (www.worldsurfaris.com). The spacious beachside bungalows are semi-open plan and made from local materials including kwila hardwood and sago palm thatch. It's a relaxed place and the large open-air restaurant is a great place to hang out with a beer and a book between bouts of surfing. Fishing, snorkelling and excursions to other breaks can all be arranged here.

Tanyuli Bungalows GUESTHOUSE **$**

(☑7230 2291; Yako village; per person without bathroom K55) These nine bungalows are in the seaside village of Yako (PMV fare K1.50), next to Baro School, on the way to the Indonesian border. Facilities are fairly basic – a mattress on the floor, but the location is superb and you'll sleep soundly, lulled by the sound of the surf. Firewood is provided if you wish to cook your own meals, otherwise give your ingredients to the staff who will prepare them for you (K20) or provide you with some local fare from their gardens (K25).

Sandaun Surf Hotel HOTEL **$$**

(☑457 1000; vanimosandaunsurfhotel@gmail.com; s/d K330/360; ❀) The hotel is reminiscent of a string of railway carriages – a series of large airy bungalows, each with a wooden floor, overhead fan, TV and fridge – and the smartest accommodation Vanimo has to offer. The bar and restaurant (mains K40) serves steaks, chicken and pork dishes. Our steak had the bejesus cooked out of it.

Vanimo Beach Hotel HOTEL **$$**

(☑457 1102; vbhotel@online.net.pg; r K275-425, apt K675; ❀) The well-trimmed gardens and traditionally inspired bungalow apartments make a pretty impression when you arrive and are very comfortable. Unfortunately, the standard rooms are a big step down – many are windowless and the small air conditioners make lots of noise but very little cool air. There's a comfortable bar and patio restaurant (mains K35), which catches the ocean breeze coming off the beach.

ℹ Information

Vanimo is built at the base of a hilly headland on a narrow isthmus. The airport's runway slashes across the neck of this isthmus from the western ports to the eastern beaches. 'The Town' can be found between the airport and the base of the headland and has all the essentials – supermarkets, post office, Westpac bank (which cashes travellers cheques), Bank South Pacific (with an ATM) and a rather unimpressive market. There are no internet cafes in Vanimo.

ℹ Getting There & Around

For information on travelling down the coast to Wewak, either by speed boat or PMV, see the boxed text (p125).

If you're heading the other way to Indonesia, see p196 for the low-down on PNG's only land border crossing.

Air

Most hotels send vans to meet arriving guests, but the two main hotels in town are only a five-minute walk from the airport, opposite the Indonesian consulate.

Air Niugini (☑ 457 1217; www.airniugini.com. pg) To avoid the queues head early to the office in town near the market. There are Wednesday, Friday and Sunday flights to Port Moresby (K925) via Wewak (K452).

MAF (☑ 7173 6703) Has irregular flights to remote airstrips and a Wednesday service to Wewak (K750) if there is enough demand. If you can't get hold of its local agent Alfred Kramer on the listed number, contact its Wewak office.

Sunbird Aviation (☑ 457 1257; Airport) Principally a charter-only company but has a few regular runs within the Sandaun Province. Generally it serves the small eastern airstrips on Monday and Tuesday and the inland airstrips around Telefomin (K680) and Oksapmin (K760) on Thursday.

Boat

The agents for both Lutheran Shipping and Rabaul Shipping are located in the same large hanger at the main wharf. They open for ticket sales about three days prior to arrival of one of their boats.

WORTH A TRIP

MAPRIK'S HAUS TAMBARANS

There isn't much to Maprik. There is a market, post office, two churches, a couple of shops selling the bare essentials and that's about it. The town has little to draw travellers but it's the logical base to explore the Prince Alexander Mountains and nearby Abelam villages notable for their yam cults, carvings and decorations. You'll also find striking, forward-leaning haus tambarans (spirit houses), an architectural style echoed in such modern buildings as Parliament House in Port Moresby. The front facade of a Maprik haus tambaran is usually brightly painted in browns, ochres, whites and blacks, and in some cases can reach 30m high.

Traditionally haus tambarans were exclusively an initiated-man's domain, but these days the rules are usually bent for Western travellers. Locals usually charge K5 to K20 to enter and an additional K5 to K10 photography fee. There isn't much to see inside anymore, most of the art was sold to collectors decades ago. The tunnel-like entrance at the front is reserved for ceremonies, so you'll be asked to enter by a door at the back.

Interesting back roads connect villages between Maprik and Lumi, some with spectacular haus tambarans and good carvings. You can walk between these villages but to explore the area thoroughly you'll need your own transport

Another good base for exploration is Apangai, 10km from Maprik, which has three haus tambarans. Another particularly fine one can be found at Kumunibis, a small village not accessible by road but by a three-hour walk from Apangai.

To get to either Maprik or Apangi from Wewak catch a 3-10PMV (K20, Monday to Saturday, three to four hours) from opposite the post office. Maprik makes for a convenient overnight stop on the way to Pagwi (K10, two hours from Maprik).

There is a hotel and two guesthouses in Maprik, and Peter Yipimi offers homestays in Apangai.

Lutheran Shipping agent (☎7201 4045) The fortnightly MV *Rita* travels along the coast to Aitape (1st/2nd class K150/102), Wewak (K180/144) and Madang (K350/300).

Rabaul Shipping (Star Ships; ☎7693 3176) Runs the MV *Kokopo Queen* twice a month to Wewak (K155, overnight) and Madang (K300, two days).

PMV

Tuesday and Thursday are shopping days at Batas, just across the border in Indonesia, and every PMV, and a good deal of the local population, will be heading that way (K10). This is great if you are Indonesia-bound but makes for a long wait if you want to catch a PMV to Lido (from the tin shelter in front of the Cash 'n' Carry supermarket; K1.50) or Yako (from in front of the main market; K2.50). Yako is actually on the way to the border, but on Tuesday and Thursday drivers would rather sell the seat to someone paying the full K10 fare to Batas.

Taxi

There are a few taxi companies in town.
Dopi Texi (☎7379 0061)
Waks Taxi (☎7383 2242)

THE SEPIK & ITS TRIBUTARIES

The mighty Sepik is the most famous geographical feature of PNG and has captured the collective imagination of adventure travellers around the world. The scale of the river, the impressive architecture of *haus tambarans,* the beautiful stilt villages, the long canoes with crocodile-head prows, flower-clogged lakes, misty dawns and spectacular sunsets make a visit unforgettable.

While photos of Sepik villages look idyllic, they don't show the heat and humidity, the mosquitoes or the basic village food. Nor do they indicate the meditative nature of travelling for hours every day in a motor-canoe, watching ibis take to the sky as you round a bend, fingers trailing in the water.

During the dry season water levels drop dramatically, cutting off villages and turning the lakes stagnant. The trapped water heats up resulting in a toxic algae bloom that kills the fish.

The Sepik is too big to cover, so pick a section and give yourself plenty of time to relax in the villages between stints on the river. Two or three Middle Sepik villages are enough for most people, and some enjoy it more when they get off the main river.

Geography & Climate

The Sepik River is 1126km long and is navigable for almost its entire length. It starts up in the central mountains, close to the source of PNG's other major river, the Fly, which flows south. The Sepik flows in a loop, first west across the West Papua border, then north before returning east across the border.

At its exit from West Papua, the Sepik is only 85m above sea level and from there it gradually winds down to the sea – a huge, brown, coiling serpent. It has often changed its course, leaving dead-ends, lagoons, oxbow lakes or huge swampy expanses that turn into lakes or dry up to become grasslands in the dry season.

The inexorable force of the river tears great chunks of mud and vegetation out of the riverbanks and these drift downstream as floating islands. There is no delta and the river stains the sea brown for 50km or more from the shore.

Early in the dry season is the best time to visit – *natnats* (mosquitoes) are less numerous and there's plenty of water in the river system. By August the level drops significantly emptying some tributaries and *barets* (artificial channels cut as shortcuts across loops in the river), and this makes travel times much longer.

Culture

The Sepik region is the best known part of PNG outside the country, and Sepik artefacts (carvings and pottery) are displayed in many of the world's great museums. Traditional art was linked to spiritual beliefs. Sepik carvings were often an attempt to make a spirit visible, although decorations were also applied to everyday items (ie pots and paddles).

Today carving is rarely traditional – it's more a mixture of long-established motifs, imagination and commercial tastes. Some villages still retain their own signature styles – Kambot makes the famous story boards but even these are not traditional. Story boards were originally painted on large pieces of bark, and now they're carved in relief from timber.

Christianity, as elsewhere in PNG, is blended with many traditional beliefs. Although most Sepik people would claim to be Christian (they go to church every Sunday), it's a very localised interpretation. The religious world is also inhabited with the spirits of ancestors and some Sepik people invest great spiritual power in crocodiles. People around Korogo village in the Middle Sepik perform an initiation rite where young men are cut with hundreds of incisions on the back, chest and buttocks (see the boxed text, p136) to imitate a crocodile's skin.

What to Bring

Only take to the Sepik what you need on the Sepik – leave your luggage with someone you trust in Wewak. A daypack is plenty.

The biggest issues on the Sepik are *nat-nats* (mosquitoes) and sunburn. You'll need to cover up for both – long sleeves and loose-fitting trousers in lightweight fabrics are ideal, although *natnats* can bite right through looser weaves and fine cottons. Covered footwear is essential as is a broad-brimmed hat.

If you're travelling on a plush cruise boat, you won't need much beyond some sensible clothes, but for everyone else, preparation is important. You will probably be sleeping rough (although some river guesthouses provide mattresses and linen) and an inflatable hiker's mattress is perfect when combined with a box-style mosquito net secured at four corners (the umbrella type are useless). You can buy good mosquito nets in Wewak. A sleeping sheet is ideal – silk is lighter and less bulky, cotton is a little cooler. A torch is essential and as there is nowhere to recharge spent digital camera batteries, bring extra and go easy on the previews.

You bathe in the river, but never nude: bring some swimmers or a *laplap* (sarong) and a towel. Bring sunscreen, sunglasses, industrial-strength insect repellent, toilet paper, a spoon and a bowl. Rain water is collected and is fine to drink, but you might want to carry bottled water to be safe. Take a basic first-aid kit and if you plan on trekking, you'll need boots as trails can get very muddy.

In Wewak or Vanimo you must stock up on food and cash. For food, pack two-minute noodles, *kundu crackers* (beef crackers), rice and *tinpis* (tinned fish). Take some cooking oil as well, as that's precious along the Sepik. Any spare food remaining can be given away and will be gratefully received. Take any money you'll need in small bills as villagers seldom have change. The only banks on the Sepik are river banks and there is no way of getting extra funds if you run short.

🛏 Sleeping & Eating
STAYING WITH LOCALS

Finding a place to stay will rely on your ability to find people willing to accommodate you. Locals often consider their dwellings below the standard acceptable to 'white' folks, and although you would gladly roll out your mattress on their floor, the feeling may not be reciprocal. This is where the knowledge of a local guide is invaluable. Villagers who have travelled beyond the Sepik are generally less reserved with foreigners. A lot depends on whom you meet and how receptive they are to an unannounced guest.

Bear in mind that you can't just pitch a tent on some deserted stretch of the river. Not only is this unsafe but like all land in PNG, none is considered deserted by the local who owns it. Landowners have a tradition of fighting over land, and their forefathers didn't spend centuries holding off marauding neighbours just to have some tourist paddle up and camp on it. Instead, ask to speak to the village chief about village guesthouses or local families willing to let you stay or camp with them.

If you stay in someone's home, compensation is expected, although you will seldom be asked directly to make a contribution. How much to give can be vexing. If you give too little, you run the risk of abusing the hospitality of some of PNG's poorest people, and if you pay too much, you'll distort the local economy, drive up the prices for other travellers and help create a myth that all tourists have money to burn. Somewhere around K15 to K25 per person, per night would be reasonable, especially if you share some of your food or buy some betel nut for your hosts. If, on the other hand, you end up eating their food, a little more would be appropriate.

VILLAGE GUESTHOUSES

Guesthouses come and go along the Sepik from one year to the next and there can be little difference in quality between staying in a guesthouse and staying with a local family. If you're lucky there may be a generator, although this is the exception rather than the rule – most won't even have beds, though some have mattresses. Like most Sepik dwellings, they are usually stilt houses constructed out of local materials and reached by a series of rickety stairs. Inside you'll be given a room, a place to keep your bag and shown where you can unfurl your sleeping mat. Most (but not all) guesthouses will provide you with a mosquito net and some even light mosquito coils for their guests at night. Typically they charge around K25 per person, except in Angoram and Pagwi, which are more sophisticated than those elsewhere and charge K50 per person but include electricity and running water. Meals can usually be arranged for a bit extra.

Travel on the Sepik

Broadly speaking you have three options. You can go it alone, hire a local guide or book a prearranged tour. Which one you choose determines the degree of comfort you can expect and ultimately how much you'll end up spending.

To experience the Sepik more economically (and, some would say, more enjoyably) base yourself in one village, live with a family, and learn the art of sago-washing, canoe-making, gardening and fishing.

Goin' Alone

While it's completely possible to travel on the Sepik independently without a guide, very few people do so. The biggest advantage of going alone is that it is considerably cheaper than the other two options.

VILLAGE CANOES & TRADERS

The river traffic is reasonably constant, although totally unpredictable, and if you've got a pretty open-ended schedule and a lot of time, you can catch rides in locals' boats or ask someone to paddle you to the next village.

Catching canoes to and from the major transport hubs of Pagwi, Timbunke and Angoram is relatively easy. There are often boats travelling to meet the buses arriving from Wewak and a canoe ride from Pagwi to Ambunti takes about two hours, depending on the outboard's horsepower and how loaded down the boat is with passengers and freight. On the Middle Sepik, Maprik's market days (Wednesday and Thursday) are prime travelling times and passing canoes work in much the same way as PMVs back on shore do. A typical two-hour ride costs about K20 but rates vary between skippers and on the current price of fuel. There is very little river traffic on weekends.

If you decide to rely on passing canoes, you will need to have plenty of time and be well prepared and provisioned. It's not uncommon to find yourself stuck somewhere for a few days before you can get a lift – leaving you up the proverbial creek without a paddle.

Guide & Boat Hire

There's nothing quite like cruising along the river sitting below the waterline in the bottom of a 20m dugout watching the world

DOS & DON'TS

There's probably too much hang-up about appropriate behaviour in the Sepik area. Good manners go a long way and locals usually forgive transgressions of local rules but try and remember the following:

» Don't wear your hat and shoes into a *haus tambaran*.

» Ask where you may wash.

» Ask before taking photographs of anybody or anything – *haus tambarans* are taboo.

» 'Best price?' Don't bargain, but objects sometimes have two prices. It's OK to ask and leave it at that.

» Alcohol can be a very sensitive thing in villages – it's probably better not to have any.

» The gender politics can be a bit confusing; it's better that men mingle with the men and women with women. There can be awkwardness if Western women are allowed into sacred *haus tambarans* when local women aren't. Couples should not overtly show affection.

THE SEPIK

slip by. If you hire a boat and guide, you'll have the peace of mind knowing that your guide will find you a place to stay, arrange some food, provide added security and have reliable transport to boot.

Ultimately the success of the trip will depend on the quality of the guide and the reliability of the boat. Because the expense of the guide and boat can be split, it's cheaper to travel in a small group.

GUIDES

Finding a reliable guide is paramount to an enjoyable trip, but doing so prior to arriving is notoriously difficult. Local guides seldom promote themselves, have unreliable telephone connections, no email addresses and invariably live in remote villages without a postal address.

It is worth asking for recommendations from other travellers and checking travel reports online at Lonely Planet's **Thorn Tree forum** (www.lonelyplanet.com) to see who is currently offering guiding services. At the very least, allow for a couple of days spent in Wewak, Angoram, Ambunti or Pagwi talking to locals and asking around. The guesthouses in Angoram, Pagwi and Ambunti are the best places to start looking and many arrange guides on the spot.

A good guide should have an extensive network of local accommodation options, know the river, and be able to accurately estimate travelling times and fuel costs. The going rate is around K50 per day and you'll need to pay your guide's PMV fares and accommodation costs in the villages.

BOATS

Your guide will be able to help you hire a canoe (with an outboard) at a reasonable price and will know how much fuel to buy. You can hire motor-canoes in Ambunti, Pagwi and Angoram.

Once you've accepted that the dugout motor-canoes (car-noo) won't tip over rounding a corner, you'll find the ride very relaxing. It takes hours getting anywhere and the experience is quite calming and meditative. Even the buzz of the outboard motor seems to fade after a while.

Budget on K200 to K300 per day to hire a motor-canoe and pilot. The fuel is the largest single contributor to the cost of the trip. Buy your fuel in Angoram and Pagwi because it costs a lot more on the river. Just like back home, the cost of fuel affects the price of most things and these rise and fall with world oil prices. A 44-gallon drum of petrol was K1000 at the time of research. Ouch! Travelling during the dry season is more expensive as various shortcuts are closed when the water level

falls. A small, light canoe (15m or so) with a 15HP to 30HP motor is more economical than a larger heavier boat. You could expect to use one 44-gallon drum of fuel in a three-day tour, two drums in a five-day tour, depending of course on how far you travel. Finally, be aware that some guides will purposely overestimate how much fuel you should buy so they can keep the unused portion at the end of the trip.

If you charter a canoe you also have to pay for the driver to return to his base, whether you go or not. It's cheaper to travel downstream as the consumption is reduced. At a leisurely pace you could travel from Ambunti to Angoram in five days.

Bearing in mind that various factors can influence the time taken, travelling downstream in a large canoe takes about 1½ hours from Ambunti to Pagwi, about six hours from Pagwi to Timbunke, and five hours from Timbunke to Angoram. Add at least 30% more time going upstream.

Taking a Tour

This is the easiest, most luxurious and expensive way to see the Sepik. Most people prearrange their Sepik itinerary with either a major inbound tour operator (see p197), or one of the smaller local-based tour companies. This latter option is perhaps the best way to go, but give operators a few weeks to make arrangements.

PNG Frontier Adventures (☎856 1584/1400; www.pngfrontieradventures.com) These guys are Sepik experts. They can

TRIBAL ART

The Sepik is synonymous with tribal art. It is often described as Papua New Guinea's 'treasure trove'; overflowing with masks, shields, figures, canoe prows and story boards, and today carving plays an important part in the river economy.

Like all art forms that are alive and vigorous, Sepik art is constantly undergoing subtle transformations, evolving from traditional forms to reflect current tastes and artistic fashions. Today, just as in the past, a master carver is regarded with considerable prestige and is quite capable of producing quality work every bit as unique as his forefathers.

The most artistic villages are concentrated on the Middle Sepik. The villages of Palambei, Kaminabit, Mindimbit, Timbunke and Tambanum are all good places to buy tribal art. Remember that a 10kg carving might cost less than K100 but excess baggage or postage charges might be twice the cost of the item.

There is also a dark side to art collecting, and over the years unscrupulous art collectors have plundered the Sepik of some of its most significant and culturally important pieces. Taking advantage of local poverty, the lucrative ethnic art market and toothless laws, traders have been able to strip the area of its cultural treasures, leaving the treasure chest, or more aptly, the skull rack, empty.

Rory Callinan's interesting article on the trafficking of human heads is worth reading at www.time.com/time/magazine/article/0,9171,1086707,00.html.

provide everything from a single guide to a full-blown tour.

Sepik Adventure Tours (Sepik Surfsite Lodge; ☑456 1516, 7259 6349; www.ambuntilodge -sepiktour.com.pg) Based in Wewak, a local operator. Friendly Alois Mateos also owns Ambunti Lodge on the Upper Sepik and specialises in all-inclusive tours based there.

Sepik Spirit (☑542 1438; www.pngtours. com; 4-day package per person all-inclusive s/tw US$3894/5562) This is a rather odd-looking vessel with its large, square, glass-covered front. It contains nine rooms, each with their own toilet and shower, as well as a communal lounge and bar area. The boat doesn't travel quickly, so guests board faster, smaller craft to explore the villages, returning each afternoon to overnight on the mother boat. From 2013 the boat will be permanently moored at Kaminabit.

Melanesian Travel Services (MTS; www. mtspng.com) The owners of the Madang Resort Hotel operate charters to the Sepik River on the super smart, 98ft *Kalibobo Spirit;* for details see p90.

❶ Getting There & Away

AIR

MAF Wewak flies twice weekly to airstrips at Amboin (K360) on the Karawari River and Ambunti (K360).

BOAT

It's possible to catch a betel nut boat from Angoram to Mandi Bay, Boroi or Awar, all very close to Bogia, where you can spend the night before catching an early morning PMV to Madang. For details, see the boxed text (p93).

PMV

The river is only accessible by road at three points – Angoram on the Lower Sepik, and Timbunke and Pagwi on the Middle Sepik. PMVs in these parts are mostly trucks, either with a tarpaulin covering bench seats down each side, or a plain open tray.

From Wewak, catch a 3-8PMV to Pagwi from the post office between 9.30pm and 11.30pm (K30, mostly on Monday, Wednesday and Thursday). These vehicles run through the night in order to meet the waiting canoes at around 6am the next morning. They return to Wewak as soon as they are full, usually between 6am and 8am.

Roads to Timbunke are impassable in the wet and this is the most unreliable of the three towns in terms of transport. The trip takes about seven hours and costs K40.

Two to four PMVs bound for Angoram leave from Wewak's market daily, except Sunday (K20, five hours). The road from Wewak to Angoram is the shortest access route to the Sepik. It branches off the Maprik road 19km out of Wewak. The 113km, all-weather road is good by Sepik standards but it's still extremely uncomfortable. If you're returning to Wewak, you start very early (around 3am) in order to get the locals to the morning market soon after dawn.

PMVs are scarce on Saturday and don't run on Sunday. Market days are the best days to travel when the trucks (and canoes) are more frequent.

Upper Sepik

Above Ambunti, the villages are smaller and more spread out. The people are friendly and hospitable and have had less contact with Western tourists. There's not the same concentration of artistic skills that you find on the Middle Sepik, but nature lovers will find this the most exciting part of the river. From Ambunti the river narrows and the land it flows through becomes hilly with denser vegetation. In many areas, trees grow right down to the water's edge.

There are few villages after Yessan and there is a long uninhabited stretch between Tipas and Mowi. The Upper Sepik is more isolated than the Middle Sepik and, as villages tend to move, there are lots of deserted settlements.

SWAGUP

Well off the main stream, east of the April River, Swagup is the home of the 'insect cult' people. Their unique art usually incorporates the figure of a dragonfly, sago beetle, praying mantis or other insects. The ferocious reputation these people earned in former times continues.

MALIWAI

This village is on a small lake off the river. The Waskuk people invest spiritual power in cassowaries and these flightless birds are carved into most things, regardless of function. It used to be customary in this village to cut off a finger joint when there was a death in the family. The *haus tambaran* here has collapsed and most artefacts are housed within people's homes.

AMBUNTI

Ambunti is an administrative centre of no great interest but there is an airstrip, police outpost, a very basic clinic and a couple of reliable people who hire motor-canoes, so this is one of the best places to start a trip.

The inaugural two-day **Crocodile Festival**, sponsored by WWF Papua New Guinea, kicked off in 2007 and was a great success. Since then the festival has grown in popularity and now attracts *singsing* (celebratory festival/dance) groups from throughout the Sepik Basin and a handful of international visitors. Usually held in August (check www. pngtourism.org.pg for exact dates), the canoe races and cultural performances aim to promote community tourism and crocodile conservation.

🛏 Sleeping & Eating

Because Ambunti gets a trickle of visitors there are various people prepared to accommodate you in their homes – you'll be expected to pay.

Ambunti Catholic Mission   GUESTHOUSE $ (per person K25) Ask the boat driver to drop you here at the bend of the river just before Ambunti Lodge. It can sometimes provide meals but bring emergency rations just in case.

Ambunti Lodge   LODGE $$ (✆456 1516, 7259 6349; www.ambuntilodge-sepik tour.com.pg; r K200; ❄) This lodge has seven double rooms, two shared bathrooms and its own generators to run the air-con. Grilled pork chop or chicken meals (K27) are served with rice and cabbage. It mainly caters to the clients of Sepik Adventure Tours (p130) but it is possible to stay here if it has rooms available. By Sepik standards it's quite comfortable. Staff can arrange half- and full-day tours, though you should be able to arrange things more cheaply if you contact the boat owners directly.

Middle Sepik

This region starts just below Ambunti and finishes at Tambanum. This area is regarded as the 'cultural treasure house' of PNG. Almost every village had a distinct artistic style but these styles are now merging. The whole Middle Sepik region is interesting but the largest concentration of villages is just below Pagwi and it's possible to visit several on a day trip.

PAGWI

Pagwi is the most important access point to the Middle Sepik. There is little of interest in Pagwi itself, and despite its vital role it's rather an ugly little place – some run-down government buildings and trade stores where you can buy basic supplies.

You can hire motor-canoes here but be mindful that there are some rogues. Day trips to Korogo, Aibom, Palambei, Yentchen and Kanganaman are all interesting and within reach. It's six hours to Timbunke and another five to Angoram. At a leisurely pace, stopping and taking side trips, you could take five or six days to get down to Angoram from where you could catch a PMV back to Wewak.

A few basic guesthouses have sprung up in the Pagwi vicinity of late and locals will direct you to them. The pick of the bunch is **Yamanumbo Guesthouse** (per person K50) on the opposite side of the river. It's fairly basic but the owner can help arrange guides and is a good source of local information. Alternatively, a two-minute walk upriver brings you to the Catholic Mission, with basic beds with mosquito nets.

KOROGO

Korogo has an impressive **haus tambaran** with a pair of carved eagles at each end of the roof. Local myth tells of two young women who, while fishing, attracted the lascivious attentions of the Crocodile Spirit. The spirit caused a flood, forcing the girls from their homes and into his waiting jaws. One sister was eaten; the other captured and duly married. The union produced two eggs from which eagles, not crocodiles, hatched.

There's a pleasant two-hour walk inland to the village of **Yamok**, home to the Sowas tribe and two smaller **haus tambarans**. You can also take a canoe to Palenqaui and walk from there (40 minutes).

In Korogo, Leo Gopmi has a small **guesthouse** (per person K30) made of bush materials. Korogo is 30 minutes by motorboat from Pagwi.

SUAPMERI

Variously spelt as Swatmeri and Sotmeri, Suapmeri is famous for its mosquitoes. There are few carvings for sale, although the area was famed for its orator's stools. Despite this, it's an attractive village and the entrance to the Chambri Lakes. There are no guesthouses but local families offer accommodation – it's just a matter of asking around.

If the water isn't too low, it's possible to take a shortcut to Kaminabit through the weed-filled *barets* from here.

Suapmeri is half an hour from Korogo by motor-canoe. To Aibom in the Chambri Lakes it's 1½ hours by motor-canoe.

YENTCHEN

The two-storey **haus tambaran** here was copied from photographs taken at the turn of the century by German explorers of the building standing at that time. The top floor is only for initiates, who climb upstairs between the legs of a female fertility symbol and are blessed in the process. Sadly the building has fallen into disrepair and there are plans to move the artefacts into the half-built structure behind the *haus tambaran* and out of the sight of the women.

Yentchen is noted for its wickerwork dancing costumes – figures of crocodiles, pigs, cassowaries and two-headed men. Male initiates have their skin cut into 'crocodile skin' (see the boxed text, p136) around Christmas. The ceremony is open to foreigners but be *very* respectful. You'll have to pay a premium (possibly even K1000, depending on who you talk to) for the privilege.

Yentchen is 2½ hours by motor-canoe from Pagwi and it is possible to stay with Jacob Kambak in his **guesthouse** (per person K25).

PALAMBEI

You can't see Palambei village proper from the river and it's easy to miss – there are a few huts and there may be some canoes on the bank. It's a hot 20-minute walk along a *baret* (which is empty in the dry season), but it is worth the effort because the village is beautiful. Built around several small lagoons full of flowering water lilies, the village has two impressive *haus tambarans* at each end of a ceremonial green. The remains of

a third **haus tambaran** can also be seen. It was bombed by the Japanese (or Americans, depending on who you ask) in WWII and all that remains are the large upright posts, two of which have sprouted.

Inside the *haus tambaran* ask to see the chair that houses the village spirit but don't photograph it. Downstairs are eight hearths bordered by eight benches, one for each of the eight clans in the village.

Stones, which must have been carried many kilometres, have been set up in the glade. Locals are great *garamut* (drum made from a hollowed log) players and you might see some beating out their powerful and complex rhythms (K10).

Palambei is 1½ hours from Suapmeri by motor-canoe and the village has two simple **guesthouses** (per person K25). One is owned by Jacob Kambak and the other by Benny Kusodimi.

KANGANAMAN

A brief walk from the river, this village is famous for the oldest **haus tambaran** on the river. Declared a building of national cultural importance, it has been renovated with help from the National Museum and is interesting to visit. It is a huge building with enormous **carved posts**.

The **guesthouse** (per person K25) in Kanganaman is cut from the same cloth as all the others – very basic without running water or electricity.

KAMINABIT

The **haus tambaran** here is in fairly good condition and it is possible to climb to the 2nd floor to view the painted beams and rafters. Skin-cutting ceremonies (see the boxed text, p136) are held here about once

---

HAUS TAMBARAN

Tambaran is a spirit, so the *haus tambaran* is the house where spirits live, inhabiting sacred carvings and *tambu* (forbidden or sacred) objects. Up to 50m long and 30m high, *haus tambarans* are often referred to as 'spirit houses' or 'men's houses' because only initiated men are allowed to enter.

Every clan has a *haus tambaran* and they are still very much the centre of local life. Men lounge around in the shade underneath the building, carving, talking or sleeping. Young male initiates remain up to nine months in the upstairs section of the *haus tambaran* while they prepare for (and often recuperate from) initiation rites. During this period they often cannot look at a woman until they are reborn as men.

The *haus tambaran* is universally a female symbol: its entrance is sometimes vaginal in shape, yet everything about them and what goes on inside them is secret men's business and *tambu* to women. These days this rule is bent for tourists and both male and female travellers are allowed to enter and look around, usually for a small fee (K5 to K10).

Middle & Lower Sepik

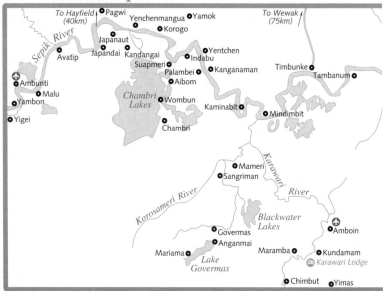

every two years, during which ancestral skulls are placed in the two large drums.

Kaminabit is divided into three villages and it's a few minutes' walk between each. There is a large, well-maintained Catholic church in the middle village, with three wings (one for each village) radiating from the central pulpit. **Sabbei Kungun and Cyril Tara** (☎ 7656 0190; sepikarts@yahoo.com.au) operate small **guesthouses** (per person K30). Cyril is also an experienced guide.

From Aibom it takes one hour to get here by motor-canoe, and from Palambei it's 1½ hours by motor-canoe.

MINDIMBIT

This village is near the junction of the Karawari and Korosameri Rivers. The Korosameri leads to the beautiful **Blackwater Lakes** region. Mindimbit is entirely dependent on carving and there is some nice work, though there is no proper *haus tambaran*.

TIMBUNKE

This is a large village with a big Catholic mission, a hospital and a number of other Western-style buildings. There are also some impressive houses.

Trans Niugini's *Sepik Spirit* calls in here, which is why there's a good range of artefacts and carvings for sale.

TAMBANUM

This is the largest village on the Middle Sepik and fine, large houses are strung along the bank for quite a distance. The people here are renowned carvers. American anthropologist Margaret Mead lived here for an extended time. From Timbunke, Tambanum is about 30 minutes by motor-canoe.

Lower Sepik

The Lower Sepik starts at Tambanum and runs down to the coast. Angoram is the most important town on the Sepik. The Marienberg Mission station, which has been operated by the Catholics for many years, is about two hours downstream from Angoram.

Near the mouth of the river, the Murik Lakes are vast semi-flooded swamplands, narrowly separated from the coast. Villages along this part of the Sepik are smaller, poorer and generally have had less Western contact than many in the Middle Sepik.

The vast volume of water and silt coming down means that the landscape around the mouth of the Sepik changes rapidly. Many villages here are only a few generations old, built on new land.

prawns are a tasty treat. The rate listed is for backpackers, others pay double.

Futulu Guesthouse
GUESTHOUSE **$**

(Jimmy's Place; ☑7121 5387; r K50) Jimmy is a well-known entrepreneur, and this guesthouse is one of the many pies his fingers are in. The basic rooms are a work in progress and surround a communal lounge decorated with mermaid murals and carved posts. When we visited, Jimmy had been drinking, though he always maintained a friendly demeanour. His brother **Jex Tatuli** (☑7301 3284) works as a guide.

Cletus Smank Guesthouse
GUESTHOUSE **$**

(☑7691 7686, 7241 7997; per person incl food K50) Local guide Cletus Smank also offers accommodation in his family home. He's in the process of building a separate guesthouse, but until it's finished guests are accommodated in rooms with mattresses (no beds) and mosquito nets. He has a small generator and canvas bag showers that he fills with rainwater (as opposed to the dirtier river water). He is located at Service Camp, a little upstream from Angoram.

KAMBOT & CHIMONDO

A good day trip from Angoram is to travel south on the **Keram River** to Kambot, stopping at Chimondo (often spelt Sumundo) on the way. These villages produce fantastic art and Kambot is the home of the **Sepik story boards**. The river is narrow and winding, and the banks are crowded with luxuriant growth that attracts many ibises.

It's possible to stay in **guesthouses** (per person K50) at both Kambot (ask for David Bamdak) and Chimondo. A traveller reported that he was allowed to pitch his tent on the platform in the Kambot *haus tambaran* and spent a magical night camped under its carved struts. It's doubtful that this invitation would be extended to women.

ANGORAM

This is the oldest and largest Sepik station. It was established by the Germans before WWII and is now a sleepy administrative centre for the Lower and Middle Sepik regions. Apparently this used to be a pretty swinging place in colonial days with banks, businesses, a hospital and an airstrip – it's hard to imagine now.

If you haven't got a lot of time to spend but you want to see some of the Sepik, Angoram is the place to visit. It's accessible by road from Wewak and there are beautiful and interesting places just a few hours away by motor-canoe.

The guesthouses listed following also arrange guides and can help find PMV boats to Bogia.

🛏 Sleeping & Eating

Wavi Guesthouse   GUESTHOUSE **$**

(☑7366 2894; per person K50) Francis Tobias operates this small guesthouse, a short walk from the Angoram market. It's made from local materials but is reasonably comfy. Francis struck us as a reliable, upfront operator who quoted sharp prices for guides and fair assessments on fuel consumption on hired boats. Meals (K18 to K35) can be arranged and, when in season, the freshwater

Tributaries & Lakes

The Sepik River becomes monotonous as it winds through its vast, flat plain, with *pit-pit* up to the water's edge. The most spectacular scenery is on the tributaries, and the villages are generally smaller, friendlier and less visited. There are three main accessible tributaries in the Lower Sepik – the **Keram**, the **Yuat** and the smaller **Nagam**.

SCAR TISSUE *NANCY SULLIVAN*

The first time I saw an initiated Iatmul man on the Sepik was in 1988. He was a guide on my first canoe trip through the region and I couldn't take my eyes off the bands of gnarly hard welts running down his shoulders and shirtless back. Years later, in the Nambaraman spirit house, I witnessed how he must have received such grizzly scars.

On that day I saw a group of young men, under the guidance of their mother's brothers, pass from youth to men, androgyny to manhood. All the initiates had their backs cut by their uncles, symbolically bleeding out their mother's postpartum blood and spilling it onto their mother's line; 'making' them into men for their fathers' clan. The uncles cradled their nephews on their laps as the gruesome scars were quickly and professionally cut. Tigaso tree oil and cooling white clay were applied and the boys were then made to lie down by smoky fires to slowly infect their wounds and produce the knobbly, keloid scars that make their skin resemble that of a crocodile's. It was during this ordeal, as the flutes and *kundu* drums played to confuse the women waiting outside, that I finally 'got' what it meant to cut skin.

Nancy Sullivan (www.nancysullivan.org), Papua New Guinea anthropologist

WASUI LAGOON

Also known as Wagu Lagoon, this is a beautiful place, with many birds. The Hunstein Range is behind **Wagu** village and the area is covered in lush rainforest. Wagu is cut off during the dry season when lake levels drop. Kaku Yamzu (Mathew) operates the **Toheyo Guesthouse** (per person K25), a simple stilt house with a shared bathroom. Simple but tasty meals are available, and Mathew's tours include trips to see the **bird-of-paradise** display tree (K15), **fishing** (K5), and **crocodile-spotting** at night (K10).

CHAMBRI LAKES

The Chambri Lakes are a vast and beautiful expanse of shallow water. Being only 4m deep, they partially empty in the dry season when things get smelly and the water is unfit for drinking unless treated.

Indabu is one of the four villages that make up the Chambri region. There is a **haus tambaran** here with a huge collection of carvings in the polished Chambri style, as well as ornamental spears. **Aibom**, another village on the lakes, produces **pottery** and has a large stone said to be that of a woman who turned to stone resisting a snake that tried to drag her into the water.

With the help of French anthropologist Nicolas Garnier and international funding, there is a new **haus tambaran** in **Wombun**. The four main totems here are eagles, flying foxes, rats and crocodiles. Although there is no guesthouse, many guides bring tourists here to stay with their *wantoks* (relatives).

When the water is deep enough there are various routes and shortcuts to Chambri, though you'll need a guide to find them. The deepest route connects the lake with the Sepik just above Kaminabit. There's another passage via Suapmeri and another via Kandangai.

From Suapmeri to Aibom takes 1½ hours by motor-canoe. From Aibom to Kaminabit takes another hour by motor-canoe. There are village boats to Kandangai from Pagwi most days.

AMBOIN

Amboin is usually reached by air and from the village it's a short distance up the river to the luxurious Karawari Lodge. The lodge river trucks will take you to nearby villages such as Maramba, Marvwak and Chimbut, where traditional Sepik-style tree houses are still used. There are also tours that travel as far as Kaminabit and some that stay in the villages. **Singsings** and re-enactments of the Mangamai skin-cutting ceremonies are all part of the deal. Special birdwatching tours to the Yimas Lakes can be organised.

The **Karawari Lodge** (☑542 1438; www. pngtours.com; s/d/tw all-inclusive US$812/1206/ 1206; @) is a luxury base, operated by Trans Niugini Tours, for exploring the Sepik near Amboin. The main building, built in the style of a *haus tambaran* with impressive carved totem poles and stools, is surrounded by 20 mosquito-proofed bungalows. The lodge has dramatic views across the Karawari River and a vast sea of jungle. Tourists are flown in as part of a larger itinerary and it's possible to opt to stay at nearby villages (far less luxurious). Like all of Trans Niugini operations, it's cheaper to come here on a package.

Island Provinces

POP 560,000 / AREA 28,450 SQ KM

Best Places to Stay

» Walindi Plantation Resort (p150)

» Rapopo Plantation Resort (p143)

» Nusa Island Retreat (p154)

» Clem's Place (p157)

» Dalom (p157)

Best Activities

» Diving Kimbe Bay (p149)

» Cycling Boluminski Hwy (p158)

» Surfing off Kavieng (p153)

» Trekking up Mt Balbi (p162)

Why Go?

Largely untamed and raw, the islands of Papua New Guinea are not your classic beach paradise. Here you'll live out your Indiana Jones fantasies, blazing a trail of your own amid wild jungles. The adventure starts by climbing the volcanoes near Rabaul, looking for WWII relics on the Gazelle Peninsula, paddling through lagoons mottled with pristine reefs near Kavieng, exploring the rugged beauty of Bougainville or escaping to an island off Lavongai (New Hanover).

The islands' bounty goes beneath the surface, with its unbeatable repertoire of diving adventures. Shipwrecks, fish life in abundance and thriving reefs are the rewards of diving here. Surfers rave about the uncrowded waves off New Ireland.

Be ready for a culture shock, too. These islands are home to tiny villages where people lead lives that have changed little over centuries. If you plan a visit in July, try to make it coincide with the authentic Warwagira Festival of masked dance.

When to Go

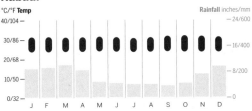

Rabaul

Dec–Mar Cyclone season, which can bring high winds and rough seas.

Nov–Apr The wet season; ideal surfing, with decent swell.

May–Oct The dry season, with slightly cooler temperatures.

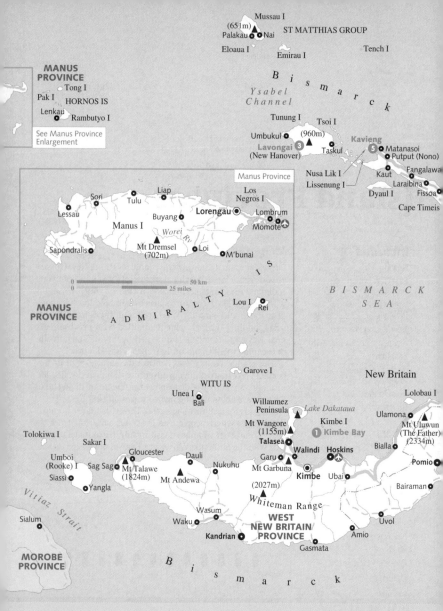

MANUS
PROVINCE

ST MATTHIAS GROUP

Mussau I
(651m) ● Palakau ● Nai
Eloaua I
Emirau I
Tench I

Tong I
Pak I
HORNOS IS
Lenkau ● Rambutyo I

B i s m a r c k

Ysabel Channel

Tunung I
Tsoi I
Umbukul ● (960m) ▲
Lavongai ❸ Taskul
(New Hanover)

Kavieng
❺ ● Matanasoi
● Putput (Nono)
Fangalawa

Nusa Lik I
Lissenung I
Kaut
Laraibina
Dyaul I
Fissoa
Cape Timeis

See Manus Province
Enlargement

Manus Province

Sori
Liap
Los
Negros I

Lessau
Tulu
Buyang
Lorengau ◉
Lombrum
Momote

Manus I
Worei R
Loi
M'bunai
Sapondralis
Mt Dremsel
(702m)

0 ——— 50 km
0 ——— 25 miles

MANUS
PROVINCE

A D M I R A L T Y   I S

Lou I
Rei

B I S M A R C K
S E A

Garove I

New Britain

WITU IS
Unea I
Bali

Willaumez
Peninsula
Lake Dakataua

Lolobau I

Mt Wangore
(1155m) ▲
Kimbe I
❶ Kimbe Bay
Ulamona
Mt Uluwun
(The Father)
(2334m)

Talasea
Walindi
Hoskins
Bialla

Tolokiwa I
Sakar I
Gloucester
Dauli
Garu ● ● Ubai
Kimbe ◉
Mt Garbuna
Pomio

Umboi
(Rooke) I
Sag Sag ● Mt Talawe
(1824m)
Mt Andewa
Nukuhu
Bairaman

Siassi
Yangla
(2027m)

Vitiaz Strait

Wasum
Whiteman Range
Uvol

Sialum
Waku
**WEST
NEW BRITAIN
PROVINCE**
Amio

**MOROBE
PROVINCE**
Kandrian
Gasmata

B i s m a r c k

Island Provinces Highlights

❶ Scuba diving some of the world's most fecund reefs in **Kimbe Bay** (p26)

❷ Scaling extinct **Kombiu** (Mt Mother; p149) and feasting your eyes on the 360-degree views of Rabaul, Gazelle Peninsula and Mt Tavurvur

❸ Relaxing with a book and a fresh coconut on a blow-your-mind beach off **Lavongai** (New Hanover; p156)

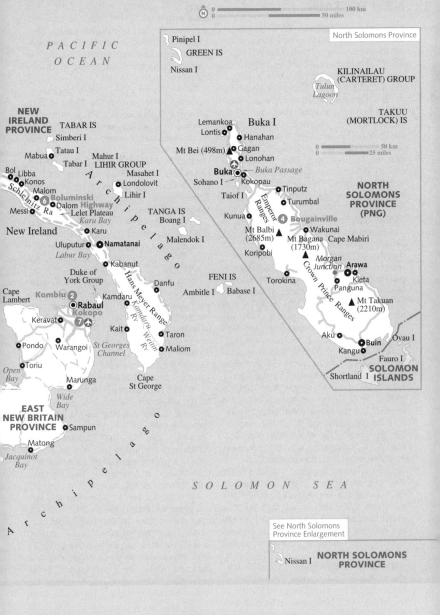

4 Blazing new territory exploring mountains, islands and villages in rarely visited **Bougainville** (p162)

5 Taking in the remarkable surfing or diving near **Kavieng** (p153)

6 Experiencing peaceful village life off **Boluminski Highway** (p157)

7 Browsing the lively market and enjoying the scenery from a relaxing stay in one of **Kokopo's** waterfront guesthouses (p141)

NEW BRITAIN

New Britain is stunning. PNG's largest island, it has a bit of everything you've come to this country for – think colonial history, remarkable traditional cultures and pristine wilderness (despite areas where there are logging and mining). The *pièce de résistance*? Volcanoes. The whole region is a rumbling, billowing string of cones and craters cloaked with virgin tropical rainforest. Some are dormant and harmless while others are scrappy villains that periodically flex their muscles. In September 1994 Mt Tavurvur and Mt Vulcan erupted and destroyed most of Rabaul, one of PNG's biggest and most alluring cities, in a furious rain of ash and rock (see boxed text, p148).

After exploring the striking landscapes, be sure to don mask and tank to delve into New Britain's sensational aquatic environs. To say that Kimbe Bay offers world-class dive sites is an understatement. Rabaul's harbour and the various bays that carve out the Gazelle Peninsula also host superlative sites, such as wrecks and psychedelic coral reefs. There is one proviso, though: don't expect to find lots of secluded white-sand beaches – not New Britain's strong point.

New Britain is divided into two provinces; each has its distinctive feel. East New Britain (ENB) Province ends in the Gazelle Peninsula, where there has been lengthy contact with Europeans, education levels are high and the people are among the most economically advantaged in the country. The other end of the island, West New Britain (WNB) Province, is sparsely populated, little developed and did not come into serious contact with Europeans until the 1960s. The migrant workers from the Highlands, the 'colonial'-flavoured expats and the dense bush give WNB the flavour that the east might have had mid-last century. It's a frontier country with many colourful, roguish Queenslanders escaping the more regulated life 'back home'.

The most easily accessible areas for travellers include the Gazelle Peninsula and Kimbe Bay. If you want to explore the rest of the island, you'll have to cut a path of your own, which means a lot of gumption, time and money.

History

The island of New Britain was settled around 30,000 years ago. The Lapita people, the world's first true ocean navigators, arrived about 4500 years ago, bringing pottery and trade with them. Several hundred years ago, the Tolai people came from southern New Ireland and invaded the Gazelle Peninsula in northernmost New Britain, driving the Baining, Sulka and Taulil people south into the mountains.

From 1874 to 1876 German traders established settlements in the Duke of York Islands and Blanche Bay. The area was renowned for cannibalism. In some districts, more missionaries were eaten than heathens converted.

On 3 November 1884 a German protectorate was declared and the German New Guinea Company assumed authority, which it held until 1914 when Australian troops landed at Kabakaul.

At the end of WWI, the German planters had their plantations expropriated and were shipped back to Germany. Meanwhile Australians evacuated German residences, but not for long.

In 1937 the Vulcan and Tavurvur volcanoes erupted, killing 507 people and causing enormous damage. Before this eruption, Vulcan had been a low, flat island hundreds of metres offshore. It had appeared from nowhere during an 1878 blast (and had been immediately planted with coconuts). When the 1937 eruptions ceased, Vulcan was a massive mountain attached to the coast.

In 1941 Rabaul was completely crushed by the advancing Japanese. At the peak of the war, 97,000 Japanese troops were stationed on the Gazelle Peninsula. But the Allies never came. More than 20,000 tonnes of Allied bombs rained down upon the peninsula, keeping the remaining Japanese forces underground and impotent. When the war ended, they were still there.

On 19 September 1994 Tavurvur and Vulcan re-awoke with relatively little warning, utterly destroying Rabaul (see boxed text, p148). Only two people died but 50,000 people lost their homes and one of PNG's most developed and picturesque cities was flattened again. In the following weeks buildings creaked under the weight of the falling ash and collapsed. There was widespread looting.

Today the region's seismic activity is measured more conscientiously than ever and the vulcanology observatory posts regular bulletins. Tavurvur's spectacular emissions of smoke and noise are not presently considered dangerous.

Gazelle Peninsula

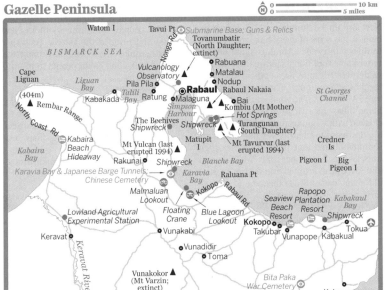

Geography & Rainfall

New Britain is a long, narrow, mountainous island. The interior is harsh and rugged, split by gorges and fast-flowing rivers, and blanketed in thick rainforest. The Pomio and Jacquinot Bay area receives more than 6500mm of rainfall each year, while annual rainfall in the Blanche Bay and Simpson Harbour area is about 2000mm.

Culture

Most of the 184,000 people in ENB are Tolai, who share many cultural similarities with southern New Irelanders. Traditional enemies of the Tolai (see p140), the seminomadic Baining people of the mountains perform fire dances, which are a spectacular event. Gigantic bark-cloth masks with emphasised eyes and features are worn by dancers who walk on – and *eat* – red-hot coals.

Secret male societies play an important role in village life, organising ceremonies and maintaining customary laws. Tolai ceremonies feature leaf-draped, anonymous figures topped by masks – *tumbuans* and *dukduks,* which are constructed deep in the bush under tremendous taboo. He who dances in the mask is no longer himself, but rather the collective *kastom* (custom) of the tribe's long history. The most feared spirits are the *masalais,* which are spirits of the bush and water that live in certain rock pools and *dewel pleses* (thickets).

Shell money retains its cultural significance for the Tolai and is used mostly for bride price. Little shells are strung on lengths of cane and bound together in great rolls called *loloi.*

East New Britain Province

A basic network of coastal roads and two towns make this the most developed province in the New Guinea islands. With the once-beautiful city of Rabaul levelled by the volcanic eruptions of 1994, Kokopo is now the main centre. Between the two, a strip of villages hug the shore of Blanche Bay. Behind them, beyond the copra plantations and the occasional town, the Baining Mountains give way to a green expanse of bush and volcanic peaks.

KOKOPO

Kokopo is an opportunistic town. It has literally risen from ashes. Kokopo started to develop just after Rabaul was flattened by the volcanic eruptions of 1994. While you can feel a palpable melancholy in Rabaul, Kokopo feels more optimistic. The town

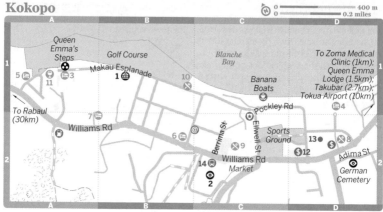

Kokopo

◎ Sights
1 East New Britain Historical & Cultural Centre...B1
2 Kokopo Market...C2

⊜ Sleeping
3 Gazelle International Hotel.....................A1
4 Kokopo Beach Bungalow Resort...........D1
5 Kokopo Village Resort.............................A1
6 Taklam Lodge..B2
7 Vavagil..A2

⊗ Eating
Kokopo Market...............................(see 2)
8 Andersons Foodland...............................D2
Breezeway Restaurant....................(see 5)

Haus Win..(see 4)
9 Paradise Food Centre..............................C2
10 Vavagil Restaurant...................................B1

⊖ Drinking
11 Ralum Country Club................................. A1

⊕ Information
12 ANZ...D2
ENB Tourist Bureau ....(see 1)
Post Office.......................................(see 12)

⊕ Transport
13 Air Niugini...D2
14 PMV Stop..C2

emanates a sense of confidence, pride and zing. But it lacks Rabaul's mysterious aura.

Kokopo is serviceable, with a good range of well-organised accommodation options, banks, government services, a couple of internet cafes and lots of businesses, but there are no big-ticket sights.

If you come from mainland PNG, Kokopo is a good base to set your body clock to island time, get your bearings and make the most of the infrastructure before heading out to rougher areas found in the New Guinea islands.

◎ Sights & Activities

The beaches around Kokopo are nothing to write home about. If you're after that perfect beach or a good snorkelling spot, it's worth considering taking a day trip to the Duke of York Islands.

East New Britain Historical & Cultural Centre   MUSEUM

(Map p142; Makau Esplanade; admission K5; ⊙9am-5pm Mon-Sat) The rewarding East New Britain Historical & Cultural Centre has a fine collection of historical objects, photographs and many WWII relics. A cassowary and a pair of blue-eyed cockatoos reside in the yard.

Blanche Bay   WATERFRONT

(Map p142) The best place to soak up the atmosphere is the waterfront, where banana boats (speed boats) pull up on the east end of the beach and their drivers wait for a fare or go fishing. These boats come and go from all over the province, the Duke of Yorks and New Ireland. The operators usually sleep through the midday heat under the big trees or gather in small groups, playing cards and string-band music on their salty ghetto blasters.

Kokopo market · MARKET

(Map p142; Williams Rd; ⊘closed Sun) The buzzing Kokopo market is also well worth a stroll. It's best on Saturday. *Buai* (betel nut) and its condiments, *daka* (mustard stick) and *cumbung* (mineral lime, which looks rather like cocaine in its little plastic wraps) account for half of the stalls, with produce such as fruit, vegetables, smoked fish and crabs accounting for the remainder. At the rear, tobacco growers sell dried leaves; home-made cigars wrapped with sticky tape at the mouth end sell for 30t each.

Kabaira Dive · DIVING

(☑982 9400, 7202 9266; kabairadive.com; Rapopo Plantation Resort) Kabaira Dive, with offices at Rapopo Plantation Resort as well as Kabaira Beach Hideaway (p149), offers a range of day trips (two dives K352). Equipment rental is K110. It's an excellent centre with professional staff. For information on diving in the area, see p26.

☞ Tours

You can arrange tours at Taklam Lodge, Kokopo Beach Bungalow Resort, Rapopo Plantation Resort and Kokopo Village Resort. Popular excursions (half-/full day from K350/650 for two people) travel from Kokopo to Rabaul, taking in all the sights along the way, including Mt Vulcan and the Submarine Base and tunnels. Harbour cruises are also available.

✯ Festivals & Events

Warwagira Festival · FESTIVAL

The Warwagira Festival (first two weeks of July) is a great occasion, the last three days of which *dukduks* and *tumbuans* (masked forest spirits; *dukduks* are the taller ones) come out of the sea from canoes at dawn to dance. At night Baining fire dancers perform, fire walking in huge masks, with a live snake. Call the ENB Tourist Bureau (p145) or one of the hotels to confirm the date and the exact location (it takes place in either Kokopo or in Rabaul).

⌚ Sleeping

Rapopo Plantation Resort · RESORT $$$

(Map p141; ☑982 9944; www.rapopo.com; r K625-825; ✳@☒) This beautifully designed resort is set amid fig and coconut trees, with immaculate lawns, a large pool and a pretty beach. Expect trim, amply sized rooms with all mod cons, and the added lure of sweeping views of the bay and Tavurvur. Other perks include a stylish open-sided restaurant and a dive centre. It's a mellow and comfortable place to stay, but far from the town centre.

Kokopo Beach Bungalow Resort · BUNGALOWS $$$

(Map p142; ☑982 8788; www.kbb.com.pg; r incl breakfast from K520-650; ✳@☒) Being a little island of subdued glamour, this well-run establishment is peacefully set amid greenery, with a pretty pool and steps leading down to a peaceful beach. The handsome wood-carved bungalows scattered in the lush garden are attractive, as are the more spacious suites. Most units have sweet vistas over the bay. There's an excellent outdoor bar-restaurant with good food and mesmerising views.

Queen Emma Lodge · LODGE $$

(off Map p142; ☑982 9206; queenemmalodge@swt.global.net.pg; r K352-385; ✳) Located 1km east of the town centre, Queen Emma has attractively designed wood-panelled rooms that open on to a common deck with garden or waterfront views. There's a good restaurant, an outdoor thatch-roof bar and a tour desk (and pricey car hire). A new wing with less-expensive budget rooms may open soon. Free airport transfers.

Taklam Lodge · HOTEL $$

(Map p142; ☑982 8870; www.taklam.com.pg; Williams Rd; r incl breakfast K225-400, without bathroom incl breakfast K185; ✳) With a good location near the town centre, Taklam is a rambling place with rooms ranging from small, tile-floored and windowless (near reception), to sunnier quarters with wood floors upstairs. You can arrange tours here, and it's run by the same management as Kokopo Beach Bungalow Resort, meaning you can catch a free lift there for a meal or to lounge by the pool or on the beach.

Seaview Beach Resort · GUESTHOUSE $$

(Map p141; ☑982 8447; seaview_bresort@global.net.pg; r K198-297, without bathroom K160-253; ✳☒) The rooms are rather institutional (cinderblock walls and fluorescent lighting) and there aren't any amenities (aside from laundry service and kitchen access), though it is just steps to a pebbly beach, where you can stroll to Rapopo Plantation Resort for a bang-up meal. Free pick-up from the airport.

Takubar · LODGE $$

(off Map p142; ☑982 8501; takubar@global.net.pg; r without bathroom with fan/air-con K140/170; ✳) Takubar has clean but basic rooms set inside a wooden bunkhouse-style building with shared bathrooms at the back. There's an outdoor bar spread along a muddy beachfront that gets quite lively on weekends (take note light sleepers). Airport transfers cost K21.

Vavagil GUESTHOUSE $
(Map p142; ☑982 9014; vavagil@global.net.pg; d K220-242, s/d without bathroom K132/143; ❋) Vavagil has a medley of rooms, from dark budget quarters with spongy beds, low ceilings and lino floors to brighter doubles with clean private bathrooms. Light sleepers should avoid rooms fronting noisy Williams Rd. Free airport transfers.

Kokopo Village Resort RESORT$$
(Map p142; ☑982 9096; www.kokoporesort.com. pg; off Williams Rd; s K160-180, d K340-500; ❋@🖙) This ageing resort consists of a series of two-storey buildings with red corrugated roofs, as well as an on-site restaurant and a tour desk. The cheaper, boxy rooms beside the reception are best avoided, though the much more appealing deluxe rooms cost a premium.

Gazelle International Hotel HOTEL $$$
(Map p142; ☑ 982 5600; www.gazelleinternational hotel.com; Makau Esplanade; r K400-560; ❋🖙🏊) New in 2010, the Gazelle has comfy, modern rooms with balconies (the best with waterfront views) and ample amenities (including a decent restaurant), though it's a rather soulless place. Heavily discounted weekend rates (from K280).

🍴 Eating

Rapopo Plantation Resort INTERNATIONAL $$$
(Map p141; ☑982 9944; mains K40-75; ☺breakfast, lunch & dinner) Kokopo's top dining spot is a beautifully designed, open-sided affair with an array of nicely prepared dishes, including mud crab, grills, lobster, daily specials and pastas.

Steak House STEAKHOUSE $$
(☑982 9206; mains K32-46; ☺breakfast, lunch & dinner) The Queen Emma Lodge serves up sizzling rump, eye fillet, T-Bone steaks and less beefy options, like sweet-and-sour pork, crumbed fish of the day, seafood laksa and even pizzas. The dining room has a wooden floor and is strung with artefacts, adding a mildly exotic tropical air to the proceedings.

Haus Win ASIAN $$
(Map p142; ☑982 8870; mains K38-88; ☺breakfast, lunch & dinner) Inside the Kokopo Beach Bungalows Resort, Haus Win serves up some of the city's best dishes. The Asian-influenced menu showcases regional delicacies such as Kavieng crab and New Ireland lobster. Other hits include coconut-coated prawns, sweet-and-sour pork and Thai chilli prawns. The photogenic dining room, complete with thatch roof and orchids on the tables, has lovely bay views.

Breezeway Restaurant INTERNATIONAL $$
(Map p142; ☑982 9096; Williams Rd; mains K30-55; ☺breakfast, lunch & dinner) Kokopo Village Resort's restaurant has an uninspiring interior, but if you dine out on the veranda you can enjoy superb views over the bay. Highlights include stir-fries, grilled steak or fish, garlic brandy prawns and Kavieng lobster.

Vavagil Restaurant PUB $$
(Map p142; Makau Esplanade; mains K20-35; ☺breakfast, lunch & dinner) This small, boxy eatery and drinking spot offers filling meals (kebabs, fish and chips, barbecue pork spareribs, pizzas) best enjoyed on the thatch-roof terrace overlooking the coast.

Kokopo market MARKET $
(Map p142; Williams Rd; ☺closed Sun) The place to head to if you want to stock up on fruit and vegetables. You can buy sausage and rice or fish, pumpkin and banana (with lots of tasty greens) wrapped in a banana leaf for K2 to K3.

Paradise Food Centre BAR $
(Map p142; Williams Rd; mains K7-8; ☺7.30am-6.30pm) This *kai* bar (cheap takeaway food bar) lures in passers-by with its rockin' music out the front (it's quiet inside), clean-ish, fan-cooled interior and belly-filling stews and fried chicken.

Andersons Foodland SUPERMARKET $
(Map p142; Williams Rd; mains K5-8; ☺8am-6pm Mon-Sat, 9am-2pm Sun) This higher-end supermarket is well stocked, with a selection of Australian imports. There's a *kai* bar near the entrance, as well as a bakery with some of the best house-made savoury pies in PNG (steak and mushroom, egg and bacon), plus muffins and cakes (try the fluffy banana cake).

🍷 Drinking

If all you need is a cold beer and a chilled-out vibe, the bars at Rapopo Plantation Resort, Queen Emma Lodge, Kokopo Village Resort and Kokopo Beach Bungalow Resort are worth investigating.

Ralum Country Club PUB

(Map p142; ⊙noon-9pm Sat-Thu, to 2am Fri) A mix of expats and nationals come to this laid-back spot with sea-fronting veranda. In addition to cold drinks (and darts!), Ralum has good-value lunch and dinner specials (mains K25 to K30). For a slice of island life, don't miss the weekly Joker Draw on Friday evening.

❶ Information

ANZ (Map p142; Williams Rd; ⊙9am-3pm Mon-Thu, to 4pm Fri) Has a guarded ATM (Visa, MasterCard), open from 7am to 7pm.

Bank South Pacific (Map p142; Williams Rd; ⊙9am-3pm Mon-Thu, to 4pm Fri) Has four guarded ATMs (Visa only), open from 6am to 7pm. Central.

ENB Tourist Bureau (Map p141; ☎982 8657; ⊙8am-4pm Mon-Fri) Located at the ENB Historical & Cultural Centre.

Police (Map p142; ☎982 8222)

Post office (Map p142; ⊙8.30am-4pm Mon-Fri)

Ngiits Internet Cafe (Map p142; per hr K25; ⊙8am-4.30pm Mon-Fri, 9am-2pm Sat) Near Taklam Lodge.

Zoma Medical Clinic (off Map p142; Williams Rd; ☎982 9356, after hours 982 9718; ⊙8am-5pm Mon-Fri, to 1pm Sat) Private clinic, east of the town centre.

❶ Getting There & Away

AIR

The Kokopo-Rabaul area is serviced by Tokua airport, 10km east of Kokopo. **Air Niugini** Kokopo (Map p142; ☎982 9033); Tokua airport (☎983 9821) has one to two daily flights to Port Moresby (K600 to K780, two hours) and three flights weekly to Hoskins (K318 to K493, 35 minutes). There are also daily flights (except Sunday) to Kavieng (K321 to K441, 40 minutes) and Buka (K400 to K550, 45 minutes, four weekly).

BOAT

Banana boats tie up on the beach near the post office and make regular departures to New Ireland (K60, two to three hours) from about 10am to 3pm. Solwara Meri is among the most reliable operators (see p158).

❶ Getting Around

CAR

Daily 4WD hire (K240, plus K1.20 per kilometre) is costly. Add another K50 to K120 per day for a driver (recommended). The following companies have offices at Tokua airport:

Avis (☎982 8179)

Budget (☎983 9391)

Hertz (☎982 9152)

Travelcar (☎982 9206; reservations@swt. com.pg) Also at Queen Emma Lodge.

PMV

The main PMV stop is just in front of the market. PMV 9, signed 'Tokua' on the windscreen, runs to the airport (K2, infrequent). This bus tends to meet the larger Air Niugini flights. Guesthouses and hotels can provide transfers (K30).

PMV 1 runs along the coast road past the Karavia barge tunnel (K2) to Rabaul (K3.10). Take PMV 2 to Warangoi (K3). PMV 3 goes to Vunadidir (K2.50) and Toma (K3.80), offering the chance to see the inland of the Gazelle Peninsula and perhaps a glimpse of the Baining mountains. PMV 5 goes to Keravat (K4) and Kabaira Bay (K5). PMV 8 goes to Vunapope and Takubar (70t). For Bita Paka War Cemetery, take PMV 9 and ask the driver to drop you there (K2). The return trip is a bit more tricky; you'll have to wait for the bus, or walk to the main coastal road. Start early.

TAXI

For metered taxis, call **Ark** (☎940 8693).

FROM KOKOPO TO RABAUL

A poignant site, **Bita Paka War Cemetery** (Map p141; ⊙dawn-dusk) contains the graves of over 1000 Allied war dead, many of them Indian slaves. The gardens are lovely. It's 8km off the main airport road; the turn-off (signposted) is about 2km east of Rapopo Plantation Resort.

The coast road goes past Raluana Point, around Karavia Bay before squeezing between Vulcan and the hills, and then around Simpson Harbour to Rabaul.

Starting from Kokopo, you'll first drive past **Blue Lagoon Lookout** (Map p141), from where you can enjoy wonderful views of Blanche Bay with Tavurvur volcano as a fantastic backdrop. About 500m to the west, you'll come across a rusty Japanese **Floating Crane** (Map p141), which was bombed by the Allies.

Along this stretch of road are countless Japanese tunnels, including **Karavia Bay Tunnels** (Map p141), which were used as a hospital, and nearby **Japanese Barge Tunnels** (Map p141), built to hold the barges out of sight from the Allies. They were hauled to the water along rails by Indian slaves (now buried at Bita Paka War Cemetery) in order to load shipping cargo. The main tunnel contains five rusty barges, lined up nose to tail; bring a torch and K5 *kastom* (custom) price. You'll also find a small **Chinese Cemetery** (Map p141) beside the Karavia Bay Tunnels.

The huge form of **Vulcan** (Map p141) rises from the roadside. The last eruption occurred in 1994. It's possible to climb up it (for a guide, ask at Rabaul Hotel).

The Burma (Vuruga) Rd leaves the Kokopo-Rabaul Rd and climbs to **Malmaluan Lookout** (Map p141), at the Telikom tower. The views are OK, and there's an anti-aircraft gun and howitzer.

As the Burma Rd begins to dip towards the coast, it passes through the Rakunai site of **Peter ToRot's cemetery and memorial church**. Peter ToRot was a village priest who was killed by the Japanese in July 1945. His remains were beatified by John Paul II in 1995. It's moving to see a multitude of families in pressed shirts, print dresses and bare feet walk many kilometres to Sunday church.

RABAUL

Walking the forlorn streets of Rabaul is like stepping into an apocalyptic film. On 19 September 1994 Mt Tavurvur, which looms ominously to the southeast, erupted, spewing huge amounts of ash over Rabaul and the Simpson Harbour and Karavia Bay area. It buried much of this once lovely city in a desert-like landscape of black and brown ash. It's still active; you can see it belch huge plumes of smoke into the sky.

Rabaul is not completely dead, though. There's a bit of life still clinging to the market and nearby streets. East of here, Rabaul is still mostly abandoned, bar one hotel that survived the Tavurvur eruption. Thanks to the deep water (and Kokopo's shallow water), Rabaul's port facilities keep the town alive.

It's definitely worth staying a day or two in Rabaul to soak up the surreal atmosphere and explore the nearby sights.

◉ Sights

Admiral Yamamoto's Bunker   HISTORIC SITE
(Map p147; admission K5) There are tunnels and caverns in the hillsides around Rabaul. Admiral Yamamoto's Bunker is interesting though austere, and the placards near it are informative. There's a map on the ceiling for plotting world domination.

New Guinea Club &
Rabaul Museum   MUSEUM
(Map p147; admission K5) Just next door to the bunker is New Guinea Club and Rabaul Museum. Established in 1933, this club was a businessmen's club with strict guidelines for

membership. It was destroyed in WWII and rebuilt in the 1950s to its former glory, only to be destroyed again by fire in 1994. It has been partly restored and is now home to a small museum. Ask at the Rabaul Hotel for the key.

Vulcanology Observatory   LOOKOUT
(Map p141) A worthwhile site is the Vulcanology Observatory, about 900m off Tunnel Hill Rd, from where you can enjoy million-dollar views over the bay and the volcanoes.

Japanese Peace Memorial   LOOKOUT
(Map p147) The Japanese Peace Memorial, the main Japanese memorial in the Pacific, is dignified and testament to the forgiveness of the local people. There's a smashing view from here.

✦ Activities

Simpson Harbour offers several first-class **wreck dives**, while the reefs off the western tip of Gazelle Peninsula are totally unspoiled and full of healthy hard and soft corals, sponges, gorgonians and a dizzying array of tropical fish: a perfect combination. For more information on diving, see p26.

For land lubbers, there are various **hiking** options around Rabaul (p149).

Kabaira Dive Rabaul   DIVING
(☑983 9266; www.kabairadive.com.pg; 1/2 dives with tanks & weights A$75/120, with full equipment A$120/165) Run by Australian expat Stephen Woolcott, Kabaira Dive Rabaul has offices at Rapopo Plantation Resort (p143) in Kokopo as well as Kabaira Beach Hideaway (p149), a few fin strokes from splendid reefs. If you're a keen diver, it's best to base yourself at the Kabaira Beach Hideaway.

☞ Tours

Rabaul Hotel   TOUR
(Map p147; ☑982 1999; www.rabaulhotel.com.pg; Mango Ave) Rabaul Hotel offers great and affordable possibilities, including local WWII heritage trips, hot-spring dips, village stays, river-rafting trips, canoe/walking trips to see the megapode colonies on Matupit Island (K70 per person) and Indiana Jones–style multiday jungle treks across the Baining Mountains, through incredibly biodiverse forests.

✦ Festivals & Events

Warwagira Festival   FESTIVAL
For details on the Warwagira Festival, see p143. Its location alternates between Kokopo and Rabaul.

Rabaul

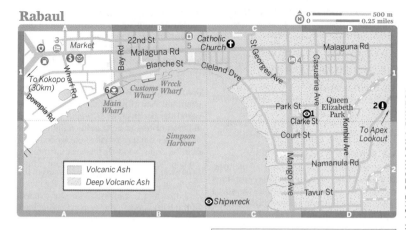

🛏 Sleeping & Eating

This is ground zero; staying here rather than Kokopo gives you that 'I was there' feeling. That said, services are limited, with dining fairly limited to the Rabaul Hotel, the market, or the food shops and *kai* bars facing the market.

Barike Lodge   GUESTHOUSE $

(Map p147; ☎982 1034; Malaguna Rd; s without bathroom with fan/air-con K80/110, d without bathroom with air-con K120; 🌣) A betel nut's throw from the market, Barike has cramped rooms with thin, battered mattresses and basic shared bathrooms. But it's tolerable and cheap (at least for PNG). There's a small bar at the back.

Rabaul Hotel   HOTEL $$

(Map p147; ☎982 1999; www.rabaulhotel.com.pg; Mango Ave; r K165-385; 🌣@🌊) Rabaul Hotel is Australian-run and has a wide array of prices, from simple, economical rooms to comfy, larger units with all the mod cons. Other strong points include the wide array of tours on offer, decent meals at the on-site restaurant (mains K32 to K60) and a convivial bar. Airport transfers cost K83 each way.

🛍 Shopping

PNG Diabetic Centre   HANDICRAFTS

(Map p147; ⊙8am-5pm Mon-Fri, to noon Sat) This place is a treasure trove for artefact hunters, with masks, necklaces, shells, carvings and other souvenirs.

❶ Information

Bank South Pacific (Map p147; ☎982 1744; ⊙8.45am-3pm Mon-Thu, to 4pm Fri) Changes cash and travellers cheques and can do cash advances on your credit card.

Rabaul

◎ Sights
1 Admiral Yamamoto's Bunker D1
2 Japanese Peace Memorial D1
   New Guinea Club & Rabaul
     Museum .... (see 1)

⊙ Activities, Courses & Tours
   Rabaul Hotel .... (see 4)

⊜ Sleeping
3 Barike Lodge A1
4 Rabaul Hotel C1

🛍 Shopping
5 PNG Diabetic Centre B1

❶ Transport
   Airlines PNG .... (see 4)
6 Rabaul Shipping (Star Ships) B1

❶ Getting There & Away

Rabaul is serviced by Tokua airport (p145). **Airlines PNG** (Map p147; ☎982 1962) has an office at Rabaul Hotel.

For information about banana-boat travel around New Britain and through the nearby islands, see p145.

Rabaul Shipping (Star Ships; Map p147) has weekly passenger boats sailing from Rabaul to Lae via Kimbe. It also sails to Buka and Kavieng. After the ferry sinking in 2012, with tragic loss of life, we don't recommend travelling on these often overloaded boats.

❶ Getting Around

Tokua airport is about 40km from the town. PMVs run out to Tokua, and Rabaul Hotel can also provide transfers.

There aren't many PMVs on Sunday. PMV 1 goes from Rabaul to Kokopo (K3.10) and back. PMV 6 goes to the Vulcanology Observatory (inform the driver), Submarine Base and Nonga Hospital. PMV 5 goes to Rakunai (Peter ToRot's memorial church) and PMV 4 goes to Malmaluan Lookout.

AROUND RABAUL

The easiest way to visit the sights around Rabaul if you're pressed for time is to take a day tour. Your hotel can arrange a vehicle and a guide.

◉ Sights

Matupit Island   ISLAND

(Map p141) The September 1994 eruptions should have destroyed little Matupit Island but the prevailing winds brought Tavurvur's load over Rabaul and left this island almost unscathed thanks, villagers say, to the local *dukduks*. The thousand-strong village community still chooses to reside right underneath the belching monster. You can hire a canoeist to get you around to see Tavurvur's southern slopes (which have giant lava flows) from the water. It's like a peek at a newborn planet. The megapode-egg hunters are here, burrowing almost 2m into the black sand to retrieve the eggs. In the same area, there's quite a smattering of Japanese aircraft wreckage scattered among the palm trees and now semi-buried in earth, including a **Japanese Betty Bomber** and a helicopter. They are close to the **Old Rakunai Airport**. The airport was completely destroyed during the 1994 eruption. *Kastom* fee is K5. From there, you can easily reach the **hot springs** – an impressive sight amid an eerie landscape that's reminiscent of the film *Mad Max*.

Beehives   LANDMARK

(Map p141) The two rocky pinnacles rising from the centre of Simpson Harbour are called the Beehives, or Dawapia Rocks, and are said to be the hard core of the original old volcano. You can visit them by boat and there is some good diving and swimming. Taklam Lodge (p143) and Rabaul Hotel (p147) can organise harbour boat trips that take in the Beehives.

Submarine Base   HISTORIC SITE

(Map p141; admission K15) For a picnic spot, nothing can beat the Submarine Base at Tavui Point. The Japanese used to provision submarines here during the war. There are tunnel and rail track remnants below and **guns and relics** (Map p141) in the hills above, but it was a 'base' in so far as the Japanese pulled their submarines up to the vertical wall and then surfaced, allowing soldiers to walk off over the reef. This site also makes for a wonderful snorkelling spot; the coral bed is flat and almost horizontal until it drops down a 75m vertical reef wall. To get there, catch PMV 6 from the central PMV stop opposite Rabaul's new market on Malaguna Rd.

DEAD TOWN

Pre-1990s Rabaul had a hustle and bustle, but it was a laid-back kind of place that was very friendly. It had the biggest market in the South Pacific, an orchid park, playgrounds and swimming pools.

There was a great music scene in Rabaul and PNG's thriving local music industry originated there. Rabaul's Pacific Gold Studios was the South Pacific's first recording studio. Now Rabaul is flattened – in 1994 it collapsed under the weight of 1m to 2m of Tavurvur's volcanic load.

For several days after the eruption, there were severe earthquakes as Tavurvur and Vulcan went at it, and Rabaul was evacuated. The dead of night would be broken by the sound of a building groaning as it eventually succumbed to the weight of ash on its roof.

However, the Rabaul Hotel is standing proof that most of the town could have been saved. Over several days the staff made a joint effort to clear the flat roof of the piling ash. Rabaul was never swamped by lava, only by slowly piling ash that weighed as much as concrete. Rabaul might have been dusted off without being very damaged with a round-the-clock shovelling effort and a bit of protection from the hundreds of looters who paraded around with new clothes and stereos immediately after the blast.

Look a few degrees higher and you can see the rim of the old caldera with its five volcanoes, one still occasionally smoking, and remember where you are. Beneath the earth, under your feet, is the old town.

🏃 Activities

Volcanoes
LANDMARK

(Map p141) For the energetic, hiking up the volcanoes can be fun and thrilling, though it's suicidal to climb the smouldering **Mt Tavurvur**. They're all tracked, but there's often a good chance of getting lost – your best bet is to take a guide from Rabaul Hotel (from K50 per person). If you want a recommendation, go for the 688m **Kombiu**. You'll be up and down in 2½ hours if you're reasonably fit. The views from the top are superb. Another must-do is the **Rabaul Nakaia**, which features the shortest climb (about 30 minutes from the base of the volcano); beware once you've reached the narrow rim of the caldera – it's easy to feel dizzy and lose your balance. The slopes of **Mt Vulcan** are a bit trickier; they are scored with deep cracks from mud-ash drying and contracting, and can be 4m to 5m deep. They can be hard to spot now they're vegetated.

Local Walks
WALKING

There are excellent walking routes around Rabaul, and you can spend hours just walking around the town overawed by its complete annihilation.

You can hike down to Matupit Island and back (although someone will probably offer you a lift) and the views from the Vulcanology Observatory also make it a rewarding walk.

If you're fit, you can climb Namanula Rd to meet the north coast road near Matalau. From here you can head north along the coast road, which rises over a pass and meets the Nonga-Submarine Base Rd. PMV 6 runs regularly to Nonga Hospital and sometimes beyond. Or you could walk the whole loop over Tunnel Hill Rd and take in the Vulcanology Observatory along the way. This would take about a day.

Rabaul Hotel
RAFTING

(Map p147; ☎982 1999; www.rabaulhotel.com.pg; Mango Ave) Rabaul Hotel offers white-water rafting trips on the scenic Warangoi River amid spectacular jungle scenery – you'll feel teletransported to the Amazon. No need to be sporty – you'll paddle at approximately 5km/h on an inflatable, a canoe, a tyre tube or manmade bamboo rafts, and there are no graded rapids. A full-day trip will set you back K350.

🛏 Sleeping & Eating

Kabaira Beach Hideaway
BUNGALOWS $$

(Map p141; ☎983 9266; www.kabairabeachhideaway. com; Kabaira Bay; s/d incl 3 meals K200/350, bungalow s/d incl 3 meals K300/450; 🖤) This quaint and laid-back Australian-run resort on the waterfront radiates a ramshackle air, and combines friendly informality and a picturesque setting. Lodgers can stay in one of four simple all-wood rooms with shared bathrooms or overnight in one of several roomier bungalows, each with a private bathroom. There's excellent swimming and snorkelling on the house reef and fantastic diving a short boat ride from the guesthouse. The cooking receives high marks. There's an on-site dive centre (p146), and a host of activities can be arranged, including Robinson Crusoe–style picnics (or overnights) on nearby islands. It's about 40 minutes from Rabaul on PMV 5 (infrequent), though you may have to transfer at Basis. Airport transfers are K50 one way. Free laundry. Reserve ahead.

West New Britain Province

If you read this section, there's a great chance that you're a diver heading to Kimbe Bay. Kimbe Bay has become a byword for underwater action, with an amazing array of marine life and sensational reefs brushing the surface. However, there is life above the water as well, with some spectacular volcanoes brooding in the background and a handful of WWII relics. WNB has the country's greatest proliferation of volcanoes – five active and 16 dormant – and you can literally smell the sulphur in the air. It's also PNG's highest timber and palm-oil exporter with consequent tension between the province's villagers and settlers.

🛈 Getting There & Away

From Port Moresby, **Air Niugini** (☎983 5287) flies to and from Hoskins (K354 to K700, once or twice daily), Kokopo (K318 to K493, twice weekly) and Lae (K376 to K542, once weekly). To reach Kavieng, you'll have to transit through Kokopo.

🛈 Getting Around

There are a few 4WD logging roads (in the dry season) leading towards the rugged and virtually unexplored mountains of the interior. PMVs go from Hoskins to Kimbe (K8, 40 minutes), where you can then transfer to a PMV towards Talasea.

TALASEA, KIMBE BAY & THE WILLAUMEZ PENINSULA

Talasea is an active volcanic region set in a dramatic landscape. Lake Dakataua, at the tip, was formed in a colossal eruption in 1884. It's worth seeing two WWII plane wrecks that lie partially disintegrated in the jungle near Talasea. There's a Mitchell B-25 Bomber and a Lockheed Vega Ventura – an impressive sight.

If you need to relax, take a dip in the **Garu Hot River**. Waters are comfortably warm and there's a mini-waterfall; the red, claylike mud on the banks has reputed health benefits. Outdoorsy types might consider **trekking** up the active Mt Garbuna. The area also offers excellent **birdwatching** possibilities.

Everything you need to know about Kimbe Bay's marine environment and coral reef habitats should become clear at the **Mahonia Na Dari Conservation Centre** (☎983 4241; www.mahonia.org; Kimbe Bay; admission free; ☉8am-4pm Mon-Sat), next door to the Walindi Plantation Resort. This marine research centre is open to the public.

Apart from the superb natural surroundings and rare birds, the main attraction here is the unsurpassable **diving** in Kimbe Bay. You might see anything from a tiny glass prawn to a pod of killer whales. The marine biodiversity is stunning, with more than 350 types of hard coral and 860 species of fish vying for your attention. Drift along the reefs and enjoy the ultimate underwater drama.

The Walindi Plantation Resort has a very professional **dive centre** (☎983 5441; www.walindi.com, www.walindifebrina.com). Expect to pay A\$182 for two dives on a day-dive boat. A multiday open-water course costs A\$540. For more information on diving, see p26.

The town of Kimbe itself is the provincial headquarters and a major centre for palm-oil production, and has no real interest for travellers.

🛏 Sleeping & Eating

Walindi Plantation Resort   RESORT $$$
(☎983 5441; www.walindi.com, www.walindifebrina.com; s/d incl 3 meals A\$204/297, s/d bungalow incl 3 meals A\$303/440; ☜) This well-established resort run by Max and Cecilie Benjamin is highly recommended for divers due to its full-service on-site dive centre and great location, and its easy access to famous dive sites in Kimbe Bay. Everything is beautifully designed here, with 12 traditional-style bungalows surrounded by jungle-like foliage that's thick with birdsong. Eight smaller but equally attractive 'plantation house' rooms provide cheaper accommodation. The service is of a high standard and the food is varied and excellent. Aside from diving, Walindi offers excellent birdwatching tours, trips up the volcano, Garu Hot Springs excursions and other activities. Airport transfers available (per person return A\$88).

Queen's Head   GUESTHOUSE $
(☎7205 0194; queensheadpng@gmail.com; r per person incl breakfast K95) This friendly, familial guesthouse has simple but clean rooms, with a shared kitchen and a mock-Tudor tavern complete with horse brasses (horseshoes). It's the best choice for budget travellers in the area and is 2km east of Walindi Plantation Resort. Airport transfers available (per person each way K50).

Mahonia Na Dari   BUNGALOWS $
(☎983 4241; www.mahonianadari.org; Kimbe Bay; dm/r per person K91/109) Next door to Walindi Plantation Resort, this place has simple but clean rooms and bungalows – when it's not booked out by scientists or school groups. There's no restaurant – either BYO and use the common kitchen, or plan to dine at Walindi.

🛍 Shopping

Le Riche Colours   GALLERY
(☎983 4990; www.picturetrail.com/leriche; Kimbe) It's worth stopping at Le Riche Colours if you are after some original souvenirs. Artist Nathalie Le Riche has very colourful hand-painted T-shirts, tribal stickers, gift cards, placemats, and other gifts that feature tribal portraits, market scenes and underwater compositions. Call ahead, as the shop keeps irregular hours.

❶ Information

The Bank South Pacific and Westpac are one block south (inland) of Kmart supermarket in Kimbe. Both are equipped with ATMs (Visa and MasterCard). East of there are the post office and daily market.

NEW IRELAND PROVINCE

Forget the 21st century in New Ireland. It really isn't important whether your friends believe that you re-enacted your Swiss Family Robinson fantasies on a remote island, discussed the fine art of carving with a master carver, acquainted yourself with the intriguing traditions of Malagan, stayed in a traditional guesthouse amid a landscape that belongs to the dinosaur age and witnessed a shark-calling ceremony. It's just important that you savour such uplifting experiences.

Few other places in PNG can boast such an interesting and accessible pick 'n' mix of nature, culture and landscapes. Sure, New Ireland doesn't offer the thrill of puffing volcanoes (in this respect, New Britain steals the show), but it boasts broad white-sand beaches and rivers of clear water tumbling down from the thickly forested central Schleinitz Range and a clutch of secluded islands off the 'mainland'.

For fans of traditional cultures, New Ireland is an unmissable destination. In the rugged south is the spiritual home of Tumbuan culture. The north is home to Malagan, while Kabai culture dominates in the central areas.

And there's the wonderfully down-to-earth, unfussy atmosphere. New Ireland is far less developed than New Britain. Once you cross St Georges Channel, which separates the islands, you'll notice the laid-back vibe, the more sedate pace of life and a greater emphasis on the old ways. Outside Kavieng and Namatanai, the only towns of consequence, there are coastal communities on each side of the island but no real settlements bigger than a trade store or two.

The good thing is that you can mix slow-paced sun-and-sand holidays with action-packed experiences. For outdoorsy types, the pursuit of choice is scuba diving, on an equal footing with surfing. Kayaking, sport fishing, snorkelling and even cycling (yes!) are available.

History

The remains of rock shelters found near Namatanai suggest that New Ireland was inhabited 30,000 years ago. Missionaries began arriving in 1875 along with blackbirders who forcibly removed many New Irelanders to work on the plantations and cane fields of Queensland (Australia) and Fiji.

A villainous crew, blackbirders often posed as missionaries to coax men aboard, killing them offhand if they revolted. One slaver even impersonated the bishop of Melanesia; the real incumbent, believed to be an imposter, was later killed in vengeance! Meanwhile, the shortage of males devastated village life in places.

Cannibalism and head-hunting were rife. Even a death from disease was often attributed, from certain 'signs', as the fault of another tribe, which might be mercilessly attacked in revenge. In some communities, relatives smeared themselves with the blood of their deceased loved ones as part of their funeral rites.

During the German reign, large copra plantations made New Ireland one of the most profitable parts of the colony. The tyrannical Baron Boluminski became district officer of Kavieng in 1910 and built the high-

way that bears his name by forcing each village along the coast to construct and maintain a section. He made villagers push his carriage over any deteriorated sections.

New Ireland fell to the Japanese in 1942 and Kavieng was developed into a major Japanese military base. Most of the Australians in Kavieng managed to escape, but some chose to stay behind as coastwatchers (spies).

The Allies made no attempt to retake New Ireland but rather bombed it into oblivion. The Japanese surrendered in Namatanai on 19 September 1945.

Geography & Climate

New Ireland is mountainous and riddled with huge, flooded caves. Midway down the island, the Lelet Plateau rises to 1481m and further south, near Taron, the Hans Meyer Range reaches 2399m. A fault line provides passage for the Weitin and Kamdaru rivers.

The area between Namatanai and Kavieng receives about 3m of annual rainfall and has a dry season between May and November. December to March is the cyclone season and can bring high seas.

Culture

The people of New Ireland are Melanesian and speak 19 local languages. The north embodies the complex system of spiritual traditions of Malagan cultures. 'Malagan' also refers to the northern New Irelanders' carvings (see boxed text, p155).

In the island's south are the Tumbuan traditions. The people from the south invaded the Gazelle Peninsula and settled the Duke of York Group several hundred years ago. *Dukduks* and *tumbuans* are common to all three cultures. Around Namatanai and central New Ireland are the Kabai traditions, which are not yet as well understood.

As in most PNG islands, traditional clan power is wielded by chiefs or *bigmen* (important men or leaders), but clan rites and land claims are passed on in a matrilineal system.

Kavieng

Being the capital of New Ireland, Kavieng is the only town of any size in the province, but we're hardly talking Shanghai – the tallest construction is the telecommunication tower, and the busiest shops operate very much on Melanesian time. If you proceed from Kokopo, you'll find it remarkably low-key

Kavieng

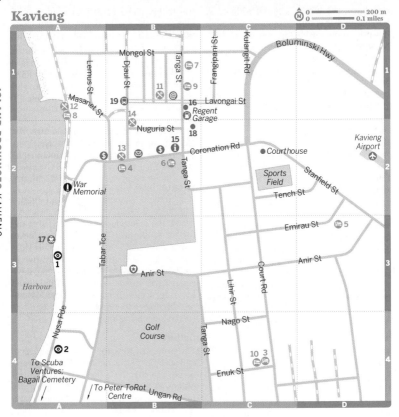

Kavieng

⊙ Sights

🛏 Sleeping

✕ Eating

ⓘ Information

ⓘ Transport

and quiet, with few cars in the streets. The seaside ambience, with its fisheries and tranquil wharf, and the bustling market in the shade of huge trees, create a dash of real life.

Kavieng itself won't fulfil all your fantasies of a tropical paradise, but it's optimally situated as a springboard to neighbouring islands, including Nusa Lik Island and Lavongai (New Hanover), and for explorations down the coast. There's good snorkelling and kayaking offshore and there's plenty of great diving in the area – not to mention excellent surf breaks.

◉ Sights

Pickings for sightseers are quite slim in spread-out Kavieng.

The northern end of **Nusa Pde** provides the setting for a lovely waterfront walk; the huge fig trees almost meet overhead. If you keep heading north of the Malagan Beach Resort, you will reach the intimate surrounds of **Patailu village**.

The southern section of Nusa Pde continues past the **market** and further along on the left are the **provincial government buildings**, built on the site of Baron Boluminski's residence.

The closest thing Kavieng has to a regular 'sight' is the **Bagail Cemetery**, where Boluminski was buried. The tough guy's grave is right before you as you enter the cemetery.

Kavieng has a large and beautiful **harbour**. You can go down to the waterfront and catch a banana boat out to one of the many islands.

🏃 Activities

Surfing

Kavieng has an up-and-coming surf scene, with a good range of reef breaks, both lefts and rights, that are easily accessible. They vary in difficulty, depending on the size and direction of the swell. From November to late April, swells of up to 2.4m are not unheard of. Even if it's growing in popularity, the **Niu Ailan Surfriders Alliance** (www.surfingpng -newireland.org.pg) ensures that the number of surfers is kept at a sustainable level thanks to a surf quota system. Among the most thrilling spots are Pikinini, Karanas, Nago Island, Edmago Island, Long Longs and Ral Island. For more information, contact the guys at Nusa Island Retreat (they are surf specialists and can arrange surf packages).

Diving

No less impressive is diving, with a wide array of high-voltage sites. Expect drift dives in action-packed passages, thriving reefs and wreck dives. For more information on diving, see p27.

Lissenung Island Resort   DIVING
(☑984 2526; www.lissenung.com; Lissenung Island; 1-/2-tank dive K220/374, equipment hire K$72) This resort has a full-service dive shop. Free pick-ups can be arranged from Kavieng.

Scuba Ventures   DIVING
(☑984 1244; www.scubakavieng.com; Nusa Pde) Dorian and Cara run Scuba Ventures, an excellent dive shop on the waterfront. A single boat dive will set you back A$88 (A$154 for a two-tank dive). Save GST (10%) by pre-booking from home. Dive packages available (with accommodation at Nusa Island Retreat).

Other Activities

Other sporting opportunities include **canoeing** and **kayaking**. You can hire a canoe from Nusa Island Retreat and paddle around Nusa Lik Island. Tailored guided kayaking trips in the Lavongai (New Hanover) area are also available.

For cycling trips, see boxed text, p158.

☞ Tours

Nusa Island Retreat can arrange tours, including snorkelling and surfing trips, and can arrange land tours.

PNG Explorer   SURFING TOUR
(☑984 1803; www.pngsurfaris.com) Offers high standard, seven- to 10-day cruises off New Ireland aboard a splendid 23m vessel that accommodates up to 12 passengers on surfaris and diving and fishing trips.

✲ Festivals & Events

Malagan Festival   FESTIVAL
The week-long Malagan Festival is usually held in July and includes dances and feasting. It sometimes takes place in Namatanai. Contact the New Ireland Tourist Bureau (p156) for details.

🛏 Sleeping

IN KAVIENG

Venbert   GUESTHOUSE $$
(☑984 1018; mnkawi9@gmail.com; Enuk St; r with/ without bathroom from K310/180; ❄) Venbert is an excellent option for its clean, airy rooms set on a quiet residential street. The fan-only rooms with shared facilities are upstairs and open on to a nicely set veranda. There's a guest kitchen, a lounge room and,

perhaps most importantly, a washing machine. Venbert is a friendly, family-run affair and warmly recommended. The big cooked breakfast (K15) is a deal.

Kalaro GUESTHOUSE $$

(☑984 2546; Enuk St; r with/without bathroom incl breakfast from K360/230; ❄) A few doors down from Venbert, Kalaro is a fine option with clean, well-maintained rooms, a lounge and a guest kitchen.

Peter ToRot Centre GUESTHOUSE $

(☑984 2684; Tabar Tce; dm K25, d without bathroom K60-100) The cheapest place in town is part of a church compound, with a long corridor of depressing, windowless rooms. Look for the weather-beaten plane parked out the front.

Kavieng Niu Lodge GUESTHOUSE $$

(☑984 2420; kaviengniulodge10@gmail.com; Tanga St; s/d from K363/413, without bathroom K253/303; ❄) This friendly 15-room guesthouse has pleasant, wood-panelled rooms and sparklingly clean bathrooms. Pricier rooms are bigger and comfier with desk and chair, mini-fridge and TV.

Kavieng Guesthouse GUESTHOUSE $$

(☑984 1165; rpaika48@gmail.com; Emirau St; s/d K300/400, without bathroom K200/300; ❄) This family-run B&B in a peaceful neighbourhood has seven clean, brightly painted rooms with either wood or lino floors. There's a small lounge with TV, and an enclosed patio where you can have dinner upon request (K45).

Malagan Beach Resort RESORT $$$

(☑984 2452; Nusa Pde; r K499; ❄) Under new management, the formerly run-down Malagan is slowly renewing itself. The potential is superb: all 16 rooms have balconies that open on to the sea. Inside, you'll find wood-floors and wood-panelling, and the usual mod cons (air-con and satellite TV). The grounds include a shady strip of beach (nothing outstanding) and a seafront restaurant.

Noxie's Place GUESTHOUSE $$

(☑7369 3331; noxiesplace@gmail.com; Tanga St; r incl breakfast K198; @) A tidy six-room guesthouse with tiled floors in the fan-cooled rooms. Guests have kitchen access and bikes are available for hire (around K50 per day).

Kavieng Hotel HOTEL $$$

(☑984 2199; kavienghotel@daltron.com.pg; Coronation Rd; s/d from K495/550; ❄) Aimed towards business travellers, the rooms are clean, modern and bland, and there's a restaurant, bar and gift shop (with an internet cafe in the works). The price for all this is absurd.

Kavieng Club HOTEL $$

(☑984 2224; kaviengclub@global.net.pg; Coronation Rd; s/d from K200/230; ❄) Offers an array of ageing rooms, most of which have saggy mattresses and painted cinderblock walls. There's a bar and restaurant.

AROUND KAVIENG

Nusa Island Retreat BUNGALOWS $$

(☑984 2247; www.nusaislandretreat.com.pg; Nusa Lik Island; s A$140-150, d A$150-200, daily meals per person A$85) This tropical haven has a heavy focus on surfers (owner Sean is a dedicated surfer himself and a mine of information), but families, couples and those who just want to chill out in a serene setting are all welcome. It's as relaxed as its sand-floor bar-restaurant suggests, and has lots of thoroughly unpretentious charm. Its traditional-style beachfront bungalows, some over water, are well maintained. There are lots of cheeky birds, too. There's a good restaurant and the staff arranges a host of activities including surfing (the core activity), kayaking, cycling, snorkelling and diving. There are surf breaks close by. It's on Nusa Lik Island, just 200m across from the international wharf. Transfers are easily arranged to Kavieng.

Lissenung Island Resort RESORT $$$

(☑7234 5834; www.lissenung.com; Lissenung Island; s/d incl 3 meals K534/770, without bathroom incl 3 meals K385/660; ☎) This lovely resort makes a great base for divers or those seeking a bit of pampering on a small island partially ringed by a ribbon of white-sand beach lapped by topaz waters. Snorkelling opportunities abound on the nearby reefs (the house reef has a staggering 300 fish species) and Lissenung runs a top-notch dive outfit. There are seven attractively designed rooms set amid several traditional, thatch-roof buildings. Each is fan-cooled, with a small front veranda; all but one have a private bathroom. Local seafood and market-fresh fare make for excellent meals (owners happily cater to vegetarians and vegans with advance notice). Dive trips, fishing excursions, surf transfers and village tours are all available. Free wi-fi.

MALAGAN DEATH RITES

For centuries, it has been *kastom* (custom) for the Malagan to carve wooden masks and sacred figures for their mortuary rites. There are a few dedicated regular carvers on Tabar Island and Libba village near Konos; otherwise, carvings are done only by secret men's societies for mortuary ceremonies or rites of passage in the villages.

Different clans have different funerary traditions, including interment, cremation and burial at sea. The *tatanu* or *tanuatu* (soul) remains close to the body after death and it cannot go to the ancestors' world until the mortuary rites are performed. The spirit of a dead person enters the ancestors' world through the places that *masalais* (spirits of the bush and water) inhabit.

Feasts are often performed for more than one person as they are terribly expensive. Those deceased long ago can be included in the rite, which includes chanting, masked dancing, clouds of lime and a huge feast.

Masks may depict the totem animal of a specific tribe in stages of metamorphosis. Such was the fearful power of the mask that, in the past, they were burned after the ceremony. Designs are strictly 'patented' according to clan rites, and a complex ritual payment must be made to pass a design on to another carver. The problem is there are simply not enough young apprentices.

✕ Eating & Drinking

IN KAVIENG

Kavieng Hotel　　　　　　INTERNATIONAL $$
(Coronation Rd; mains K35-66; ☺breakfast, lunch & dinner) The dining area is nothing glam and the menu serves decent if unimaginative dishes: lamp chops, T-bone steaks, pan-fried fish. The Friday night seafood buffet (K77), however, is a worthy splurge.

Malagan Beach Resort　　INTERNATIONAL $$
(☑984 2452; Nusa Pde; buffet K30-60; ☺breakfast, lunch & dinner) Kavieng's most alluring setting is this eatery, with a breezy terrace facing the sea. The cooking formerly received low marks, though a new chef may bring quality cuisine to match the picturesque location. Regardless, Malagan is a great spot for a sundowner.

Bilas Restaurant　　　　　PIZZERIA $$
(Lavongai St; mains K30-45; ☺11am-10pm) Better known as Bamboo, this low-key spot is best known for its pizzas, though it also serves fish and chips and barbecued chicken. Seating is in the enclosed patio ringed with bamboo fencing.

Grab 'n' Go　　　　　　　BAR $
(Nusa Pde; mains K7-9; ☺lunch Mon-Sat) Next to Malagan Beach Resort, this *kai* bar serves sandwiches, roast pork rolls and other unfussy fare. Outdoor seating, or take it to the beach.

New Ireland Supermarket　　　　　　BAR $
(Coronation Rd; mains K6-8; ☺Mon-Sat) One of several well-stocked supermarkets in town,

this one also has a good *kai* bar next door, with tender fried chicken, piping hot chips, and the usual rice and stews.

Market　　　　　　　　　MARKET $
(Nusa Pde; ☺Tue-Sat) The bustling market has a good range of fresh fruit and vegetables, including the giant, yellow hand-grenade-like pandanus fruit.

Tsang Sang　　　　　　　BAKERY $
(Djaul St; ☺6am-5pm Mon-Fri, to 2pm Sat) This basic and inexpensive bakery has fresh bread and sweet cakes available early in the day.

AROUND KAVIENG

Nusa Island Retreat　　　INTERNATIONAL $$
(☑984 2247; Nusa Lik Island; lunch mains K30-40; ☺breakfast, lunch & dinner) Nonguests are welcome at Nusa Island Retreat (call ahead to arrange transfers). Indeed, it would be a shame to miss out on its dinner buffet (K65; by reservation). Or you could tuck in to a copious burger, red curry or Thai fish cake at lunchtime and take a dip once you've digested your meal. The laid-back, toes-in-the-sand dining area is first-rate.

ℹ Information

Kavieng is the only place on the island where you can change/procure money – stash cash before heading further afield.

Bank South Pacific (Coronation Rd; ☺8.45am-3pm Mon-Thu, to 4pm Fri) ATM that takes most foreign cards, plus changes cash and travellers cheques.

Bisi Works (1st fl, Lavongai St; per min 80t; ⊙8am-5pm Mon-Fri) Internet cafe with slow, pricey connections.

New Ireland Tourist Bureau (☑984 2441; www.newirelandtourism.org.pg; Tanga St; ⊙9am-4pm Mon-Fri) Can arrange bookings for village stays.

Police (☑984 2044, 984 2054)

Post office (Coronation Rd)

Scuba Ventures (☑984 1244; Nusa Pde; per hr K30; ⊙7.30am-5pm) Has one computer, as well as wi-fi access.

Westpac (Coronation Rd; ⊙9am-3pm Mon-Thu, to 4pm Fri) Changes cash and travellers cheques, and can do cash advances on your credit card (MasterCard or Visa).

❶ Getting There & Away

Air

Air Niugini (☑984 2135; Lavongai St) has flights to Kokopo/Rabaul (K321 to K441, 40 minutes, once daily Monday to Saturday), where you can also connect to Hoskins. There are also daily flights to Port Moresby (K621 to K910, two hours).

Boat

Banana boats and work boats run to the nearby islands. Boats to Lavongai Island (K30) and nearby depart weekday mornings.

Car & PMV

There are PMVs leaving Kavieng for Namatanai (K50, six to seven hours, six weekly) daily except Sunday. There are also passenger trucks and PMVs that head some or all the way to Namatanai, or elsewhere, daily except Sunday. Ask around in town.

There are a few car-hire companies in town. Depending on the rains, a 2WD will make it to Namatanai, though you'll have to take it slow on the unpaved section past Dalom. Count on K250 per day plus K1.10 per kilometre. Following are recommended options:

Drimas (☑984 1792; Tanga St)

Kavieng Hotel (☑984 2199; kavienghotel@ daltron.com.pg; Coronation Rd) Also rents 4WDs.

❶ Getting Around

PMVs around town cost K1. The airport is close to town; most accommodation offers free transfers, though there's also an airport bus (door-to-door K10). Kavieng Niu Lodge has a **taxi** (☑7274 5232, 7274 5239).

Lavongai (New Hanover) & East Islands

Is this the province's best-kept secret? Hop on a banana boat in Kavieng and check it out yourself. Volcanic, ruggedly beautiful Lavongai Island, as well as the string of islands that lie scattered to the east, are the kind of places that seem to emit a magnetic force. If you're searching for paradise in its raw form, void of luxurious trappings (not a TV or hot-water shower in sight), look no further than this fascinating archipelago. Lavongai is a truly wild island, complete with dense rainforest, mountains, waterfalls and rivers. With just a handful of modest, homespun guesthouses, tourism in Lavongai and East Islands remains on a refreshingly humble scale.

🛏 Sleeping & Eating

There is no formal accommodation on Lavongai. The following guesthouses are on nearby islands, from where you can easily access Lavongai by dinghy. There's no phone, no electricity (except the odd generator, if you're lucky) and no shops (but you wanted a Robinson Crusoe experience, right?).

LIFE IN A (NEW) IRISH VILLAGE

You'll attract a lot of attention when you show up, but it'll trail off; there's a quiet respect for your privacy in most villages. Take something (preferably lasting and useful) for the kids if you can, but give it to the local school or *bigman* (leader) to redistribute. A football (there's no describing the joy), swimming goggles (you can carry quite a few and they're functional) and pens are all good gifts. Salt, sugar and tea will be appreciated by your hosts in the more remote places, but don't worry about this if you're on the tarmac road. If you're way off the beaten track, BYO rice or you'll eat your hosts out of house and home.

A torch (flashlight), sleeping sheet, mosquito net, hammock, thongs (flip-flops; coral is sharp), book and roll of toilet paper are useful items to take along. Most villages have pit toilets these days, but if not, ask about the customary spot in the river or sea.

If you can, stay for Sunday. Whether you're religious or not, you can't fail to be moved by the whole community dressing up and heading off to church, then returning to discuss the sermon.

Clem's Place
BUNGALOWS **$$**

(☑7151 2318; www.clemsplace.com; Tunung Island; r per person incl 3 meals K200) On tiny Tunung Island, Clem's Place is a magnificent getaway – 'end of the world, beginning of paradise' is how Clem Anton, the friendly and travel-savvy owner, describes it. Days are spent surfing good breaks, snorkelling (there's a nearby WWII wreck) and blissing out amid the tropical verdure of this 80-strong island village. Clem's has six simple but charming bungalows made from woven sago leaves, and a clean ablution block (with flush toilets), amid a lovely property a few steps from the beach. Fishing or river trips to Lavongai can also be arranged. There are no public boats from Kavieng; contact Clem to arrange transport, which takes three hours and costs K700 each way – split evenly among the travellers coming or going.

Lumeuas Cove
GUESTHOUSE **$**

(☑7213 6861; Tsoi Island; r per person incl 3 meals from K100) Leah and Jethro Usurup provide a friendly welcome at this familial and charming spot near the waterfront. Accommodation is in one of four private rooms, set in a long, thatch building nicely decorated with *bilums* (string bags), weavings and baskets. In the works are several private bungalows. Attractions in the area include snorkelling the reef (BYO gear), surfing waves off the northern end of the island and hanging out with the friendly islanders who live nearby.

Tsoi Lik Lagoon Guesthouse
GUESTHOUSE **$$**

(Tsoi Island; r per person incl 3 meals K180) A good place to kick off your shoes for a few days. This little morsel of paradise is owned by the provincial administrator and has a lovely beachfront location. The two rooms and the ablution block are in good nick. One proviso: there's not much shade on the property (don't forget your sunscreen).

❶ Getting There & Away

To Tsoi Island, banana boats usually head off in the morning (around 8am to 10am Monday to Friday) from the market wharf (one way K30). It takes about two hours to get to Tsoi Island.

East Coast

Outside Kavieng, the plunge into a more traditional world is immediate. Though the east coast feels more 'developed' than the west, with the Boluminski Hwy running most of its length, it still retains a rough diamond type of rural edge to make it special. It has lots of aesthetic appeal, shown in its numerous beaches, limestone pinnacles jutting out of the ocean and lagoons of surpassing beauty.

Adventure and nature may stir your blood, but what will really sweep you off your feet are the stimulating people that live here. The coast is liberally sprinkled with communities where locals haven't moved away from subsistence traditions. It's a great idea to ditch your guidebook, remain for a few days and experience a village stay. Digs are in basic bush-material huts, with no electricity and no running water. Meals are simple but nourishing (we hope you like taro). Otherwise there are small trade stores around but they sell mostly *tinpis* (tinned fish) and rice.

Now it's your turn to delve in, but take your time: you won't get to more than one, maybe two, places a day by public transport, and none on Sunday.

BOLUMINSKI HIGHWAY

Yes, New Ireland has a highway, which runs the 263km from Kavieng to Namatanai, making exploration easy along the east coast. It is surfaced from Kavieng to shortly after Dalom, 180km away. Further south, it's a potholed gravel road, usually passable in 2WD (take it slow). There are a number of villages along the way where you can break up your journey.

Leaving Kavieng, the first major settlement is Matanasoi (or Liga) village, about 5km along the highway from Kavieng airport. There's a limestone cave filled with crystal-clear water. The Japanese used this grotto for drinking water.

Twenty-three kilometres further is Putput and the trippy Treehouse Village Resort (☑945 1464; www.treehouse.com.pg; bungalow s/d K185/260, daily meals per person from K138), which has a series of traditional-style, fan-cooled bungalows on stilts overlooking the beach. One unit is perched up a 200-year-old *Calophyllum* tree, above the dining room. Here you can arrange village visits, rainforest walks, canoe trips in the mangroves and snorkelling excursions. This quirky venture is owned by Alun Beck, a New Zealander, who has become a local chief. Overall, it's rustic and overpriced (try to get a discount), but amusing.

At Km 90 it's worth pulling over to see Cathy Hiob's Eels at Laraibina (ask for Munawai village). Here you can see the hand-feeding of huge eels in the river, which slither right over your toes. Bring a tin of fish and K5.

BOLUMINSKI HIGHWAY FROM THE SADDLE

Feel like enjoying the scenery and atmosphere from the saddle instead of a seat in a car or PMV? **Cycling** is an ecofriendly and cheap way to discover New Ireland's east coast along cycle-friendly Boluminski Hwy. You can pick your own pace and become intimate with local communities. Boluminski Hwy seems to have been purpose-built for cycling, with very little traffic, no pollution, a surfaced road that's perfectly flat and a number of guesthouses conveniently located along the way. You can cover the whole stretch in four to five days.

Guided cycling tours around Kavieng and down the Boluminski Hwy can be organised through **Tabo Meli's Rainbow Tours** (984 2441; www.newirelandtourism.org.pg; New Ireland Tourist Bureau, Tanga St; daily bicycle hire K100; 7.45am-4pm) and **Nusa Island Retreat** (984 2247; www.nusaislandretreat.com.pg; Nusa Lik Island; daily bicycle hire K105).

Fancy a dip? Try the crystal-clear, natural swimming pool upstream from the bridge at **Fissoa** (admission per vehicle K10-25) in the grounds of the Fissoa Vocational Centre.

A the village of **Bol**, about 120km from Kavieng, you can bunk down in the **Panatalis Dodor Beach Peles** (Bol's Guesthouse; s/d incl 3 meals K100/120), which is a good place to see community life. It's run by Demas Kavavu, an interesting character who knows anything and everything on Malagan culture. The rooms are very simple but right on the beach, with Tabar Island looming on the horizon. The weak points are the toilets (pit) and the showers (nonexistent; prepare to bathe in the river).

Located 4km south of Bol, **Libba** village is a great place to look at **Malagan art** and stock up on handicrafts. The village is home to master carver Ben Sisia. Ben charges K8 to see the Malagan house where a piece might sell for upwards of K300. Even the village church is carved in the local style.

In **Malom** village, 25km south of Konos (and 181km from Kavieng), the well-run **Malom Guesthouse** (7234 4279; r per person incl 3 meals K150) is a good place to rest your head. The setting is lovely, with lots of greenery, and it's a short stagger from the beach. Your gracious host, Cathy Benson, is a good cook too.

There's a village **guesthouse** (7251 6321; r per person from K80) further down at **Dalom**. It's a serious contender for the title of best place to stay on the east coast, with welcoming hosts and an enchanting setting – right on a gorgeous beach by a turquoise stream. It has a modernish ablution block, tidy rooms and good surf out the front. Try not to turn up on Saturday (the Adventists' Sabbath).

Another kilometre further is **Rubio Guesthouse** (984 1305, 7216 6566; www.newirelandsurf.com/rubio.html; r per person incl 3 meals from K230), a surf-loving spot with the most

amenities (including refrigeration) on the east coast. Attractive bungalows with verandas all face the sea, and the cooking is good and varied. It's run by Shane Clark, a savvy surfer with American roots. BYO beer.

At Km 263, you reach Namatanai, a ramshackle town with a few simple guesthouses and a supermarket. Most folks come here just to transit by boat, to or from Kokopo in New Britain. The **Namatanai Hotel** (/fax 984 3057; r from K160) by the waterfront has decent rooms and a few bungalows, as well as a restaurant (mains around K35). Other options include the **Boluminski Guesthouse** (984 3077; s/d without bathroom K85/120), a B&B-like venture 3km from the town centre with clean fan-cooled rooms, and meals and guided walks available upon request. **Brentbino Guesthouse** (984 3043; s/d without bathroom K100/110) has basic rooms right next door to Solwara Meri.

❶ Getting There & Away

PMVs for Kavieng leave from Namatanai at 9am to 10am and arrive from Kavieng at about 5pm (K30).

Banana boats travel between New Britain and New Ireland. The well-organised **Solwara Meri** (7253 8592) runs a truck (K2) from Namatanai down to Uluputur on the west coast, where it connects with boats making the crossing to Kokopo (K60). Trucks leave Namatanai at 6am, 11am, 1pm and 3pm Monday to Saturday. Returning boats depart from Kokopo to Uluputur from 10am until about 3pm. Go early for the calmest seas.

NORTH SOLOMONS PROVINCE

Welcome to what is possibly the most special province in the country. In many ways, the islands that comprise the North Solomons (Buka, Bougainville and a scattering of smaller atolls) feel different, and the influence of the PNG mainland is a distant memory. Look at a map, and you'll see why: the North Solomons are closer to the neighbouring Solomon Islands than they are to PNG. The international border between the two countries passes just a few kilometres south of Bougainville Island. The Shortland and Choiseul islanders in the Solomons are very close to Bougainvilleans, culturally and ethnically – both have jet-black skin. Around PNG, Bougainvilleans are known as 'blackskins' or 'bukas', and often the whole North Solomons region is referred to as Bougainville.

This province is best known for its tumultuous history. Until the secessionist rebellion, it had the most productive economy, best education and well-run government. Between 1972 and its 1989 closure, the Panguna mine made 45% of PNG's export earnings. But 'the Crisis' shattered all progress and much infrastructure was devastated (for details, see boxed text, p161).

After 10 years of conflict, life has largely returned to normal. There is no longer any fighting and most of the province is safe to explore. Once-forbidden routes are opening up. Gone is the rather sullen, oppressed atmosphere that prevailed several years ago, even if the civil war still looms large in the psyche of many islanders. The province is now poised for a great regeneration, thanks to a wealth of natural resources, including gold and cocoa, and its status within PNG – it has brokered a special autonomy status to control its own destiny. There's huge potential for ecotourism, diving, surfing, trekking, caving, cycling, kayaking, birdwatching and fishing, but there's little in the way of infrastructure and organised activities (for now).

Wherever you go in this province, you're unlikely to cross paths with other travellers. All the better for you: this less-visited part of the country remains something of a 'secret', which adds to the sense of adventure. Go now.

History

There's evidence that humans settled on Bougainville at least 28,000 years ago.

Spanish mariner Luis Vaez de Torres passed through in 1606, but Bougainville acquired its name from French explorer Captain Louis-Antoine de Bougainville, who sailed up the east coast in 1768.

European settlements were established as the German New Guinea Company began trading in the late 1890s. Bougainville and Buka were considered part of the Solomons group, a British possession, until 1898 when they were traded to Germany. Australia seized the North Solomons, with the rest of New Guinea, at the start of WWI.

The Japanese arrived in 1942, swiftly defeating the Australians and holding most of the island until the end of the war. Buka became an important air base, and Buin, at the southern tip of Bougainville, was a base for ground troops. In 1943 American troops captured the port of Torokina and Australian forces fought their way south towards Buin. Of 80,000 Japanese troops only 23,000 were taken prisoner; 20,000 are thought to have been killed in action and the remaining 37,000 died of disease and starvation in the jungles. There's a moving monument to the Japanese dead atop Sohano Island's cliff.

In 1964 a major copper discovery was made at Panguna and more than K400 million was invested in a mine and its ancillary operations. A new town, roads, a power station and a port were constructed, and thousands of workers descended.

Geography
Bougainville is volcanic, about 200km long and covered in jungle. The Crown Prince, Emperor and Deuro ranges make up the central spine and Mt Bagana frequently erupts. Mt Balbi, the island's highest point at 2685m, is a dormant volcano; Benua Cave is perhaps the world's largest at 4.5 million cubic metres. The island has many natural harbours, and large swamps on its western edge.

Buka Island is formed almost entirely of raised coral. It's separated from Bougainville Island by Buka Passage, a tidal channel only 300m wide and a kilometre long. Buka Island is generally low-lying, apart from a southern hilly region. Another 166 islands spread over 450,000 sq km of sea. It's the most earthquake-prone area of the country.

Culture
Intricately woven Buka baskets are made all over the country except here, it seems, where they originated. The baskets are made from jungle vine, and the variation in colour is achieved by scraping the skin off the vine. They can be simple drink coasters or giant laundry baskets, and they're the most skilfully made, solid and durable baskets in the Pacific. They were originally made by the Siwai and Telei people of southwest Buka Island.

There are 23 languages in the North Solomons; Tok Pisin is the second main language but most people speak English well.

The people of Takuu (Mortlock) and Nukumani islands are Polynesian.

North Solomon Islanders have a matrilineal system of clan membership and inheritance rights. Most still live in bush-material housing in villages and grow cash crops.

Buka Island

Buka Island is mostly covered with copra plantations. To the southern tip of the island, Buka is the centre of activity in the province and the main gateway to the islands.

BUKA

An ambitious town, Buka used to be a tiny place but it has boomed in the last 15 years, during the war and afterwards, and now has many new buildings and residents. Although tourist sights are as scarce as hen's teeth, it's worth spending a day or two soaking up the atmosphere and chatting with the locals. It feels so exotic to be the only foreigner wandering in the streets, and people are genuinely interested in talking with a 'real' tourist. Most of the shops and services are on, or just off, the main waterfront strip of Buka.

Buka remains an important port for copra and cocoa; but for travellers, it serves primarily as a point of departure to Bougainville.

◉ Sights & Activities

Passage
WATERFRONT

A particular highlight in Buka is the passage, which refers to the channel that separates Buka Island from Bougainville Island. The water runs at about 6 knots when the tide is fast, making deep undulations on the water's surface. Banana boats congregate near the animated market (⊙ Tue-Sat).

Sohano
ISLAND

You can also take a boat ride to explore the idyllic islands near the southern mouth of the passage and beyond. Good swimming spots are on these islands. The most easily accessible island is Sohano Island, a few minutes by boat from Buka. It was the provincial capital from WWII until 1960. It's a beautiful place with lawns and gardens, a Japanese monument and war relics, steep craggy cliffs, and panoramic views over town, the passage and Bougainville Island. There are some colonial-period buildings. The weird Tchibo Rock stands just offshore from Sohano's northernmost point and figures in many local legends. It's said to have magical properties. The banana-boat fare to Sohano Island is K2.

Other Islands
ISLAND

Further south, Madehas Island, Christmas Island, White Island and Sal Island, blessed with lovely reefs and gorgeous beaches, are well worth the 20- to 30-minute boat ride from Buka. If you want to snorkel, seek permission first from the locals. Tours can be arranged with Kuri Village Resort.

🛏 Sleeping & Eating

All lodging except for the budget options have restaurants and offer airport transfers.

The Bougainvillea
RESORT $$$

(✆ 7129 5674; Sohano Island; r from K500; ❄) Enormous effort was put into this stunning new resort, with 12 beautifully designed rooms in an octagonal building perched high atop Sohano Island. All rooms have verandas (some with waterfront views) and the trappings of luxury (some even have full kitchens). The restaurant (with delectable Italian cooking) is first class.

Madehas Island Resort
RESORT $$$

(✆ 973 9063; Madehas Island) This new resort is being developed by the MacNabs, an Australian family that settled in here a few decades ago. Half complete when we last passed through, the resort has attractive, modern bungalows set amid idyllic island views and a backdrop of coconut trees (it's a copra plantation) beside a picturesque lagoon.

Kuri Village Resort
BUNGALOWS $$

(✆ 973 9151; Buka; r K250-275, bungalow K285-395; ❄) Run by Laurens, a local politician, this resort is somewhat of an institution in the province. Many reconciliation agreements between rival factions were signed in the restaurant after 'the Crisis' (see boxed text, p161). The quarters consist of plain rooms (best upstairs) in a building across the road, and slightly more appealing bungalows scattered in the garden. The best feature is the bar-restaurant with a wide deck overlooking Buka passage. Good place to arrange boat tours.

Destiny Guest Haus
GUESTHOUSE $$

(✆ 973 9048, 7395 8151; destiny.guesthaus@yahoo.com; Buka; r K325-370; ❄) New in 2011, Destiny has seven attractively designed rooms with wood-floors, peaked ceilings and hot showers. The best feature: all have small verandas over the water. There's a restaurant (mains around K35) as well as a kai bar (mains around K15).

Lynchar Guest Haus
GUESTHOUSE $$

(✆ 973 9449, 7237 6571; Buka; r K280-398; ❄) Lynchar has clean but unexceptional rooms,

SECESSION, WAR & PEACE

In the 1960s and early 1970s, the North Solomons began a push to break away from Australian colonial control, climaxing in land disputes over the proposed Panguna mine.

Before PNG independence, Bougainville pushed for an independent grouping of the Bismarck Archipelago. In 1974 secessionist movements sprang up.

In 1987 the Panguna Landowners Association was formed, led by Pepetua Sereo and Francis Ona. It demanded better environmental protection, huge back payments of profits from the mine and US$10 *billion* in compensation. These demands were not met and in 1988 the Bougainville Revolutionary Army (BRA), an offshoot of the landowners' association, began to sabotage the mine. Relations between the locals and police sent to protect the mine deteriorated sharply. The BRA's numbers were bolstered by sympathisers from other parts of the country and even a religious cult.

Increasing attacks on mine workers resulted in the mine's closure in 1989 – an enormous blow to the PNG economy. A state of emergency was declared, the PNG army moved in and the conflict spread to the rest of the island. Whole villages were moved into 'care centres', areas outside BRA control. To ensure that the people moved, the army burned their villages and stories about rape and murder flooded out of Bougainville. The Panguna issue became a civil war – at the height of the conflict, there were 60,000 people displaced.

In 1990 the PNG government withdrew its forces and began a blockade, leading to great hardship for Bougainvilleans. The BRA declared independence, forming the Republic of Meekamui on 17 May. Bougainville slipped back into primitivism. The BRA brought over supplies from the nearby Solomon Islands and the PNG army, in retaliation, caused international tension by raiding suspected BRA bases in the Solomon Islands, killing innocent people.

In February 1997 the Sandline Affair hit the headlines. In a highly secret operation then-prime minister Julius Chan contracted a mercenary company to put down the rebels. The plan was exposed and there was an international outcry. Days of heavy tension in Port Moresby saw rioting and looting in the streets, with people calling for Chan to stand down. He did and the mercenaries – South Africans mostly – were deported. This act of lunacy hastened efforts to find a peaceful outcome for Bougainville.

In March 2002 the PNG parliament passed legislation to give legal effect to the autonomy arrangements contained in a peace agreement, which includes a referendum for an independent Bougainville state by 2020. The PNG Defence Force (PNGDF) withdrew for the last time in April 2003. Weapons were surrendered to the UN, and certain amnesties and pardons were granted. In mid-2004 the first divisions of local police graduated their training. Francis Ona, leader of the BRA, died in 2006.

At the time of writing the situation had stabilised except in the 'no-go zone' near Panguna (for the latest developments, see p172).

---

with all the mod cons (fridge, hot water, cable TV). Pricier quarters add space, but are probably not worth the extra kina. Decent restaurant (mains around K48).

Lumankoa   GUESTHOUSE $$
(☎973 9779; Buka; s/d incl 3 meals from K180/280) This weatherboard house has dimly lit rooms short on charm (and natural light), but it's clean and the spacious garden makes a nice retreat.

Hani's Inn   GUESTHOUSE $$
(☎973 9358, 7346 4435; hanisinn@daltron.com.pg; Buka; s/d K180/250, s without bathroom K150; ❄) A lacklustre option, with cramped rooms, joyless greyish walls and average beds.

Liberty Lodge   GUESTHOUSE $
(☎7364 1008; Buka; s/d with fan K100/130, with air-con K110/140; ❄) A bare-bones cheapie, with 10 basic rooms with lino floors, wafer-thin mattresses and shared facilities.

Tamari Foods   BAKERY, BAR $
(Buka; meals K8-12; ❉6am-5pm) In an unsigned corrugated building on the main street, Tamari whips up tasty *kai* bar fare (chicken, chips, rice and stews), plus light fluffy lamingtons in the morning (arrive around 8am).

❶ Information
Bank South Pacific Has ATMs.
KaguCom (per hr K20; ❉8am-5pm Mon-Fri, to noon Sat) Internet access.

❶ Getting There & Around

Air Niugini (📞973 9655; ⊙8am-4pm Mon-Fri) has flights to Rabaul (K400 to K550, 45 minutes, four weekly) and Port Moresby (K504 to K1083, two hours, four weekly), two of which go via Rabaul.

Rabaul Shipping (Star Ships; 📞982 1070; Rabaul) sails once a week to Rabaul (K150 to K300), but the schedule is erratic so double-check it.

Water taxis are the way to get around the Buka passage area (K2). PMVs (Land Cruiser Troop Carriers) ferry people down the coast road of Bougainville to Arawa (K50, 3½ hours) and on to Buin (K100, eight hours). You have to go to Kokopau across the passage and then book a seat by 9am, even though the vehicles leave at 11am or noon (no services on Sunday).

Bougainville

Once at the centre of PNG's worst regional armed conflict, Bougainville has put aside its troubled past and is slowly recovering.

Green, rugged and little developed, this large volcanic island has a dramatic setting, with thick forests, towering volcanoes, tumbling rivers, azure lagoons, plunging waterfalls, giant caves and impenetrable valleys that slither into the mountains. For now, visitors can have the island pretty much to themselves. There's huge potential for small-scale tourism, but little in the way of organised activities; it's DIY travel.

Starting from Kokopau, you'll head due south and traverse several coastal communities where time seems to have stood still. Why not pull over in picturesque Tinputz, a one-hour drive to the south? There's a friendly guesthouse; for guided hikes up to Namatoa Crater Lake get in touch with Osborne (📞7112 0637).

A good base, Wakunai is where you can arrange a three-day trek to Mt Balbi (2685m), or follow the Nooma Nooma track that crosses the island to Torokina, on the west coast (count on a three-day minimum). From Mt Balbi, you can see the active Mt Bagana (1730m).

Continuing south, you'll drive past the infamous Morgan Junction, where you can catch a glimpse of the former 'no-go zone' and Panguna. High in the centre of the island, this dormant mine is one of the world's largest artificial holes. Copper was discovered here in 1964, and Bougainville Copper Limited was the operator of the open-cut mine. The Arawa Women's Centre Lodge can help arrange visits to the mine.

About 10km south of Morgan Junction, you'll reach Arawa and Kieta, which are virtually contiguous. Both were severely damaged during the conflict (see boxed text, p161), and whole neighbourhoods have been abandoned. In Arawa, Zhon Bosco Miriona (📞626 3583, 7162 6393; www.bougtours.com) leads guided day- and multiday tours of the area (birdwatching, trekking, village visits).

About 260km south of Buka, Buin really feels like the end of the line. It suffered less damage than Kieta and Arawa during the conflict. During WWII, Buin hosted a large Japanese army base and the area has many rusting relics. Admiral Yamamoto's aircraft wreck is the area's most historically interesting wreck. Admiral Isoroku Yamamoto, who planned the attack on Pearl Harbour, left Rabaul in a 'Betty Bomber' on 18 April 1943 with a protective group of Zeros, not realising that US fighters were waiting for him near Buin. The wreckage of the bomber still lies in the jungle a few kilometres off the Panguna-Buin road. It's signposted, near Aku, 24km before Buin.

🛏 Sleeping & Eating

Buin has a few basic guesthouses.

Taga Guest Haus   GUESTHOUSE $
(📞7381 8899; Tinputz; r per person incl 2 meals K115) Rooms are small and basic (with shared bathrooms), but Gladys and Paul, your hosts, will make you feel at home. Paul is the leader of the Sinamo community based in Namatoa, way up in the mountains, and can arrange a hike to Namatoa Crater Lake.

Arawa Women's Centre Lodge GUESTHOUSE $$
(📞342 5603, 7197 6976; Arawa; r per person incl 2 meals K180-190; ❄) The obvious choice in Arawa is a peaceful spot with tidy rooms, crisply dressed rooms and well-maintained shared bathrooms. The wood-panelled restaurant serves tasty market-fresh fare. There's also a grassy lawn and a *haus win* (wooden open-air structure).

❶ Getting There & Around

The most convenient way to get around Bougainville Island is by PMV. There's only one main gravel road, running down the east coast to Arawa and Kieta, and on to Buin to the south. It's in fair condition, with new bridges (built by the Japanese) to replace the currently forded river crossings.

Regular PMVs ply the route between Kokopau and Arawa (K50, 3½ hours), where you can continue on to Buin (K50, another four to five hours).

Understand PNG

population per sq km

PNG   AUSTRALIA   USA

≈ 3 people

Papua New Guinea Today

A Chaotic Political Atmosphere

» Population: 6.31 million

» GDP: US$16.7 billion

» Languages spoken: 820

» Highest point: Mt Wilhelm (4509m)

» Bird species: 781

» Literacy rate: 57.3%

» Parliamentary political parties: 33

» Indigenous counting systems: more than 50 (one is based on joints of the body and the nose)

» Number of airports: 562

Politics is a topsy-turvy affair in Papua New Guinea, with a parliament often mired in dysfunction. This is perhaps not surprising, given the nation's bewildering political complexities – where 109 MPs representing 820 languages regularly cross the floor to vote with the opposition, often showing little or no allegiance to their political party. As a consequence, since 1975 (when PNG became independent) only one prime minister has served a full five-year term without being brought down in a no-confidence vote. Survival, not policy, tends to be the focus of PNG politics.

The chaotic political scene sometimes takes a turn for the absurd, as happened in late 2011, when two men each claimed to be the legitimate prime minister. The problems began when Prime Minister Michael Somare took leave from the country in 2011 to receive medical care abroad and remained away for nearly five months. During his absence, MPs officially removed Somare from his post and installed Peter O'Neill as prime minister.

Mutiny!

When Somare returned to PNG, he tried to reclaim his position, which led to a ruling by the Supreme Court in his favour. O'Neill and MPs refused to recognise the court order, resulting in deadlock until January 2012, when 'a mutiny' was carried out. Soldiers loyal to Somare seized key military barracks and placed military chief Brigadier-General Francis Agwi under house arrest. The whole affair greatly discredited Somare in the eyes of many Papuans, who felt that after his 43 years in parliament, 18 as prime minister, it was time to move on.

Top Books

» **Beyond the Coral Sea** (Michael Moran) A fascinating portrait of PNG's island cultures.

» **Throwim Way Leg** (Tim Flannery) Enjoyable account of Flannery's adventures as a biologist in remote New Guinea.

» **Into the Crocodile's Nest** (Benedict Allen) A masochist-adventurer becomes the first Westerner initiated into a crocodile cult on the Sepik River.

» **Mister Pip** (Lloyd Jones) Moving story of a white teacher in Bougainville during the war.

Top Docos

» **First Contact** Extraordinary film about the 1933 discovery of PNG's Highlanders.

» **Joe Leahy's Neighbours** A traditional society coming to terms with the modern world.

» **Shark Callers of Kontu** About the ancient art of shark-calling.

belief systems
(% of population)

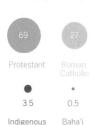

69	27
Protestant	Roman Catholic
● 3.5	· 0.5
Indigenous religions	Baha'i

if Papua New Guinea were 100 people

87 would live in a rural area
13 would live in an urban area

A New Path

O'Neill has promised a new era in PNG government: better education and health care, major investment in infrastructure and a more inclusive environment for women. He also aims to clean up corrupt government practices, and revitalise relationships with Australia and other countries.

Tragic Events

Volcanic eruptions, earthquakes, landslides and tsunamis are among the natural disasters PNG has suffered over the years. More recent misfortunes have been of the man-made variety. In early 2012 the *Rabaul Queen* sunk in heavy seas on its voyage from Kimbe to Lae, taking the lives of some 180 passengers.

Lae, PNG's second-largest city, erupted in rioting in 2011. Rising crime levels in the city and increasingly brazen acts of violence spurred Lae residents to take matters into their own hands. What started as a peaceful march degenerated into ethnic violence as locals clashed with Highlanders – often blamed for the surge of social problems in the city. Nine people were killed, dozens injured and thousands of homes destroyed before police restored order.

Gas-Powered Economy

On the economic front, the letters on everyone's lips are LNG. The US$15 billion resource-extraction project – run by the US company Exxon Mobil – is PNG's biggest commercial endeavour ever. Centring on the Hides gas fields in Hela Province in the remote Southern Highlands, the massive project (with the first deliveries estimated for 2014) could double the country's GDP. Whether it ends up benefiting the masses or the few is the multibillion-dollar question (see the boxed text, p113).

Must-Dos

» Dancing at a Highland *singsing*.

» Playing *garamut* (a hollowed log) and *kundu* (hourglass-shaped, lizard-skin) drums.

» Chewing betel nut.

» Sleeping in a *haus tambaran* (spirit house).

» Buying a Sepik carving.

Must-Haves

» **Bilums** Colourful string bags – strong and expandable.

» **Bowls & Stools** Elaborately carved pieces from the Trobriand Islands and Tami Islands.

» **Tapa Cloths** Bark cloth painted with elaborate designs from Oro Province.

» **Buka Baskets** Some of the finest wickerwork in the Pacific, originally from Bougainville.

» **Cult Hooks** Richly carved anthropomorphic pieces from the Sepik region.

History

The first humans in the area arrived from Asia some 60,000 years ago, settling the coasts and lower elevations of the Highlands. Around 9000 years ago, Papua New Guineans began cultivating local crops, becoming some of the world's earliest farmers. The first Europeans arrived in the 16th century; Portugal named the area, while Spain started several colonies that ended in disaster. Due to hostile territory and fierce natives, Europeans weren't very interested in the region, though in 1660 the Dutch claimed sovereignty over unexplored parts to help protect its Dutch East Indies Empire.

In the 18th century the British and French explored various parts, though it wasn't until the Germans arrived on the scene in the late 1800s that the Brits got serious, 'claiming' most of New Guinea as an official British protectorate in the 1880s. In 1906 the Australians took over colonial administration and later cemented their power by driving out Germany during WWI.

The discovery of gold brought a rush of settlers to the north coast in the 1920s. The following decade, expeditions to the interior led to the jaw-dropping discovery of more than a million Highlanders living unknown to the outside world. In WWII the region formed the backdrop to horrific battles on sea and land, particularly when Australian forces repelled the Japanese advance along the tortuous Kokoda Track.

Following the war, New Guinea marched slowly towards self-rule, finally gaining independence in the 1970s. From the 1980s onward, developers exploited Papua New Guinea's huge gold and copper deposits. Mineral riches, however, did little to eradicate poverty, and indeed helped fuel resentment at Bougainville's Panguna mine, leading to a bloody war on the island. Meanwhile, the 1990s also saw tragic natural disasters, including a volcanic eruption that buried Rabaul.

The 21st century began with promise: the brokering of a state treaty with the newly formed Autonomous Bougainville Government finally brought peace (and the future possibility of self-rule) to the island. Sir Michael Somare retained power for a third term as prime minister of

TIMELINE

60,000 BC	30,000 BC	7000 BC
The Ice Age of the Pleistocene period allows the first humans to island-hop their way from Asia across the Indonesian archipelago to New Guinea and the Solomon Islands.	Papuan-speaking hunter-gatherers from New Guinea settle islands in the eastern Solomons before the sea levels rise with the end of the Ice Age in 10,000 BC.	The use of food gardens – breadfruit, sago, coconuts, yams and sugar cane – and domesticated pigs makes New Guineans among the world's first agriculturalists.

PNG, promising electoral reform. However, after years of Somare rule New Guineans seemed ready for a change, and parliament voted to remove him following a five-month absence from the country in 2011. The power struggle continues (see p164 for more on this).

The First Arrivals

Archaeological evidence suggests humans first reached New Guinea, and then Australia and the Solomon Islands, by island-hopping across the Indonesian archipelago from Asia at least 60,000 years ago. The migrations were made easier by a fall in the sea level during the Pleistocene period, or Great Ice Age, and by a land bridge that linked PNG with northern Australia. The descendants of these people speak non-Austronesian (or Papuan) languages and are today called Melanesians.

The World's First Agriculturalists

Evidence of early New Guinea coastal settlements includes 40,000-year-old stone axes found in Morobe Province. Humans probably climbed up to settle in the Highlands about 30,000 years ago. At Kuk (or Kup) Swamp in the Wahgi Valley in Western Highlands Province, archaeologists have found evidence of human habitation going back 20,000 years and there is evidence of gardening beginning 9000 years ago. They cultivated breadfruit, sago, coconuts, yams and sugar cane (which originated in New Guinea). New Ireland, Buka and the Solomon Islands were probably inhabited around 30,000 years ago and Manus Island 10,000 years ago.

Elsewhere in the world, the development of agriculture resulted in the establishment of cities and an elite class, but this did not happen in New Guinea or the Solomon Islands. Perhaps this was because basic food crops could not be stored long so food couldn't be stockpiled. It's not known when pigs and more productive starch crops (Asian yams, taro and bananas) were introduced, but New Guineans have had domesticated pigs for at least 10,000 years. People lived in small villages on well-established tribal lands practising shifting cultivation, fishing and hunting. Coastal people built canoes, and feasting and dancing were regular activities. Each settlement comprised just one extended family as well as the captives from raiding neighbouring settlements – ritual head-hunting, slave-raiding and cannibalism were common. People worshipped ancestors, not gods.

Polynesians & Malay Traders

Between AD 1200 and AD 1600 some Polynesians started heading westward again and, finding most of the islands of New Guinea already inhabited, settled some of the remaining isolated islands and atolls. They travelled vast distances in small canoes.

Top PNG History Reads

» *A Bastard of a Place*, Peter Brune

» *Fortress Rabaul*, Bruce Gamble

» *The Bone Man of Kokoda*, Charles Happell

» *The Sandline Affair*, Sean Dorney

HISTORY THE FIRST ARRIVALS

1000 BC	1526	mid-1500s	1660
The second great wave of migration in the Pacific associated with proto-Polynesian 'Lapita people' colonises islands east of the Solomons. The last isolated atolls remain unsettled for another 2000 years.	Jorge de Menezes, Portuguese explorer and governor of Ternate in present-day Indonesia, becomes the first European to land on the New Guinea mainland; he names the region Ilhas dos Papuas.	Malay traders introduce sweet potatoes into western New Guinea (present-day Indonesian Papua), sourced from the Spanish and Portuguese exploits in South America.	The Dutch East India Company claims Dutch sovereignty over still-unexplored New Guinea in order to protect its profitable business interests in modern-day Indonesia. It remains Dutch-owned for the next century.

By the mid-16th century, sweet potatoes were being taken from South America into southeast Asia by the Portuguese and Spanish, and Malay traders brought them to the western part of the New Guinea island. The high yield of sweet potatoes in cold climes allowed for the colonisation of still higher altitudes in the Highlands and the domestication of many more pigs. Around this time steel axe-heads were traded into the Highlands from the coast. These developments saw huge rises in population, and an increase in war, slave-trading and head-hunting.

The First European Contact

The first definite European sighting of the New Guinea island was in 1512, when Portuguese sailor Antonio d'Abreu sighted the coast. However, it wasn't until 1526 that another Portuguese, Jorge de Menezes, became the first European to set foot on the main island – he named it Ilha dos Papuas. But New Guinea was regarded as a large, daunting place with no obvious wealth to exploit and very hostile natives, so it was largely left alone while European colonists plundered the Americas.

European Exploration

Eager to protect incursions into the eastern end of their fabulously profitable Dutch East Indies Empire (modern-day Indonesia), the Dutch East Indies Company claimed sovereignty over unexplored New Guinea in 1660. And so it remained for more than a century.

In 1768 Louis-Antoine de Bougainville discovered Buka, Bougainville and Choiseul islands. Many British, French and American explorers followed and from 1798 whalers sailed through the islands. Sandalwood and *bêche-de-mer* (sea cucumber) traders brought iron and steel tools, calico and fish hooks, but ultimately it was treachery and resentment that they left. European diseases were devastating in New Guinea, and the guns the traders brought resulted in an explosion of warfare and head-hunting.

The British East India Company explored parts of western New Guinea in 1793 and even made a tentative claim on the island but in 1824 Britain and the Netherlands agreed the latter's colonial claim to the western half of the New Guinea island should stand (and it did until 1963). A series of British 'claims' followed, which were repudiated each time by Queen Victoria's government.

By the late 1860s the sandalwood had been exhausted and resentment toward Europeans led to the murder of several missionaries. The islands quickly became notorious as the most dangerous place in the Pacific, inhabited by head-hunters and cannibals. There were violent and unpredictable attacks on foreigners, and several savage massacres.

EARLY EXPLORERS

Sixteenth-century Portuguese explorers named New Guinea *Ilhas dos Papuas* (Islands of the Fuzzy-Hairs) from the Malay word *papuwah*. Later, Spanish navigator Ynigo Ortis de Retez likened it to West Africa's Guinea and named it New Guinea. The names were combined at independence in 1975.

1699	1768	1790s	1876
Swashbuckling Englishman William Dampier charts the southeastern coasts of New Britain and New Ireland and discovers the Dampier Strait between the New Britain and the New Guinea mainland.	Louis-Antoine de Bougainville sails through the Solomon Islands and names Bougainville after himself; Choiseul after French diplomat Étienne-François duc de Choiseul; and Buka after an Islander word.	The British explore the western part of the New Guinea mainland, while sandalwood and *bêche-de-mer* (sea cucumber) traders and whalers sail through the islands of New Guinea and the Solomons.	Italian adventurer Luigi d'Albertis charts the Fly River in a tiny steamer, the *Neva*, taking eight weeks to travel 930km upriver and using fireworks to scare off menacing-looking locals.

SUMMARY JUSTICE – SECRET LYNCHINGS OF WWII

It's been a dark secret until recently but, as Australian Paul Ham, amongst other writers, has pointed out, Australian troops summarily hanged New Guineans during WWII for co-operating with the Japanese – perhaps as many as 213. Hundreds of children were made to watch the execution of 17 men in a single day in 1943 near Higaturu in Oro Province to 'learn a lesson' about cooperating with the Japanese. Many of the 'fuzzy wuzzy angels', as they were affectionately known – the New Guinean stretcher-bearers who carried wounded Australian Diggers along the Kokoda Track – were actually press-ganged into service.

Towards Independence

Masses of abandoned war equipment were put to use in developing New Guinea. Even today you can see how Marsden matting is used for fencing and building material, and many WWII-era Quonset huts are still standing. However, the war's main impact proved to be social and political.

An influx of expatriates to Papua and New Guinea, mainly Australians, fuelled rapid economic growth. The expat population grew from about 6000 to more than 50,000 in 1971. (Today it's around 20,000.)

Colonialism wasn't popular in the 1950s and '60s and Australia was urged to prepare Papua and New Guinea for independence. A visiting UN mission in 1962 stressed that if the people weren't pushing for independence, then it was Australia's responsibility to do so. Australia's policy of reinforcing literacy and education was part of a concerted effort to create an educated social group that could run government.

In 1964 a House of Assembly with 64 members was formed. Internal self-government came into effect in 1973, followed by full independence on 16 September 1975.

Troubled Young Nations

Law and order became a more serious issue in the 1990s, when mineral-rich PNG began to develop large-scale mining operations. These fast became the greatest contributors to the economy, but also social, environmental and political burdens that, in the 1980s and '90s, took a heavy toll. First the giant Ok Tedi gold-and-copper mine poisoned much of the Ok Tedi and Fly Rivers, and then conflict over profits from the Panguna copper mine in Bougainville led to war (see p161). Rebel leader Francis Ona and the Bougainville Revolutionary Army (BRA) fought for independence from PNG.

The Bougainville war drained resources and divided PNG along tribal lines for years, it also strained relations with the Solomons. In 1997 the government of Sir Julius Chan hired mercenaries to try to crush the separatists. What became known as the Sandline Affair was

Barely recovered from the devastation of WWII, in 1951 the district headquarters of Central Province, Higaturu, was flattened when Mt Lamington erupted, killing more than 3000 people. The new capital, Popondetta, was built further from the volcano.

Colonialism

German interest in New Guinea's northeast coast finally spurred Great Britain to get serious about its own colonial ambitions. In September 1884, when the British announced that they intended to claim part of New Guinea, the Germans quickly raised the flag on the north coast. A compromise was reached – an arbitrary line was drawn east–west through the 'uninhabited' Highlands between German and British New Guinea.

New Guinea was now divided into three sections: a Dutch half protecting the eastern edge of the Dutch East Indies; a British quarter to keep the Germans (and everybody else) away from Australia; and a German quarter that would ultimately become a highly profitable outpost of German plantation agriculture. The Germans eventually decamped to New Britain, where German-initiated plantations still operate today.

Government by Patrol

In 1888, when Sir William MacGregor became British New Guinea's administrator, he established a native police force to spread the benefits of British government. He instituted the policy of 'government by patrol', which continued through the Australian period. In 1906 British New Guinea became the Territory of Papua and its administration was taken over by newly independent Australia.

Despite being in decline elsewhere, slavery was thriving in New Guinea during the late 19th and early 20th centuries. Known as 'blackbirding', men were carted off to provide plantation labour in northern Australia and Fiji.

1914–41

When WWI broke out in 1914, Australian troops quickly overran the German headquarters at Rabaul and for the next seven years German New Guinea was run by the Australian military. In 1920 German New Guinea was officially handed over to Australia as a mandated territory.

Australia was quick to eradicate the German commercial and plantation presence, baulking only at the German missions. Australia enacted legislation aimed at restricting the commercial exploitation of Eastern New Guinea to British nationals and, more particularly, Australians. Copra, rubber, coffee and cocoa were the main earners.

The discovery of large deposits of gold at Edie Creek and the Bulolo Valley in the 1920s brought men and wealth to the north coast. After 400 years of coastal contact, some of those white men finally made it into the interior (see the boxed text, p170).

Under the Australian administration, *kiaps* (patrol officers) were usually the first Europeans to venture into previously 'uncontacted' areas, and were also responsible for making the government's presence felt on a regular basis. This situation continued until independence.

In 1880 the Marquis de Ray, having never been to New Guinea, sent 340 would-be settlers to his New France 'colony' near Cape St George in New Ireland. Instead of fertile land and friendly natives, emigrants confronted impenetrable jungle, malaria, starvation and cannibals. Only 217 survived.

In 1927 an 18-year-old Errol Flynn arrived in New Guinea. He worked as a cadet patrol officer, gold prospector, slaver, plantation manager, copra trader, charter-boat captain, pearl diver and a diamond smuggler for six years. He called New Guinea one of the great loves of his life.

1997
The Sandline Affair makes headlines worldwide, as PM Julius Chan hires South African mercenaries to put down Bougainville rebels; Chan resigns but the affair hastens negotiation of a peace agreement.

1998
On 17 July, a 10m tsunami hits the coastal region west of Aitape in Sandaun Province, killing more than 2200 people and causing injuries to another 1000.

1999
Australian mining giant BHP admits to causing major environmental damage in the operation of the gold-and-copper Ok Tedi mine. Deforestation and decimated fish stocks lead to various class-action lawsuits.

March 2005
A diplomatic spat between PNG and Australia erupts after Prime Minister Michael Somare is asked to remove his shoes at a routine security screening in Brisbane airport.

1884
Germany hoists the flag on the north coast of the New Guinea mainland and establishes the German *Neuguinea Kompanie* at Finschhafen. An arbitrary line divides German and British New Guinea.

» PNG villagers (1885)

JOHN WILLIAM LINDT

1906
British New Guinea becomes the Territory of Papua and its administration is taken over by newly independent Australia. Progressive Sir Hubert Murray is governor from 1907 until 1940.

1914
Australia seizes German New Guinea at the outbreak of WWI and is officially given German New Guinea in 1920 as a mandated territory by the League of Nations.

WWII & the Birth of the Kokoda Legend

Having raced south through Asia and the Pacific, the Japanese occupied Rabaul in New Guinea in January 1942. However, Japanese successes in New Guinea were short-lived. Australian troops fought back an advance along the rugged Kokoda Track, which the Japanese were using in an attempt to reach and take Port Moresby, the only remaining Australian stronghold on the island. In a flanking move, the Japanese landed at Milne Bay but were repulsed after a bloody 10-day battle with Australian troops.

The Japanese came within 50km of Port Moresby, but an unsustainably extended supply line and heroic resistance by Australian soldiers with local help turned the course of the whole Pacific war. By September 1942 the previously undefeated Japanese were in a slow and bloody retreat. Over the next 16 months, Australian and US forces battled their way towards the Japanese strongholds along the north coast at a cost of thousands of lives.

The Japanese refused to surrender. It took until 1945 to regain all the mainland from the Japanese but New Ireland, New Britain and Bougainville were not relieved until the official Japanese surrender. For years after the end of WWII there were stories – some apocryphal, some true – about Japanese soldiers still hiding out in the jungle.

Most Melanesians were initially militarily neutral in the conflict, although they were used extensively on both sides as labourers, guides, carriers and informers – sometimes press-ganged by the Japanese and Australians. But some were heavily involved with the Allies, operating behind enemy lines as 'coastwatchers'. A number of Papua New Guineans were decorated for their bravery. It is estimated that almost a third of Tolais from northern New Britain were killed.

On 2 July 1937 aviator Amelia Earhart and her navigator Fred Noonan left Lae on PNG's north coast and flew off into oblivion.

THE LAND THAT TIME FORGOT

When Mick Leahy ventured inland in 1930 he was looking for gold. Instead, on that and nine subsequent expeditions over the next five years, Leahy, his brother Dan and Jim Taylor 'discovered' about a million people living in the secluded valleys of the New Guinea Highlands.

New Guinea's white colonialists had thought the area uninhabited, but it was the most densely populated part of the country. In an age of aeroplanes, radio and international telecommunications, the discovery was stunning. It didn't take long for the 'land that time forgot' to be dragged into the 20th century. The Leahy brothers introduced coffee, and before long missionaries and aircraft were also arriving. The Highlanders, who had only known a barter economy, were quick to adapt to cash.

Mick Leahy's meticulous recording of events – in his diary, several hours of 16mm film and more than 5000 photographs – can be seen in the 1983 documentary *First Contact*.

CARGO CULTS

To many New Guineans, it seems the strange ways and mysterious powers of the Europeans could only have derived from supernatural sources. Cult leaders theorised that Europeans had intercepted cargo that was really intended for the New Guineans, sent to them by their ancestors in the spirit world. One cultist even suggested that the white people had torn the first page out of their bibles – the page that revealed that God was actually a Papuan.

If the right rituals were followed, the cult leaders said, the goods would be redirected to their rightful owners. Accordingly, docks were prepared and crude 'airstrips' laid out for when the cargo arrived. Other leaders felt that if they mimicked European ways, they would soon have European goods – 'offices' were established in which people passed bits of paper back and forth. But when locals started to kill their own pigs and destroy their gardens, the colonial government took a firm stand. Some leaders were imprisoned while others were taken down to Australia to see with their own eyes that the goods did not arrive from the spirit world.

Seeing black American troops during WWII with access to desirable goods had a particularly strong impact. In Manus Province in 1946, a movement started by Paliau Moloat called the New Way, or Paliau Church, was initially put down as just another cargo cult. But Paliau's quasi-religious following was one of PNG's first independence movements and a force for modernisation. He opposed bride prices, for example, and sought to dissuade the local populace's belief in the arrival of actual cargo from the sea.

Paliau was imprisoned in the early days, but in 1964 and 1968 he was elected to the PNG House of Assembly. He was seen by his followers as the last prophet of the world. He died on 1 November 1991.

Postwar Experience

The Melanesian experience of WWII caused a sharp resurgence in cargo cultism (see box). The war's sudden arrival and its massive impact could not have been more profound. US soldiers – many of them black – treated locals as equals and shared food with them. This was something that locals had never experienced from their colonial overlords. The postwar profligacy of the massive US war machine – where boats were scuttled and guns and jeeps were dumped in the sea before the soldiers disappeared in giant transport planes – sent very strange messages to people who were living subsistence lifestyles.

Every year, 23 July is commemorated as Remembrance Day for the Papua New Guineans who died in WWII. It's also the anniversary of the 1942 battle between the Papuan Infantry Battalion and the Japanese invaders that took place near the Kumusi River in Oro Province.

1930

The Leahy brothers walk into and 'discover' the Highlands – and about one million people living completely unaware of the outside world. It's a monumental anthropological breakthrough.

1942

The invading Japanese establish a base in Rabaul in January, by April they've taken most of New Guinea and the Solomons and by September they've begun their retreat along the Kokoda Track.

» Burned out village, WWII

BETTMANN/CORBIS©

1957

Kiaps (Australian patrol officers) organise the first Goroka Show. It grows to become one of the largest and best-known singsings in the country, attracting scores of participating tribes.

1963–69

The Dutch pull out of western New Guinea, transferring control to Indonesia subject to a UN-administered plebiscite – the sham 'Act of Free Choice' legitimises brutality towards independence-seeking Papuans.

1975

Papua New Guinea gains full independence from Australia on 16 September. Michael Somare, who helped lead the nation towards self-government, becomes the first prime minister.

1989

The first PNG Defence Force (PNGDF) soldiers are killed as civil war breaks out in Bougainville; the following year PNGDF troops are withdrawn from Bougainville and the island is blockaded.

Two of R volcanoes and Tavurvu burying the town in th volcanic Kokopo b new c a disaster, but ironically the fall-out brought world attention to the conflict and forced the protagonists to find peaceful solutions.

The 1980s and '90s saw PNG face a series of challenges: a volcanic eruption in 1994 buried much of Rabaul (see p148); ongoing border problems involving the Organisasi Papua Merdeka (Free West Papua Movement) strained relations with Indonesia and saw thousands moved to refugee camps in PNG; and a growing level of corruption and government misspending sucked money away from where it was needed most – education and health. All this served as a backdrop to the revolving door of prime ministers and no-confidence motions that characterised politics in PNG.

The New Millennium

In March 2002 the PNG government passed legislation that brought into effect autonomy arrangements of the Bougainville Peace Agreement (BPA), which guarantees a referendum for Bougainvillean independence by 2020. The Autonomous Bougainville Government was sworn into office on 15 June 2005 with Joseph Kabui as its president.

Francis Ona, leader of the BRA and staunch opponent of the BPA, died of malaria barely a month later on 24 July 2005. Ona's supporters continued to defend the so-called No-Go Zone around the abandoned Panguna mine. The proliferation of weapons in the No-Go Zone remains serious. For more on the Bougainville conflict and the Sandline Affair, see p161.

The area around Tuno in the No-Go Zone is also where Noah Musingku maintains his own fiefdom. Musingku operated an illegal pyramid fast-money scheme called U-Vastrict that left investors all over PNG empty-handed. He fled to Bougainville in 2005 where he feted Francis Ona, proclaiming him King of Papala and then assumed this bogus title himself when Ona died. Musingku hired eight Fijian mercenaries as bodyguards and to train his private army, offering them US$1 million each. In November 2006 there was armed confrontation between the Fijian ex-soldiers and their trainees on one side, and pro-government Bougainville Freedom Fighters on the other. To date, all but one have either returned to Fiji or turned themselves over to the PNG police – none received the money promised to them. These bizarre circumstances aside, the UN regards the negotiated peace agreement on Bougainville as one of the most successful anywhere in the world in modern times.

'Grand Chief' Sir Michael Somare, PNG's 'father of independence', returned in 2002 for a third stint as prime minister and introduced electoral reforms to create a more stable political climate, and in turn to help the economy. Somare was the first prime minister in the country's history to avoid the familiar no-confidence motion and then be re-elected in July 2007 as an incumbent prime minister. However, Somare returned to the prime ministership under strained relations with Australia.

CIVIL WAR

The 10-year secessionist war in Bougainville claimed an estimated 20,000 lives.

June 2005	2007	August 2011	October 2011
Peace at last returns to troubled Bougainville. The Autonomous Bougainville Government is sworn into office on 15 June 2005 with Joseph Kabui as its president.	Michael Somare (whose face appears on the K50 note) assumes the role of prime minister for the fourth time, capping nearly four decades in politics.	After spending months away on medical leave, Prime Minister Michael Somare is replaced by Peter O'Neill. Somare's return causes a power struggle, leading to a failed pro-Somare coup in 2012.	Following discoveries of enormous gas fields, work commences on an 850km-long pipeline – part of the US$15 billion LNG (liquefied natural gas) project, which could potentially double the country's GDP.

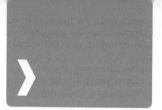

Environment

By Tim Flannery

Tim Flannery is a naturalist, ecologist, environmental activist and author. He has been Director of the South Australian Museum, professor at the University of Adelaide, Principal Research Scientist at the Australian Museum in Sydney and was awarded the 2007 Australian of the Year. He is currently an adjunct professor at Macquarie University.

The island of New Guinea, of which Papua New Guinea is the eastern part, is only one-ninth as big as Australia, yet it has just as many mammal species, and more kinds of birds and frogs. PNG is Australia's biological mirror-world. Both places share a common history going back tens of millions of years, but Australia is flat and has dried out, while PNG is wet and has become mountainous. As a result, Australian kangaroos bound across the plains, while in PNG they climb in the rainforest canopy.

PNG – A Megadiverse Region

PNG is one of earth's megadiverse regions, and it owes much of its diversity to its topography. The mountainous terrain has spawned diversity in two ways: isolated mountain ranges are often home to unique fauna and flora found nowhere else, while within any one mountain range you will find different species as you go higher. In the lowlands are jungles whose trees are not that different from those of Southeast Asia. Yet the animals are often startlingly different – cassowaries instead of tapirs, and marsupial cuscus instead of monkeys.

Papua New Guinea is still very much a biological frontier, so it's worth recording carefully any unusual animal you see. In little-visited regions, there's a chance that it will be an undescribed species. There are still lots of species – especially frogs, reptiles and insects – waiting to be discovered.

The greatest diversity of animal life occurs at around 1500m above sea level. The ancestors of many of the marsupials found in these forests were derived from Australia some five million years ago. As Australia dried out they vanished from that continent, but they continued to thrive and evolve in New Guinea, producing a highly distinctive fauna. Birds of paradise and bowerbirds also abound there, and the forest has many trees typical of the forests of ancient Gondwana. As you go higher the forests get mossier and the air colder. By the time you have reached 3000m above sea level the forests are stunted and wreathed in epiphytes. It's a formation known as elfin woodland, and in it one finds many bright honeyeaters, native rodents and some unique relics of prehistory, such as the giant long-beaked echidna. Above the elfin woodland the trees drop out, and a wonderland of alpine grassland and herbfield dominates, where wallabies and tiny birds, like the alpine robin, can often be seen. It is a place where snow can fall and where early morning ice coats the puddles.

Lowlands

Flying into Port Moresby you'll encounter grassland – a far cry from the eternally wet forests that beckon from the distant ranges. Such habitats exist in a band of highly seasonal rainfall that exists across southern

New Guinea, and the fauna you'll see there is much like that of northern Australia. Magpie geese, brolgas and jabirus occupy the floodplains, as do sandy-coloured agile wallabies, Rusa deer (which were introduced a century ago) and saltwater crocodiles.

Where the dry season is shorter, however, the savannah gives way to lowland jungles and there you are in another world. The largest native land animal you'll encounter is not a mammal or a reptile, but a bird – New Guinea's southern cassowary.

It's the nature of rainforests that their inhabitants form intimate relationships, and the cassowary stands at the centre of an intricate web. It eats the fruit of rainforest trees, and it can fit objects as large as a grapefruit down its throat. Its stomach strips the pulp from the fruit but passes the seeds unharmed, and from them new forest trees can grow – unless a sinister-looking parrot is nearby. The vulturine parrot is a cockatoo-sized bird with the colours of an Edwardian gentleman's morning suit – a sombre black on the outside, but with rich vermilion linings. Its head is naked and bears a long, hooked beak, hence its common name. Until recently no one knew quite why its head was so odd – then one was seen neck-deep in cassowary faeces. The bird specialises, it seems, in picking apart reeking cassowary droppings in search of the seeds, and for such an occupation a bald head (which prevents the faeces from sticking) and a long pincer-like beak are essential requirements.

New Guinea's snake fauna includes some extremely venomous species, such as the taipan and king brown snake, which are limited to the savannahs. Generally speaking the higher up the mountains you go, the fewer venomous snakes there are.

Mountain Forests

The forests of New Guinea's mountains, including its high-mountain elfin woodland, are, on first acquaintance, more sedate places. There is often a distinct chill in the air at dawn, and out of the mist you might hear the pure tones of the New Guinea whipbird, or the harsher calls of any one of a dozen birds of paradise. Just why New Guinea is home to such an astonishing variety of spectacular birds has long puzzled biologists. Part of the answer lies in the lack of mammalian predators on the

---

Top Wildlife Reads

» *Throwim Way Leg*, Tim Flannery

» *Birds of Northern Melanesia*, Jared Diamond and Ernst Mayr

» *Birds of New Guinea*, Bruce Beehler et al

» *Mammals of New Guinea*, Tim Flannery

ENVIRONMENT PNG – A MEGADIVERSE REGION

WILDLIFE SPOTTING

Good places to see wildlife:

» **Ambua Lodge** (p115) In comfort; in the Tari Gap, Southern Highlands.

» **Kumul Lodge** (p109) Specialist birders' lodge 40 minutes from Mt Hagen.

» **Crater Mountain Wildlife Management Area** (p103) For the more adventurous; in the Southern Highlands area.

» **Karawari Lodge** (p136) In pristine lowland rainforest in the foothills of East Sepik Province.

» **Walindi Plantation Resort** (p150) Famous among divers, Walindi also offers superb birdwatching.

» **Kamiali Wildlife Management Area** (p84) Huge hawksbill and leatherback turtles nest here between November and March.

» **Sibonai Guesthouse** (p69) An excellent place to see Goldie's Bird of Paradise and other unique avian species.

» **Ohu Butterfly Habitat** (p91) Community conservation project breeding butterflies, including PNG's huge birdwing varieties.

» **Jais Aben** (p91) Easy access for divers and snorkellers to a stunning variety of marine wildlife.

Australia and New Guinea have the world's only macropods and monotremes. The agile wallaby is found in New Guinea and Australia, but most of New Guinea's macropods are endemic tree kangaroos that are quite distinct from Australia's species of kangaroos and wallabies.

There are 42 species of birds of paradise, of which 36 are unique to New Guinea. Two species are found in both New Guinea and northern Australia. The male Raggiana decorates the flag of PNG. Birds of paradise first appeared in European literature in 1522.

island. The largest – a marsupial known as the New Guinea quoll – is only kitten-sized. Thus there are no foxes, leopards or similar creatures to prey on the birds, which as a consequence have developed such astonishing colours and spectacular mating rituals as to beggar belief.

If you can get well away from the villages, perhaps by accompanying experienced bushmen on a two- or three-day walk to distant hunting grounds, you might get to see a tree kangaroo. These creatures are relatives of Australia's rock wallabies which, five million years ago, took to the treetops. There are eight species in New Guinea, but in the central ranges you are likely to see just two. Goodfellow's tree kangaroo is a chestnut-coloured creature the size of a Labrador. Higher up you may encounter the bearlike Doria's tree kangaroo. It is shaggy, brown and immensely powerful, and lives in family groups.

Alpine Regions

Where the woodland gives way to the alpine regions another world unfolds. There the tiger parrot calls from stunted umbrella plants. Rhododendron bushes and tufted orchids are covered with flowers, and any woody plants are festooned with ant plants. In a perfect example of the intimate ecological relationships that abound in the forest, the ant protects the plant, while the plant provides shelter for its tiny defenders.

You'll see well-worn tracks winding through the alpine tussocks. Some are made by diminutive wallabies, others by giant rats. New Guinea is home to a spectacular diversity of rats, which comprise fully one-third of the mammal fauna. These distant relatives of the laboratory rat are spectacularly varied: some look like miniature otters and cavort in mountain streams, others resemble small, tree-climbing possums, while still others look, and smell, like rats from elsewhere.

In two of the highest mountain regions in PNG – the Star Mountains in the far west and Mt Albert Edward near Port Moresby – one of the country's most enigmatic birds can be seen. Known as McGregor's bird of paradise, it is a velvet-black bird the size of a large crow that makes a distinctive rattling sound as it flies. Under each wing is a large orange spot, and behind each eye a fleshy, flapping orange wattle of skin.

The Kokoda Story

By Peter FitzSimons
Journalist, ex-Wallaby and author of *Kokoda*

Walking in Diggers' Footsteps

Each year around 5000 Australians walk the Kokoda Track. For them it is part pilgrimage, part opportunity to pay homage to the soldiers of WWII and part extraordinary challenge. For it is not for the fainthearted. It's 96km of steep terrain: humid, slippery and potentially dangerous. Local guides are needed to ensure safety and to provide stories and a connection to the environment.

For myself, I knew I couldn't write my book without having experienced the Kokoda Track personally, so in November 2002 I set off with 17 other blokes from Sydney, scrambling up and down the same ravines as those men of yore, battling much the same conditions they had, to get from Owers' Corner just north of Port Moresby all the way to Kokoda. From the beginning of the journey, the heat, the humidity and the enduring sense that we were a long, long way out of our depth was indescribable, and that was just Port Moresby airport.

By the time we were on the track proper, it was (and I write as one who knows what it is to have an entire All Black pack dance a jig on my back) far and away the hardest thing I have ever done, and all of us on my trek felt the same.

Yet all of us were conscious that as we kept pushing north, we were walking in the footsteps of the greats. We Sydneysiders sweated, we strained, we whinged, we whined. We forded rivers that could have swept us to our deaths had we lost our footing, walked along precipices where any slip meant oblivion. We clambered up mountains that were anything but a stairway to heaven, and then faced the agony of getting down the other side. Our lungs wheezed, our hearts pumped 19 to the dozen, our feet began to slide around in our boots on balloons of blisters mixed with blood and sweat. Never, not once, could we lose ourselves in our thoughts, for the track would not allow it – you had to fiercely concentrate on the here and now...or risk the hereafter.

KOKODA TIMELINE

7 December 1941
The Japanese bomb Pearl Harbor.

15 February 1942
Singapore falls to the invading Japanese forces.

4 May–8 May 1942
In the Battle of the Coral Sea, around the eastern tip of New Guinea, the US Navy and Imperial Japanese Navy savage each other to such an extent that the only way left for the Japanese to take Port Moresby is overland, via the Kokoda Track.

21 July 1942
Japanese forces land on the north coast of New Guinea, at the top of the Kokoda Track.

28 July 1942
The Japanese take the small outpost of Kokoda – significant because its airstrip is the only one in the area – and in the process kill the commander of Australia's 39th Battalion, the key force opposing them.

26 August 1942
The Battle of Isurava begins. It ends on 30 August, as the Australians, bloodied but unbowed, pull back.

8 September 1942
The Battle of Brigade Hill. Again, the Japanese eventually prevail, but are severely weakened. Before the month is out, the Japanese at Ioribaiwa Ridge, overlooking Port Moresby, receive orders from Tokyo to 'advance to the rear'.

22 January 1943
The last Japanese at the head of the track surrender; the Kokoda campaign is finally over.

Always, for us, the best thing was the night, when we would usually make camp in the wilderness in small tents. We could stop then. Gather around the fire, talk, recuperate the best we could, have a bit of a laugh, speculate on what it had been like for the Diggers when they were doing it, and maybe even sing a few songs.

Anyway, at last the moment came: complete rest. Blessed sleep. Look, we *thought* that we had perhaps six to eight hours before *reveille,* but my own experience was that my sleep was so profound that it *felt* like I was being awakened just 10 minutes after closing my eyes.

For at dawn the following day, we were back into it.

Every half-day or so – sometimes more, sometimes less – we would go through a village where there would oft be sweet respite. The villagers were generally generous-hearted and pleased to see us, if slightly bemused at why we were putting ourselves through such an ordeal. They knew that they had been born and raised to walk the track – and they practically skipped along with a song in their hearts – but there was little we could do to hide our own extreme discomfort, and our reluctance to leave them.

And then we were back into it. Always, back into it. The jungle pressed, the leeches sucked, the mountain rose and fell, the green nightmare got ever more vivid. Was there some kind of light in the foliage above to indicate that we were near the summit? No, just a false dawn. We counted 20 of them before we finally got there, screamed, and then began the descent. Keep going. It is all we could do. And always we remembered that at least we didn't have to face bullets and bayonets, at journey's end, like the Diggers did.

If you wish to tackle the track, see p59 for details on preparation, gear, guides and tours.

A Historical Synopsis

Written on your thumbnail, the story of the Kokoda Track goes like this...

The Japanese bombed Pearl Harbor on 7 December 1941, and was at war with the Allies, including Australia, almost immediately thereafter. From there, Japan's superbly trained army swept through Southeast Asia knocking over country after country, stronghold after stronghold, including most notably Singapore on 15 February 1942. By late July '42, the first of an initial wave of 13,000 Japanese soldiers landed on the north coast of New Guinea and set off south along a jungle track that passed through the tiny outpost of Kokoda before coming out near Port Moresby – which it was their intention to occupy. The Australian military and political leadership was alarmed at the possibility that, if successful, the Japanese would be able to use Port Moresby as a base from which to launch south,

TOP KOKODA READS

There is a reasonable choice of publications about Kokoda available. Here are some of our recommendations:

» *Kokoda* by Paul Ham (2004) – War history told from both the Japanese and Australian perspective.

» *Those Ragged Bloody Heroes* by Peter Brune (1992) – The Kokoda battle through the eyes of the soldiers who fought there, raising questions about the leadership.

» *The Kokoda Trail: a History* by Stuart Hawthorne (2003) – A 130-year history of Kokoda: colonial, missionary and adventurer presence along the trail.

» *Kokoda* by Peter FitzSimons (2004) – Gripping account of the WWII battle.

» *Blood and Iron* by Lex McAuley (1991) – The battle tale researched by an ex-Australian Army serviceman.

RECENT INTEREST

In recent times interest in Kokoda has surged, as Australians have learnt more about what occurred. It is a compelling story, an extraordinary story, and it makes Australians proud. And it was for a very good reason that, as Australian Prime Minister, Paul Keating kissed the ground when he arrived at Kokoda in 1992, to pay tribute. It was a symbol of the fact that Australia was finally recognising what had been achieved in this place. Here, Mr Keating said, the Australian soldiers were not fighting for Empire; they were fighting 'not in defence of the Old World but the New World. Their world. They fought for their own values.' Which was why, he explained, 'for Australians, the battles in Papua New Guinea were the most important ever fought.'

perhaps landing in Queensland, Australia. However, in the first instance only 400 inexperienced militia soldiers of the 39th Battalion could be mustered to stop the Japanese invaders, or at least hold them up long enough for the more experienced veterans of the Australian Imperial Force (AIF) – who were being rushed forward – to get there.

The legend of the Kokoda Track, thus, concerns firstly the story of what happened when those two forces met in the middle, at a place called Isurava, and then the subsequent actions up and down the length of the track, with the 'front line' – such as it was – often being judged by where the pointy end of the bayonet of the most forward troops of each army could be found.

The fighting at Isurava was savage and without mercy from either side. And yet, while through sheer weight of numbers and an almost suicidal courage the Japanese finally prevailed at Isurava, in so doing they used up much of their fighting force. Certainly, the Japanese soldiers nevertheless pressed on, down the track – being ambushed all the way by the Australians, who now set out to weaken them further – but ultimately the invaders were all but exhausted by the time those that remained could get to within rough sight of Moresby.

It was there, at Ioribaiwa Ridge, that the Japanese military leadership (having no word for 'retreat') ordered their soldiers to 'advance to the rear'. The Australians were able to chase the Japanese back down the same track whence they came, all the way back to where they had first landed. More bitter fighting ensued as the Japanese dug in with fresh reinforcements, but at last, with the help of newly arrived American forces, it was all over on 22 January 1943. That was the day that the last Japanese resistance was wiped out at the head of the track, and the Australian flag was raised in those parts once more.

In the course of the previous six months in New Guinea, Australia had lost 2165 troops, with 3533 wounded. The US, which had only come into action very late in the piece, had lost 671 troops, with 2172 wounded. It was the Japanese, operating so far from their homeland, with military officers perhaps less concerned with the sanctity of their soldiers' lives, who suffered most. Some 20,000 Japanese troops landed in Papua, of which it is estimated the Japanese lost 13,000.

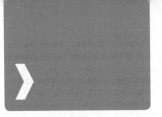

The People of PNG

Population

PNG people are closely related to people from other parts of the Pacific. There are Papuans, the first arrivals; Melanesians, who represent 95% of people and are related to people from the Solomon Islands, Vanuatu, Fiji and New Caledonia; Polynesians, related to New Zealand Maoris, Tongans, Samoans and Hawaiian islanders; and Micronesians, related to people in the Marshall Islands, Kiribati and Nauru.

Only 15% of people live in urban areas, while most of the rest are subsistence farmers. Nearly two million people live in the Highlands, the most densely populated part of the country.

Most cities have many people who weren't born there. Many Highlanders migrate to Port Moresby and elsewhere, but few coastal people move into the Highlands. Melanesian people still identify more strongly with their clan links and their origins than with the people they come to live with, so enclaves exist in the settlement areas of the big cities, and there is a traditional distrust between Highlanders and coastal people.

Lifestyle

Some people have typical urban lifestyles with cars and comfortable homes. Others inhabit remote areas and may never have seen a town or a white person. Urban or rural, they almost all chew *buai* (betel nut), go to church, worship dead ancestors and fear *masalais* (malevolent spirits).

Melanesians are laid-back, at least on the coast where it's too hot to get overly fussed. Highlanders are a bit more feisty and passionate. Everyone seems to walk slowly, but they've got this climate worked out – cling to the shade, sleep through the midday heat and save physical exertion for village rugby late in the day.

By Western standards most people live very simply. In the bush people have very few possessions and often no cash income. In the cities a number of educated people lead sophisticated middle-class lives, but other people live in squalor in city-fringe settlements. PNG lifestyles range from the rarefied cold-weather climes of the Highlands to life on the coast in stilt houses above the shifting tide.

Both PNG and the Solomons are changing quickly and locals want development. Particularly in PNG, people have married outside their traditional clans and homelands, and *tok ples* (local language, pronounced 'talk place') is increasingly being replaced in the villages with Tok Pisin (the Pidgin language). Isolated communities are suddenly being confronted with huge mining and logging operations. These bring new roads and facilities and remote areas are opened to Western influences – both good and bad.

Linguistic Diversity

PNG is the most linguistically complex country in the world with more than 12% of the world's living languages – well over 800 living languages – but many are dying out. In the Solomon Islands alone, more than 70 languages are spoken.

Cargo Cults

After the great American military machine left at the end of WWII, cargo cults began to sprout. People built runways for imaginary planes to land on and deliver *kago* (material goods).

Traditional Lifestyle

Ownership in the Western sense didn't exist in traditional societies; instead ownership was a concept tied up in family and clan rights, controlled by the male elder.

In traditional Melanesian culture there are three main areas of everyday importance – prestige, pigs and gardening. A village chief shows wealth by owning and displaying certain traditional valuables, or by hosting lavish feasts where dozens of pigs are slaughtered. *Bigmen* (important men or leaders) don't inherit their titles, although being the son of a chief has advantages. *Bigmen* must earn their titles by accolades in war, wisdom in councils, magic-practice skills and the secret arts that are *tambu* (taboo) for women. Particularly in the Highlands, people have to be made aware how wealthy *bigmen* are, so ceremonial life in this region focuses on ostentatious displays and in giving things away. There are various ways in which this is formalised; it's part of a wide circle of exchange and interclan relationships. Wealth is never really given away in the Western sense. Your gifts cement a relationship with the receiver, who then has obligations to you. Obligation and payback are deadly serious in Highlands culture; Melanesia has no privileged classes, but individuals still inherit land through their parents (often their mother). Village life in PNG and the Solomons is usually egalitarian, and ownership continues to be a concept tied up in family and clan rights.

Pigs are extremely valuable; they're regarded as family members and lactating women sometimes suckle piglets. People can be seen taking their pig for a walk on a leash, patiently waiting as the pig grazes and digs by the roadside. Large pigs can be worth K1000. Dogs, on the other hand, are mangy, fly-blown creatures left to scavenge for food.

Bride Price

Bride price is the formalised gift-giving of money and traditional valuables to the father of a would-be bride. It might include shell money, cash, pigs and even SP Lager. Part of becoming a man and commanding respect is working hard to raise a bride price so you can marry.

THE PEOPLE OF PNG LIFESTYLE

Animism, Christianity & Spirit Houses

People in both countries still maintain animist beliefs. Despite the inroads of Christianity, ancestor worship is still important. The netherworld is also inhabited by spirits, both protective and malevolent, and there are creation myths that involve animal totems. This is stronger in certain areas: islanders from Malaita in the Solomons worship sharks

THE WANTOK SYSTEM

Fundamental to Melanesian culture is the idea of *wantoks* (meaning 'one talk' in Tok Pisin) and your *wantoks* are those who speak your *tok ples* (language) – your clan or kinfolk. Every Melanesian is born with duties to their *wantoks* but they also have privileges. Within the clan and village, each person can expect to be housed and fed, and to share in the community's assets.

Some say that the *wantok* system is the best and worst thing about PNG and the Solomon Islands. For villagers, it is an egalitarian way for the community to share its spoils. In rapidly changing circumstances, the village and the clan provide basic economic support as well as a sense of belonging.

When these ideas are transposed to politics and social affairs, it becomes nepotism and, at worst, corruption. Candidates don't get to run without the support of their fellow *bigmen* (important men or leaders), who expect that when 'their' candidate is elected, their generosity will be repaid. The *wantok* system is also the greatest disincentive to enterprise.

The *wantok* system is a microcosm of the battle being waged between the modern and the traditional in PNG and the Solomons. It is so deeply entrenched that some educated youngsters choose to move away from their families to avoid the calls for handouts. And without it, life would be much harder for many others. Just saying 'no' to a *wantok* is rarely an option.

while some Sepik River people revere crocodiles. Christianity has a tight grip on most people, but it hasn't supplanted traditional beliefs. They coexist – Jesus is alive in people's hearts and minds without conflicting with their traditional ideas.

Men's cults are widespread throughout Melanesia and involve the ritualised practice of 'the arts' and ancestor worship in men's houses and *haus tambarans* (spirit houses). This can involve the building and display of certain ceremonial objects, song and dance, and the initiation of boys into manhood. It manifests in different ways in different societies, but it is very secretive and deadly serious – in the Sepik boys are cut with crocodile markings as part of their initiation, while Tolais boys are visited by *dukduks* (spiritual costumes) to perform their initiation rites. It's ironic and hard to fathom for outsiders, but while men's business and *haus tambarans* are *tambu* for women, men's cults and their initiation rites are all about rebirthing – the *haus tambaran* is like a womb and in some places its entrance is actually shaped like a vagina.

Women's Roles

Sexual politics is complicated in traditional Melanesian society. In some places in the Highlands husband and wife don't live together at all, and sexual relations are not to be taken lightly. Some Melanesian men have two or more wives. In many belief systems women are considered dangerous, especially during menstruation. Women often live in a house alone with the young children, or with sisters and their nieces and nephews. In many places land rights pass through the mother, and older women can wield great power in the villages.

Women carry *kago* (cargo) in *bilums* (string bags) home from the market while the man walks unburdened. Women do most of the food gardening, although men grow magnificent decorative gardens. Traditionally, men practise arts that are exclusively their domain and, although these can sometimes be shown to women travellers, they are still *tambu* for local women.

Arts

PNG's arts are regarded as the most striking and varied in the Pacific, and Solomon Islanders, being great carvers, are part of the same cultural tradition. The lack of contact between different villages and groups of people has led to a potent array of indigenous art.

In traditional societies, dance, song, music, sculpture and body adornment were related to ceremonies. Art was either utilitarian (such as bowls or canoes) or religious. Since European contact, art has become objectified. There have always been master carvers and mask-makers, but their role in traditional cultures was to enable the ceremonies and rituals to be performed correctly, and to serve the clan and chief.

The production of artefacts is itself often ceremonial and ritualistic. On some of the islands, secret men's societies build *dukduks* or carve *malangan* masks (totemic figures honouring the dead). Women are forbidden to look upon a *dukduk* or *malangan* until it is brought to life in a ceremony by a fierce anonymous character.

Bill Bennett's *In a Savage Land* (1999), filmed in the Trobriands, is about a couple of anthropologists in the 1930s and their take on the 'Islands of Love'. Australian musician David Bridie's soundtrack won a bunch of awards.

Top Singers & Albums

» Narasirato, *Tangio Tumas*

» George Telek, *Serious Tam*

» Hausboi, *Diriman*

» O-Shen, *Faya*

» Sharzy, *Hem Stret*

» Litol Rastas, *Dollar Man*

» Tipa, *Maiae*

Survival Guide PNG

Directory A–Z

Accommodation

Papua New Guinea offers poor value in terms of accommodation. When compared with the cheap-as-chips places of nearby Indonesia, or even with the developed-world prices of neighbouring Australia, hotel rates make for grim reading.

Top-end hotels are required to charge a 10% value added tax (VAT; but sometimes called GST), and all

PRICE RANGES

All room prices include bathrooms unless specified otherwise, and when meals or breakfasts are included, 'incl breakfast' or 'incl meals' is shown in the accommodation listings. Price ranges are for twin or double rooms and are defined as follows:

$ <150
$$ K150–400
$$$ >K400

prices in this book are inclusive of this tax. If you book and pay for your PNG accommodation from outside the country, it is VAT exempt.

Booking ahead is also a good idea during festival times when everything is packed. Apart from festival weekends (see p19) and national holidays (see p191), tourists make up such a small percentage of hotel guests that there is no clearly defined high or low season.

Camping

Camping is not a traditional part of Melanesian culture. Travellers are welcomed into whatever dwelling is available, and refusing such hospitality in favour of pitching a tent can be quite offensive. All land has a traditional owner somewhere and you need to seek permission to camp – finding the landowner could take awhile, and chances are that when you do they'll offer you room in a hut anyway. So unless you're planning on doing some seriously off-the-beaten-track trekking, don't bother bringing a tent.

Hotels & Resorts

The vast majority of hotels fall into the midrange and

top-end categories in terms of price if not quality. They principally cater to the large mining consortiums and their notoriously deep pockets. In major towns, hotels are equipped with a bathroom, cable TV, phone and air-con, and might include a fridge, tea- and coffee-making facilities, breakfast, and free transport to and from the airport. Despite their hefty five-star price tags, don't expect much beyond three-star quality.

Truly top-end resorts are few and far between. Prices for such style can be as high as K1400 for a plush suite. You'll usually have access to a swimming pool and a range of pricey bars and restaurants at this level. Service is usually pretty good, and tariffs may include some activities as most tourist-orientated resorts revolve around diving, birdwatching, trekking, fishing or cultural visits. **Trans Niugini Tours** (www.pngtours.com) is the largest such operator with six luxury lodges scattered throughout the mainland.

Wherever you head, don't forget to ask about specials, and corporate and weekend rates.

Missions, Hostels & Guesthouses

The cheapest accommodation options are usually the region's many mission guesthouses, community-run hostels and private guesthouses. These can be good value for money. Mission guesthouses are mainly for church types, but the lodgings are generally clean, homey and open to travellers. Quality varies and the cheaper ones have no air-con and shared bathrooms. You'll have to put up with a few rules – drinking and smoking are discouraged (or banned) and you can expect to hear grace before meals. But the managers are usually pretty interesting people and great sources of information – best described as Bible-handlers rather than bashers. Among the missions, the Lutheran guesthouses are consistently good.

Rental Accommodation

Large numbers of expats come and go and there is no shortage of long-term rental accommodation. Much of it is attached to midrange and, more often, top-end hotels, but there are some less expensive alternatives. The formula is simple enough: provide large walls, plenty of security guards and the facilities of a hotel, and people will come. Weekly, monthly and yearly rates are very attractive when compared with hotel prices. Check www.pngbd.com/forum/f74s.html on the Papua New Guinea Business Directory. Alternatively, contact some of the volunteering organisations (p194) or try the diplomatic representative of your country in Port Moresby.

Village Accommodation

One of the great experiences of travelling in PNG is taking the opportunity to stay in a village. Village accommodation comes in all manner of guises. It might be a basic hut in a highland village; a tiny thatched stilt house in the Trobriand Islands; or one of the simple village guesthouses on the Huon Gulf coast, or around Tufi, Milne Bay, the Sepik or New Ireland. It might not be a village house at all, but a spare room in a school, space in a police station, in a church house or just about any building you see. Just ask.

Village accommodation can be pretty rough but it's the cheapest way to see the country, and in most villages you'll find a local who'll put you up. You must pay; K30 to K50 is a fair amount to offer a family providing you a roof and *kai* (food). But ask locals before you head out of town what might be appropriate compensation – a live *kakaruk* (chicken) could be

BOOK YOUR STAY ONLINE

For more accommodation reviews by Lonely Planet authors, check out http://hotels.lonelyplanet.com. You'll find independent reviews, as well as recommendations on the best places to stay. Best of all, you can book online.

the go. But a live *kakaruk* can be a hassle to lug around, so maybe a sack of rice, or some bully beef, salt, tea or sugar might be better. In some instances a carton of beer is good currency, but alcohol can be a very sensitive issue in some communities, so proceed with caution.

In some villages couples might be asked to sleep in separate buildings to observe local custom. Most rural villages have a men's house and these spaces often function as domiciles for elderly or widowed men and young male initiates, as resthouses for male guests and as places where men practise 'the arts'. Men's houses are *tambu* (forbidden) to women – female travellers will be enthusiastically 'adopted' by the village women and quickly engaged with the womanly affairs of the community. In some villages there's a *haus kiap* – a village house set aside for travellers to stay in. These were originally erected for accommodating visiting *kiaps* (government patrol officers) and some remain today. You might be asked to stay in one of these, but it's more enjoyable to stay with a family in a traditional house than sleeping by yourself.

Activities

Travel to PNG is all about being outdoors in the elements and part of the natural environment – let's face it, there's precious little shopping and very few galleries and museums!

Birdwatching

PNG is home to thousands of species of flora and fauna and seeing some of it, especially

the rich bird life, is becoming easier as local guides learn what birders want.

Birders report that in a three-week trip you'll see about 300 species. A small number of local guides are well worth seeking out. You can plan and execute your trip with these guys for a fraction of the cost of a tour. Samuel Kepuknai from **Kiunga Nature Tours** (☎675-548 1451; kepuknai@online.net.pg) is *the* man in remote Western Province, while former hunter **Daniel Wakra** (☎675-688 0978; danielwakra@yahoo.com) knows the sites around Port Moresby very well. Kumul Lodge (see boxed text, p109) in Enga Province, Warili Lodge (p115) and Ambua Lodge (p115) both in Tari, all have programs specifically for birdwatchers and excellent guides.

For practical planning tips and inspiration, it's worth reading the field reports posted on the following sites:

Travelling Birder (www.travellingbirder.com)

Fat Birder (www.fatbirder.com/links_geo/australasia/papua_new_guinea.html)

The following tour companies all offer specialist birding tours in PNG:

Bird Quest (www.birdquest-tours.com) UK based.

Eagle Eye Tours (www.eagle-eye.com) US based.

Field Guides (www.fieldguides.com) US based.

Kirrama Wildlife Tours (www.kirrama.com.au) Australia based.

Rockjumper Worldwide Birding Adventures (www.rockjumperbirding.com) South Africa based.

PRACTICALITIES

Newspapers

» PNG has two daily English-language newspapers: the *Post Courier* (www.postcourier.com.pg) and the *National* (www.thenational.com.pg). The weekly *Wantok Niuspepa* is written entirely in Tok Pisin, while the weekend *Sunday Chronicle* is PNG's only locally owned newspaper.

Radio

» PNG has two government-funded national radio stations: Karai on the AM band and Kalang on FM. National commercial stations include NauFM (96.5FM) broadcasting in English and YumiFM (93FM) broadcasting in Tok Pisin. BBC World Service can be heard in Port Moresby on 106.7FM. There are numerous regional radio stations mostly devoted to local pop music.

» For a full list of stations and frequencies see http://radiostationworld.com.

TV

» EmTV and Kundu 2 are the only free-to-air stations in PNG. There are seven 'cable' (actually satellite) channels plus a range of stations from rural Australia that can also be picked up by those with the capabilities.

Weights & Measures

» PNG uses the metric system, except by trade boat skippers who buy and sell fuel by the gallon. This is particularly true on the Sepik.

Boating

Few roads. Lots of rivers. More islands. It's a combination that makes boating in one form or another almost inevitable in PNG. The one ingredient you need for almost every boat trip is time, not just to reach the journey's end, but most often to get the journey underway! Local dinghies and motor-canoes seem to take an eternity to get their *cargo* loaded up – cartons of beer, margarine, rice and Kundu crackers – and then, of course, the boat's pilot must be found (who'll be asleep under a tree somewhere) and his cousin's sister who's catching a ride.

RIVER JOURNEYS

PNG has some of the world's largest and most spectacular rivers. The Sepik is often compared to the Amazon and Congo Rivers and local people use the river as a highway. For details, see p127.

SEA JOURNEYS

If you don't own a cruising yacht (and when you see PNG's islands and harbours you'll wish you did), there are four alternatives: use the regular coastal shipping; take a tour; charter a boat; or crew a yacht. For more on these options, see p198.

With a dense scattering of beautiful islands, PNG is a great place for sea kayaking. **Southern Sea Ventures** (www.southernseaventures.com) offers an amazing 11-day guided sea-kayaking voyage from Rabaul to Alotau. Apart from this, and a few kayaks at some of the diving resorts, it's BYO everything.

Caving

Caves in the limestone regions of the Southern Highlands may well be the deepest in the world, but actually getting into them requires something approaching a full-scale expedition. The Mamo Kananda in the Muller Range (near Lake Kopiago) is reputed to be one of the longest caves in the world at 54.8km. There are also caves around Bougainville (Benua Cave is thought to be the world's biggest cavern at 4.5 million cubic metres),

Pomio (East New Britain Province) and Manus Province.

While there are no tour operators offering caving as an activity, caving expeditions from the UK, USA and France have been exploring PNG caves in recent years.

Diving & Snorkelling

PNG offers some of the most interesting, exciting and challenging underwater activities on earth. Those who like diving on wrecks will find dozens of sunken ships – either as a result of WWII or the maze of spectacular coral reefs. And the reefs are not only for divers – excellent visibility and an abundance of fish make them perfect for snorkellers.

See the diving chapter (p25) for an overview on what's up down below.

Fishing

Fishing, and particularly sportfishing in PNG's many river estuaries, is one of the country's major tourist drawcards. There are dozens of virtually untouched rivers brimming with fish, including species such as barramundi, mangrove jack and the legendary Papuan black bass. And off the coasts there's no shortage of big fish either. Yellowfin tuna, mackerel, sailfish, and blue, black and striped marlin are just some of monster fish hooked by die-hard anglers that come here from all over the world.

You can't just get in a boat and go. Everything and every piece of PNG is owned by someone, including streams and reefs, and unless you have permission from traditional owners, you could easily get yourself into trouble. It's obviously a lot easier to arrange your fishing via a tour company or lodge.

The **Game Fishing Association of Papua New Guinea** (www.gfa.com.pg) has an excellent website with lots of information on events, local clubs and competitions, and the contact details of fishing charters and fishermen-friendly lodges throughout PNG.

Surfing

The southern coast of the PNG mainland gets swell from June to September when Hula Beach, 100km east of Port Moresby, gets 1m to 2m waves. However, the best waves are during the monsoon season from late October to April along the north coast and in the islands. Beach, point- and plenty of reef-breaks are out there, and reaching them is becoming easier. You'll only need one good all-round board, and a rash vest to keep the sun off.

The best places to head are Kavieng (p151) and the western end of New Ireland, Wewak (p117) and Ulingan Bay (p92), both on the northern coast of the PNG mainland and, the pick of the lot, Vanimo (p124), on the north coast near the border with Indonesian Papua.

The **Surf Association of Papua New Guinea** (⌨326 0884 in Port Moresby; www. surfingpapuanewguinea.org. pg) has a decent website

with links to surfing tours. It has recently introduced the Surf Area Management Plan (SAMP) that levies a K30 per person, per day fee to all international surfers. The proceeds are split between the local land and reef owners, board rider clubs and the surf association itself, which hopes to ensure a sustainable future for surf tourism and fund future growth.

Besides the surf camps listed in the locations earlier in this section, it's worth looking at the following websites for their all-inclusive surfing charters and packages:

World Surfaris (www.world surfaris.com)

PNG Surfaris (www.pngsur faris.com)

Adventures in Paradise (www.adventuresinparadise. com.pg)

Trekking

PNG is a trekking paradise. The country is crisscrossed with tracks, many of which have been used for centuries by the local population, and it is rarely more than a day's walk between villages.

Your major costs will be paying for guides, where they are necessary. Expect to pay a guide around K100 per day and a porter anything between K50 and K90 per day. You'll also have to provide or pay for their food. The best way to find a reliable guide is to ask around the local expat population – they will usually be able to put you in touch with someone who knows someone. All of the tour companies can provide guides or at least information on where you might procure one.

The Kokoda Track (p34) is the most popular trek in PNG. Mt Wilhelm (p104) is climbed fairly often, and some people then walk from there down to Madang (p105). The Black Cat Trail (p84) and the Bulldog Track (p87) will appeal to those with a military or historical bent...and a wide masochistic streak.

Windsurfing

The lagoons of PNG are ideal for windsurfing. There are many sheltered harbours and strong winds between June and August. If you don't have your own board, ask around the yacht clubs and resorts.

Business Hours

Opening and closing times can be erratic, but you can rely on most businesses closing at noon on Saturday and remaining closed all day Sunday. In this book, hours accord with the following details unless stated otherwise.

Banks (⊙8.45am-3pm Mon-Thu, 8.45am-4pm Fri)

Government offices (⊙7.45am-12.30pm & 1.45-4pm Mon-Fri)

Post offices (⊙8am-4pm Mon-Fri, 8-11.30am Sat)

Restaurants (⊙lunch 11.30am-2.30pm, dinner 6pm or 7-10pm or whenever the last diner leaves)

Shops (⊙9am-5pm or 6pm Mon-Fr, 9am-noon Sat)

Children

People who bring their *pikininis* (children) to PNG are often overwhelmed by the response of local people, who will spoil them mercilessly given half a chance. Childrearing in Melanesian culture is a communal village activity and just when you're starting to fret about your missing two year old he/she will turn up being carried on the hip of a six-year-old girl.

There are few really child-friendly sights – no theme parks or carousels – but the practicalities of travelling with children aren't too bad.

» Top-end and midrange hotels should have cots, and most restaurants have high chairs. You'll be lucky, however, to find dedicated nappy-changing facilities anywhere, and forget about safety seats in taxis – working safety belts are a novelty.

» As you'd expect in a country where bare breasts are everywhere, breastfeeding in public is no problem.

» A limited range of nappies and baby formula is available in larger towns.

» There are no daycare centres catering to travellers, though larger hotels can usually recommend a babysitter.

Customs Regulations

Visitors to PNG are permitted the following:

» 200 cigarettes (or 50 cigars or 250g of tobacco)

» 2L of alcohol

» 1L or 1000g of perfume

» New goods to the value of K1000. Exceed this K1000 threshold and things get ugly. One shifty way to get around this is to ditch the packaging before you board the PNG-bound plane and act as if the goods are *not* new when you disembark at Port Moresby's Jacksons Airport.

Since most people fly into and out of PNG from Australia, the customs and quarantine restrictions that apply in Australia are particularly pertinent. If anything you are carrying is deemed a quarantine risk, you'll have to pay to have it fumigated, a process that can take several days, and if you have a same-day onward connecting flight, you can kiss your artefacts goodbye. Places such as PNG Arts (p51) in Port Moresby or the Melanesian Arts Gallery (p79) in Lae can arrange (for a fee) fumigation and certification, but Australian customs officials won't take any notice of these documents and will want to either confiscate or fumigate your goods to their own exacting standards. Post can be a good alternative.

Items that will see you starring in an Aussie border-security reality TV show include the following:

» Animal parts, such as skin (often used on Kundu drums), teeth or feathers.

» Polished wood won't cause much alarm, but anything with bark is deemed risky.

» Bukaware itself is fine, but small bugs love to hide in the weaving, so this sometimes raises alarms.

» Betel nuts, fruit and other plant material.

Finally, anything created before 1960, including traditional stone tools, certain shell valuables, and any item incorporating human remains or bird of paradise plumes, cannot be exported. If you are uncertain of what your purchases are made of, get them checked at the National Museum in Port Moresby (p44).

Electricity

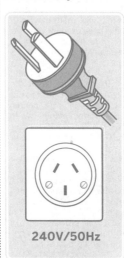

240V/50Hz

Embassies & Consulates

All embassies are in Port Moresby.

Australia High Commission (Map p48; ☎325 9333; www.png.highcommission.gov.au/pmsb/home.html; Godwit St, Waigani); Honorary Consul (Map p78; ☎472 2466; Trukai Industries, Mataram St, Lae)

France (Map p44; ☎321 5550; www.ambafrance-pg.org; Defens Haus, cnr Champion Pde & Hunter St)

Indonesia Consulate (☎457 1371; Vanimo); Embassy (Map p48; ☎325 3544; fax 325 0535; Kiroki St, Waigani)

Japan (Map p44; ☎321 1800; 1st fl, Cuthbertson House, Cuthbertson St, Town)

New Zealand (Map p48; ☎325 9444; nzhcpom@dg.com.pg; Magani Cres, Waigani)

Solomon Islands (Map p48; ☎323 4333; sihicomm@daltron.com.pg; Unit 3, GB House, Kunai St, Hohola) Poreporena Fwy.

UK (Map p48; ☎325 1677, emergency 683 1627; www.ukinpng.fco.gov.uk; Kiroki St, Waigani)

USA (Map p44; ☎321 1455; www.portmoresby.usembassy.gov; Douglas St, Town)

Food

Although the culinary scene has improved markedly in recent years, PNG is not going to excite the gourmet traveller. Apart from the wonderful seafood found on the coast, the traditional diet consists largely of bland, starchy vegetables. Which bland vegetable is served depends on where you are. In the Highlands it will probably be *kaukau* (sweet potato); on the islands, it's taro or yam; and in the Sepik and other swampy areas of PNG *sak-sak* (sago) is all the rage. Rice *(rais)* is universally popular.

Pigs are the main source of meat protein, although they are generally saved for feasts. Chicken *(kakaruk)* is also quite popular. A legacy of WWII is the prevalence and popularity of canned meat and fish. Locals prefer tinned fish *(tinpis)* to fresh fish, and whole supermarket aisles are devoted to bully beef *(buli)*.

Although local cuisine seems monotonous and unimaginative, produce available at markets is varied and excellent. You'll see capsicums (bell peppers), tomatoes, peanuts, avocados and spectacular fresh tropical fruit. In the Highlands you can sometimes get strawberries, cauliflower and broccoli.

Where to Eat & Drink

Where you eat will depend on your budget. In towns and cities the ubiquitous *kai* bar will probably lure you in for a snack at least once. *Kai* bars look and taste like Australian milk bars of the late 1970s; that is, they sell meat pies, sausage rolls, deep-fried dough balls and, probably your best bet, pre-prepared meals of indeterminable Asian origin (K12). We haven't listed many *kai* bars – just look for people milling around.

Other than those found in hotels, there are few stand-alone eateries outside of Port Moresby. If there is, it's usually Chinese that tend to offer better value (K25 to K45) and tastier meals than the pricier hotel restaurants (K45 to K70).

Gay & Lesbian Travellers

It's quite noticeable that recently gay men are more prepared to express themselves. These days you do see effeminate Melanesian men, and while they may not be strident or provocative about it, there's nothing ambiguous about their sexual orientation. And that's pretty gutsy – homosexuality is illegal and homophobia is quite palpable (unlike in Polynesia where there are strong traditions of transgenderism and homosexuality). Local women, on the other hand, don't seem so prepared to 'fly the flag' in public. Any local 'gay scene' that exists is closeted and underground. This is not surprising given that the churches have been reinforcing the idea that homosexuality is morally reprehensible for years.

You'll see many local people hold hands as they walk down the street – women with women and men with men. But don't misunderstand – this is simply an expression of friendliness and affection that's common in Melanesian societies.

Health

With sensible precautions and behaviour, the health risks to travellers in PNG are low. Mosquito-transmitted disease is the main problem.

Recommended Vaccinations & Prophylactics

The World Health Organisation (WHO) recommends that all travellers be covered for diphtheria, tetanus, measles, mumps, rubella and polio, regardless of their destination.

Vaccination for yellow fever (and the certificate to prove it) is required if you are entering from a yellow fever–endemic country. Vaccinations are also recommended for hepatitis A, hepatitis B, typhoid fever and Japanese B encephalitis.

Malaria, both malignant (falciparum) and the less threatening but relapsing forms, are found in all areas of PNG below 1000m. Since no vaccine is available you'll have to rely on mosquito-bite prevention (including exposing as little skin as possible, applying topical insect repellents, knockdown insecticides and, where necessary, bed nets impregnated with permethrin) and taking antimalarial drugs before, during and after risk exposure.

Availability of Health Care

In Port Moresby and Lae you can expect primary care of a high standard but limited by the lack of access to sophisticated medical equipment.

Specialists in internal medicine, surgery and obstetrics/gynaecology are also available in these centres, while in Port Moresby there are also paediatric, orthopaedic, dental and psychiatric specialists.

In secondary centres (eg Madang), the quality of service can be lower – often because of lower-quality diagnostic and treatment facilities. Small hospitals, health centres and clinics are well placed throughout these centres but staffing and facilities will vary.

Drinking Water

The municipal water supply in the capital and in the majority of major towns can be trusted. If you're trekking, drink only from streams at a higher altitude than nearby villages. Otherwise a sensible precaution is to boil, filter or chemically disinfect (with iodine tablets) all water.

Insurance

In a country where help is often a helicopter ride away, a travel insurance policy to cover theft, loss and an emergency flight (medivac) home is essential. Read the small print to check it covers potentially 'dangerous activities' such as diving and trekking.

Internet Access

Although there is still virtually no internet in PNG, there is usually at least one (and often only one) internet cafe

---

PRICE RANGES

Tipping is not required or expected in PNG and prices listed in this book include tax. The following price ranges refer to standard mains:

$	<20
$$	K20–40
$$$	>K40

in most major towns. Rates are often laughably high, anything from K15 to K30 per hour. Hotels and restaurants that do offer internet services are denoted throughout the book with a @ symbol for standard connections and a 🛜 symbol for wi-fi.

If you need to stay in regular contact with the online world or plan to spend a lot of time in small villages, it may be worth buying a modem data stick (K99) from either of the countries' mobile phone providers, **Digicel** (www.digicelpng.com) or **B-Mobile** (www.pacificmobile. com.pg). This will enable your laptop or iPad to receive mobile broadband – although 'broadband' in PNG is more like dial-up speeds elsewhere.

Legal Matters

Most police are courteous enough (even friendly!) but don't expect them to do much about any crime perpetrated against you. For years police have been outnumbered, out-gunned and out-motivated by gangs of *raskols* (bandits), and the number of crimes solved is piteously low. Police frustration is common, and don't be surprised to hear of swift justice being applied when a *raskol* is caught. If you need the police to go anywhere, you might need to pay for their fuel.

Maps

For the most up-to-date maps of PNG towns you need look no further than the nearest telephone book. It features a colour map section that covers all the major centres and it's free.

There are two country maps of PNG that should be available to purchase online, if not necessarily at your local bookshop. Hema Maps' *Papua New Guinea* (1:2,600,000) 2nd Edition (1992) is the most common, and is readily available in

PNG as well. More recent is ITMB's *Papua New Guinea* (1:2,000,000). This is probably the pick of the two.

If you're planning on trekking, or just want more detailed maps, you're advised to contact the **National Mapping Bureau** (NMB; ☑327 6222; www.lands.gov.pg/ Services/National_Mapping_ Bureau; Melanesian Way, Waigani), order the maps you want and then collect them from the office in Port Moresby when you arrive. The topographic maps range in scale from 1:2000 through 1:50,000, 1:100,000 and 1:250,000. They have the whole country covered, though they're often out of stock, out of paper or out of date.

If you're planning to walk the Kokoda Track, the NMB's *Longitudinal Cross Section of the Kokoda Trail* (1995) is very useful. It's been reproduced many times and is available at the **Kokoda Track Authority** (Map p47; ☑325 1887; www.kokoda trackauthority.org; 1st fl, Brian Bell Plaza, Boroko; ⊙8.30am-4.30pm Mon-Fri).

Money

After years of decline the kina has risen in value against major currencies thanks to the massive investment pouring in to the country from the LNG Project (see boxed text, p113) in the Highlands.

See the Quick Reference (inside front cover) for exchange rates.

ATMs

ATMs are fairly common in cities, and those at **ANZ** (www. anz.com/png/importantinfo/ atmlocations.asp), **Bank South Pacific** (BSP; www. bsp.com.pg) and **Westpac** (www.westpac.com.au) allow you to withdraw cash against your Visa or MasterCard on the Cirrus, Maestro and Plus networks. If the machines are broken, head inside and you

should be able to get a cash advance against your credit card over the counter.

Cash

PNG's currency is the kina (*kee*-nah), which is divided into 100 toea (*toy*-ah). Both are the names of traditional shell money and this connection to traditional forms of wealth is emphasised on the notes – the K20 note features an illustration of that most valuable of village animals, the pig.

You don't need to go too far off the track before you're fully reliant on cash. In remote areas, having enough small bills is important. People are cash poor and won't have change for K50.

Traditional currencies, such as shell money and leaf money, are still occasionally used. You'll see women in the Trobriand Islands carrying *doba* (leaf money), which is dried banana leaves with patterns incised on them.

Credit Cards

Credit cards are only accepted in top-end hotels and by a few restaurants and shops in Port Moresby and other larger towns. Visa and MasterCard are the favourites, with Amex, JCB and Diners Club not so widely accepted. Credit card payments often incur an additional charge.

Travellers Cheques

Travellers cheques are widely accepted at banks throughout PNG, though commission rates vary not only from bank to bank but also from branch to branch. The biggest drawback with using travellers cheques is that you'll be forced to join insanely long queues that snake through the bank and, on occasion, clean out the door.

Photography

PNG is pretty close to a photographer's nirvana. The stunning natural colours and locations are just the start, and shooting a cultural show could end up a career highlight. A few points to consider when shooting in PNG:

» Negative film is widely available but you'll need to bring your own slide film.

» If you're shooting digital it's worth bringing some sort of portable storage device, as you'll have a hard time finding an internet cafe (or the like) where you can download images and burn to a CD.

» You'll find people are generally happy to be photographed, even going out of their way to pose for you, particularly at *singsings* (celebratory festivals/dances). But ask permission before shoving a camera in someone's face, especially around the markets of the bigger cities – Port Moresby, Lae and Mt Hagen – as people can get a little testy about this.

» Some people, usually men dressed in traditional style, might request payment if they are photographed – K10 is a popular price. If you've gone ahead and taken a photo without getting permission and establishing a price, you may well find yourself facing an angry, heavily armed Highlander demanding K20 or more in payment. It would take some nerve to argue.

» *Never* take a photograph of, or even point a camera in or at, a *haus tambaran* (spirit house) without asking permission from a male elder.

For more tips see Lonely Planet's *Travel Photography*.

Post

PNG has an efficient postal service and you can usually rely on your mail or parcels getting home, even if it takes quite a while. Note that there is no postal delivery in PNG, so everyone and every business has a PO Box.

» **International aerograms** cost K2.50.

» **Letters or postcards** up to 50g cost K5 to Australia

and the Pacific, K7 everywhere else.

» **A 5kg package** costs K160 to Australia and K320 to the USA or Europe. You might've been feeling impetuous when you bought that 20kg skull rack, but you'll be thinking long and hard about the cost of posting it home – K315 to Australia, K590 to either the UK or USA. All parcels are shipped via airmail as surface mail is a thing of the past.

Public Holidays

In addition to the following national holidays listed, each province has its own provincial government day (usually a Friday or Monday) and there is usually a *singsing* to mark the occasion.

New Year's Day 1 January

Easter March/April, variable dates. Includes Good Friday and Easter Monday.

National Remembrance Day 23 April

Queen's Birthday Second Friday of June

PNG Independence Day 16 September

Christmas Day 25 December

Boxing Day 26 December

Safe Travel

It's very difficult to get the balance right about the dangers of travelling in PNG. If you believe the hype, you'll never go and you'll never understand that Melanesians are by nature among the most gentle, hospitable and generous people in the world. While urban drift has undoubtedly caused 'law and order' issues, it's not like the Wild West where gun-law rules and stepping outside is to put your life in danger.

If you use your common sense, especially in larger towns, the chance of encountering the notorious *raskols* is small. That said, when things do go wrong in PNG, it can be pretty frightening. Violent

crime is not unusual, but the victims are rarely tourists.

So what does this mean for the traveller? Most importantly, don't be paranoid. Those who have travelled to developing countries in the past probably won't be overly concerned, but for inexperienced travellers the lack of structure and the number of unemployed standing idly around the cities can be intimidating.

Bear in mind that everything is much more relaxed outside Port Moresby, Lae and Mt Hagen. Tribal fighting is still common deep in the Highlands, and while this can make things unpredictable it rarely embroils outsiders. In villages people quickly get to know you and you rapidly lose the anonymity that makes a stranger a target. Expats will tell you not to ride the buses and PMVs, but that's just silly. They'll regale you with stories of rape and

GOVERNMENT TRAVEL ADVICE

For the latest travel warnings and advice log onto the following (overly cautious) websites:

Australian Department of Foreign Affairs & Trade (www.dfat.gov.au/travel)

Japanese Ministry of Foreign Affairs (www.mofa.go.jp/anzen)

New Zealand Ministry of Foreign Affairs & Trade (www.safetravel.govt.nz)

UK Foreign & Commonwealth Office (www.fco.gov.uk/en/travel-and-living-abroad)

USA Department of State/Bureau of Consular Affairs (www.travel.state.gov)

pillage and plunder (even murder), but these tales are often urban legends that can have very tenuous connections to real events.

It's pretty simple – it would be highly unusual to encounter any trouble in the main areas where travellers are likely to go in the daytime with people around. The mantra is common sense. Fortunately, common sense is not rocket science, but here are some tips:

» Don't flaunt your wealth – wear unremarkable clothes and keep your camera hidden. Carry a *bilum* (string bag) rather than a daypack.

» Always keep at least K50 'raskol' money in your pocket to appease any would-be thief. Hide the rest of your money in a money belt or your shoe.

» Speak to people rather than being aloof.

» Be especially careful on the fortnightly Friday pay nights when things can get pretty wild.

» If you get held up, as in this situation anywhere, stay calm. Most robberies are fairly unsophisticated affairs.

Shopping

There is no shortage of wonderful artefacts and craft objects to take home. The best advice to shoppers is to buy one good piece you really like – it might even cost several hundred kina – rather than armfuls of small inferior carvings and artefacts.

See Customs Regulations (p188) for information about getting PNG and Solomons artefacts through Australian customs.

Bargaining

There is no tradition of bargaining in Melanesian culture, so don't expect to be able to cut your costs much by haggling. Bargaining is, however, starting to creep into some aspects of society, souvenir shopping

being one. It's a rather grey area and impossible to give definitive advice, but if you tread sensitively you should be OK. For example, artists who are used to dealing with Westerners (eg at Port Moresby's markets) will have experienced bargaining to some degree, so probably won't be too offended if you make a lower bid for their work. But forget about the old 'offer one-third and work up to a half' maxim; it's more like they ask K300, you offer K200 and you get the piece for K250. Maybe. Some artists are used to being asked for a 'second price' but few will appreciate being asked for a 'third price'.

Telephone & Fax

Telecommunications can be very unreliable and in the more remote parts of the country a working telephone line is pretty rare. Dialling out of PNG can also be problematic as the limited number of international lines fill quickly. PNG's country code is ☎675 and, as there are so few phones, there are no area codes.

Some useful codes:

Dialling outside PNG ☎00
International directory assistance ☎1517
PNG directory assistance ☎1513
International reverse-charge calls ☎1516
National reverse-charge calls ☎1511
Ships at sea ☎300 4646
To call a HF radio phone ☎1572

PNG has different emergency numbers for each city. They're all listed on the inside cover of the phonebook and in our relevant chapters.

FAX
Kwik piksa leta (fax) remains pretty big in PNG, where email is still in its infancy. You can send faxes from post offices for a few

kina and they can be a useful way of making accommodation bookings. The cost of sending a fax from a post office within PNG is K6 for one page, with each additional page costing a further K1.

MOBILE PHONES
Almost everyone in PNG has a mobile phone, often two; one from each of the two mobile phone companies **Digicel** (www.digicelpng.com) and **B-Mobile** (www.pacificmobile.com.pg). Sim cards (K15 to K25) and prepay top-up cards (from K3) are readily available and basic handsets start at K99.

Off-peak calls cost K0.11 to K0.49 per minute and peak time (8am to 10.59pm) calls cost K0.99 per minute.

Considering the mountainous terrain, mobile phone coverage is fairly good and being continuously expanded as new phone towers are built.

When dialling from a B-Mobile phone you need to add a '7' in front of any old-style numbers starting with '6'. If you forget, an automated prompt will remind you. All Digicel numbers already start with '7'.

PHONECARDS & TELIKAD
Most PNG cities have phonecard public phones, but people rarely buy a phonecard that needs to be inserted into a phone. Almost everyone has a Telikad, which are available in K5, K10, K20 and K50 denominations.

Telikads are widely available and easy to use. Just dial ☎123 from *any* fixed-line phone, including any type of public phone, then '1' for English, and follow the voice prompts to enter your 12-digit code and the number you're calling. Telikads are great for using in hotels, but only for long-distance calls as most hotels will still charge you K1 for the call, even though you're paying for it.

SATELLITE PHONES

There are two functioning networks: **Iridium** (www.iridium.com), which is worldwide and uses a Motorola phone; and **Aces** (Asia Cellular Satellite; www.acesinternational.com), which only covers parts of Asia and uses Ericsson phones. Aces is a fair bit cheaper, but less reliable.

Time

The time throughout PNG is 10 hours ahead of UTC (GMT). When it's noon in PNG it will be noon in Sydney, 9am in Jakarta, 2am in London, 9pm the previous day in New York and 6pm the previous day in Los Angeles. There is no daylight saving (summer time) in PNG.

You will inevitably encounter 'Melanesian time' at some point, the habit throughout Melanesia (and all the South Pacific) of putting a low premium on punctuality.

Toilets

In remote villages you might find a long-drop consisting of a pit with a hollow palm trunk on top, and a toilet seat on top of that. And that's relatively extravagant. If you're in a village and can't spy the loo, be sure to ask someone; if you accidentally take a crap in the village garden, the locals might get shitty.

Tourist Information

There is little in the way of organised, Western-style tourist offices that hand out maps and brochures, and a lack of funding has seen some of the best offices closed in recent years.

The **PNG Tourism Promotion Authority** (☎320 0211; www.pngtourism.org.pg) mainly focuses on marketing campaigns, but it's excellent and beautifully designed

website has boatloads of useful info and links.

Following are the three remaining regional tourism offices:

The East Highlands Province Tourism Bureau (Goroka)
Madang Visitors & Cultural Bureau (☎422 3302; www.tourismmadang.com)
Milne Bay Tourism (☎641 1503)

Travellers with Disabilities

Unfortunately there is little infrastructure that caters for the needs of disabled travellers. Access ramps are virtually nonexistent and only the most upmarket hotels are likely to have lifts (elevators).

Visas

All nationalities require a visa to visit PNG and must have a valid passport or internationally recognised travel document valid for at least six months beyond the date of entry. There are heavy penalties for overstaying any visa.

TOURIST VISAS

There are two ways to get a tourist visa.

» **On Arrival** Western Europeans, Americans, Australians, New Zealanders and citizens of most Pacific countries can obtain a 60-day tourist visa on arrival for K100. The process is simple enough: once inside the terminal change money to get your K100, fill out a form, take your cash and one passport photo to the immigration desk. Note that on weekends or at random other times the exchange bureau inside immigration can be closed and you'll be sent into the arrivals hall to change at the Bank South Pacific. This process can be fraught, however, if you have a same-day connecting flight out of Port Moresby into the

provinces – the queues can be *very* long and the process can take hours.

» **In Advance** A 60-day tourist visa can also be obtained at any PNG diplomatic mission. In Australia the cost of a tourist visa is A\$35. Skippers (but not crew) arriving by yacht, regardless of nationality, should also arrange a visa (A\$90) in advance and pay a K300 customs clearance fee when they leave.

WORKING VISAS

Applying for a business visa requires all manner of letters from home (including letters of invitations from businesses) and PNG, as well as details of your business. Approval can take months, so start early. A Business Short-Term Multiple-Entry visa is valid for 12 months and allows stays of up to 60 days each time and costs A\$220. If you are seeking an employment visa, you must provide certain medical results, details for a police clearance, a copy of your employment contract and a copy of a Work Permit issued by the PNG Department of Labour & Employment.

Church and aid volunteers can enter on a special A\$25 visa (plus A\$50 'transmission fee') but the issuing authorities are required to wait for special immigration department approval. Researchers, filmmakers and journalists must submit their visa applications with a special application form from the **National Research Institute** (☎326 0300; fax 325 0531; PO Box 5854, Boroko). They cost A\$25 (visas for journalists cost A\$220).

VISA EXTENSIONS

Tourist visas can be extended once only, for one month, for a K200 fee. To do it yourself, go to the Department of Foreign Affairs' **immigration section** (☎323 1500; ground fl, Moale Haus, Wards Strip, Waigani; ⊗9am-noon Mon-Fri), where you'll battle hordes of agents who are on first-name terms with the staff. Extending a visa takes one to two weeks, though occasionally travellers do it faster.

If money is not too tight, using an agent will save you a lot of grief. Agents can be found in the *Yellow Pages* under 'Visa Services'.

SEAMAN PASS

Cruise ship passengers do not need a visa provided they have a seaman pass. If you do not have this pass, you will be required to pay for a K100 tourist visa.

Volunteering

There are several organisations operating volunteer projects. These are often in remote communities, so this sort of work is not for those who will faint at the sight of a spider.

Activities range from teaching and medical assistance to advisory roles with local area councils. Most are either associated with the churches or with international volunteer organisations.

Lonely Planet's **volunteering website** (www.lonelyplanet.com/volunteer/index.cfm) has excellent resources for those interested in making a contribution to PNG or elsewhere.

Most of the following organisations have projects in PNG.

Australian Business Volunteers (www.abv.org.au)

Australian Volunteers International (AVA; www.australianvolunteers.com)

Canadian University Service Overseas (CUSO; www.cusointernational.org)

German Development Service (DED; ☎325 5380; www.ded.de)

Japan International Cooperation Agency (JICA; ☎325 1699; www.jica.go.jp/png)

Voluntary Service Overseas (British VSO; ☎852 1924; www.vso.org.uk)

Volunteer Service Abroad (NZ VSA; ☎325 4136; www.vsa.org.nz)

Two other useful websites that have details for those interested in volunteering:

Global Volunteers (www.globalvolunteers.org)

Volunteer Abroad (www.volunteerabroad.com)

Women Travellers

Plenty of women travel to PNG and while doing so with a man, or a friend, is usually safer than doing so alone, quite a few solo women have written to us with glowing reports of their trips. Of course, women travelling alone need to be more aware of where they go, what they wear and how they act.

» Three-quarter-length pants and T-shirts will attract far less attention than skimpy tops or revealing clothing.

» Showing your thighs is considered sexually provocative, so shorts are best avoided. You won't see local women in Western-style swimwear, and unless you're at a resort it's best to wear a *laplap* (sarong) while swimming.

» At night, don't go *anywhere* alone, and avoid secluded spots at all times. Rapes and attacks are not uncommon, especially in urban centres, so you should avoid any situation where you're alone with a man you don't know well.

» In some parts of PNG tribal beliefs about women and their menstrual cycles persist. In the Sepik, for example, women are thought to have powerful energies that can be harmful to men. It is *tambu* in many places for a woman to pass over a man – to step over a seated man's outstretched legs or even over his possessions, and a man mustn't swim under a woman in a canoe. If you're menstruating – it's better not to mention it.

Transport

GETTING THERE & AWAY

Entering the Country

The vast majority of visitors to Papua New Guinea arrive by air at Port Moresby's Jacksons Airport with nothing more than a passport with six months' validity, an onward ticket and enough money to buy a visa on the spot (see p193) and to support themselves for the length of their stay. Mining charter flights aside, the only other option is to cross PNG's only land border from Jayapura (Papua Province, Indonesia) to Vanimo in the Sandaun Province (p196).

Flights and tours can be booked online at lonely planet.com/bookings.

Air

Airports & Airlines

The good thing about flying into PNG is that you don't have to shop around too much looking for a ticket. Currently, the only international airport is Port Moresby's **Jacksons Airport** (POM). For years (and years) there has been talk of Mt Hagen, Lae and Alotau reopening for international flights – if they do, flights will probably be to/from Cairns (Australia).

Presently only the following three companies sell tickets to PNG but it looks likely that newbie **Travel Air** (www.travelairpng.com) will join them sometime in the next year or two.

Air Niugini (Australia ☎1300 361 380, PNG ☎327 3444; www.airniugini.com.pg). PNG's national airline flies to Australia (Cairns, Brisbane and Sydney), Japan (Tokyo), Philippines (Manila), Singapore, Fiji (Nadi), China (Hong Kong) and Solomon Islands (Honiara).

Airlines PNG (Australia ☎1300 002 764, PNG ☎180 2764; www.apng.com) Flies to Cairns and Brisbane in Australia.

Qantas (www.qantas.com) A code-share agreement with Air Niugini that means even though you book and pay for your ticket with Qantas and are issued with a Qantas boarding pass, the aircraft may actually be run by Air Niugini. Regardless, Qantas Frequent Flyer points are awarded and can be redeemed for any flight with a Qantas flight number.

Tickets

ASIA

There are no flights between PNG and neighbouring Indonesia. Garuda Indonesia and a couple of Indonesia's new budget airlines do fly to Jayapura, just across the border from PNG.

Air Niugini has weekly flights between Port Moresby and Manila, Singapore, Hong Kong and Tokyo. Apart from Tokyo (Saturday only), there are at least three flights a week to and from these cities.

CLIMATE CHANGE & TRAVEL

Every form of transport that relies on carbon-based fuel generates CO_2, the main cause of human-induced climate change. Modern travel is dependent on aeroplanes, which might use less fuel per kilometre per person than most cars but travel greater distances. The altitude at which aircraft emit gases (including CO_2) and particles also contributes to their impact. Many websites offer 'carbon calculators' that allow people to estimate the carbon emissions generated by their journey and, for those who wish to do so, to offset the impact of the greenhouse gases emitted with contributions to portfolios of climate-friendly initiatives. Lonely Planet offsets the carbon footprint of all staff and author travel.

FLIGHTS TO PORT MORESBY

The prices given are for return Air Niugini flights and include all taxes. Bookings made well in advance can be up to 40% cheaper ('*wantok*' fares) than the standard 'paradise' rates listed here.

FROM	FREQUENCY	COST (A$)	CARRIER
Brisbane	11 weekly	$624	Air Niugini, Airlines PNG, Qantas
Cairns	9 weekly	$485	Air Niugini, Airlines PNG, Qantas
Honiara	3 weekly	$1020	Air Niugini
Hong Kong	3 weekly	$1092	Air Niugini
Nadi	3 weekly	$865	Air Niugini
Manila	3 weekly	$1138	Air Niugini
Singapore	4 weekly	$1028	Air Niugini
Sydney	2 weekly	$1076	Air Niugini, Airlines PNG, Qantas
Tokyo	1 weekly	$1005	Air Niugini

AUSTRALIA & NEW ZEALAND
Papua New Guinea is well connected to three Australian cities: Cairns, Brisbane and Sydney. Australians and New Zealanders will need to make their way to one of these cities for an onward flight to Port Moresby.

THE PACIFIC
Air Niugini flies to Nadi (Fiji) via Honiara (Solomon Islands). The only other way of getting to PNG from the Pacific is via Australia.

EUROPE
Flying via Australia is the obvious way to get to PNG from the UK, Ireland or continental Europe, and is especially attractive given the plethora of cheap deals on offer.

The other option is flying to Singapore, then on to Port Moresby. There is normally some sort of deal. The Singapore option is obviously shorter, but coming via Australia gives you far more flexibility with onward connections. In 2011 AirFrance and KLM Royal Dutch Airlines signed an e-ticketing agreement that allows baggage to be checked through to Port Moresby.

THE USA & CANADA
There are a couple of options from North America: fly to Australia, then on to Port Moresby; or fly to Narita (Tokyo), Hong Kong, Manila or Singapore, then on to Port Moresby.

Land
Border Crossings
The only land **border crossing** (PNG ⊙9am-5pm, Indonesia ⊙8am-4pm) is between Vanimo in Sandaun Province and Jayapura in Papua Province (West Papua), Indonesia.

Leaving PNG for Indonesia is relatively straightforward. If you haven't already got an Indonesian visa in Port Moresby (p188) you'll need to get one at the **Indonesian Consulate** (☑457 1371; fax 457 1373; ⊙9am-noon & 2-4pm Mon-Fri) in Vanimo. It takes 24 hours to issue a nonextendable 30-day (K70) or 60-day (K135) visa. You'll need two photos, a completed application form (which you get there), a passport valid for at least six months and, occasionally, proof of onward travel. It's best to say you're heading for Bali or Manado as they are less controversial destinations than anywhere in Papua.

On Tuesday and Thursday locals travel by PMV (K10, 1½ to two hours) to the Batas Market on the Indonesian side of the border to stock up on cheaply made goods. Immigration officials turn a blind eye to shopping day-trippers although this courtesy is seldom extended to foreigners. Tuesdays and Thursdays aside, only occasional PMVs travel all the way to the border from Vanimo's main market. If you are desperate and PMVs are conspicuously absent, Sandaun Surf Hotel (p125) will drive you there for K200.

To get from the border to Jayapura catch a shared taxi (400,000Rp for the whole car) or hitch.

To enter PNG requires a visa which (in theory) can be obtained from the **PNG Jayapura Consulate** (☑967-531 250; Blok 6 & 7, Ruko Matoa, Jl Kelapa Dua, Entrop; ⊙9am-noon & 1-2pm Mon-Fri). Unfortunately this office seems to be in a constant state of disarray and its backwards slide seems set to continue. If they do agree to issue a visa, it will take at least a week and you will need two passport-sized photos, 225,000Rp, a typed letter requesting a visa and an onward ticket out of PNG. A far safer ploy is to obtain your visa from another PNG mission in advance.

Remember: foreigners are required to obtain a travel permit known as a *surat keterangan jalan* (or more commonly, *surat jalan*) to travel to most places outside of Jayapura. This is easily obtained at the police station (Jl Yani 11; ⊗7am-3pm, Mon-Fri) in Jayapura. Take your passport, two passport photos, a photocopy of your passport pages showing your personal details and Indonesian visa and a list of every place you intend to visit in Papua.

Sea

There are plenty of boats plying the waters around PNG but very few are actually scheduled services to other countries.

Unless you are a Torres Strait Islander, it is illegal to island hop between Thursday Island (TI to locals) and PNG. You can exit Australia from TI but you must go directly to PNG, usually Daru, where you can pass through immigration if you already have a visa.

PRIVATE BOATS
PNG and the Solomons are popular stopping points for cruising yachts, either heading through Asia or the Pacific. In PNG you can clear immigration at Alotau, Daru, Kavieng, Kimbe, Lae, Lorengau, Madang, Misima Island, Port Moresby, Rabaul, Samarai and Vanimo. You must get a visa before you arrive. See **Noonsite** (www.noonsite.com) for a full rundown.

CRUISE SHIPS
The following companies offer luxury cruises that incorporate some of the PNG islands – usually those in the Milne Bay Province.
Aurora Expeditions (www.auroraexpeditions.com.au)
North Star Cruises (www.northstarcruises.com.au)
Orion Expeditions (www.orionexpeditions.com)
Coral Princess (www.coralprincess.com.au)

Tours

The following are the main PNG-based inbound tour operators. They offer a wide variety of tours but prices are usually disconcertingly high. For smaller operators and special-interest tours, see p185. For Kokoda Track tours, see p31.
Eco-Tourism Melanesia (www.em.com.pg) Focuses on village-based tours, and cultural, wildlife, birdwatching and trekking trips.
Melanesian Tourist Services (www.mtspng.com) Operates several high-end resorts, which you'll stay at on its tours.
Niugini Holidays (www.nghols.com) Probably the biggest range of tours, from specialised family tours to surfing, fishing, diving, trekking, war-veterans tours and more.
Trans Niugini Tours (www.pngtours.com) Based in Mt Hagen, Trans Niugini operate the *Sepik Spirit* and several luxury lodges. There are general tours, wildlife tours, treks, cruises and tours of the cultural shows.

GETTING AROUND

Air

About 2000 airstrips have been cut out of the bush or into hill tops and coral islands during the last 80 years or so. Although less than a quarter of these airstrips are regularly used today, PNG is heavily reliant on air transport to connect its isolated and scattered population. It is worth remembering the following points when travelling by air around PNG:

» For lighter aircraft, the baggage limit is 16kg (but 20kg is usually accepted). Excess-baggage charges are reasonable but can add up.

» Some remote strips have no facilities, just a guy with a two-way radio who meets the flights, and at many of these remote strips you'll have to buy your ticket direct from the pilot – cash only.

» Outside the main centres (or when the phones lines are down) don't rely on being able to pay for anything by credit card.

» Unpredictable weather combined with mechanical problems and complex schedules can frequently lead to delays or cancellations.

Airlines in the Region
The following is a list of airlines operating scheduled flights in PNG. Local offices are listed on the airline websites or under the relevant destinations in the regional chapters.
Air Niugini (☑327 3444; www.airniugini.com.pg) The major carrier in PNG operating larger planes to the larger centres.
Airlines PNG (☑180 2764; www.apng.com) The main secondary airline in PNG with the largest route map other than Air Niugini.
MAF (Mission Aviation Fellowship; ☑545 1506; www.maf.org.au) Deals with small isolated highland communities. Based in Mt Hagen.
North Coast Aviation (☑472 1755; norco-lae@global.net.pg) Covers remote destinations out of Lae.
Travel Air (☑422 3009; www.travelairpng.com) The country's newest airline, with a rapidly expanding network.

Fares
Nobody pays the full fare for Air Niugini or Airlines PNG domestic flights. Both airlines have a number of different pricing tiers and each flight usually has a limited number of seats at discounted rates. Obviously the cheap seats are the first to go so book as early as possible to get the cheapest rate. *Wantok* fares are an exception – these can

only be bought three weeks in advance.

It's worth remembering that the cheaper fares are usually subject to all manner of restrictions (including nonrefundable cancellations or penalties for date changes). Take the time to read the fine print. Air Niugini's cheapest fares are called 'Wantok' fares and Airlines PNG fares are known as 'Wild Fares'.

Boat

Boat Charter

Many dive operators charter their boats, some for extended cruises. For more on dive boats, see p25. **Melanesian Travel Services** (MTS; www.mtspng.com), owners of the Madang Resort Hotel, operate charters to the Sepik River and throughout the islands on the supersmart, 30m *Kalibobo Spirit*.

Cargo Boats

Sailing from one exotic locale to the next – via who-knows-where – on a slowly rolling freighter has a certain Joseph Conrad–style romance to it. While cargo boats generally don't take travellers, it's worth trying your luck. Lae on the north coast is the main shipping hub in PNG, and it's the best place to look; ask around the port to see what's going where. You'll almost always have more luck getting on a freighter by talking directly to the ship's captain (and perhaps investing in a few SP Lagers) rather than the office people.

Passenger Boats

There are no passenger vessels linking the north and south coasts or any running along the south coast. Things are a little better on the northern coast and from the mainland to the island provinces with scheduled, if slightly erratic, services offered by the two companies listed below. Boats carry both cargo and passengers and have tourist class (air-conditioned seats and berths) and deck class (air-vented seats and berths). Deck class can get crowded; both classes have video 'entertainment' and it's worth avoiding bunks near the video. There are sometimes simple snack bars that might just be someone with soft drinks in a cooler and a carton of kundu crackers. Students are sometimes entitled to discounts. Details (timetables, fares etc) for routes are given in the regional chapters.

Lutheran Shipping (Luship; Lae ☎ 472 2066, fax 472 5806, Madang 422 2577, Wewak 456 2464; luship@global.net.pg) Based in Lae, Lutheran Shipping has a virtual monopoly on passenger shipping along the Morobe coast. Boats run at least once a week from Lae to Finschhafen, Madang, Kimbe and Rabaul. There is also a weekly service between Wewak and Vanimo.

Rabaul Shipping (Star Ships; Rabaul ☎ 982 1070/1071, fax 982 1955, Lae 472 5699, Wewak 456 1160; rabship@starships.com.pg). At the time of research (see boxed text), Star Ships connected Lae with Rabaul via Kimbe, and Lae with Alotau via Oro Bay. There was also a weekly service between Madang and Wewak that, on occasion, travelled to Vanimo.

Small Boats

Trade boats – small, wooden boats with thumping diesel engines – ply the coast, supplying trade stores and acting as ferries. They are irregular but if you're prepared to wait, they can get you to some off-the-track places. Don't expect comfort, bring your own food and make sure the operator is trustworthy before you commit yourself to a day or two aboard. If you're in a major centre, such as Alotau, ask around the port and at the big stores, which might have a set schedule for delivering supplies to the area's trade stores. Negotiate the fee before you leave.

THE 2012 FERRY DISASTER

On 2 February 2012, Rabaul Shipping's MV *Rabaul Queen* capsized and sank in rough seas as it travelled between Kimbe (New Britain) and Lae. Of the 350 passengers and 12 crew on board only 238 survived, although some passengers maintain the true fatality rate is far higher, and that the boat was carrying in excess of 500 people that day. Whatever the case, it is becoming clear that in addition to the bad weather and giant waves, overcrowding played a part in the tragedy. The sinking of the *Rabaul Queen* is ranked as PNG's worst maritime disaster and will have far-reaching implications beyond the anguish felt by families of lost loved ones. Sea transport is a major communication lifeline in the PNG archipelago, and the *Rabaul Queen* was one of the mayor players. To further compound matters, grieving families demanding *belkol* (peace money or compensation) torched three other Rabaul Shipping boats in Bougainville shortly after the tragedy and Rabaul Shipping services were suspended.

It's worth noting that our research was conducted just prior to this disaster and undoubtedly the fate of Rabaul Shipping will hinge on the official inquiry and their ability to get a replacement boat should their license to operate be reinstated. In PNG, this could take years.

For shorter distances, there are dinghies with outboard motors, often known as speedies or banana boats. These are usually long fibreglass boats that leap through the waves and are bone-jarringly uncomfortable. They operate in much the same way as regular PMVs, only leaving when full. Travellers are increasingly using these boats to get from Angoram (on the Sepik River) to Bogia (from where you can travel to Madang) and between Aitape and Vanimo.

Note, banana boats are no fun at all when the wind picks up, and the wind can pick up with little warning. People die reasonably frequently in open-sea banana-boat crossings and you will need to exercise common sense before boarding one. Don't contemplate a trip in rough weather or if the boat is dangerously overloaded. Remember that these boats do not carry life jackets or any kind of safety equipment.

Car & Motorcycle

Driving yourself around PNG is not really a viable way of travelling because the country only has one road – the Highlands Hwy – that connects two or more places you might want to visit.

Driving Licence

Any valid overseas licence is OK for the first three months you're in PNG.

Hire

Four-wheel drives can be hired in most PNG cities, including on the islands, and in Lae and Port Moresby you can hire a plain old car. You must be 25 to hire a car and have either a credit card or K2500 cash as a deposit. Hiring anything will cost you an arm and probably both legs, and the rates are even higher when you add the per-km charges, insurance and tax. For example, a compact car (the cheapest option) costs from K250 per day, plus

K1 per kilometre, plus 10% VAT, plus any fee for personal insurance.

One-way rentals are available at locations along the Highlands Hwy but may be subject to one-way drop-off fees. The following companies have offices around PNG but you will also find a number of smaller agencies based at the major airports.

Avis (☎324 9400; www.avis.com.pg)
Budget (☎323 6244; www.budget.com.pg)
Hertz (☎325 4999; sales@leasemaster.com.pg)
Travel-Car (☎323 9878; queenemmalodge@daltron.com.pg)

Road Conditions

Perhaps the most pertinent point about the roads in PNG is that there aren't many. Port Moresby, for example, is not linked by road to any other provincial capital except Kerema, and that road is subject to seasonal difficulties. The most important road is the Highlands Hwy, which runs from Lae to Lake Kopiago, via Goroka, Mt Hagen and Tari. Madang is also connected to it via the Ramu Hwy.

Road conditions are variable, to say the least. Many are full of potholes and only passable by 4WD, and only then in the dry. Others are recently sealed, all-weather affairs. If you're planning on getting out of the towns, a 4WD is a necessity.

Road Hazards

Roads in PNG come with a range of hazards. There is the deterioration factor: many are becoming almost impassable due to lack of maintenance. There's the wet-season factor: it rains, you get bogged. And then there's that one you can't do much about: the *raskol* (bandit) factor. Your chances of being held up are admittedly quite slim, but it's worth reading the Safe Travel section (p191) for tips on what to do if it happens to you.

If you are involved in an accident: don't stop, keep driving and report the accident at the nearest police station. This applies regardless of who was at fault or how serious the accident (whether you've run over a pig or hit a person). Tribal concepts of payback apply to car accidents. You may have insurance and you may be willing to pay, but the local citizenry may well prefer to take more immediate and satisfying action.

Road Rules

Cars drive on the left side of the road. The speed limit is 60km/h in towns and 80km/h in the country. Seat belts must be worn by the driver and front-seat passengers. Most cars won't have seat belts in the back.

Hitching

Hitching is an important mode of travelling in the region. The lack of scheduled transport means jumping onto a bus, truck, canoe, freighter, plane – or whatever else is going your way – is a time-honoured way of getting around. You'll often be expected to pay the equivalent of a PMV fare. If your bag is light, it's also sometimes possible to hitch flights at small airports.

Keep in mind that hitching is never entirely safe in any country. Travellers who decide to hitch are taking a small but potentially serious risk, and solo women should absolutely *not* hitch in PNG. People who choose to hitch will be safer if they travel in pairs and let someone know where they are planning to go.

Taxi

Considering PNG's reputation for nocturnal danger, it's surprising there are not more taxis. Port Moresby and Alotau have plenty and there are two in Madang and another two Vanimo. That's it.

If you do manage to get a taxi you'll find most of them are complete clunkers – windscreens that look like road maps, broken seats and no radios or meters – you'll have to negotiate the fare before you get in. The one shining exception is **Scarlet Taxis** (☑323 4266) in Port Moresby.

PMV

PMV (public motor vehicle) is the generic term for any type of public transport and wherever there are roads, there will be PMVs. Whether it's a dilapidated minibus, a truck with two facing wooden benches, a pick-up with no seats whatsoever but space in the tray, or any other means of transport (boats are also referred to as PMVs), the PMV is one of the keys to travelling cheaply in PNG. It's also one of the best ways to meet local people.

There's no real science to using PMVs; just turn up at the designated departure point and wait for it to fill up, although the following tips are worth keeping in mind.

» Many rural routes have only one service a day so ask around a day ahead for when and where it leaves (usually the local market).

» From small towns, PMVs often start out very early in the morning, drive to another (usually larger) town, then wait a couple of hours while the morning's passengers go to market before returning.

» Out of town you can assume that anything with lots of people in it is a rural PMV. If you want to get off before the end, just yell 'stop driver!'

» In most urban areas PMVs travel along a network of established routes. Stops are predetermined and are often indicated by a yellow pole or a crowd of waiting people; you can't just ask to be let off anywhere. The destination will be indicated by a sign inside the windscreen or called out

by the driver's assistant in a machine-gun-style staccato.

» Market days (usually Friday and Saturday) are the best days for finding a ride.

» Most of the time, travelling in a PMV is perfectly safe; your fellow passengers will be most impressed you're with them and not in some expensive 4WD. There is, of course, a risk of robbery, especially on the Highlands Hwy. Lone women travellers are also at greater risk and should think twice about travelling by PMV. If you do, find a vehicle with women passengers and get a seat nearby.

» PMVs have a crew of two: the driver, who usually maintains an aloof distance from the passengers; and the conductor, who takes fares and copes with the rabble.

» Don't be surprised if you have to wait for your change; it will come when the conductor gets his change sorted.

Solomon Islands

Solomon Islands

Best Historical Sites

» US War Memorial (p207)
» Mt Austen (p212)
» Vilu Open-Air Museum (p213)
» Skull Island (p219)

Best Places to Stay

» Tavanipupu Private Island Resort (p217)
» Tetepare Island (p221)
» Uepi Island Resort (p216)
» Sanbis Resort (p222)
» Oravae Cottage (p221)

Why Go?

For those seeking an authentic Melanesian experience or an off-the-beaten-track destination, the Solomons are hard to beat. From WWII relics scattered in the jungle to leaf-hut villages where traditional culture is alive, there's so much on offer. Then there's the visual appeal, with scenery reminiscent of a Discovery Channel documentary: volcanic islands that jut up dramatically from the cobalt blue ocean, croc-infested mangroves, huge lagoons, tropical islets and emerald forests.

Don't expect white-sand beaches, ritzy resorts and wild nightlife – the Solomons are not a beach-holiday destination. With only a smattering of traditional guesthouses and comfortable hideaways, it's tailor-made for ecotourists. For outdoorsy types, lots of action-packed experiences can easily be organised: climb an extinct volcano, surf uncrowded waves, snorkel pristine reefs or kayak across a lagoon. Beneath the ocean's surface, unbeatable diving adventures await.

The best part is, there'll be no crowds to mar the experience.

When to Go
Honiara

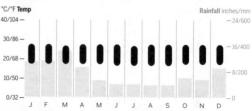

Dec–Mar Intervals of calm weather broken by storms makes for good reef breaks and diving.	**Jun–Sep** Mild weather (but rough seas); good for hiking, less ideal for diving. Great festivity time.	**Apr–May & Oct–Nov** The shoulder seasons are relatively dry and aren't a bad time to visit.

Connections

Solomon Airlines' domestic wing offers scheduled flights to about 20 airstrips throughout the archipelago. Honiara is the main hub. From the capital there are frequent flights to the main tourist gateways, including Seghe, Munda and Gizo.

There are regular passenger boat services between Honiara and Auki (Malaita). There's also a scheduled weekly service between Honiara and Gizo (via Marovo), but it's more erratic.

ITINERARIES

One Week

Go west! Skip Guadalcanal and the nearby islands (Savo and Tulagi) in favour of Marovo Lagoon, Munda and Gizo – the three unmissable destinations in 'the West'. Thanks to reliable inter-island boat and plane services, they can easily be combined. That said, you won't cover more than two destinations in a week – Munda and Gizo are the easiest to tackle.

Two Weeks

Split your time between three provinces – Guadalcanal, Central Province and Western Province. Devote three days to Guadalcanal (four days if you're a diver), then catch a boat to Savo or Tulagi and settle in for a couple of days of relaxation. Grab a flight to Gatokae or Seghe for a few days of exploring Marovo Lagoon. Afterwards, fly to Gizo where two days can easily be spent messing around in and on the water. You might also make time for a hike on Kolombangara.

Three Weeks

Stretch the two-week itinerary into a saner 16 days. Use the extra time for a stay at Munda, which offers great diving options and excellent day tours to some must-see WWII relics, or book a back-to-nature trip to Tetepare Island. Fly back to Honiara and catch a boat to Malaita where you can chill out in Langa Langa Lagoon. Or you could round out your trip with a romantic stay at Tavanipupu Private Island Resort on Guadalcanal.

Resources

» **Solomon Islands Visitor Bureau** (www.visitsolomons.com.sb) Official tourism site with oodles of information about activities, accommodation and services.

» **Welkam Solomons** (www.welkamsolomons.com) Packed with loads of useful information about hotels, cultural sites, transport, history and activities.

» **Solomons Travel Portal** (www.solomonislands-hotels.travel) Has a wealth of information on accommodation, with online bookings, as well as other practical information for visitors.

AT A GLANCE

» **Currency** Solomon Islands dollar (S$)

» **Language** Solomon Islands Pijin

» **Money** A few ATMs in the major urban centres

» **Visas** Not required for most Western countries for stays of up to one month

» **Mobile phones** Local SIM cards are available and can be used with unlocked GSM phones.

Fast Facts

» **Land area** 27,540 sq km
» **Population** 538,000
» **Capital** Honiara
» **International telephone code** ☎677
» **Emergency** ☎999

Exchange Rates

Australia	A$1	S$7.41
Canada	C$1	S$7.28
Euro	€1	S$9.49
Japan	¥100	S$8.82
New Zealand	NZ$1	S$5.83
UK	UK£1	S$11.60
USA	US$1	S$7.18

For current exchange rates see www.xe.com.

Set Your Budget

» **Twin room in a resort** S$1200
» **Two-course evening meal** S$180
» **Ticket Honiara–Gizo (one-way)** S$1380
» **Two-tank dive** S$1300

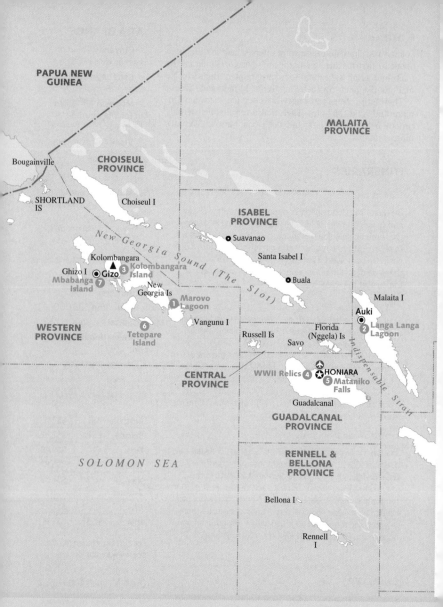

PAPUA NEW GUINEA

Bougainville

CHOISEUL PROVINCE

SHORTLAND IS

Choiseul I

MALAITA PROVINCE

ISABEL PROVINCE

Suavanao

Santa Isabel I

Buala

New Georgia Sound (The Slot)

Kolombangara

Ghizo I
Gizo ③
Kolombangara Island

Mbabanga Island ⑦

New Georgia Is

① **Marovo Lagoon**

Vangunu I

⑥ **Tetepare Island**

WESTERN PROVINCE

Russell Is

Florida (Nggela) Is

Savo

CENTRAL PROVINCE

WWII Relics ④ ✈ ★ **HONIARA**
⑤ **Mataniko Falls**

Guadalcanal

Malaita I

Auki

② **Langa Langa Lagoon**

Indispensable Strait

GUADALCANAL PROVINCE

SOLOMON SEA

RENNELL & BELLONA PROVINCE

Bellona I

Rennell I

Solomon Islands Highlights

① Diving and snorkelling in fish soup in **Marovo Lagoon** (p214)

② Feeling free in an intimate lodge at **Langa Langa Lagoon** (p226)

③ Huffing to the top of the mount on **Kolombangara Island** (p222)

④ Spending the day spotting rusty **WWII relics** around Honiara (p212)

⑤ Taking a dip in a natural pool at **Mataniko Falls** (p213)

⑥ Assisting rangers in tagging marine turtles on ecofriendly **Tetepare Island** (p221)

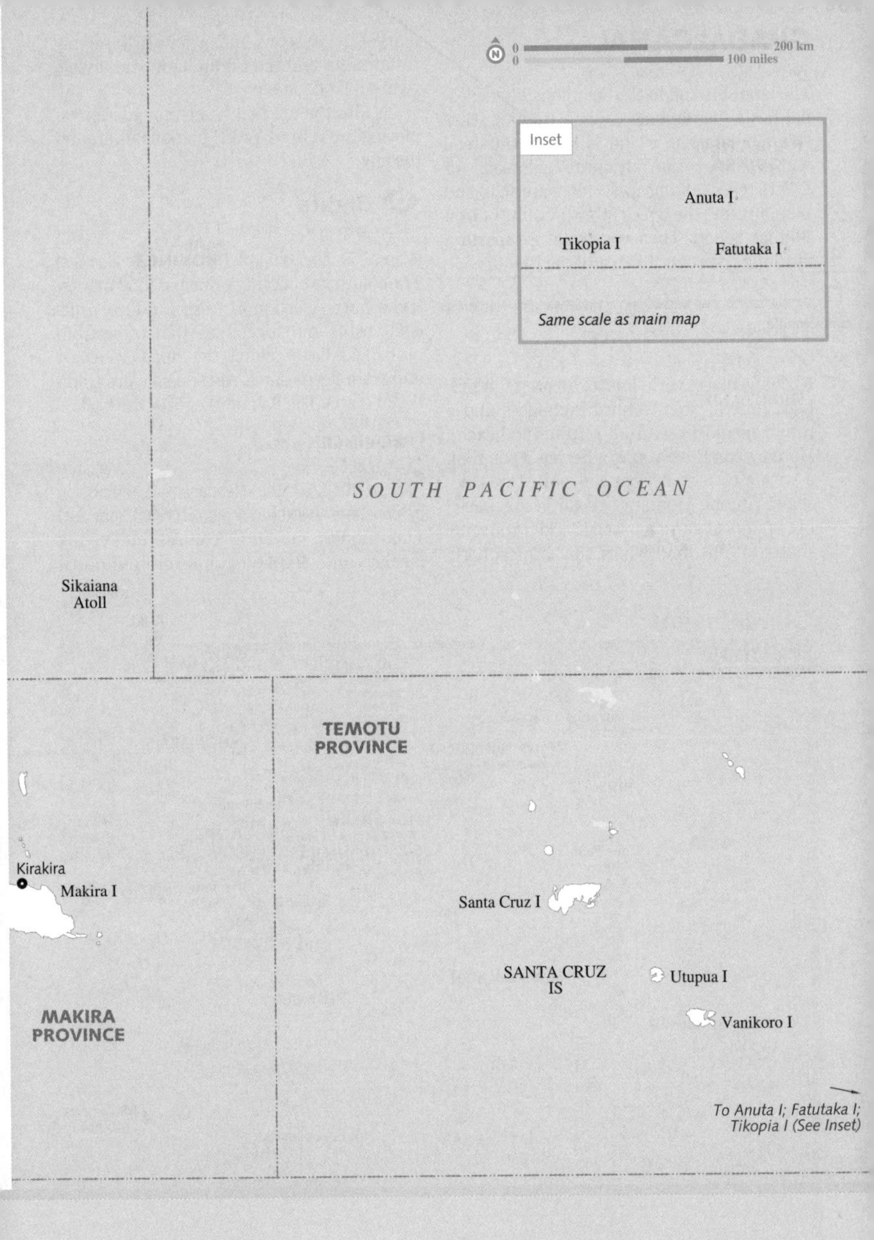

Inset

Anuta I

Tikopia I   Fatutaka I

Same scale as main map

200 km
100 miles

SOUTH PACIFIC OCEAN

Sikaiana
Atoll

TEMOTU
PROVINCE

Kirakira
Makira I

Santa Cruz I

SANTA CRUZ   Utupua I
IS
                        Vanikoro I

MAKIRA
PROVINCE

To Anuta I; Fatutaka I;
Tikopia I (See Inset)

7 Chilling out at a laid-back
resort on **Mbabanga Island**
(p222)

GUADALCANAL

POP 104,000 / AREA 5336 SQ KM

The largest island in the Solomons, Guadalcanal hosts the national capital, Honiara. Outside Honiara, the island is largely untamed and raw. Start your adventure by looking for WWII relics, hiking to scenic waterfalls and plunging into the wreck-strewn waters of Iron Bottom Sound. Then you could escape to a far-flung resort on the east of the island.

Honiara

POP 57,000

A dusty place with lots of decrepit buildings, no real architectural highlights and a rather mediocre seafront setting (no beach), Honiara can leave you wondering if you took a wrong turn at Brisbane airport. Don't despair! Among Honiara's rewards are pleasing botanical gardens, well-stocked souvenir shops, a bustling wharf, an atmospheric market, a museum and a few high-quality restaurants and bars. Plus fantastic diving, right on its doorstep.

It's also the optimal launching pad for exploring the various WWII battlefields around the city.

◉ Sights

Central Market   MARKET
(Map p209; Mendana Ave; ☺dawn-dusk Mon-Sat) The country's bubbling principal food market has a huge selection of fresh produce, especially fruits and vegetables, that come from outlying villages along the northern coast and from Savo island. Also on sale are traditional crafts. The fish market is at the back.

National Museum &
Cultural Centre   MUSEUM
(Map p210; ☎24896; Mendana Ave; admission by donation; ☺9am-4pm Mon-Fri, 9am-2pm Sat) This modest museum features interesting displays and old photographs on traditional

Guadalcanal

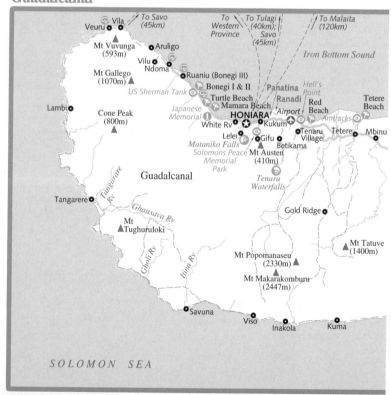

dance, body ornamentation, currency, weaponry and archaeology.

National Parliament PUBLIC BUILDING
(Map p210; Lower Vavyaya Rd; ⊙8am-4pm Mon-Fri)
The conical-shaped concrete building that's perched on the hill above Hibiscus Ave is the National Parliament. Inside, the dome boasts a rich tapestry of traditional art, including arching frescoes.

US War Memorial HISTORIC SITE
(Map p209) Skyline Dr has commanding views over the town and leads to the US War Memorial, a steep 30-minute walk up from Mendana Ave. The compound has marble slabs bearing detailed descriptions of battles fought during the Guadalcanal campaign.

Botanical Gardens GARDENS
(Map p209; ☎24032; Lenggakiki; admission by donation; ⊙8am-4.30pm) These lovely grounds on the hills located above the city provide a green haven for nature lovers.

🏃 Activities

Diving is Honiara's trump card, with a fantastic collection of WWII wrecks lying offshore in an area known as Iron Bottom Sound, including Bonegi I & II to the west, and the *John Penn* to the east. See p27 for more information on diving.

Tulagi Dive DIVING, SNORKELLING
(off Map p209; ☎7475043, 26589; www.tulagidive.com.sb) This highly professional dive shop based in White River is run by Australian Neil Yates, who adheres to strict safety procedures for deep dives. Prices start at S$250 for a shore dive. He organises day trips to Florida Islands (S$1100 including two dives and lunch) and snorkel trips (S$150). Gear hire is S$550 per day.

🛏 Sleeping

Honiara is expensive and excepting a few basic guesthouses, hotels catering mainly to business people dominate the market.

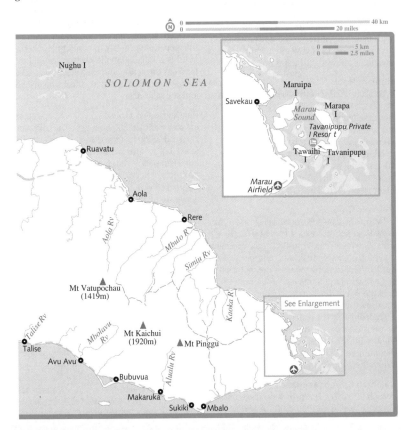

SOLOMON ISLANDS HONIARA

Heritage Park Hotel
HOTEL $$$

(Map p210; ☎24007; www.heritageparkhotel.com.
sb; Mendana Ave; d S$2200-2400; ❋@☎❋) By
some degree the fanciest big hotel in the
Solomons, this hotel and conference centre
is where you'll find the richest businessmen
and international consultants. It's right in
the centre and on the waterfront. Nearly all
the small but tastefully designed rooms have
a sea view and a sunny balcony; angle for
one on the upper floors for the most privacy
and best views. Heritage Park offers plenty
of amenities, including two restaurants, two
bars, a small pool and a disco.

Chester Resthouse
GUESTHOUSE $

(Map p210; ☎26355; mbhches@solomon.com.sb;
Lower Vayvaya Rd; r with shared/private bathroom
S$220/500) This budget set-up is popular
with travellers and local families because
it's spitting distance from the action. In the
older wing, fan-cooled rooms are tiny and
lack intimacy (windows open right onto the
corridor and communal area, where guests
slump on couches in front of the TV). For
more space and privacy, upgrade to a room
with private facilities in the newer wing. It's
also a safe choice for women travellers. No
alcohol is allowed on the premises.

Honiara Hotel
HOTEL $$

(Map p209; ☎21737; reservation@honiarahotel.com.
sb; Chinatown; d S$750-1900; ❋☎❋) While it's
not exactly city central, this sprawling place
has a genuine ace up its sleeve – a large pool.
Other pluses include a bar, a gym and three
good restaurants. Go for the more recent
rooms, which are better equipped and get
more natural light. The cheaper rooms in the
older wings aren't such a good deal.

Raintree Café
B&B $$

(off Map p209; ☎7444383; www.raintreehoniara.com;
White River; s/d incl breakfast from S$450/550; ☎)
This fair-value cafe-cum-B&B has excellent
bedding, copious breakfasts, and occupies a
verdant plot right by the seashore, but it's not
perfect: it's about 3km west of the centre just
past the White River market (a not-so-inviting
area), and two rooms – the Orchid and the
Frangipani – face a concrete wall. The moral
of the story: try for the aptly named Ocean
View, within earshot of the sea. During the
day, numerous vans ply the route between the
White River market and the city centre.

Solomon Kitano Mendana
HOTEL $$$

(Map p210; ☎20071; reserv@mendana.com.sb;
Mendana Ave; d S$1000-1600; ❋☎❋) The
Mendana scores high on amenities, with two
restaurants, a bar, an airy foyer and a small
pool. All rooms have undergone a major reno-
vation in 2011 and 2012 and are equipped to a
high standard, so you can expect bright interiors, modern furnishings and prim bathrooms.
Be sure to ask for a room with a sea view.

King Solomon
HOTEL $$$

(Map p210; ☎21205; www.kingsolomonhotel.info; Hi-
biscus Ave; d S$800-1300; ❋☎❋) Anchored on a
steep hill with a kinky funicular that shunts
people between the rooms and the recep-
tion area, this longstanding venture features
a variety of spacious units scattered amid
beautifully landscaped grounds and boasts a
stress-melting swimming pool built into the
hill. Most bungalows are self-contained. Not
all rooms have an ocean view. Compared with
its competitors, the 'King Sol' has a more laid-
back feel. Avoid the onsite restaurant and
instead head to Bamboo Bar Cafe next door.

Sanalae
APARTMENTS $$

(off Map p209; ☎39218; sanalae.apart@solomon.
com.sb; Panatina Ridge; r S$750-1100; ☎) A well-
guarded secret among long-term visitors,
this pert little number in a quiet neighbourhood is a reliable abode despite being a bit
far from the action and up a steep road. The
rooms are self-contained, nicely furnished
and squeaky clean.

Pacific Casino Hotel
HOTEL $$

(off Map p209; ☎25009; www.solomon-hotel.com;
Kukum; d S$750-1300; ❋@☎❋) You certainly
won't fall in love with this large waterfront
hotel complex at the eastern end of town (the
neon-lit corridors are a bit oppressive), but
it's stocked with loads of amenities, including
a swimming pool, an internet cafe, a restau-
rant and a bar. Ask for a room with a sea view.

✗ Eating

TOP
CHOICE **Bamboo Bar Cafe**
CAFETERIA $$

(Map p210; ☎21205; Hibiscus Ave; mains S$50-200;
☺7am-4pm Mon-Fri, 8am-2pm Sat; ☎) Perfect for
a comforting breakfast, lunch (daily specials
are chalked up on the blackboard) or a snack
attack any time of the day, this cheerful place
next door to King Solomon Hotel is the snaz-
ziest spot in town. Good news: it's licensed,
and there's a cosy terrace. It should be open
for dinner by the time you read this.

TOP
CHOICE **Club Havanah**
FRENCH $$$

(Map p209; ☎21737; Honiara Hotel, Chinatown;
mains S$180-350; ☺dinner) The G-spot for local

Greater Honiara

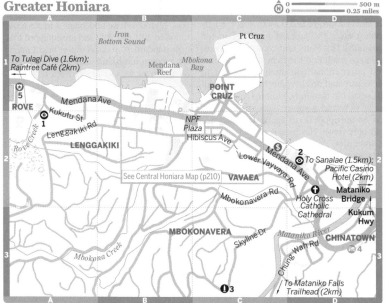

gourmands. Georges, the adept French chef, is a true alchemist, judging from the ambitious *confit de canard maison* (duck cooked and preserved in its own fat). Leave room for the decadent *marquise aux deux chocolats* (white and black chocolate mousse). Next to the pool, a cheaper alternative is the **Oasis Restaurant** (mains S$75-270; ⊙breakfast, lunch & dinner). The Sunday 'Buffet Roast Night' (S$180) is a steal. Honiara Hotel's third restaurant, **Mandarin** (mains S$70-150; ⊙dinner) is well known for its mile-long menu featuring excellent Chinese dishes.

Lime Lounge CAFETERIA **$**
(Map p210; ☏23064; off Mendana Ave; mains S$40-90; ⊙7am-5pm Mon-Fri, 8am-3pm Sat, 9am-3pm Sun; ☏) Funky little Lime Lounge is highly popular with expats. There's everything from satisfying breakfasts to palate-pleasing salads, well-made sandwiches and yummy pastries. No view and no terrace, but the walls are adorned with paintings by local artists, which gives the place a splash of style.

Raintree Café CAFETERIA **$$**
(off Map p209; ☏7444383; www.raintreehoniara.com; White River; mains S$60-220; ⊙7am-9.30pm; ☏) A very relaxing spot. Picture a lovely waterfront location, ample views of Savo, and organic food with vegetarian options. It also

Greater Honiara

⊙ Sights
1 Botanical Gardens A2
2 Central Market D2
3 US War Memorial C3

⊟ Sleeping
4 Honiara Hotel D3

⊗ Eating
Club Havanah ....(see 4)
Mandarin ....(see 4)
Oasis Restaurant ....(see 4)

ⓘ Information
5 Police Headquarters...........................A1

offers lovely tea, coffee and juices, though it's a shame the service is so slow. It's in White River, about 3km west of the centre.

Hakubai JAPANESE **$$**
(Map p210; ☏20071; Solomon Kitano Mendana Hotel, Mendana Ave; mains S$90-300; ⊙lunch & dinner) If you have a sashimi or yakitori craving that must be met, head to Hakubai inside the Mendana Hotel for authentic Japanese food. Next door, the **Capitana** (mains S$90-250; ⊙lunch & dinner) serves classic Western dishes and boasts a terrace overlooking the sea.

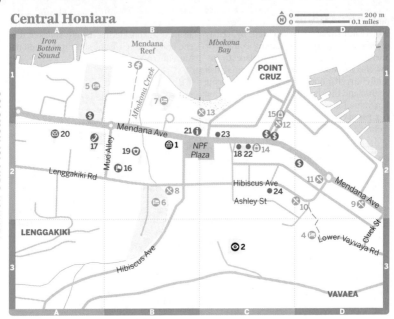

Central Honiara

◎ Sights
1 National Museum & Cultural
 Centre B2
2 National Parliament C3

◇ Activities, Courses & Tours
3 Extreme Adventures B1

⊜ Sleeping
4 Chester Resthouse D3
5 Heritage Park Hotel A1
6 King Solomon B2
7 Solomon Kitano Mendana B1

✕ Eating
8 Bamboo Bar Cafe B2
 Capitana .... (see 7)
9 Frangipani Ice D2
 Hakubai .... (see 7)
10 Hong Kong Palace D2
11 Honiara Hot Bread Kitchen D2
12 Lime Lounge C2
13 Point Cruz Yacht Club C1

◇ Drinking
 Bamboo Bar Cafe .... (see 8)
 Lime Lounge .... (see 12)

✿ Entertainment
 Club Xtreme .... (see 5)

⌂ Shopping
14 King Solomon's Handicraft C2
15 Melanesian Handicrafts C1

ⓘ Information
16 Australian High Commission B2
17 Our Telekom A2
18 Point Cruz Chemist C2
19 Police Station B2
20 Post Office (Solomon Post) A2
21 Solomon Islands Visitors
 Bureau (SIVB) B2

ⓘ Transport
22 Guadalcanal Travel Services
 (GTS) C2
 MV 360 Discovery .... (see 14)
23 MV Lady Wakehurst C2
 MV Pelican Express .... (see 15)
24 Solomon Airlines C2

Point Cruz Yacht Club   FISH & CHIPS $$
(Map p210; 22500; Mendana Ave; mains S$60-90; ☺lunch & dinner) Frequented by crusty expats and yachties, the ageing Point Cruz Yacht Club is an interesting place to enjoy a cold Solbrew and well-prepared fish and chips. It's nothing fancy (think plastic chairs) and the choice is limited, but sizzling hot value for what you get. There's a member fee of S$30, of which S$20 is deducted from your meal.

Ocean View Restaurant   INTERNATIONAL $$
(off Map p209; ☑25009; Pacific Casino Hotel, Kukum; mains S$100-250; ☺breakfast, lunch & dinner) The big dining room lacks character, but the seafront terrace is inviting, with great views north over the Florida Islands. Pizzas, meat dishes and seafood feature prominently on the menu.

Hong Kong Palace   CHINESE $
(Map p210; ☑23338; Hibiscus Ave; mains S$50-300; ☺lunch & dinner) For comforting Chinese fare, head to this unmissable blood-red pagoda on Hibiscus Ave.

Frangipani Ice   ICE CREAM $
(Map p210; Mendana Ave; ice cream from S$4; ☺8am-6pm) This ice-cream parlour is very popular with locals.

Honiara Hot Bread Kitchen   BAKERY $
(Map p210; Mendana Ave; ☺6am-7pm) Has freshly baked bread and buns. Come early; by 10am the buns are sold out.

Drinking & Entertainment

If you've just arrived in the Solomon Islands, you'll find the bar scene pretty dull in Honiara. But those who've just arrived from several weeks in the provinces will feel like they're in Ibiza!

Check out the bars at Honiara's top-end hotels, which are popular and often offer live entertainment once or twice a week – bamboo bands, Micronesian hula dancers and karaoke. For a fruit juice or a cuppa, head to Lime Lounge (p209) or Raintree Café (p209). Bamboo Bar Cafe (p208) is another mellow spot and, joy of joys, it's licensed.

Honiara's sole decent club is the elegant Club Xtreme (Map p210; ☺Wed-Sat), inside Heritage Park Hotel.

Shopping

There are a few prominent stores with better-than-average crafts on and around the main drag, including Melanesian Handicrafts (Map p210; ☑22189; Point Cruz) and King Solomon's Handicraft (Map p210; Mendana Ave). It's also worth considering the gift shops at top-end hotels, as well as the shop at the National Museum (p206).

ℹ Information

Dangers & Annoyances
Be sure to use your common sense and avoid walking alone in deserted streets. Beware of pickpockets at the market and in crowded areas. At night, take a taxi.

Internet Access
You'll find a few internet cafes in the NPF Plaza building. There's a small internet outlet at the post office, too. Rates average S$20 per hour. The Pacific Casino Hotel and the Heritage Park Hotel also offer internet access. Wi-fi is available at most hotels as well as at the Lime Lounge, Raintree Café and Bamboo Bar Cafe.

Medical Services
National Referral Hospital (off Map p209; ☑23600; Kukum)
Point Cruz Chemist (Map p210; ☑22911; Mendana Ave; ☺8am-5pm Mon-Fri, 8am-1pm Sat) A well-stocked pharmacy.

Money
You'll find a good dozen 24-hour ATMs in the centre. There's a small bureau de change at the airport.
ANZ (Map p210; Mendana Ave; ☺9am-4pm Mon-Fri) Changes all major currencies. Has an ATM inside. Other ATMs are located outside the post office and next door to Lime Lounge.
Bank South Pacific (Map p210; BSP; Mendana Ave; ☺8.30am-3pm Mon-Fri) Changes all major currencies. Has ATMs. Other ATMs are in the main BSP office near Heritage Park Hotel; there's also one ATM beside the reception at Heritage Park Hotel.
Westpac (Map p210; Mendana Ave; ☺9am-4pm Mon-Fri) Changes all major currencies except Euros. Has an ATM. Another ATM is outside the Our Telekom office.

Post
Solomon Post (Map p210; Mendana Ave; ☺8am-4.30pm Mon-Fri, 8am-noon Sat) Also houses a Western Union counter and a small internet cafe.

Telephone
Our Telekom (Map p210; Mendana Ave; ☺8.30am-4.30pm Mon-Fri, 9am-noon Sat) Next to the post office. Sells prepaid phonecards, Bumblebee cards (for wi-fi access) and prepaid mobile phonecards.

Tourist Information

Solomon Islands Visitors Bureau (SIVB; Map p210; ☑22442; www.visitsolomons.com.sb; Mendana Ave; ☺8am-4.30pm Mon-Fri) There's little printed material, but staff can provide advice and contact isolated lodges and villages (by two-way radio) to make bookings. Also sells a useful map of the country.

Getting There & Away

Air

International flights land at Honiara's Henderson Airport, and all domestic routes begin and end in Honiara. See p230 for details of international flights. **Guadalcanal Travel Services** (GTS; Map p210; ☑22586; guadtrav@solomon.com. sb; Mendana Ave; ☺8am-4.30pm Mon-Fri, 9am-noon Sat) represents most international and regional airlines. From Honiara, **Solomon Airlines** (Map p210; ☑23562, 20031; www. flysolomons.com; Hibiscus Ave; ☺8am-4pm Mon-Fri, 8.30-11.30am Sat) flies to most islands in the country.

Boat

The passenger boat **MV Pelican Express** (Map p210; ☑28104) offers a weekly service between Honiara and Gizo via Marovo Lagoon (Seghe and Mbunikalo). The 12-hour Honiara–Gizo trip costs S$600. It generally plies this route on Sunday (return on Monday); check while you're there. The office is next door to Lime Lounge. The passenger boat **MV 360 Discovery** (Map p210; ☑20957, 7442802; City Centre Bldg) operates daily between Honiara and Auki (S$220 one-way, three to four hours); four days a week it makes a stop at Tulagi (S$160). The **MV Lady Wakehurst** (Map p210; ☑7592006; Solomon Motors, Mendana Ave) also travels between Honiara and Auki (S$150, five to six hours, twice weekly).

Island hopping on the cargo boats that sail between Guadalcanal, Malaita and the Western Province is an adventurous and inexpensive way to travel. Departure times and dates are unscheduled and the best way to find out what's available is to ask around at the docks. Try the **Kosco**, which runs between Honiara and the Western Province.

ⓘ GETTING AROUND THE NORTH COAST

Exploring the north coast by public transport is feasible, but it's not really convenient. Most sights are not signed and are not easy to find. We suggest hiring a taxi in Honiara; count on S$100 per hour.

ⓘ Getting Around

From the airport, the standard taxi fare into town is S$100.

Honiara's minibuses are cheap, frequent (in daylight hours) and safe. The flat S$3 fare will take you anywhere on the route, which is written on a placard behind the windscreen of the bus.

There are taxis everywhere in Honiara. They don't have meters, so agree on a fare before hopping in – S$10 per kilometre is reasonable.

Rental cars can be arranged through the Pacific Casino Hotel.

East of Honiara

One of the star attractions in Honiara's hinterlands is **Mataniko Falls**, which feature a spectacular thundering of water down a cliff straight into a canyon below (see p213).

The road to Mt Austen begins in Kukum and climbs up to the historical sites where Japanese troops doggedly resisted the US advance. The **Solomons Peace Memorial Park**, about 3.5km from the main coastal road, was built by Japanese war veterans in 1981 to commemorate all who died in the WWII Guadalcanal campaign. Further south you'll go past the **Gifu**, named after a Japanese district by its wartime Japanese defenders, before reaching the summit of **Mt Austen** (410m). A dirt track leads to a former **Japanese Observation Point**. Americans in WWII dubbed this spot Grassy Knoll. There's a plaque that explains the strategic importance of Mt Austen during WWII.

About 6.5km from Honiara is the turnoff south to the **Betikama SDA Mission**. The sprawling property comprises a large handicraft shop and a small **museum** (S$25) with an outdoor collection of WWII debris.

A memorial at **Henderson Airport** honours US forces and their Pacific islander allies. About 100m to the west of the terminal is the scaffold-style **US WWII control tower**.

About 4km past the airport, you'll find a marble monument on a private property near a deserted black-sand beach at **Hell's Point**. The Japanese Colonel Kiyono Ichiki and his 800 men 'died with courage' here on 20 August 1942 after a banzai attack from the eastern side of the creek against US machine guns and artillery mounted on its western bank.

A few hundred metres further east, a road heads inland and follows the west bank of the Tenaru River. After 1.5km you'll come to Marine Hospital No 8, the first wartime hospital in Guadalcanal, in **Tenaru Village**.

Tenaru is the launching pad for the Tenaru Waterfalls (see p213).

Back to the main coastal road, continue further east until you reach Red Beach. Here you'll find a lonely, very rusted Japanese gun, placed here by US veterans and pointing forlornly out to sea. This is the only reminder of the US landings here in 1942.

Continue east to Tetere, where a dirt track leads to a beach and 30 or more abandoned amtracks (amphibious troop carriers). There's a S$50 *kastom* fee.

West of Honiara

Life becomes very sedate as one heads west through some of the north coast's delicious scenery. Urban existence is left behind once the road traverses White River and crawls its way along the scenic coastline.

The area boasts a high historical significance. The seas between Guadalcanal's northwestern coast and Savo island were the site of constant naval battles between August 1942 and February 1943. By the time the Japanese finally withdrew, so many ships had been sunk it became known as Iron Bottom Sound.

Popular with locals and expats at weekends, Mamara Beach (S$25) has black sand and is OK for swimming and bathing. About 1km further west is Turtle Beach (S$25), an appealing strip of white coral sand fringed with coconut trees.

Just past the Bonegi II site (see p214), there's a bush track that heads inland and runs about 400m to a well-preserved US Sherman tank (S$30) called *Jezebel*.

At Ruaniu (also known as Bonegi III), about 4.5km west from Bonegi II, there's a 6500-tonne Japanese transport ship, believed to be the *Kyushu Maru*, that lies just offshore – another superb playground for divers.

About 25km from Honiara, a turn to the south from the coastal road brings you to the Vilu Open-Air Museum (S$50). Here there are US and Japanese memorials, four large Japanese field guns and the remains of several US aircraft.

CENTRAL PROVINCE

Another world awaits just a two-hour boat ride from Honiara, either in the Nggela (Florida) group or on Savo.

DON'T MISS

TAKE A DIP!

Short of dreamy expanses of white sand on Guadalcanal, you can take a dip in lovely natural pools. But you've gotta earn these treats, as they are accessible on foot only.

Mataniko Falls

The hike starts in Lelei village with a steep ascent to a ridge, followed by an easier stretch amid mildly undulating hills. Then you'll tackle a gruelling descent on a slippery muddy path to reach the floor of the little canyon where the Mataniko flows. It takes roughly two hours return to do this walk. You'll find guides in Lelei.

Tenaru Waterfalls

The gorgeous Tenaru Waterfalls are a fairly easy four-hour walk (return) from a tiny settlement about 2km south of Tenaru Village. The path follows the floor of the river valley and cuts across the river's many bends. Guides are available at Tenaru Village.

❶ Getting There & Away

Small cargo boats take two hours to ply between Tulagi (or Savo) and Honiara, charging about S$250 one way. In Honiara, they leave from the little beach next to Point Cruz Yacht Club. Lodgings can organise private transfers.

Florida (Nggela) Islands

POP 21,600 / AREA 1000 SQ KM

The Floridas' main draws? Diving, snorkelling, surfing and an ultra-chilled atmosphere. The two main islands, Tulagi and Nggela Sule, have rugged interiors, long white-sand beaches and mangrove swamps. In the middle of the Floridas, Tulagi was the Solomons' former capital; it was also a Japanese base during WWII.

🏃 Activities

There's superb snorkelling off Maravagi Resort and fabulous diving off Tulagi, including world-class wrecks (see p27). Contact Tulagi Dive (🕾7475043, 26589; www.tulagidive.com.sb) in Honiara.

Maravagi is also an increasingly popular venue for surfing.

Extreme Adventures BOAT TOURS
(☑23442, 749541; excursion per person from S$1200) Based in Honiara, Extreme Adventures runs boat excursions to the Florida Islands most weekends. They include snorkel stops and a beach barbecue lunch.

🛏 Sleeping & Eating

Maravagi Resort BUNGALOWS $$
(☑29065, 23179; www.maravagiresort.com.sb; Mangalonga Island; s/d A$60/102) Honiara's expats come to this small island near the northern end of the Florida group to enjoy the stunning location, with gorgeous coral pinnacles that extend just off the dining room. The rustic, beachfront leafhouse bungalows feature private bathrooms (cold-water showers), breezy terraces, mozzie nets and electricity. Avoid the six charmless, dorm-style rooms at the back. Food (meals A$55 per day) is tasty. Village visits, surfing and snorkelling trips can be organised. Private boat transfers from Honiara cost from A$110 return. Credit cards are accepted.

Vanita Motel GUESTHOUSE $
(☑32074; Tulagi; r without bathroom S$220, r with bathroom from S$350) A no-frills but well-kept guesthouse.

Savo

POP 3500 / AREA 31 SQ KM
Though lying just 14km north of Guadalcanal, Savo is a world away from the capital. Imagine an active volcano with a pair of dormant craters, coconut groves, a narrow strip of grey-sand beach and a few hot springs that are accessible by foot. The island also features a megapode field where

---

DON'T MISS

BONEGI

About 12km west from Honiara, **Bonegi** (S$25) is music to the ears of divers and snorkellers. Two large Japanese freighters sank just offshore on the night of 13 November 1942, and make for a magnificent playground for scuba divers, who call them Bonegi I and Bonegi II. As the upper works of Bonegi II break the surface, it can also be snorkelled. For more information on diving these sites, see p207 and p27. There's also a black-sand **beach** that is suitable for a picnic.

---

hundreds of female birds lay their eggs in holes scratched into the hot sand.

Savo is also one of the most dependable locations in the Solomons to spot pods of dolphins, which usually congregate off the west coast.

🛏 Sleeping & Eating

Sunset Lodge HOTEL $$
(☑22517, 28071, 7498347; Kuila; r per person incl 3 meals S$500) Features 20 tidy rooms, some with private bathrooms, in a fairly bland concrete building on a hillside. The setting is enchanting, with the added appeal of tasty meals; transfers can be arranged from Honiara (from S$600). Various excursions and tours can be organised.

WESTERN PROVINCE

Marovo Lagoon, Munda and Gizo are the three unmissable destinations in the Western Province. Thanks to reliable inter-island boat and plane services, they can easily be combined and toured at a comfortable, leisurely pace.

Marovo Lagoon

On New Georgia's eastern side, Marovo Lagoon is the world's finest double-barrier-enclosed lagoon, bordered by the large New Georgia and Vangunu Islands on one side and a double line of long barrier islands on the other. It contains hundreds of beautiful small islands, most of which are covered by coconut palms and rainforest and surrounded by coral.

Here you can visit laid-back villages and explore *tambu* (sacred) sites, picnic on deserted islands, take a lagoon tour, meet master carvers, dive in fish soup, kayak across the lagoon or take a walk through the rainforest or up awesome summits.

Don't expect paradise on earth, though. Truly idyllic stretches of sand are almost nonexistent, and years of intense logging have left their scars, literally.

🏃 Activities

Diving & Snorkelling

Marovo Lagoon offers plenty of exhilarating dives for both experts and novices. Here's the menu: channels, caves, drop-offs, coral gardens, clouds of technicolour fish and a few wrecks thrown in for good measure. See

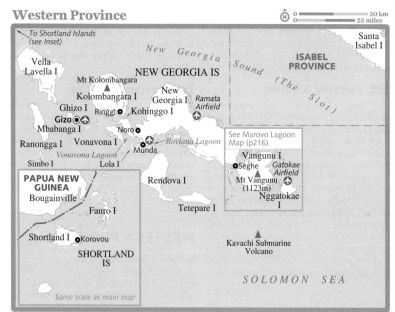

the diving chapter (p28 & p28) for more information.

With hundreds of lovely sites scattered throughout the lagoon, snorkelling is equally impressive. Lodges can organise lagoon tours and snorkelling trips, which cost anything from S$50 to S$300 per person depending on distance and duration. Bring your own gear.

Solomon Dive Adventures
DIVING, SNORKELLING
(www.solomondiveadventures.com; Peava, Gatokae Island) This small outfit is based at Vuana Guesthouse in Peava (South Marovo). The ebullient American owner, Lisa Roquette, runs dive trips to Mbulo, Kicha and Male Male Islands. Introductory dives cost S$1000 (including gear), shore dives are S$400 and one-/two-tank dives run at S$550/1100. Two-tank outings to Kicha Island with a picnic lunch cost S$1300. Rental gear is available (S$240 per day). They also offer snorkelling excursions (from S$400). Cash only.

Uepi Island Resort
DIVING, SNORKELLING
(www.uepi.com; Uepi island) This outfit has a great reputation for service and professionalism and offers stunning dives (from A$75) for all levels of proficiency throughout Marovo Lagoon. Equipment hire is A$40 per day. It's also renowned for its certification courses and dedicated snorkelling trips. It caters mainly to the resort's guests; non-guests may be accepted – space permitting and by prior arrangement only.

Dive Wilderness
DIVING
(www.thewildernesslodge.org; Peava, Gatokae Island) This operation, launched in early 2012, caters to guests staying at the Wilderness Lodge. A single dive costs A$75.

Kayaking
Kayaking is probably the most entrancing way to explore Marovo Lagoon. Uepi Island Resort can arrange multiday kayaking trips.

Walking
If you've got itchy feet, don't forget your walking shoes. Consider scaling Mt Mariu (887m) on Gatokae (two days), climbing the hill that lords over Chea Village on Marovo island (two hours) or tackling Mt Reku (520m) on Vanguntu (half a day).

Tours
All kinds of tours and activities, including village visits, guided walks, picnic trips and lagoon excursions can be arranged through the region's lodges.

Marovo Lagoon

N
0 —————————— 10 km
0 —————————— 5 miles

Marovo Lagoon

⊙ Activities, Courses & Tours
Dive Wilderness ....(see 6)
Solomon Dive Adventures...........(see 5)
Uepi Island Resort ....(see 4)

⊜ Sleeping
1 Charapoana Lodge B1
2 Matikuri Lodge A3
3 Ropiko Lodge...D4
4 Uepi Island Resort B1
5 Vuana Guesthouse D4
6 Wilderness Lodge D4

🛏 Sleeping

There's a small network of ecolodges on the lagoon. These rustic, family-run establishments are great places to meet locals and offer an authentic cultural experience. If you want to pamper yourself, opt for Uepi Island Resort or the Wilderness Lodge.

Most places overlook the lagoon, but there's no beach.

TOP CHOICE Uepi Island Resort RESORT $$$
(www.uepi.com; Uepi Island; s incl 3 meals A$220-290, d incl 3 meals A$380-500; 🛜) This extremely well-run resort is very popular with Australian divers, who stay here to get thrilled by the sensational dive sites right on their doorstep. Snorkellers will get a buzz on the house reef that spreads from the end of the short jetty. The best thing is that it also appeals to honeymooners and families. The spacious bungalows are comfortable, but not flash (no air-con, ordinary furnishings), and are scattered amid lovely bush gardens and coconut palms. The ethos here is laid-back, ecological and activity-oriented. Perks include a bar, a breezy dining room with excellent meals, a full dive shop and a good excursion program. Boat transfers to Seghe are A$105 per person return.

TOP CHOICE **Wilderness Lodge**   BUNGALOWS $$$

(www.thewildernesslodge.org; Peava, Gatokae Island; r/bungalow per person incl 3 meals A$155/185) Nestled in a coconut grove right by the lagoon, this 'lodge' features a large leafhouse with two bedrooms that share a bathroom as well as two luxurious seafront bungalows with private facilities. Meals incorporate locally grown fruit and vegetables and there's 24-hour solar-generated electricity. Adventurous travellers can forgo relaxing on the pontoon in favour of snorkelling along the magnificent house reef, spear fishing in the bay, diving off Kicha Island (there's a small onsite dive centre), hiking and crocodile-spotting – all of which can be organised by the lodge. Boat transfers to Gatokae airstrip cost A$56 per person return.

Matikuri Lodge   BUNGALOWS $$

(7467177, 7541016; Matikuri Island; dm incl 3 meals S$350, bungalow per person incl 3 meals S$470) Matikuri Lodge's drawcard is its soothing sense of isolation, sitting on the western arc of Marovo Lagoon. Digs are in three island-style bungalows that face the sea; the four dorm-style rooms in the main house are rudimentary. There's good swimming just offshore. No electricity, but kerosene lamps are provided. The dining area has a large deck on stilts. A host of guided walks, village visits and lagoon tours can be organised, and there are kayaks for hire. One-way boat transfers to Seghe airstrip (20 minutes) are S$250 per person.

Vuana Guesthouse   GUESTHOUSE $$

(www.solomondiveadventures.com; Peava, Gatokae; r per person incl 3 meals S$700-800) Divers couldn't ask for a better base than this well-run guesthouse with an onsite dive centre and a sensational house reef. There are two simple bungalows with fabulous waterfrontage as well as one room in the owner's house. Aim for the slightly dearer 'Breeze' unit, which is more charming and better laid out. Toilets and showers (cold water) are shared. Most guests are here on dive packages, though the guesthouse is also a great place to decompress. It takes a genuine interest in sustainability, composting food and supporting local projects. If only there was a beach! Instead of sand at the front, it's ironshore – a sharp rock made of coral and limestone. Not exactly a great tanning spot, but don't fret – there's a nice strip of sand a short walk away. Boat transfers to Seghe airstrip are S$250 (for two people) one way. Cash only.

WORTH A TRIP

TAVANIPUPU ISLAND

If you've ever dreamed of having your own island paradise, **Tavanipupu Private Island Resort** (36081, 36082; www.tavanipupu.com; d incl 3 meals A$550), on a small island off Guadalcanal's eastern tip, has all the key ingredients – exclusivity, seclusion, atmosphere. Digs are in six tastefully decorated, spacious bungalows scattered in a well-tended coconut grove that overlooks the beach. The restaurant uses only the freshest seafood. Snorkelling is excellent (gear provided), as is fishing, and you can work your tan on sandy beaches or pamper yourself in the spa. Solomon Airlines flies three times a week from Honiara to Marau (S$1600 return, 30 minutes), from where it's a 15-minute boat ride to the resort.

Charapoana Lodge   BUNGALOWS $$

(30156, 7409634, 7403714; kanikilasana@gmail.com; Charapoana Island; r per person incl 3 meals S$370) Just across the passage from Uepi Island, this well-regarded ecolodge exudes a Melanesian family atmosphere. Guests are accommodated in a large wooden house with three basic rooms. There are also a few bungalows right on a little stretch of sand, offering more privacy. The shared 'mangrove toilet' is something that has to be used to be believed (you'll see). Food is copious and varied. Sunbathing, swimming and snorkelling are top-notch – there's even a manta rays' cleaning station just a short swim away. Boat transfers to Seghe airstrip cost S$1100/700/570 for one/two/three people. Cash only.

Ropiko Lodge   BUNGALOWS $$

(7495805, 28065; rolandpiko@yahoo.com; Gatokae Island; r per person incl 3 meals S$400) This charming place grows on you quickly, with a well-proportioned bungalow facing the lagoon. Lovely setting: the property is filled with colourful orchids and there's a small beach lapped by turquoise waters. The decent

DAY OFF

Take note that Marovo Lagoon is strongly Seventh Day Adventist, so you can't do much on Saturday.

ablution block has flush toilets. When we visited, the owner had started to build additional bungalows with private facilities. Enjoy excellent swimming and snorkelling on the nearby reef. Boat transfers to Gatokae airstrip cost S$200 per person return. Cash only.

 ## Information

The mobile phone network doesn't cover Marovo Lagoon entirely; at the time of writing, South Marovo wasn't yet covered. Bookings for resorts and lodges can be made online or through SIVB in Honiara (p212).

 ## Getting There & Away

AIR There are two main gateways to Marovo: Seghe (for North Marovo Lagoon) and Gatokae Island (for South Marovo Lagoon). **Solomon Airlines** (www.flysolomons.com) connects Seghe with Honiara (S$1200, daily), and Munda (S$685) and Gizo (S$790) about six days a week. Gatokae is serviced from Honiara (S$1200, three times weekly). All prices are one way.

BOAT The passenger boat **MV Pelican Express** (☎28104 in Honiara) offers a weekly service between Honiara and Gizo via Marovo Lagoon; it stops at Mbatuna (one way S$460) and Seghe (one way S$500) on its way to Gizo. Check while in Honiara, as the schedule is erratic.

 ## Getting Around

If you have booked accommodation, your hosts will arrange airport transfers. Costs will depend on the distance travelled and the number of passengers.

Public transport does not exist. To get from South Marovo to North Marovo (or vice versa), you'll need to charter a boat; as an indication of price, a ride between Gatokae and Uepi should set you back around S$2000.

Munda

West New Georgia has its fair share of attractions as well as reliable accommodation options, a hatful of historic sites – from

MONEY MATTERS

Marovo Lagoon has no ATMs and no banks, and credit cards are only accepted at Uepi Island Resort, so you'll need to bring a stash of cash to cover your entire bill (including accommodation, meals, activities and transport), plus some extra for surprise add-ons.

WWII relics to skull shrines – and thrilling dive sites. The largest settlement, the little town of Munda on New Georgia itself, makes a convenient, if not glamorous, base for exploring the area's attractions.

 ## Sights & Activities

Museums   WWII RELICS
(S$25 each) History buffs should consider the two small private 'museums' of WWII relics. The one closest to Agnes Lodge is run by Gordon Beti (no sign; ask for exact location); the second, and most interesting, is further east along the road, near the soccer field, a 20-minute walk from Agnes Lodge. Run by Alphy Barney Paulson, it features lots of utensils, ammunition, machine guns, shells, crockery, helmets, shavers and knives, all left behind by the Japanese and Americans.

Dive Munda   DIVING, SNORKELLING
(☎62156; www.mundadive.com; Agnes Lodge) Munda is a destination of choice for demanding divers, who have the pick of lots of superlative dive sites (see p27), with an exciting selection of wrecks, drop-offs, reefs and underwater caves. Run by a friendly British couple, Dive Munda offers two-tank dives (A$200 with all equipment) and certification courses. At most dive sites snorkelling (A$50) is also possible.

Tours

The easiest way to get a broad look at the delights around West New Georgia is to take a half- or one-day tour. Based at Agnes Lodge, **Go West Tours** (☎62180) offers a wide range of excursions. Prices start at S$800 for two people.

Sleeping & Eating

Agnes Lodge   INN $$
(☎62133, 62101; www.agneslodge.com.sb; s with shared bathroom S$220-280, d with shared bathroom S$440-550, d S$800-1100, ste S$1200-1400; ❄❂) This long-established venture right on the waterfront (no beach) has a variety of rooms for all budgets, from fan-cooled, two-bed rooms to comfy self-contained units with air-con. Downside: rooms are tightly packed together. The place isn't luxurious but is in top nick, the onsite bar is good for discovering essential local gossip, and the **restaurant** (mains S$80-300; ☺breakfast, lunch & dinner) serves excellent food. It's a short walk from the airstrip. Credit cards are accepted.

Zipolo Habu Resort
RESORT $$$

(☑62178, 7471105; www.zipolohabu.com.sb; Lola Island; bungalow with shared bathroom A$140-190, deluxe bungalow A$230-340; 🛜) On Lola Island, about 20 minutes by boat from Munda, this small resort with a casual atmosphere satiates the white-sand beach, coconut-palm, azure-lagoon fantasy, with six spacious, fan-cooled bungalows. The cheaper ones are fairly basic leafhouses, while the two deluxe units boast private bathrooms and unobstructed views over the lagoon. The restaurant (meals per day A$80) gets good reviews. This place offers village tours, lagoon excursions, sportfishing and surf charters. Return boat transfers to Munda cost A$120 per boatload. Divers can be picked up at the resort by Dive Munda. Credit cards are accepted.

Qua Roviana
GUESTHOUSE $$

(☑62123; quaroviana@gmail.com; s with shared bathroom S$220, r with shared bathroom S$550; ❄🛜) Just across the road from Agnes Lodge, this family-run abode is great value. The nine rooms are simply furnished but serviceable, and the common lounge, bathrooms and kitchen are clean, comfortable and well fitted out. Qua Roviana will accept cash only.

ℹ Information

Check your emails at **Telekom** (per hr S$20; ⏱8am-noon & 1-4.30pm Mon-Fri).

The **Bank South Pacific** changes currency and has an ATM. The **ANZ** branch, near the post office, also has an ATM.

ℹ Getting There & Away

AIR **Solomon Airlines** (☑62152; www.fly solomons.com) connects Munda with Honiara (S$1250, daily), Gizo (S$685, daily) and Seghe (S$685, six weekly).

BOAT **Go West Transport** (☑62180), based at Agnes Lodge, has a shuttle service to Gizo (S$240, two hours, two to three weekly) stopping at various places en route, including Zipolo Habu Resort and Lolomo Eco Resort.

Around West New Georgia

Fancy a dip? Head to the 10m **Holupuru Falls**, east of Munda. If you've got itchy feet, you can hike up **Mt Bau**, about 9km inland. You'll need a guide to show you the way (ask at Agnes Lodge, p218).

In **Baeroko Bay** you'll see the *Casi Maru*, a sunken **Japanese freighter** near the shore (and a dive site). Its rusty masts protrude from the water. It was bombed as its crane was loading cargo on to an adjacent barge. **Enoghae**, at the jutting northern lip of the bay, has several large **Japanese WWII anti-aircraft guns** still hidden in the scrub.

Skull Island, on Vonavona Lagoon, is the final resting place for the skulls of countless vanquished warriors, as well as a shrine for the skulls of Rendovan chiefs.

On **Kohinggo Island**, there is a wrecked **US Sherman tank** on the northern shore. It was lost in action in September 1943 when US marines overran a Japanese strongpoint.

🛏 Sleeping

Lolomo Eco Resort
BUNGALOWS $$

(☑8519774, 22902; warren.paia@gmail.com; Kohinggo Island; r with shared bathroom S$660; ❄🛜) Halfway between Munda and Gizo, this supremely relaxing place, opened in 2011, offers something different, with three large, smartly finished thatched-roof bungalows on stilts, but it's a bummer it's not suitable for swimming; the shore is fringed with mangroves. For a dip, the owners will happily take you to a nearby sandy island. The ablution block is squeaky clean and equipped with flush toilets and hot-water showers. The meals package costs S$300 per day. Lolomo is very isolated but convenient nonetheless, as the shuttle operated by Go West Transport stops here when it travels between Munda and Gizo. Private boat transfers to either Munda or Gizo cost S$1200 per boatload return. Cash only.

Gizo

Little Ghizo Island is dwarfed by its neighbours, but it has the Solomons' second-biggest 'city', Gizo (pronounced the same, spelt differently), the most developed area outside the capital.

Gizo is the hub around which the Western Province revolves. Sprawled along the waterfront with its steep hills behind, the town is not devoid of appeal, although the architecture is charmless. Most places of importance are on the main street. Apart from the bustling market on the waterfront, there are no specific sights, but there are some appealing lodgings a short boat ride away. Gizo is also a good base for divers, surfers and hikers.

Gizo

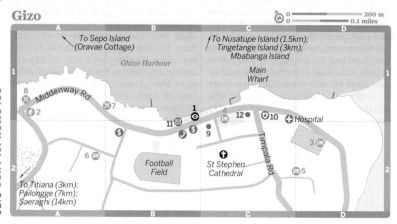

Gizo

⊙ Sights
1 Market...B1

⊕ Activities, Courses & Tours
2 Dive Gizo...A1

⊟ Sleeping
3 Cegily's Guesthouse............................D2
4 Gizo Hotel...C1
5 Nagua Resthouse.................................D2
6 Rekona Moamoa Lodge........................A2

⊗ Eating
7 Lamasa...B1
Nuzu Nuzu Restaurant ....(see 4)
8 PT 109..A1

⊜ Drinking
Gizo Hotel...(see 4)
PT 109..(see 8)

⊛ Entertainment
Bamboo...(see 4)

ⓘ Information
9 Immigration Office................................C2
10 Police...C1
11 Post Office...B2

ⓘ Transport
12 Solomon Airlines...................................C1

⊙ Sights

Market   MARKET
(⊙Mon-Sat) Villagers from neighbouring
islands (and even from the Shortland Islands) arrive each morning by boat to occupy their little stands under the shade of
tall trees. It's at its liveliest Monday and
Friday mornings.

World Fish Centre   CLAM FARM, SNORKELLING
(☑60022; Nusatupe island; ⊙by reservation) On
Nusatupe island (Gizo's airstrip), this clam
farm and research centre is a good spot if
you want to snorkel over giant clams of up
to 1m long in the lagoon (bring your own
gear). Boat transfers from Gizo cost about
S$200, or you can take the Solomon Airlines
shuttle (S$60 one-way).

🏃 Activities

Diving & Snorkelling
Gizo has made a name for itself in diving.
Sure, large tracts of reefs were battered
when the 2007 tsunami hit the Gizo area,
but overall the level of destruction was relatively low and most sites have now recovered. Most dives are less than a 20-minute
boat ride from Gizo and include wrecks and
reef dives. See p28 for more information on
dive sites.

In the mood for snorkelling? Kennedy Island, just off Fatboys (p222), is your answer.
Take the shuttle to Fatboys (S$100), hire
snorkelling gear at the resort and snorkel
to your heart's content. Dive Gizo also runs
snorkelling trips (S$40, including lunch and
snorkel set).

Dive Gizo
DIVING, SNORKELLING

(60253; www.divegizo.com; Middenway Rd) This solid professional outfit at the western end of town charges A$140 for an introductory dive (including equipment hire) and A$150 for a two-tank dive, including picnic (add an extra A$30 for gear rental). An open-water certification is A$680. We love their two-tank dive organisation; you spend your surface interval picnicking on a secluded island or having lunch at Fatboys (p223).

Swimming & Surfing

The main road out of Gizo skirts the shore to **Saeraghi** at the island's northwestern end, which has lovely beaches. There's excellent point surfing off **Pailongge**, on Ghizo's southern coast. The October-to-April swell rises to 2m or more. There's a great left-hander near **Titiana** village, with a long paddle out to the reef's edge, and a right at Pailongge. Gizo Hotel is a good source of information. To get to the spots, take a taxi from Gizo. Bring your own boards.

Hiking

If you're a hiking fiend, we'd unhesitatingly recommend the climb up Kolombangara (see p222).

Sleeping

GIZO

Nagua Resthouse
GUESTHOUSE $$

(60012; s with shared bathroom S$150-350, r S$400-500) A short (uphill) walk from town, this family-run guesthouse features plain, functional well-scrubbed rooms with air-con, and there's a nice communal kitchen. Overall the whole place is well maintained, linen is fresh and the staff is friendly. A safe bet.

Cegily's Guesthouse
GUESTHOUSE $$

(60035, 60935, 7467982; r with shared bathroom S$290-350) This small guesthouse with only three fan-cooled rooms could just be the best choice for those on a tight budget. It's a study in simplicity, but it's also clean, calm and secure. There's a well-kept communal kitchen, a tidy lounge area and a terrace with good ocean views. It's just past the hospital, on a hillside.

Rekona Moamoa Lodge
GUESTHOUSE $$

(60368; dm S$160, d with shared bathroom S$250, d S$350-690; ❄☎) Good value for its quiet and central location on a street which sees little traffic. The cheaper rooms are fairly Spartan, but at these rates you know you're not getting the Ritz. The dearer ones – especially rooms 16 to 20, upstairs – are much more inviting and come with private bathrooms and air-con. There's a kitchen area for common use.

Gizo Hotel
HOTEL $$$

(60199; www.gizohotel.com; Middenway Rd; r S$1000-1200; ❄☎⌨) Gizo Hotel is a perennial favourite for its central location, salubrious yet unflashy rooms and wide array of facilities (wi-fi, air-con, gift shop, bar and restaurant). Popular with expats and business-people, it can't quite shake that just-a-motel feeling, despite a swimming pool amid lush vegetation at the back. Some rooms have sea views, others open onto the garden and the pool. Excursions to Kennedy Island are organised most Sundays.

SEPO ISLAND

Oravae Cottage
BUNGALOWS $$

(66621, 66619; www.oravaecottage.com; cottage incl 3 meals per person from A$100) Look at the homepage on the website: it's truly like this.

WORTH A TRIP

TETEPARE ISLAND

This large rainforest island is one of the Solomons' conservation jewels and a dream come true for ecotourists. The **Tetepare Descendants' Association** (62163 in Munda; www.tetepare.org; r per person incl 3 meals S$500), which manages the island, welcomes visitors in its simple yet genuinely ecofriendly leafhouses (no air-con, solar power, shared facilities). There are plans to build another two bungalows with private facilities. What makes this place extra special is the host of environmentally friendly activities available, including snorkelling with dugongs, spotting crocodiles, birdwatching and turtle-tagging. They're free (except the ones that involve boat rides), and you'll be accompanied by trained guides. Food is fresh and organic. No alcohol is available, but it's BYO. Minuses: the cost and duration of transfers (S$1900 per boatload one-way, two hours from Munda), but there are plans to arrange cheaper transfers with Go West Transport (p224) – ask when you book.

DON'T MISS

HIKING IN KOLOMBANGARA

Growing weary of water activities? Consider climbing up to the crater's rim on Kolombangara (the big island facing Gizo). It's an exhilarating two-day/one-night hike. Take note that it's an arduous walk – it's wet and muddy all the way up, it's steep, and the path is irregular – so you'll need to be fit. But the atmosphere and views are surreal.

You'll need guides and porters. Dive Gizo (p221) and **Kolombangara Island Biodiversity Conservation Association** (KIBCA; ✆60230, 7400544; www.kolombangara.org) can arrange logistics. Plan on S$1600 to S$2000 per person, excluding boat transfers from Gizo (S$1600 per boatload return).

Kolombangara also has less challenging hikes, including crater walks and river walks.

Just 10 minutes from Gizo, this lovely retreat has two handsomely designed traditional houses with private facilities (cold-water showers). The bigger cottage can sleep up to eight people; the smaller one is suitable for couples. Both units have a terrace opening onto the lagoon. Luxury it ain't, but it has charm in spades. The atmosphere is delightfully chilled out and meals get high marks from travellers. Swimming and snorkelling are excellent.

TINGETANGE ISLAND

At the time of writing, a new resort was being built on this islet lying a five-minute boat ride from Gizo. The owners had plans to name it **Imagination Island** (ward_geoscience@yahoo.com). It will comprise seven bungalows, a six-room house, a bar and a restaurant.

MBABANGA ISLAND

A mere 10-minute boat ride south of Gizo, this island has a brochure-esque appeal, with an expansive lagoon and a string of white-sand beaches.

Sanbis Resort   RESORT $$$
(✆66313; www.sanbisresort.com; d S$1500, lodge A$1000; ☎) A place of easy bliss. Relax in your creatively designed bungalow, snorkel over healthy reefs just offshore, snooze in

a hammock, treat yourself to a tasty meal at the laid-back over-the-water restaurant or kayak over translucent waters. The icing on the cake is the ultra-exclusive Lodge, which is outstandingly positioned at the tip of the island. No air-con, but the location benefits from cooling breezes. The beach is thin but attractive, and the whole place is ecofriendly. It's a good base for honeymooners, divers (there's a small on-site dive shop) and fishermen (professional equipment is available for rent). No kids under 12.

Fatboys   RESORT $$$
(✆60095, 7443107; www.fatboysgizo.com; d from A$230; ☎) This small complex has suffered in recent years from a lack of maintenance and TLC, but at the time of writing, capable new managers were working to get the place back into shape. It consists of five spacious waterfront bungalows that blend tropical hardwoods and traditional leaf. It's quite spread out so you can get a decent dose of privacy. The defining factor, however, is the lovely bar and restaurant directly over the exquisite waters of the lagoon. The narrow beach is average, but the snorkelling is sensational.

🍴 Eating

Gizo has several well-stocked supermarkets, open Monday to Saturday.

Lamasa   SEAFOOD, CHINESE $$
(Middenway Rd; mains S$50-110; ⊙lunch & dinner Mon-Fri) Lamasa is nothing more than a few tables, but it's hygienically kept and the fish and chips are brilliant value. No alcohol, but the smoothies are to die for.

SB Bar   INTERNATIONAL $$
(✆66313; Sanbis Resort, Mbabanga Island; mains S$60-130; ⊙from 11am) Sanbis Resort's over-water restaurant is an atmospheric place to sample a well-executed pizza or a burger at lunchtime. Call the reception to arrange transfers from Gizo.

Nuzu Nuzu Restaurant   INTERNATIONAL $$
(✆60199; Gizo Hotel, Middenway Rd; mains S$90-150; ⊙breakfast, lunch & dinner) The breezy open-air dining room is suitably exotic, with wood-carved posts, wooden tables and wicker seating. The choice of dishes on offer is pretty limited, but fish is ultrafresh, the daily specials are well-prepared and the wood-fired pizzas are tasty. Breakfast is average.

PT 109
SEAFOOD $

(Middenway Rd; mains S$60-120; ⊙lunch & dinner Mon-Fri) Named after John F Kennedy's WWII patrol boat that sank off Gizo, and situated in a great waterfront location, this place has a relaxed vibe. A blackboard displays a few simple dishes, such as local fish or chicken, as well as lobster.

Fatboys
INTERNATIONAL $

(📞60095; Mbabanga Island; mains S$50-120; ⊙lunch) What a sensational setting! The dining room is on a pier that hovers over the turquoise waters of Vonavona Lagoon. Food-wise, it's a bit less overwhelming – fish and chips, grilled fish and salads. There are billiard tables and a reading library. After your meal, rent snorkelling gear and swim over sandy shallows that extend to Kennedy Island. From Gizo, take the daily shuttle at 11am (S$60 one-way). It's best to reserve.

Market
MARKET $

(⊙Mon-Sat) For organic fruit and vegetables, as well as fresh fish, nothing can beat the market on the waterfront.

Drinking

The best drinking dens include the bar at the Gizo Hotel and PT 109. During the day, nothing can beat a frothy tropical cocktail or a cold beer at Sanbis Resort or Fatboys, on Mbabanga Island.

Entertainment

If you want to relive *Saturday Night Fever* island-style, try **Bamboo**, which is part of the Gizo Hotel, or PT 109, which has a dance floor. Both get busy on Thursday, Friday and Saturday evenings.

Shopping

Dive Gizo and Gizo Hotel have a rather wide selection of stonework and woodcarvings.

ℹ Information

ANZ Bank (Middenway Rd; ⊙9am-4pm Mon-Fri) Currency exchange. Has an ATM.

Bank South Pacific (BSP; Middenway Rd; ⊙8.30am-3.30pm Mon-Fri) Currency exchange. Has an ATM.

Daltron BeMobile (Middenway Rd; per hr S$30; ⊙8.30am-4.30pm Mon-Fri, 8am-noon Sat) Internet access. Beside the entrance of Gizo Hotel.

Gizo Internet Cafe (per hr S$25; ⊙8am-8pm) Same location as Lamasa restaurant.

Hospital (📞60224; Middenway Rd)

Immigration Office (⊙8-11.30am & 1-4.30pm Mon-Fri) Behind ANZ Bank. Can issue a visitor's permit for yachties proceeding from PNG and the Shortland Islands.

BEST OF THE REST

If, after visiting Guadalcanal, Malaita, Central and Western Provinces, you still feel the urge for more off-the-beaten-track adventures, and if time is really no object, consider travelling to the other provinces.

Choiseul One of the least-visited provinces in the Solomons, Choiseul has two airfields, on Taro Island and in Kagau.

Shortland Islands Like Choiseul, the Shortland Islands are culturally closer to Bougainville in PNG, which lies only nine kilometres to the north.

Makira-Ulawa An untouched world only one hour from Honiara. Kirakira is the main gateway. Sensational surfing off Star Harbour.

Temotu Temotu Province lies at the Solomons' most easterly point. Lata, the provincial capital, on Santa Cruz island, is the main launching pad for outlying islands, such as Reef Islands, Utupua and Vanikoro.

Rennell & Bellona Both islands are Polynesia outliers, sharing similar languages and cultures. Geologically they're both rocky, uplifted-coral atolls.

Isabel This province is a castaway's dream come true, especially if you can make it to the Arnarvon Islands, off the northwestern tip of Isabel. This conservation area managed by **Nature Conservancy** (📞20940, 28095 in Honiara; www.nature.org) is one of the world's largest nesting grounds for the hawksbill turtle. Isabel has an excellent place to stay, **Papatura Island Retreat** (www.papatura.com), which offers snorkelling, fishing and surfing outings. The gateways to Isabel are Buala and Suavanao.

Our Telekom (Middenway Rd; per hr S$20; ⊗8.30am-12.30pm &1-4.30pm) Sells phonecards, SIM cards and Bumblebee cards. Internet access is available, too (two computers only).

⊕ Getting There & Away

Air

Solomon Airlines (☑60173; www.flysolomons.com; Middenway Rd; ⊗8.30am-4pm Mon-Fri) has up to three daily flights between Gizo and Honiara (from S$1380). There are also daily flights between Gizo and Munda (from S$685), and three weekly flights between Gizo and Seghe (from S$790). From Gizo you can also fly to the Shortland Islands and Choiseul. The airfield is on Nusatupe island (boat transfer S$60).

Boat

The **MV Pelican Express** (☑28104 in Honiara) has a weekly service between Gizo and Honiara via Marovo Lagoon (S$600, 12 hours).

Go West Transport (☑62180; Agnes Lodge, Munda) runs a shuttle boat connecting Gizo to Munda (S$240, two hours, two to three weekly) stopping at various places en route, including Zipolo Habu Resort and Lolomo Eco Resort.

Islands Around Ghizo

A perfect cone-shaped volcano that rises to 1770m, **Kolombangara** looms majestically on the horizon, northeast of Ghizo Island. It's a scenic two-day hike to the top and back if you are fit and have the energy (see p222). It rises from a 1km-wide coastal plain through flat-topped ridges and increasingly steep escarpments to the rugged crater rim of Mt Veve. For history buffs, there are WWII Japanese relics scattered around the island. **Vila Point** was an important WWII Japanese base and you can still see guns in the bush.

Definitely worth a visit is **Simbo Island** for its megapode hatcheries and its easily climbable volcano. There's also a sulphur-covered crater lake.

Both Kolombangara and Simbo offer accommodation in the form of village stays.

⊕ Getting There & Away

The islands around Ghizo have no regular boat services. Your best bet is to find a shared ride at Gizo market. Dive Gizo (p221) can arrange excursions to Simbo and Kolombangara islands.

MALAITA

Malaita Province is named after the largest island in the region. Easily reached from Guadalcanal, Malaita is a hauntingly beautiful island with narrow coastal plains, secluded bays and a rugged highland interior. As well as having a host of natural features to explore, Malaita has an equally fascinating ethnic heritage. It's a rare combination of being both an adventure island as well as a stronghold of ancient Melanesian traditions and cultures.

Unlike in Guadalcanal and the Western Province, the development of tourism is still in its infancy here. In the main destinations (Auki and Langa Langa Lagoon) there's enough infrastructure to travel safely on your own. Elsewhere it's virtually uncharted territory.

Auki & Around

Curled around a wonderfully shaped bay and surrounded by jungle-clad hills, Auki is the Solomons' third-largest town. It's a nondescript little port town, with a few low-slung buildings and a smattering of houses on stilts. Everything moves slowly except at the lively market and the bustling wharf, at the town's southern end.

⊙ Sights & Activities

Lilisiana   FISHING VILLAGE
With its traditional-style houses raised on stilts over the shore, the friendly fishing village of Lilisiana, about 1.5km from Auki, is photogenic to boot. Lilisiana's peaceful beach is a narrow, long, golden sand spit beside coral shallows. Beside the beach is Osi Lake, which is home to colonies of seabirds.

Riba Cave   CAVE
(S$25) An hour's walk east of Auki is Riba Cave, with stalagmites, several large subterranean chambers and an underground river.

Kwaibala Waterfall   WATERFALL
(S$25) If you need to refresh yourself, head to Kwaibala Waterfall, about 3km from Auki. Expect modest cascades with a few pools where you can take a bracing dip.

Marata Man   TOUR GUIDE
(☑7458201; marataman1@yahoo.com.au) You'll need a guide to visit Riba Cave and Kwaibala Waterfall, which are on private land

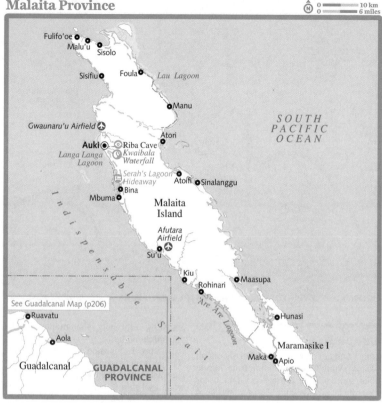

and difficult to find. Silas Diutee Malai is a freelance guide who charges S$200 for Riba Cave, S$200 for Kwaibala Waterfall and S$100 for Osi Lake. Make sure that *kastom* fees are included in the prices he quotes.

🛏 Sleeping & Eating

Auki Motel HOTEL **$$**
(✒40014, 40208; Loboi Ave; r S$250-660; ✳🛜) Auki Motel has the best facilities in town. Bathrooms are in good nick and it features a range of rooms to suit all budgets. Downstairs rooms are a tad cramped but have private bathrooms and shared air-con. The menu at the **restaurant** (mains S$50-70; ☺breakfast, lunch & dinner) varies according to what's available.

Rarasu SEAFOOD **$**
(✒40280; off Maasina Rulu Pde; mains S$40-65; ☺lunch & dinner Mon-Sat, dinner Sun) Choice is very limited, but the dishes are fresh and

copious. The vaguely barn-like surrounds ooze a ramshackle charm.

ℹ Information

Get online at **Telekom** (per hr S$20; ☺8.30am-noon & 1-4pm Mon-Fri).

An **ANZ** (off Loboi Ave; ☺9am-4pm Mon-Fri) and a **Bank South Pacific** (BSP; off Loboi Ave; ☺8.30am-3pm Mon-Fri) are in the town centre and change major currencies. Both have an ATM (Visa and MasterCard).

ℹ Getting There & Away

Because of land disputes, flights were indefinitely suspended between Honiara and Auki at the time of writing.

The passenger boats **MV Pelican Express** (✒28104), **MV 360 Discovery** (✒20 957, 7442802) and **MV Lady Wakehurst** (✒7592006) have regular services between Honiara and Auki (from S$150, four to six hours).

Auki

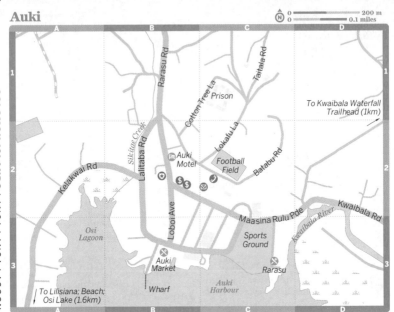

SOLOMON ISLANDS LANGA LANGA LANGA LAGOON

Langa Langa Lagoon

Langa Langa Lagoon is indisputedly one of Malaita's highlights. Extending from 7km to 32km south of Auki, the lagoon is famous for its artificial islands built of stones and dead corals. It's also a strong centre for traditional activities, especially shell-money making and shipbuilding.

One proviso: 'lagoon' is a bit misleading. If it has recently rained, waters may be more chocolate than bright turquoise, and you won't find stunning beaches to sun yourself on. People rather come here for the laid-back tempo and the magical setting.

WORTH A TRIP

SERAH'S LAGOON HIDEAWAY

Scene: Langa Langa Lagoon at dusk. Close up: you're sipping a glass of bush lime on your private terrace at **Serah's Lagoon Hideaway** (☎7472344; se rah_kei@yahoo.com.au; r per person incl 3 meals S$550-650). Run with flair by Serah Kei, this retreat comprises two bungalows on stilts embellished with a few feminine touches as well as a three-room house. The ablution block is tip-top, with a proper shower and flush toilets, and the meals are memorable. Your host can arrange lagoon tours as well as cultural shows (from S$300). Call Serah and she will arrange transfers from Auki (about S$600 per boatload one-way).

UNDERSTAND THE SOLOMON ISLANDS

Solomon Islands Today

RAMSI (Regional Assistance Mission to Solomon Islands) remains in the Solomons in an ongoing capacity while the country slowly rebuilds, but it's hoped that all RAMSI police will have withdrawn by 2015.

Due to highly unstable parliamentary coalitions, changes of government are frequent in the Solomons. In August 2010, Danny Philip was elected Prime Minister by a majority of one. He had to resign in November 2011 following a vote of no confidence, and his former Minister for Finance and Treasury, Gordon Darcy Lilo, was elected Prime Minister a week later. The next elections will be held in 2014.

With restored security and increased stability, the economic outlook is positive. Thanks to better air connections from Australia, tourism is slightly on the rise, and the Gold Ridge Mine, 40km southeast of Honiara, which was closed in 2000 due to civil unrest, recommenced commercial operations in 2011. The Solomon Islands is to host the 11th Festival of Pacific Arts in July 2012, a major cultural event in the region.

JFK

In 1960 John F Kennedy invited two Solomon Islanders to his presidential inauguration in Washington DC. They were turned away because they spoke no English. In 1943 these two islanders rescued 26-year-old skipper JFK and 10 survivors after their boat was sunk by Japanese during WWII.

History

Papuan-speaking hunter-gatherers from New Guinea were the only inhabitants of the Solomons for thousands of years, until Austronesian-speaking proto-Melanesians began moving in around 4000 BC. The Lapita people appeared between 2000 and 1600 BC. Polynesians from the east settled the outer islands such as Rennell, Bellona and Ontong Java between AD 1200 and 1600.

The first European visitor was Spaniard Don Alvaro de Mendaña y Neyra in 1568. He returned in 1595 with four ships and 450 would-be colonists. He came upon and named Santa Cruz, and established a settlement before dying there of malaria. After two months the settlement was abandoned and the survivors limped back to Peru.

There was almost no further contact with Europeans until 1767, when the British Captain Philip Carteret came upon Santa Cruz and Malaita. British, French and American explorers followed, and whalers began arriving in 1798. Sandalwood traders visited from the 1840s to late 1860s.

On 6 October 1893, Britain proclaimed a protectorate over the archipelago's southern islands, which was extended in 1897 and again in 1898. In 1899, Britain relinquished claims to Western Samoa, and in return Germany ceded the Shortlands, Choiseul, Ontong Java and Santa Isabel to Britain.

Between 1871 and 1903 blackbirders (slave traders) took 30,000 men from the Solomons to work in the cane fields of northern Australia and Fiji.

The year 1942 marked a turning point: in April the Japanese seized the Shortland Islands. Three weeks later Tulagi was taken and the Japanese began building an airstrip on Guadalcanal. United States troops landed on Guadalcanal in August 1942, but were severely defeated by a Japanese naval force that had left Rabaul in New Guinea to attack the US transports. However, the US forces gradually gained the upper hand. During the Guadalcanal campaign, six naval battles were fought and 67 warships and transports sunk – so many ships were sunk off the northern coast of Guadalcanal that this area is now called Iron Bottom Sound. Around 7000 American and 30,000 Japanese lives were lost on land and at sea. The Allies recovered all islands after the official Japanese surrender in 1945. (In 1965, after 20 years of hiding in the bush after the end of WWII, the last Japanese soldier surrendered on Vella Lavella island in the Solomons. He returned home to full military honours.) The town of Tulagi was gutted during the war and the Quonset-hut township of Honiara replaced it as the capital.

A proto-nationalist postwar movement called Marching Rule sprang up in Malaita, opposed to cooperation with the British authorities, whose rule had been restored after WWII. Britain began to see the need for local government, and a governing council was elected in 1970. The British Solomon Islands Protectorate was renamed the Solomon Islands five years later and independence was granted on 7 July 1978.

Ethnic tensions started to fester; the Gwale people (people from Guadalcanal) resented the fact that their traditional land was being settled by migrants from Malaita. Early in 1999, the inevitable happened. Civil war broke out, and hundreds died in the fighting. Following mediation by Australia and New Zealand, the Townsville Peace Agreement was signed between the two factions in October 2000. However, what began as ethnic tension descended into general lawlessness. Though the conflict was confined to Guadalcanal, 'events' started happening elsewhere, including in the Western Province. The whole country was crippled and traumatised, and the fragile economy collapsed.

On 24 July 2003, the RAMSI, an Australian-led coalition of police from Pacific island states, was deployed throughout the whole country to restore law and order. However, this progress was seriously undermined in April 2006, when the election of controversial Snyder Rini as prime minister resulted in two days of rioting in the streets of Honiara, despite the presence of RAMSI. Australia flew in reinforcements for the RAMSI personnel. Rini resigned and the subsequent ascension of Manasseh Sogavare as prime minister brought calm to the Solomons' capital.

In early April 2007, a tsunami struck Western and Choiseul provinces. Gizo, the Solomons' second-largest city, was at the centre of the disaster, and Ghizo's southwest coast was worst hit, leaving Gilbertese villagers between Titiana and Saeraghi homeless. Aid workers arrived en masse to help rebuild the local economy. All things considered, the destruction was fairly limited and the effects of the tsunami are almost no longer visible on land.

The Culture

Solomon Islanders' obligations to their clan and village bigman (chief) are eternal and enduring, whether they live in the same village all their lives or move to another country. As in most Melanesian cultures, the *wantok* system is observed here. All islanders are born with a set of obligations to their *wantok*, but they're also endowed with privileges that only *wantok* receive. For most Melanesian villagers it's an egalitarian way of sharing the community assets. There's no social security system and very few people are in paid employment, but the clan provides economic support and a strong sense of identity.

Melanesian culture is deeply rooted in ancestor worship, magic and oral traditions. Villagers often refer to their traditional ways, beliefs and land ownership as *kastom;* it's bound up in the Melanesian systems of lore and culture.

The Solomons' 2005 population was estimated at 538,000. Melanesians represent 94% and Polynesians 4%. The large Micronesian communities who were resettled from Kiribati by the British in the 1960s are still called Gilbertese. The remainder of the population is made up of Asians and expats, mainly Aussies and Kiwis. Most of the population lives in rural villages.

About 96% of the population is Christian. Of these, 35% are members of the Anglican-

affiliated Church of Melanesia and 20% are Roman Catholics.

Islanders still practise pre-Christian religions in a few remote areas, particularly on Malaita; in other places traditional beliefs are observed alongside Christianity.

Arts

Solomon Islanders are incredibly musical people – it's a must to go to a local church service to listen to the singing. The Malaitan pipe bands (or bamboo bands) are amazing. In ensembles of 12 or so members, the band plays bamboo pipes in all sizes bundled together with bushvine. They're played as panpipe and flutes, and as long tubes whose openings are struck with rubber thongs to make an unusual plinketty-plonk sound. One of the most famous panpipe groups is Narasirato (www.narasirato.com), from Malaita; this group has gained international recognition. They mix classic Malaitan panpipe music with contemporary beats.

There are also strong carving traditions in the Solomons. Carvings incorporate human, bird, fish and other animal motifs, often in combination, and they frequently represent deities and spirits. Woodcarvings are inlaid with nautilus or trochus shell. Carvings of *nguzunguzu* (canoe figureheads, also carved in miniature) and animals are produced from kerosene wood and ebony. Decorated bowls and masks are widely available, as are stone replicas of traditional shell money.

Shell money is used in Malaita, while in the Temotu Islands red-feather coils are still used.

Environment

The country is largely covered by tropical rainforest, but much of it has been degraded by logging operations. Excessive logging threatens the rich diversity of flora and fauna as well as the traditional lifestyle of villagers. Other possible negative effects include erosion, climate changes, loss of water resources and disruption to coral reefs. In Marovo Lagoon, Isabel and other islands, the effects of logging are clearly being felt. That said, there are plans to encourage sustainable logging and thus reduce the pressure on the environment.

The spectacular marine environment is home to a rich variety of fish, corals, anemones

SOLOMONS ENDEMICS *TIM FLANNERY*

The Solomon Islands represent a whole other environment, for they are an ancient island archipelago that has never been connected to a continent. The cuscus (tree-dwelling marsupial) found there only reached the islands a few thousand years ago with people. The true endemics are giant rats, monkey-faced bats and unusual birds such as the Guadalcanal honeyeater. The giant rats are rare now, but you might be fortunate enough to spot one of the half-dozen species in dense, virginal forest. One of the largest species makes nests like those constructed by eagles in the tallest rainforest trees. One other aspect of the Solomons fauna is a radiation of frogs that is unique. Some look like dead leaves, others like lumps of moss, while one genus, which is often found in caves, is gigantic, reaching over 20cm long.

Tim Flannery is a naturalist, ecologist, environmental activist and author. He is currently an adjunct professor at Macquarie University.

and many other creatures, including eight species of venomous sea snakes. Several islands are breeding grounds for green and hawksbill turtles.

The Solomons has 173 bird species, 40 of them endemic.

Native reptiles include the 1.5m-long monitor lizard, freshwater crocodiles and the very dangerous saltwater crocodile.

More than 130 butterfly species are found locally, and 35 are endemic.

SURVIVAL GUIDE

Directory A-Z
Accommodation
Tourist-class hotels are confined to Honiara, Gizo and Munda. Although basic by international standards, these hotels generally have rooms with or without private shower and air-con. Most have restaurants and bars, offer wi-fi service (or internet facilities) and take credit cards. There's also a handful of plush resorts in Honiara and the Western Province. A few high-end places quote their rates in Australian dollars.

Elsewhere accommodation is offered in basic leafhouse-style lodges or private houses, usually with only basic shared bathrooms.

The visitor information centre in Honiara (p212) can make suggestions and organise bookings. Online bookings can be made with the Solomons Travel Portal (www.solomonislands-hotels.travel).

Activities
Diving The highly reputable live-aboard dive boat MV Bilikiki (www.bilikiki.com)

offers regular cruises around the Russell Islands and Marovo Lagoon. Australian-based specialist companies offering package dive tours include Allways Dive Expeditions (www.allwaysdive.com.au), Dive Adventures (www.diveadventures.com.au) and Diversion Dive Travel (www.diversionoz.com).

Surfing Two ecofriendly operators organise community-based surfaris to Guadalcanal, Malaita, Isabel and Makira islands: Surf Solomons (www.surfsolomons.com) and Sol Surfing (www.surfingsolomonislands.com).

Business Hours
The following are common business hours in the Solomons; exceptions are noted in reviews.

Banks & post offices (8.30am-3pm Mon-Fri)

Government offices (8am-noon & 1-4pm Mon-Fri)

Restaurants (11am-9pm)

Shops (8.30am-5pm Mon-Fri, 8.30am-noon Sat)

Embassies & Consulates
Australia (Map p210; 21561; www.solomonislands.embassy.gov.au; Mud Alley, Honiara)

France & Germany (22588; tradco@solomon.com.sb; Tradco Office, City Centre Bldg, Honiara)

NZ (21502; www.nzembassy.com/solomon-islands; City Centre Bldg, Honiara)

PNG (20561; Anthony Saru Bldg, Honiara)

UK (21705; www.ukinsolomonislands.fco.gov.uk; Tanuli Ridge, Honiara)

Food

Tipping is not required or expected in the Solomons and prices listed in this book include tax. The following price ranges refer to standard mains:

$	less than S$60.
$$	S$60 to S$120.
$$$	more than S$120

Holidays

New Year's Day 1 January

Easter March or April

Whit Monday May or June

Queen's Birthday First Monday in June

Independence Day 7 July

Christmas 25 December

National Thanksgiving Day 26 December

Internet Access

You'll find internet cafes in Honiara and in Gizo. Solomon Telekom (www.solomon.com. sb) has public email facilities in Honiara, Gizo, Munda and Auki.

Wi-fi is also available at the better hotels and at a few cafes in Honiara, Munda and Gizo thanks to the prepaid 'Bumblebee' card. It's available in some shops and hotels or at Solomon Telekom offices.

Money

ATMs There are ATMs at the ANZ, Bank South Pacific (BSP) and Westpac banks in Honiara, as well as in Auki, Munda and Gizo.

Credit cards The main tourist-oriented businesses, the Honiara branch of Solomon Airlines, a few dive shops and most upmarket hotels and resorts accept credit cards (usually with a 5% surcharge), but elsewhere it's strictly cash.

PRACTICALITIES

» **Newspapers & Magazines** The Solomons Star (www.solomon starnews.com), the National Express and the web-only Solomon Times Online (www.solomontimes.com)

» **Electricity** The Solomons uses 240V, 50Hz AC and Australian-style three-pin plugs.

» **Weights & Measures** The imperial system is used here.

Currency The local currency is the Solomon Islands' dollar (S$). A supply of coins and small-denomination notes will come in handy in rural areas, at markets, and for bus and boat rides.

Moneychangers The Bank South Pacific, Westpac and ANZ will change money in most major currencies.

Taxes There's a 10% government tax on hotel and restaurant prices, but more basic places often don't charge it. All prices given in this book are inclusive of tax.

Tipping & bargaining Tipping and bargaining are not traditionally part of Melanesian culture.

Telephone

Solomon Telekom (www.telekom.com.sb) operates the country's telephone system. Public phones are reasonably common in the larger centres and phonecards are widely available. Solomon Island's country code is ☑677 and first hit ☑00 to dial out of the country.

MOBILE PHONES
Solomon Telekom and BeMobile offer GSM mobile phone service in most areas (but Marovo isn't entirely covered yet). Prepaid SIM cards are available for purchase. Both operators have international roaming agreements with Telstra and Optus (Australia).

Visas

Citizens from most Western countries don't need a visa to enter the Solomon Islands, just a valid passport, an onward ticket, and sufficient funds for their stay. On arrival at the airport, you will be given an entry permit for up to one month.

Women Travellers

Exercise normal caution in Honiara – after dark, take a taxi and stay in busy areas.

Melanesians are very sensitive about the show of female thighs so shorts and skirts should be knee-length and swimwear should incorporate boardshorts rather than bikini bottoms.

Getting There & Away

Air

The Solomons' only international airport is Henderson Airport, 11km east of Honiara.

The following airlines have regular scheduled flights to the Solomon Islands.

Air Pacific (www.airpacific.com) Connects Honiara with Nadi and Honiara with Vila. As we went to print, Air Pacific – Fiji's national carrier – was rebranding itself as Fiji Airways , and the airline information in this book may be subject to change.

Air Niugini (www.airniugini.com.pg) Has flights between Port Moresby and Nadi to Honiara.

Our Airline (www.ourairline.com.au) Operates from Nauru to Honiara (and on to Brisbane).

Pacific Blue (www.flypacificblue.com) Has services to/from Brisbane.

Solomon Airlines (www.flysolomons.com; Mendana Ave, Honiara) The national carrier. Has services between Honiara and Brisbane, Nadi, Port Moresby and Vila.

Sea

The Solomons is a favourite spot for yachties who take refuge in the lagoons during cyclone season. Along with Honiara, Korovou (Shortland Islands), Gizo, Ringgi, Yandina, Tulagi and Graciosa Bay are official ports of entry where you can clear customs and immigration.

Getting Around

Air

Solomon Airlines (www.flysolomons.com) services the country's 20-odd airstrips. The main tourist gateways, including Gizo, Seghe (for North Marovo Lagoon) and Munda are serviced daily from Honiara, but be sure to confirm your flight at least 24 hours before your departure.

The baggage allowance is set at 16kg per passenger.

Boat

DINGHIES

Outboard-powered dinghies are the most common means of transport in the Solomons. People pay a fare to travel a sector. Charters cost around S$1500 per day for the boat and a driver; fuel is often not included (S$20 per litre in remote areas).

PRICE RANGES

The following price ranges refer to a double room with bathroom, unless specified otherwise in the accommodation listings:

$	less than S$250
$$	S$250 to S$800
$$$	more than S$800

PASSENGER BOATS

Go West Transport Operates a thrice-weekly shuttle between Munda and Gizo (Western Province).

MV 360 Discovery Has regular services between Honiara, Tulagi and Auki (Malaita).

MV Pelican Express Has a weekly service between Honiara and the Western Province (including Marovo Lagoon and Gizo).

Bus

Public minibuses are found only in Honiara. Elsewhere, people pile into open-backed trucks or tractor-drawn trailers.

Car & Motorcycle

The country has around 1300km of generally dreadful roads. International driving permits are accepted, as are most driving licences. Driving is on the left side of the road.

Hire cars are available only in Honiara. Contact Pacific Casino Hotel (p208).

Hitching

If you want a ride through the countryside, flag down a passing vehicle and ask the driver the cost of a lift. In rural areas most vehicles double as public transport.

Taxi

Taxis are plentiful in Honiara and there are small fleets in Gizo and Auki. They are meterless, so agree on the price before you set off.

Language

WANT MORE?
For in-depth language information and handy phrases, check out Lonely Planet's *Pidgin Phrasebook*. You'll find it at **shop .lonelyplanet.com**, or you can buy Lonely Planet's iPhone phrasebooks at the Apple App Store.

After the national pidgins of Papua New Guinea and the Solomon Islands, English is the most widely understood language, but while it's quite common in the cities and large towns, in rural areas you'll need some basic pidgin in order to communicate. Luckily pidgins are fairly straightforward for English speakers to get a handle on.

TOK PISIN (PAPUA NEW GUINEA)

More than 800 languages are spoken in Papua New Guinea – a whopping 12% of the world's indigenous languages. Linguists divide these languages into 14 major groups. Austronesian languages are spoken by a sixth of the population and dominate the islands and the coastal areas. Enga is spoken by about 165,000 speakers in the Highlands region, and is the predominant spoken native language in Papua New Guinea. Kuanua has about 60,000 speakers.

In the early days of British New Guinea and then Australian Papua, the local language of the Port Moresby coastal area, Motu, evolved into Police Motu, and was spread through Papua by the native constabulary. It's still widely spoken in the southern Papuan part of Papua New Guinea.

Tok Pisin (or as it has also been called, New Guinea Pidgin English, Tok Boi, Neo-Melanesian) has its origins in the Pacific labour trade and shows influences of German. It is now learned as a second language in most villages, while in the big towns it is becoming creolised (adopted as the first language). As the national language of independent Papua New Guinea, it is used regularly by more than two million speakers.

Tok Pisin is used in all areas of daily life, including the administration, education, churches and the media. It has been a written language since the 1920s, and although an official writing system exists, nonstandard spellings still abound.

Most Tok Pisin words are of English origin, but many words referring to local phenomena originate in local languages. Second-language Tok Pisin speakers are often influenced in their pronunciation and grammar by the conventions of their mother tongue.

Pronunciation

Note that *p* and *f* are virtually interchangeable in both spelling and pronunciation, as are *d* and *t*, *j* and *z*. The combination *kw* represents the English 'qu'. Vowels and vowel combinations are pronounced clearly, even when unstressed and at the end of a word, as follows: *a* as in 'art', *e* as in 'set', *i* as in 'sit', *o* as in 'lot', *u* as in 'put', *ai* as in 'aisle', *au* as the 'ou' in 'house' and *oi* as in 'boil'.

Basics

Hello.	*Gude.*
Goodbye.	*Lukim yu.*
Yes.	*Yes.*
No.	*Nogat.*
Please.	*Plis.*
Excuse me./Sorry.	*Sori.*
Thank you (very much).	*Tenkyu (tru).*
How are you?	*Yu stap gut?*

I'm well.	*Mi stap gut.*
What's your name?	*Wanem nem bilong yu?*
My name is ...	*Nem bilong mi ...*
Where are you from?	*Ples bilong yu we?*
I'm from ...	*Ples bilong mi ...*
What's your job?	*Wanim kain wok bilong yu?*
I'm (a/an) ...	*Mi ...*
I (don't) understand.	*Mi (no) save.*
More slowly, please.	*Yu tok isi isi plis.*
I need help.	*Mi laikim sampela halp.*

a little	*liklik*
big	*bikpela*
brother	*brata*
child	*pikinini*
man/woman	*man/meri*
relative	*wantok*
sister	*susa*

Accommodation

Do you have a single/double room?	*Yu gat rum slip long wanpela/tupela man?*
How much is it per night?	*Em i kostim hamas long wanpela de?*
Can I see the room?	*Inap mi lukim rum pastaim?*
I like this room.	*Mi laikim (tru) dispela rum.*
Is there a mosquito net?	*I gat moskita net i stap?*
Is there a bath/shower?	*I gat rum waswas i stap?*
Is there a laundry?	*I gat rum bilong wasim (ol) klos?*
Where's the toilet?	*Haus pekpek i stap we?*
I want to stay ... days.	*Mi laik stap ... de.*
I'd like to check out today/tomorrow.	*Mi laik bai mi lusim hotel tede/tumora.*

Eating & Drinking

Is the restaurant open/closed?	*Haus kaikai i op/pas?*
Do you have an English menu?	*Yu got menyu long Tok Inglis?*
Does this dish have meat?	*I gat abus long dispela kaikai?*
I don't eat beef/ pork/chicken/ dairy products.	*Mi tambu long bulmakau/ pik/kakaruk/ susu samting.*
I'd like...	*Mi laikim...*

Numbers – Tok Pisin

1	*wan*
2	*tu*
3	*tri*
4	*foa*
5	*faiv*
6	*sikis*
7	*seven*
8	*et*
9	*nain*
10	*ten*
20	*tupela ten*
30	*tripela ten*
40	*fopela ten*
50	*faivpela ten*
60	*sikispela ten*
70	*sevenpela ten*
80	*etpela ten*
90	*nainpela ten*
100	*wan handet*

The bill, please.	*Mi laik peim kaikai bilong mi.*
I enjoyed the meal.	*Mi laikim tumas dispela kaikai.*

food	*kaikai*
meat	*abus*
soft drink	*loli wara*
vegetables	*sayor/kumu/kumis*
water	*wara*

Shopping & Services

I'd like to buy ...	*Mi laik baim ...*
How much is it?	*Hamas long dispela?*
What's that?	*Wanem dispela?*
I'm just looking.	*Mi lukluk tasol.*
That's very cheap.	*Pe/Prais i daun (tru).*
Is that your lowest price?	*I gat seken prais?*
I'll take it.	*Bai mi kisim.*

I'm looking for ...	*Mi painim ...*
a bank	*haus mani/benk*
the church	*haus lotu*
the hospital	*haus sik*
the market	*maket/bung*
the police	*polis stesin*

Time & Dates

What time is it?	*Wanem taim nau?*
It's (eight) o'clock.	*Em i (et) klok.*
morning	*moningtaim*
afternoon	*apinun*
evening (7pm–11pm)	*nait*
night (11pm–4am)	*biknait*
yesterday	*asde*
today	*tede*
tomorrow	*tumora*
Monday	*Mande*
Tuesday	*Tunde*
Wednesday	*Trinde*
Thursday	*Fonde*
Friday	*Fraide*
Saturday	*Sarere*
Sunday	*Sande*

Transport & Directions

Is transport available?	*I gat bas, teksi samting?*
How much is it to ... ?	*Em i hamas long ... ?*
How long is the journey?	*Hamas taim long go long ... ?*
I'd like a ... ticket.	*Mi laik baim tiket long ...*
one-way	*i go long tasol*
return	*go na i kambek*
What time does the ... arrive?	*Wanem taim ... i kamap?*
What time does the next ... leave?	*Long wanem taim neks ... i go?*
boat	*bot*
bus	*bas*
plane	*balus*
Where is ...?	*... i stap we?*
Can you draw a map?	*Inap yu wokim/droim map?*
Straight ahead.	*Stret.*
Turn left/right.	*Tanim lep/rait.*
How far is it?	*Em i longwe o nogat?*
behind	*bihain long*
in front of	*ai bilong*
near	*klostu*
far	*longwe*

PIJIN (SOLOMON ISLANDS)

Officially, there are 67 indigenous languages and about 30 dialects in the Solomon Islands. It is quite common for people from villages separated by only a few kilometres to speak mutually incomprehensible languages. As a result, the national language of the Solomons is Solomon Islands Pijin, or Pijin for short.

Early 19th-century sailors stimulated the evolution of Pijin. The recruitment of labour (including Solomon Islanders) from the 1860s to 1900s to work in mines, and in Oceanic canefields and plantations, spread the language all over the Pacific. By the 1930s Pijin was being spoken by missionaries in many areas, helping to spread it further. While English is now the official language of the administration, many government staff use Pijin in everyday conversation.

Pijin speakers use two versions. One is a simplified form used by islanders for the purpose of communication with their English-speaking employers. The second is the 'true' Pijin, which they use among themselves.

Pronunciation

Pijin pronunciation varies a lot because most speakers are influenced by the sounds of their own native languages. Pijin has five vowels, pronounced as follows: *a* as the 'a' in 'father', *e* as the 'e' in 'bet', *i* as the 'ee' in 'deet', *o* as the 'o' in 'gone' and *u* as the 'oo' in 'soon'. When two different vowels are joined, both vowels are pronounced. Doubled vowels have a longer vowel sound than single ones.

Basics

Hello.	*Halo.*
How are you?	*Hao?/Oraet nomoa?*
Fine.	*Oraet nomoa.*
Goodbye.	*Bae-bae.*
See you later.	*Lukim iu (bihaen).*
Yes./No.	*Ia./Nomoa.*
Excuse me.	*Ekskius plis.*
Thank you.	*Tanggio tumas.*
What's your name?	*Hu nao nem blong iu?*
My name is ...	*Nem blong mi ...*
Where are you from?	*Iu kam from wea?*
I'm from ...	*Mi kam from ...*
Say it again.	*Talem kam moa.*
Where's the toilet?	*Wea nao toelet?*
Help me!	*Iu mas helpem mi!*

Eating & Drinking

I want to book a table (for four).	*Mi laek fo bukim wanfala tebol (fo fofala).*
What do you have on your menu for today?	*Wanem nao iufala garem long lis fo kaikai tude?*
What do you have to drink?	*Watkaen dring nao iufala garem?*
I want ...	*Mi laekem ...*
Do you have beer?	*Waswe, iu eni bia?*

Shopping & Services

Do you sell ...?	*Waswe, iufala salem ...?*
What's this?	*Wanem nao diswan?*
How much is this?	*Hao mas nao diswan?*
I want to buy this/that.	*Mi laek baem diswan/ datwan.*
I don't want this/that.	*Mi no wandem diswan/ datwan.*

Time & Dates

What time is it?	*Hemi wataem nao ia?*
It's (one) o'clock.	*Hemi (wan) klok.*
this morning	*tude moning*
this evening	*tude ivining*
yesterday	*iestade/astade*
today	*tude*
tomorrow	*tumoro*
Monday	*Mande*
Tuesday	*Tiusde*
Wednesday	*Wenesde*
Thursday	*Tosde*
Friday	*Fraede*
Saturday	*Satade/Sarere*
Sunday	*Sande*

Transport & Directions

I want to go to ...	*Mi laek go long ...*
How long will it take to get to ...?	*Hao long nao bae hemi tekem fo kasem ...?*
What does it cost to go to ...?	*Hao mas nao fo go long ...?*
Where can I buy a ticket for ...?	*Wea nao mi save peim tiket fo tekem go long ...?*
When does the ... leave?	*Wataem nao ... hemi aot?*

Numbers – Pijin

1	*wanfala*
2	*tufala*
3	*trifala*
4	*fofala*
5	*faefala*
6	*sikisfala*
7	*sevenfala*
8	*eitfala*
9	*naenfala*
10	*tenfala*
20	*tuenti/tuande*
30	*teti/toti*
40	*foti*
50	*fifti*
60	*sikisti*
70	*seventi*
80	*eiti*
90	*naenti*
100	*handred*

When will we arrive at ...?	*Wataem nao bae iumi kasem ...?*
Where is a/the ...?	*Wea nao ...?*
bus stop	*bas stop*
hospital	*hospitol*
market	*maket*
pharmacy	*famasi*
post office	*pos ofis*
Is it near/far?	*Waswe, hemi kolsap/ farawe?*
How long would it take to walk?	*Hao long nao bae hemi tekem fo wakabaot go?*
It's near the ...	*Hemi kolsap long ...*
It's on the opposite/ right/left side.	*Hemi long narasaet/ raetsaet/lefsaet.*
Turn left/right here.	*Tane lef/raet long hia.*

GLOSSARY

arse tanket – a bunch of tanket leaves stuck into a belt to cover a man's backside, also called arse gras (Highlands)

bagarap – broken; literally 'buggered-up'
bagi – red shell necklace used for trade in the kula ring islands
banana boat – trade boat or dinghy
baret – artificial channel or canal constructed across loops in a river (Sepik)
bigman – important man, a leader
bilas – jewellery, decorations, finery
bilum – string bag
BRA – Bougainville Revolutionary Army (Solomon Islands)
buai – betel nut
bukumatula – bachelor house (Trobriand Islands)
buli – tinned (bully) beef

dim dims – white people
diwai – wood
doba – leaf money from Milne Bay Province
dobu – long house
dukduk – spirit and ritual costume

garamut – drum made from a hollowed log
GRA – Guadalcanal Revolutionary Army (Solomon Islands)

haus – house
haus tambaran – spirit house
haus win – open-air structure like a gazebo; literally 'house of wind'

kai bar – cheap takeaway food bar
karim leg – courting ceremony involving crossing legs with a partner; literally 'carry leg' (Highlands)
kastom – custom
kaukau – sweet potato
kiap – patrol officer (of colonial origin)
kina – unit of PNG currency; large shell traded from the coast as an early form of currency
kula ring – ring of trading islands in Milne Bay Province
kumul – bird of paradise
kunai – grass, grassland
kundu – hourglass-shaped drum covered with lizard or snake skin
kwik piksa leta – fax; literally 'quick picture letter'

laplap – sarong
loloi – rolls of shell money strung on lengths of cane (East New Britain)

malangan – ritual of making totemic figures (also called malangans) to honour the dead; also known as malagan
meri – wife, woman
Motu – the indigenous people of the Port Moresby area; the language spoken by these people

nambawan – number one, the best
natnat – mosquito

payback – compensation paid for a wrongdoing, but in reprisal more than revenge
pikus tri – fig tree
pinis – finish
pis – fish
pitpit – wild sugar cane

PMV – public motor vehicle
pukpuk – crocodile

raskol – bandit, criminal or thief
ria – volcanic fjord, as found near Tufi

saksak – sago
singsing – celebratory festival/dance
solwara – ocean, sea
story board – narrative carving done on a wooden board

tambaran – ancestral spirit, also called tambuan, tabaran or tabuan
tambu – forbidden or sacred; shell money (Tolai)
tapa – beaten bark cloth
taro – tuberous root vegetable similar to a sweet potato
toea – unit of PNG currency (100 toea = 1 kina); a shell necklace also used as currency
Tok Pisin – the Pidgin language
tok ples – local language; first language; pronounced 'talk place'
Tolai – the main inhabitants of East New Britain's Gazelle Peninsula, pronounced 'tol-eye'
tumbuan – large, feather-draped body mask

voluntia – volunteer

wantok – fellow clanspeople, kith and kin; literally 'one talk' or 'one who speaks the same language'

yam – tuberous root vegetable similar to a sweet potato

behind the scenes

SEND US YOUR FEEDBACK

We love to hear from travellers – your comments keep us on our toes and help make our books better. Our well-travelled team reads every word on what you loved or loathed about this book. Although we cannot reply individually to postal submissions, we always guarantee that your feedback goes straight to the appropriate authors, in time for the next edition. Each person who sends us information is thanked in the next edition – the most useful submissions are rewarded with a selection of digital PDF chapters.

Visit **lonelyplanet.com/contact** to submit your updates and suggestions or to ask for help. Our award-winning website also features inspirational travel stories, news and discussions.

Note: We may edit, reproduce and incorporate your comments in Lonely Planet products such as guidebooks, websites and digital products, so let us know if you don't want your comments reproduced or your name acknowledged. For a copy of our privacy policy visit lonelyplanet.com/privacy.

OUR READERS

Many thanks to the travellers who used the last edition and wrote to us with helpful hints, useful advice and interesting anecdotes:

Dianna Adler, Douglas Adler, Ruth Attard, Emily Barker, Fabienne Becker, Valerie Cheah, Caroline Chow, Melanie Dean, Roderick Eime, Carla Ewin, Barbara Fische, Denzel Fohonibari, Paul Folley, Thomas Fox, Michal Gonnen, Shaila Goodman, Ken Green, Connie Hanley, Jan Hasselberg, Manuel Hetzel, Bernhard Hoisl, Chris Houston, Gillian Hoyer, Stanley Jacob, Christian Janiesch, Henry Jedelsky, Georgios Kechagioglou, Marm Kilpatrick, Mark King, Wancy Lam, Zach Leigh, Sean Linton, Martin Lutterjohann, Karin McCollum, Larry McGrath, Jason Mcilvena, Dorothy Merriott, Annette Potts, Nikki Purkiss, Robert Schoenfeld, Wanda Serkowska, Uli Terheggen, Mannis Van Oven, Ian Veinot, Sigurd Volk, Gene Waddell, Jack Wang, Jonas Wernli, Teresa Widmer, Andrew Wilkins, Mark Wolfsbauer, Tim Worth, Andrey Yakobson.

AUTHOR THANKS
Regis St Louis

Big thanks to the many Papuans, travellers and expats who helped along the way.

Thanks to Rowan McKinnon and my hard-working co-authors for helpful advice and stellar work on previous editions. Other thanks go to Grace and family at Kokoda, Laurens in Buka, Josephine in Arawa, Ralph in Kokopau, Gretta in Alotau, Sean and staff at Nusa, Clem on Tunung Island, Solwara Meri, the paramount chief and friends on the Trobriands, the fantastic villagers at Tumari and Horia Diaconescu for Bougainville tips. Thanks also to my wife Cassandra and daughters Magdalena and Genevieve for their support.

Jean-Bernard Carillet

Heaps of thanks to the South Pacific team at Lonely Planet, especially Maryanne and Errol, for their trust, and to the editorial and cartography teams. Coordinating author Regis gets the thumbs up for his support, and Dean is, as always, a great co-author. In the Sollies, special thanks to Kerrie, Danny, Richard, Chris, Freda, Roland (who helped me when I was stuck in Gizo), Sue, Don, Allen and Serah. On the homefront, well-deserved *bisous* to my daughter, Eva, and Christine, who are always supportive.

Dean Starnes

PNG isn't the kind of country where you can spend months on the road without help. *Tenkyu tru* to all the people who pointed me in the right direction, especially Danielle Vincent, Andy Philip, Horia Diaconescu, my fellow authors and the hard work by the team at Lonely Planet. Thanks too to my parents, Julie and Alan Starnes, and my *nambawan meri*, Debbie, for holding down, fixing up and paying the bills for the fort in my absence.

ACKNOWLEDGMENTS

Climate map data adapted from Peel MC, Finlayson BL & McMahon TA (2007) 'Updated World Map of the Köppen-Geiger Climate Classification', *Hydrology and Earth System Sciences*, 11, 163344.

Cover photograph: Papua New Guinean tribesman in ceremonial garb, Rob Howard/ Corbis ©
Many of the images in this guide are available for licensing from Lonely Planet Images: www.lonelyplanetimages.com.

THIS BOOK

This 9th edition of *Lonely Planet's Papua New Guinea & Solomon Islands* guidebook was researched and written by Regis St Louis, Jean-Bernard Carillet and Dean Starnes. The previous edition was written by Rowan McKinnon, Jean-Bernard Carillet and Dean Starnes. Andrew Burke, Rowan McKinnon and Arnold Barkhordarian wrote the 7th edition. Lonely Planet co-founder Tony Wheeler researched and wrote the first two editions of *Papua New Guinea*. Environmental scientist Tim Flannery wrote the Environment chapter and best-selling author Peter FitzSimons wrote the Kokoda Story chapter, both updated this edition by Regis St Louis. This guidebook was commissioned in Lonely Planet's Melbourne office, and produced by the following:

Commissioning Editor Maryanne Netto

Coordinating Editors Erin Richards, Ross Taylor

Coordinating Cartographers Hunor Csutoros, Sophie Reed

Coordinating Layout Designer Virginia Moreno

Managing Editor Barbara Delissen

Senior Editors Andi Jones, Susan Paterson

Managing Cartographers David Connolly, Corey Hutchison

Managing Layout Designer Jane Hart

Assisting Editors Kristin Odijk, Saralinda Turner, Gordon Farrer

Cover Research Naomi Parker

Internal Image Research Rebecca Skinner

Language Content Branislava Vladisavljevic

Thanks to Ryan Evans, Larissa Frost, William Gourlay, Annelies Mertens, Trent Paton, Peter Shields, Gerard Walker

000 Map pages
000 Photo pages

how to use this book

These symbols will help you find the listings you want:

- 👁 Sights
- 🏖 Beaches
- 🏃 Activities
- 🐢 Courses
- 👉 Tours
- 🎊 Festivals & Events
- 🛏 Sleeping
- 🍴 Eating
- 🍺 Drinking
- ☆ Entertainment
- 🛍 Shopping
- ℹ Information/Transport

Look out for these icons:

- **TOP CHOICE** Our author's recommendation
- **FREE** No payment required
- 🍃 A green or sustainable option

Our authors have nominated these places as demonstrating a strong commitment to sustainability – for example by supporting local communities and producers, operating in an environmentally friendly way, or supporting conservation projects.

These symbols give you the vital information for each listing:

- 📞 Telephone Numbers
- ⊙ Opening Hours
- P Parking
- ⊖ Nonsmoking
- ❄ Air-Conditioning
- @ Internet Access
- 🛜 Wi-Fi Access
- 🏊 Swimming Pool
- ✔ Vegetarian Selection
- 📖 English-Language Menu
- 👶 Family-Friendly
- 🐾 Pet-Friendly
- 🚌 Bus
- ⛴ Ferry
- M Metro
- S Subway
- 🚊 Tram
- 🚆 Train

Reviews are organised by author preference.

Map Legend

Sights
- Beach
- Buddhist
- Castle
- Christian
- Hindu
- Islamic
- Jewish
- Monument
- Museum/Gallery
- Ruin
- Winery/Vineyard
- Zoo
- Other Sight

Activities, Courses & Tours
- Diving/Snorkelling
- Canoeing/Kayaking
- Skiing
- Surfing
- Swimming/Pool
- Walking
- Windsurfing
- Other Activity/Course/Tour

Sleeping
- Sleeping
- Camping

Eating
- Eating

Drinking
- Drinking
- Cafe

Entertainment
- Entertainment

Shopping
- Shopping

Information
- Bank
- Embassy/Consulate
- Hospital/Medical
- Internet
- Police
- Post Office
- Telephone
- Toilet
- Tourist Information
- Other Information

Transport
- Airport
- Border Crossing
- Bus
- Cable Car/Funicular
- Cycling
- Ferry
- Metro
- Monorail
- Parking
- Petrol Station
- Taxi
- Train/Railway
- Tram
- Other Transport

Routes
- Tollway
- Freeway
- Primary
- Secondary
- Tertiary
- Lane
- Unsealed Road
- Plaza/Mall
- Steps
- Tunnel
- Pedestrian Overpass
- Walking Tour
- Walking Tour Detour
- Path

Geographic
- Hut/Shelter
- Lighthouse
- Lookout
- Mountain/Volcano
- Oasis
- Park
- Pass
- Picnic Area
- Waterfall

Population
- Capital (National)
- Capital (State/Province)
- City/Large Town
- Town/Village

Boundaries
- International
- State/Province
- Disputed
- Regional/Suburb
- Marine Park
- Cliff
- Wall

Hydrography
- River, Creek
- Intermittent River
- Swamp/Mangrove
- Reef
- Canal
- Water
- Dry/Salt/Intermittent Lake
- Glacier

Areas
- Beach/Desert
- Cemetery (Christian)
- Cemetery (Other)
- Park/Forest
- Sportsground
- Sight (Building)
- Top Sight (Building)

Contributing Author

Peter FitzSimons Peter writes for the *Sydney Morning Herald* and the *Sun-Herald*. He has played for the Wallabies, written 18 books and was Australia's best-selling nonfiction author in 2001 and 2004, the latter with his book *Kokoda*. Married to television presenter Lisa Wilkinson, Peter has three children and lives in Sydney.

Tim Flannery Tim is a scientist, explorer and writer. He has written several award-winning books including *The Future Eaters*, *Throwim Way Leg* (an account of his work as a biologist in New Guinea) and *The Weather Makers*. He lives in Sydney where he is a professor in the faculty of science at Macquarie University.

DA FEB 1 4 2013

OUR STORY

A beat-up old car, a few dollars in the pocket and a sense of adventure. In 1972 that's all Tony and Maureen Wheeler needed for the trip of a lifetime – across Europe and Asia overland to Australia. It took several months, and at the end – broke but inspired – they sat at their kitchen table writing and stapling together their first travel guide, *Across Asia on the Cheap*. Within a week they'd sold 1500 copies. Lonely Planet was born.

Today, Lonely Planet has offices in Melbourne, London and Oakland, with more than 600 staff and writers. We share Tony's belief that 'a great guidebook should do three things: inform, educate and amuse'.

OUR WRITERS

Regis St Louis

Coordinating Author; Port Moresby; Central, Oro & Milne Bay Provinces; Island Provinces A big fan of off-the-beaten-path travel, Regis has fallen hard for the tropical islands and remote villages of Papua New Guinea. On this trip, he took over a dozen flights hopping across the New Guinea Islands, walked a long stretch of the Kokoda Track and took countless banana boat rides across often-rough seas. He also celebrated with Alotau residents at the magnificent Milne Bay Canoe and Kundu Festival, lingered on deserted islands in Kimbe Bay and caught an impromptu *singsing* at the paramount chief's village in the Trobriands. A longtime travel writer, Regis has contributed to over 30 Lonely Planet titles. He lives in Brooklyn, New York.

Read more about Regis at:
lonelyplanet.com/members/regisstlouis

Jean-Bernard Carillet

Solomon Islands Paris-based journalist and photographer Jean-Bernard is a die-hard island lover and diving instructor. He has clocked up numerous trips to the South Pacific, including four assignments to the Solomon Islands. On this research gig he searched for the best dive sites, the most thrilling adventure tours and the best value accommodations. His favourite experiences included swimming with dugongs off Tetepare Island, diving the reefs around Kicha Island and crossing Marovo Lagoon by boat. Jean-Bernard has contributed to many Lonely Planet titles, in French and in English, and coordinated Lonely Planet diving guides. He also writes for travel and dive magazines.

Dean Starnes

Morobe & Madang Provinces, The Highlands, The Sepik Dean first visited PNG in 2007 when he worked on the 8th edition of this guide and has been biding his time until he could return ever since. No stranger to off-the-map travel (he has also worked on Lonely Planet guides covering Rwanda, the Democratic Republic of the Congo, Kyrgyzstan, Burundi and Mongolia), he finds the cultural diversity, genuinely hospitable people and rugged scenery hard to beat. When he's not writing for Lonely Planet, Dean lives in New Zealand with his wife and his wife's cat (the cat's not thrilled about that arrangement). His website, www.deanstarnes.com, features photography and stories about his wayfaring ways.

Read more about Dean at:
lonelyplanet.com/members/dean_starnes

OVER PAGE — MORE WRITERS

Published by Lonely Planet Publications Pty Ltd
ABN 36 005 607 983
9th edition – Sep 2012
ISBN 9 78174179 321 5
© Lonely Planet 2012   Photographs © as indicated 2012
10 9 8 7 6 5 4 3 2 1
Printed in China

Although the authors and Lonely Planet have taken all reasonable care in preparing this book, we make no warranty about the accuracy or completeness of its content and, to the maximum extent permitted, disclaim all liability arising from its use.

All rights reserved. No part of this publication may be copied, stored in a retrieval system, or transmitted in any form by any means, electronic, mechanical, recording or otherwise, except brief extracts for the purpose of review, and no part of this publication may be sold or hired, without the written permission of the publisher. Lonely Planet and the Lonely Planet logo are trademarks of Lonely Planet and are registered in the US Patent and Trademark Office and in other countries. Lonely Planet does not allow its name or logo to be appropriated by commercial establishments, such as retailers, restaurants or hotels. Please let us know of any misuses: lonelyplanet.com/ip.